CORPUS-BASED SOCIOLINGUISTICS

In the last decade, the availability of corpora and the technological advancements of corpus tools have increased dramatically. Applied linguists have greater access to data from around the world and in a variety of languages through Web sites, blogs, and social networking sites, and there is a high level of interest among these scholars in applying corpora and corpus-based methods to other research areas, particularly sociolinguistics.

This innovative guidebook presents a systematic, in-depth account of using corpora in sociolinguistics. It introduces and expands the application of corpora and corpus approaches and tools in sociolinguistic research, surveys the growing number of studies in corpus-based sociolinguistics, and provides instructions and options for designing and developing corpus-based studies. Readers will find practical information on such contemporary topics as workplace registers, megacorpora, and using the Web as a corpus. Vignettes, case studies, discussion questions, and activities throughout further enhance students' involvement with the material and provide opportunities for hands-on practice of the methods discussed. *Corpus-Based Sociolinguistics* is a comprehensive and accessible guide, a must read for any student or scholar interested in exploring this popular and promising approach to sociolinguistic research.

Eric Friginal is an Assistant Professor in the Applied Linguistics and ESL Department at Georgia State University.

Jack A. Hardy is a doctoral candidate in the Applied Linguistics and ESL Department at Georgia State University.

CORPUS-BASED SOCIOLINGUISTICS

A Guide for Students

Eric Friginal and Jack A. Hardy
Georgia State University

Routledge
Taylor & Francis Group

NEW YORK AND LONDON

First published 2014
by Routledge
711 Third Avenue, New York, NY 10017

Simultaneously published in the UK
by Routledge
2 Park Square, Milton Park, Abingdon, Oxon OX14 4RN

Routledge is an imprint of the Taylor & Francis Group, an informa business

Library of Congress Cataloging-in-Publication Data

Friginal, Eric.
Corpus-based sociolinguistics: a guide for students / by Eric Friginal and
  Jack A. Hardy.
      pages cm
   Includes bibliographical references and index.
   1. Sociolinguistics.   I. Hardy, Jack A.   II. Title.
P40.F75 2014
306.44—dc23
2013026990

ISBN: 978-0-415-52955-6 (hbk)
ISBN: 978-0-415-52956-3 (pbk)
ISBN: 978-0-203-11482-7 (ebk)

Typeset in Bembo
by Apex CoVantage, LLC

Printed and bound in the United States of America by
Edwards Brothers Malloy

TABLE OF CONTENTS

LIST OF FIGURES

LIST OF TABLES

ACKNOWLEDGEMENTS

Kandil, M. (2008). *The Israeli-Palestinian conflict in American, Arab, and British media: Corpus-based critical discourse analysis.* Unpublished doctoral dissertation proposal, Department of Applied Linguistics and ESL, Georgia State University, Atlanta.

Friginal, E. (2013a). 25 years of Biber's multi-dimensional analysis: Introduction to the special issue. *Corpora, 8*(2) pp. 137–152. [Permission from Edinburgh University Press.]

Reiter, J. (2011). *Lexical variation in inaugural addresses: A research proposal and preliminary results.* Unpublished manuscript, Department of Applied Linguistics and ESL, Georgia State University, Atlanta.

Figure C3.3. Comparison of *god* words in presidential inaugurals across historical periods, from Reiter, Feinberg, and Thompson (2011)

Figure C4.2. Emotive words used as a percentage of total word use in King's and X's speeches, from Pinkasovic (2013)

Figure C4.3. King's and X's use of words of anxiety, anger, and sadness, from Pinkasovic (2013)

Figure C4.4. King's and X's use of words referring to family, friends, and religion, from Pinkasovic (2013)

Table C1.1. Composition of the parenting subcorpus, from Roberts and Murphy (2012)

PREFACE

We view *corpus linguistics* as a research approach that facilitates practical investigations of language variation and use, producing a range of reliable and generalizable linguistic data that can be extensively interpreted. The corpus approach follows methodological innovations that allow scholars to ask research questions about the patterns of linguistic phenomena across many social situations. The findings these questions generate produce important perspectives on language variation from those taken in traditional sociolinguistic investigations. In addition, corpora can also provide a strong support for the view that language variation is systematic and can be described using empirical, quantitative methods. This argument is important because sociolinguistic studies, even with their deep roots in ethnographies or qualitative analysis, also require extensive technical, multifaceted data that explain the interface between linguistic parameters existing within social groups. One important contribution of corpus linguistics to sociolinguistics, therefore, which we explore and highlight in this book, is the documentation of the existence of social constructs that strongly (i.e., *statistically*) influence language variation and use.

According to McEnery and Wilson (2001),

> while sociolinguistics has traditionally been based upon empirical data, the use of standard corpora in this field has been limited. The expansion of corpus work in sociolinguistics appears to have been hampered by three problems: the operationalization of sociolinguistic theory into measurable categories suitable for corpus research, lack of sociolinguistic metadata encoded in currently available corpora, and lack of sociolinguistically rigorous sampling in corpus construction. (p. 116)

We agree, for the most part, with these scholars. Admittedly, there are very important sociolinguistic theories and constructs that are just not suited for corpus-based investigations. For example, the study and analysis of accents, pronunciation, and especially sociophonetic features of speech may not yet be completely possible in corpus-based sociolinguistics, given obvious procedural and technical limitations. There are also many areas of study in sociolinguistics that simply do not require the use of corpora (e.g., language policy and planning, diglossia, and analysis of linguistic discrimination and prejudice). Objections to corpora in language studies in general also often focus on what type of language is actually represented in a static corpus and how a variable such as gender can be properly accounted for in corpus-based analysis. Some of these theoretical arguments are difficult to address here. However, there have been major developments, at least in the last 10 years, to answer these and other "problems" hampering corpus-based research in sociolinguistics. Sociolinguistic metadata have been encoded in the updated version of the British National Corpus (BNC) and its Web interface, and controlled demographics and parallel registers are provided in the International Corpus of English (ICE). In addition, recently available or published specialized corpora such as the Hong Kong Corpus of Spoken English or HKCSE (Cheng, Greaves, & Warren, 2005), prosodically transcribed using Brazil's (1985, 1997) model, offer functional, social, and textual information that are readily available for corpus-based analysis within the confines of sociolinguistics.

Many researchers involved in the study of linguistic variation across groups of speakers or writers have developed models of corpus design that emphasize **representativeness** and **generalizability** of corpora, which may support (and possibly operationalize) sociolinguistic theories from these corpora. Spoken texts from interviews have also been carefully designed to capture at least some of the lexico/syntactic features of speech for various demographic comparisons. For example, a "sociolinguistics corpus" collected by Tagliamonte (2006, 2008) was obtained from oral narratives to capture vernacular language and annotated for speakers' demographic characteristics. The Linguistic Innovators Corpus or LIC (Kerswill, Cheshire, Fox, & Torgersen, 2008) also utilized sociolinguistic interviews collected from 100 working-class adolescents (who were college students) and 18 elderly speakers in two English boroughs, Hackney and Havering. The LIC corpus has been used to test whether or not London is the center of linguistic innovation in southeastern England (i.e., a dialect study). A related sociolinguistic objective for the LIC corpus focuses on the role of ethnicity and social networks (or "friendship networks") in the analysis of language change in England (Gabrielatos, Torgersen, Hoffman, & Fox, 2010). Finally, the creation and availability of "mega corpora" such as Google Lab's Google Books Ngram Viewer and Mark Davies's COCA and COHA (Corpus of Contemporary American English and Corpus of Historical American English), which all provide information suitable for temporal studies (both synchronic and diachronic studies), contribute to the increasing number of research that can directly describe sociolinguistic variation and change. In summary, although corpus-based sociolinguistics has not yet been fully integrated into the larger field of sociolinguistics, there is no denying its important contribution and increasing influence.

Corpus-Based Sociolinguistics: A Guide for Students focuses on the application of corpora and corpus-based approaches in sociolinguistic research. We introduce and expand the productive merging of corpus tools and sociolinguistic interpretations in the study of variation in language. We survey the growing number of published articles that combine corpora, quantitative data, and sociolinguistic analyses, and we also provide instructions and suggestions for how to design and develop corpus-based sociolinguistics studies. In all these, we emphasize the importance of well-developed research questions to guide the collection of sociolinguistic corpora or use existing texts that can be adapted to form convincing and accurate interpretations of linguistic variation. We believe that this book can effectively guide student-researchers in upper-level undergraduate and graduate courses in sociolinguistics. Specifically, this book focuses on the following six major themes:

1   corpora and the study of languages, dialects, and social varieties
2   language variation and change (diachronic studies of change)
3   lexico-syntactic variation across speaker/writer groups
4   variation in discourse: politeness, stance, and vague reference
5   workplace discourse
6   social media and Web registers.

We acknowledge the support and guidance of Douglas Biber and Randi Reppen, our mentors, in writing this book. Special thanks to Mike Cullom for his perceptive reviews of many drafts of this book and for his constant encouragement. We are grateful for our Routledge editors and reviewers who provided insightful comments and suggestions in developing this book to include additional themes and suggested activities. We recognize Edward Finegan, Paul Baker, Tony McEnery, Sali A. Tagliamonte, Jack Grieve, Richard Xiao, Susan Conrad, Winnie Cheng, Martin Warren, James Pennebaker, Shlomo Argamon, and especially Laurence Anthony and Mark Davies for leading the way with their groundbreaking projects that effectively demonstrated the application of corpora in sociolinguistic research. We thank the many authors whose works are cited and synthesized in this book, especially Wolfgang Teubert, Federica Barbieri, Paulo Quaglio, David "Forrest" Caskey, Lucy Pickering, Stephanie Lindemann, Dennis Preston, Ute Römer, Don Rubin, Magdi Kandil, Kristen Precht, Jená Burges, Ashley Titak, Audrey Roberson, Pamela Pearson, Laura Di Ferrante, Carrie Bruce, Hans J. Ladegaard, the Google *Culturomics* group, Jacob Eisenstein, Mike Scott, and Michael Barlow.

We are grateful to our former students at the Department of Applied Linguistics and ESL at Georgia State University who helped us in developing and critiquing corpus-based sociolinguistic research questions and shared their ideas and pilot studies: John Reiter, Oksana Waugh, Marsha Walker, Janet Beth Randall, Ben Pinkasovic, Jennifer Roberts, Cindy Murphy, Iris Feinberg, Nathalie Thompson, Joohyun Chun, and Carolyn Monteilh. We also thank our colleagues at Georgia State University, Northern Arizona University, Ateneo De Manila University, Aurora State College of Technology, Universidad de las Américas Puebla, and Oxford College of Emory University. A very special thanks to Ken Carter for his patience and encouragement and to Donna and Ela Friginal for their support.

Eric Friginal and Jack A. Hardy,
January 2014

Introduction to Corpus-Based Sociolinguistics

A1

SOCIOLINGUISTIC INVESTIGATIONS OF VARIATION

A1.1 Sociolinguistics

Here are some ways people have responded to the words *thank you* in spoken interactions:

you're welcome	*no worries*	*my pleasure*	*yep/yeah*
sure	*don't mention it*	*anytime*	*uh-huh*
no problem	*not at all*	*you bet*	*of course*
thanks	*cheers*	*ditto*	*alright*

"No response" or "No, *thank* You" (i.e., don't thank me, it's you who should receive *thanks*) are also relatively common.

Have you used *you bet* or *ditto* as a response to *thank you*? Who do you think uses these two responses and in what interactional settings would they be commonly heard? What do you think is the most typical response to *thank you* in a service encounter—in a café, for example? Do women in general express gratitude more than men? Which among the responses on this list is preferred by British English speakers?

Your responses to the questions above support the concept of **variation** in language. Variation exists in how we express a response, a reaction, or an idea following what we have heard or read. We often do not think about the different ways we use words or phrases in speaking and writing. Although we have preferences, and we have formed individual speech mannerisms and expressions, our everyday use of language varies. What are the causes of variation in language? How do we study these variations? What are the practical applications of these studies in understanding the nature of human communication? The answers to these questions are provided to us by sociolinguistics.

Sociolinguistics is the study of variation in language *form* and *use* that is associated with social, situational, attitudinal, temporal, and geographic influences. Studies in sociolinguistics have investigated why and how individuals across varying backgrounds speak and write differently. They have also explored the effects of all aspects of society, which include societal expectations, cultural norms and traditions, and historical backgrounds on the way language is used.

The **social, situational, attitudinal** and **relational, temporal,** and **geographic** factors influencing everyday linguistic variation are broadly defined in this context of research. Sociolinguistics does not necessarily focus on a definitive, singular cause of variation in speech and writing. In fact, an overlap between and among these variables is commonly explored in many sociolinguistic investigations to further understand the unique merging and interplay of factors that influence explicit and implicit linguistic variation. For example, social influences which include personal demographic information such as **gender** can be used together with **nationality**, as identified by geographic locations, in studying the use of *slang* words. Thus, we can compare how American and Canadian men and women make use of particular words identified as *slang* in various speech events.

What is clear in sociolinguistic studies is that there are two primary variables under investigation: (1) *linguistic variables*, which focus on the presence of variation in language use—from observable shifts or changes in how these linguistic forms are utilized in speaking and writing and (2) *societal variables*, which include the social, situational, attitudinal and relational, temporal, and geographic influences, and any combination of these influences, that potentially account for these linguistic shifts or changes. It is important to know how these two groups of variables are defined or operationalized in many sociolinguistic studies. We further describe these linguistic and societal variables below:

Linguistic Variables Investigated in Sociolinguistics

- **sounds, words, and grammatical features of a language**—include a range of differences in the pronunciation of sounds, intonation of utterances, and the use of words and phrases (e.g., the *thank you* responses above), and grammatical structures of language;
- **discoursal features**—include spoken and written characteristics of style, formality/informality of discourse, and textual structures (e.g., use of cohesive devises in writing; interruption, latching, or overlaps in face-to-face conversation);
- **pragmatic features**—include spoken and written expressions of politeness in language, stance and hedging, the use of respect markers or cuss words, and features of agreements and disagreements in interactions;
- **specific communicative features**—include spoken and written manifestations of friendliness, affection, loyalty, or disgust; various speech acts (e.g., requests, commands, and declarations); and pauses, backchannels, greetings and leave-takings;

- **paralanguage features**—include pitch and volume in speech and non-verbal elements of language such as silence, gasp, laughter in conversations; paralanguage may also include the use of visuals, emoticons, or punctuation marks in writing.

Societal Variables in Sociolinguistics

- **social**—speaker/writer demographic information such as gender and sexuality, age, occupation, educational background, annual income, group networks, social class, or social status;
- **situational**—various communication contexts and **registers** (see Section A2.4 for the operational definition of registers we use in this book); speech events such as conversation, interview, or broadcast;
- **attitudinal and relational**—speaker/writer perceptions and attitudes (including prejudice), identity and identity construction, power, relationships and roles, solidarity;
- **temporal**—time periods, change in societal and cultural perspectives over time, major historical events including influences from wars, natural calamities, and migration patterns over time;
- **geographic**—particular locations, geographic regions, and boundaries;
- **other societal variables**—more specific personality factors, sociological distinctions; think also about "uncommon" or new/emerging societal variables that are still not extensively explored in research.

In sum, by studying the influence of societal items on language form and use, we can further comprehend and also experience the reality that our everyday language is remarkably varied and influenced by numerous factors. No one speaks the same way all the time, and people constantly exploit the nuances of the languages they speak for a wide variety of purposes. This recognition of variation implies that we must see language as not just some kind of abstract object of study. Language is pragmatic, practical, evolving, and unique to individuals or groups of connected individuals. We can form our own generalizations about these variations and their practical implications—how do they influence policies or our own attitudes? How do we address these differences to make sure that our reactions are valid or constructive, especially as we try to define what is proper or correct language in contrast to improper or substandard language (does "substandard" language exists in the first place?). Ultimately, we can take advantage of how we interpret and use these everyday variations in language to help us understand our own special ways of communicating with people around us.

Understanding variation in language has definitive functions and concrete applications that can eventually lead to our greater **sociolinguistic competence**. The concept of sociolinguistic competence implies that we know *when*, *where*, and *how* to use the appropriate forms of language—to fully express our ideas and emotions, respond to questions accurately, and avoid misunderstandings

TABLE A1.1 Linguistic and societal items

Linguistic Items	Societal Items
Sounds (e.g., *phonemes, accents, intonation*)	Identity
Words (e.g., *cuss words, respect markers, pronoun use*)	Power/Relationships/Role
Grammatical Structures (e.g., *quotative like, that deletion, information density markers*)	Social Class/Status
	Gender
Paralinguistic Markers (e.g., *laughter, gestures, silence, emoticons*)	Occupation
	Solidarity
Discourse/Pragmatic Structures (e.g., *politeness and stance, turn-taking and interruption, requests*)	Age
	Social Networks
Other linguistic items?	Geographical Origin
	Personality Factors (e.g., introverts vs. extroverts)
	Others societal items?

or miscommunications to obtain optimal outcomes. It is certainly not going to be easy, given the complications of language, to achieve sociolinguistic competence in various contexts of spoken and written communication. Everyday interactions with our parents, spouses or partners, children, friends and coworkers, acquaintances, bosses or subordinates, and every Facebook friend or follower on Twitter will require a particular form of discourse in order for us to successfully participate and contribute. It will be a guessing game and sometimes we will not *get it*. The good thing about language is that, we are not expected to get it all the time and we can clarify, ask, or negotiate to move forward.

Reflective Break

- What potential studies can you investigate that could show the interaction between societal items and linguistic items from the comparison table (Table A1.1) above? What do you think are the pragmatic or practical applications of these studies? What are your goals and research questions in conducting these studies and how will you collect data?
- **Here's a sample research question**: Does the gender of speakers (as interviewer vs. interviewee) influence the distribution of politeness markers (e.g., *thanks, thank you, appreciate, please*) during job interviews? Try to provide hypotheses to this research question.

A1.2 Applications of Sociolinguistic Research

Sociolinguistics also focuses on extensive language contact situations—in which groups of speakers or writers using different languages with a variety of backgrounds interact with one another on a day-to-day basis. Sociolinguistic research has explored the attitudes of writers/speakers; educators; professionals in other fields such as media, politics and economics; and the public toward the forms and uses of language. Over the years, sociolinguists have extensively identified the linguistic markings of speaker characteristics and the linguistic choices of speakers and writers that are affected by varying purposes, topics, and settings. This dynamic field has also covered issues in the sociology of language, including the following:

- cross-cultural interaction
- language in education and literacy
- standardization of language
- technology and language
- English for globalization
- multilingualism, bilingual education, and language planning.

A1.3 Sociolinguistic Investigations

Sociolinguistic investigations follow technical and scientific procedures in obtaining and analyzing a range of linguistic data. In order to obtain these data for sociolinguistic research, many studies have utilized ethnographic and anthropological approaches. Investigators have accumulated an extensive collection of spoken texts from interviews with informants accompanied with detailed observations and documentation of societal norms and events during the time of these interviews. Over the past 50 years, a number of different approaches to the empirical study of variation in language have emerged and have developed their own unique methodologies (Macaulay, 2009). Coding interview and observational data has become highly scientific, making use of computer-based tools and multimedia equipment. Newer technical approaches from the study of actual interactional events to the analysis of behaviors within simulated settings have also produced additional descriptions of distinctive variation in the use of language in numerous and widely diverse communicative contexts.

Sociolinguistic studies are generally classified according to the following research models.

Ethnography of Communication

Various linguistic studies conducted by Dell Hymes from the 1960s paved the way for Ethnography of Communication (EOC) as an independent method of discourse analysis that explores the interactional patterns of members of a particular speech community. EOC is influenced by the anthropological field of ethnography (i.e., linguistic anthropology), which conceptualizes speech communication as a continuous flow of information from a broader perspective and not just as a segmented exchange of messages. EOC studies (e.g., Cameron, 2001; Philipsen, 1975; Saville-Troike, 1982) look at cultural values and how these influence speech (or writing) and perceptions about contextual appropriateness, intent, and group judgments. In these studies, local cultural patterns and norms must be understood for analysis and interpretation of the appropriateness of speech situated within specific communities.

Interactional Sociolinguistics

Interactional sociolinguistics explores how speakers negotiate and interpret meaning within a particular social interaction. Social contexts include a range of settings, speaker relationships, social purposes of talk in interactions, and other intangibles (e.g., time of interaction, locations, and personal demographics). Research topics in interactional sociolinguistics may focus on cross-cultural (mis)communication (referred to as "crosstalk"), agreement/disagreement, requests and refusals, and politeness. The study of interactional sociolinguistics was developed and popularized by linguistic anthropologist John J. Gumperz. In terms of research methods, interactional sociolinguists typically analyze audio or video recordings of conversations or other specialized interactions. Their analyses focus not only on linguistic forms such as words and sentences but also on subtle cues such as prosody, facial expressions, and the influence of culturally specific settings.

Conversation Analysis

Conversation analysis (CA) focuses on very detailed observations of communication events matched by a clear method for collecting, analyzing, and organizing speech patterns across instances of a phenomenon (e.g., turn-taking, pausing, questions). Over the years, CA has gone through a combination of approaches originally developed by sociologist Harvey Sacks to account for the role of talk in wider social processes. For example, studies of repair structures and organization in speech (Sidnell, 2009); use of personal references (Levinson, 2006); institutional talk, doctor's office, courtroom trials (Heritage & Clayman, 2010); or critical engagements (Hutchby & Wooffitt, 2008), among many other methodologies, have extended the systematic study of conversation from CA's historical beginnings into more detailed investigations of "trajectories of action" (Sidnell, 2009). These trajectories of action often involve people who are engaged in explicitly accomplishing a goal or getting something done (Schegloff, 2005). CA's focus on business meetings, business negotiations, and decision-making (or "task-focused talk") provides a model for the analysis of professional interactions on macro- and microlevels.

Experimental Sociolinguistics

Researchers studying constructs such as prejudice in language, linguistic attitudes and interpretation, and linguistic perception may conduct actual experiments to obtain behavioral data to illustrate variation. Settings can be simulated to record informants' reactions to particular linguistic input—that is, a word, sentence, or utterance that may or may not produce behaviors that represent a social group or a speech community. Experimental research questions guide participant sampling, data collection, and subsequent analysis. Drager (forthcoming) proposed that for a question such as the following, "Can listeners accurately identify speakers' ethnicity based only on hearing their voices?" it is recommended to explore theories of speech production and establish a link between linguistic variables (e.g., accent, pronunciation) and the social characteristics associated with these variables. These linguistic variables could then be used in the experiment to extract perceptions of and attitudes about such qualities as the speakers' friendliness, level of education, and accuracy of speech patterns.

Variationist Sociolinguistics

In general, many sociolinguistic studies deal with linguistic variation, but those that specifically focus on comparisons of linguistic distributions across social groups have been referred to as variationist sociolinguistic studies. Variationist sociolinguistic studies are also called "Labovian Sociolinguistics," at least in the United States, as a tribute to American linguist William Labov. Labov conducted one of the very first and most influential variationist investigations of language in the United States in the 1960s (see Section B1.5.1 for a description of William Labov's Martha's Vineyard study). The use of corpora is very common in variationist sociolinguistics. The works of Douglas Biber and Edward Finegan have influenced many corpus-based analyses of historical discourse, regional dialects of English, and cross-linguistic comparisons of multilingual corpora. Variationist studies also utilize quantitative data and applications of statistical techniques in further describing linguistic patterning and usage.

A1.4 Qualitative Approaches in Sociolinguistics

Qualitative approaches in sociolinguistic research include *ethnographies* (such as field studies and field interviews), *case studies, phenomenology, narrative research, grounded theory, historical research, critical social research*, and *ethical inquiry*. An ethnographer may live with a particular group of people to document observable sociocultural behaviors, use of language in various contexts, and, from these observations, describe data that can be used to develop a theoretical framework.

When audio and video recorders became available to researchers, data gathering of speakers' actual pronunciation, patterns of speech, paralinguistic markers, and other recorded variables helped tremendously to further facilitate and enrich research in sociolinguistics. More and more available information about languages has been synthesized over the years through recorded and archived data, documenting phenomena such as language change, the standardization of a language, or language death.

Qualitative sociolinguistic research methods have emphasized systematic data collection and careful documentation of speaker/writer characteristics. In this line of research, patterns of language use are coded and analyzed to comprehensively describe the nature of linguistic variation. Research questions are clearly established from the start, and data collection is based on logical and efficient methodologies. Among the many possible research questions in sociolinguistics, Meyerhoff (2005, p. 3) listed the following questions that broadly combine linguistic and social items to direct a qualitative sociolinguistic inquiry:

- Who uses those different forms of language varieties?
- Who do they use them with?
- Are they aware of their choice?
- Why do some forms of language "win out" over others? (And is it always the same ones?)
- Is there any relationship between the forms in flux in a community of speakers?
- What kind of social information do we ascribe to different forms in a language or different language varieties?
- How much can we change or control the language we use?

These general questions suggest a range of methods to analyze linguistic patterns and identify speaker/writer attitudes toward languages or language contact situations. For example, to investigate a question such as the third question from Meyerhoff's (2005) list above, "Are they aware of their choice?" (i.e., choice in using the different forms of language), researchers need to utilize interpretive techniques that will have to be supported by a sound theoretical framework and evidence from collected data. In this sense, a sociolinguist will have to further explore factors such as personality, identity, and social perceptions based on the particular speaking or writing context. Participant interview questions may be tailored to address this item, and behavioral data could be coded to match how participants actually use these various linguistic patterns.

Researcher observations and interviews with informants provide a wealth of evidence of how social contexts influence the use of language. Many qualitative sociolinguistic studies are conducted by following only a few informants to obtain data that could be analyzed in-depth for extensive coding. **Narrative studies**, for example, focus on participants' personal stories and the retelling of chronological events conducted by the researcher. These stories are coded for emerging linguistic themes and patterns.

For example, a **narrative study** conducted by Ladegaard (2012) looked at the discourse of "powerlessness and repression" from stories and responses to interviews of abused female foreign domestic helpers (FDH) in Hong Kong (HK) who had sought shelter at a church when they had been mistreated by employers. The stories of these FDHs focused primarily on trauma narratives about physical assault, underpayment, exploitation, and starvation. Ladegaard carefully analyzed these stories to explore the linguistic structure of repression from the point of view of abuse victims. This study also investigated how narratives may be used as a means for identity construction (e.g., repression of voice, gaining power) and also potentially to empower FDHs to retell their stories and become agents of change in their own lives. Ladegaard suggested that linguistic resources can be used to index different identities and expose functionally how ideologies of moral exclusion, or the local codes of argument, serve to legitimize dehumanization of abused FDHs in HK.

Narrative studies such as Ladegaard's (2012) are deeply rooted in sociolinguistics research. Sociolinguistics has, in fact, paved the way for conceptual models of narratives and storytelling, and many similar studies have used Labov's (1972a) framework of narrative structure described below to identify the key components of an oral narrative:

- *abstract* (a brief summary of the general propositions the story will make)
- *orientation* (essential background information like time, place, and people involved)
- *complicating action* (key events of the story)
- *evaluation* (highlighting the point of the story)
- *resolution* (how the crisis was resolved)
- *coda* (concluding remarks)

Data collection (recording, interviewing participants, and transcription) in qualitative studies, especially narrative studies, is very tedious, and it requires sufficient training and experience to make sure that ethical considerations are properly considered and addressed. Participant consent is required, and the privacy and confidentiality of information and experiences shared by informants will have to be ensured. Once stories and interviews are collected, researchers have various options to code and analyze data. Spoken narratives, especially group narratives, could be analyzed using discourse or conversation analysis to focus specifically on linguistic patterns that support emerging themes. (Please note that **discourse analysis** and **conversation analysis** are two different approaches, each with a specifically defined set of procedures.) In Ladegaard's (2012) study, interviews were transcribed using conventions from conversation analysis. Group stories featured multiparty conversations that glossed, clarified, and amplified aspects of a topic introduced by a speaker. As a consequence, group identities are constructed with the evaluation, resolution and pragmatic intent of the stories becoming collaborative endeavors of the group of speakers. Text Sample A1.1 shows the importance of verbal support from speakers (FDHs) sharing a common identity.

Text Sample A1.1. Group Narrative

Participants: Aya, 22 years old, Indonesian helper, three months in HK, two years in Brunei before HK; Nadia, 22 years old, Indonesian helper, one month in HK, two years in Malaysia and two years in Singapore; Suleima, 25 years old, Indonesian helper, 18 months in HK, two years in Singapore; Ronia, 37 years old, seven years in HK. Four other Indonesian helpers were in this sharing session. The women are explaining why they are at the shelter. Original in Bahasa; English translation in brackets.

1 Aya:		*saya, saya di rumah majikan saya cuman bersih-bersih,*
2		*tujuh mobil*
		[I, I worked in my employer's house as a house keeper, I clean seven cars]
3 Nadia:		**cuma tujuh**//[laughter]//
		[**seven only**] //[laughter]//
4 Aya:		//*tujuh mobil*// *tujuh mobil, terus yang saya*
5		*nggak suka majikan kalau kita nggak salah kan harus tanya*
6		*tapi dia malah mukul (1.0) terus sehabis mukul dia nyuruh*
7		*senyum* [laughter]
		[//seven cars// seven cars, then the only thing I don't like about them is, even though I wasn't wrong, instead of clarifying they just beat me (1.0) and then after they hit me they ask me to smile] [laughter]
8 *Suleima:*		*gila*
		[crazy]
9 Aya:		*habis itu, habis itu, pokoknya berat, setiap pekerjaan dimenitin*
		[and then and then, everything is tough, they count all my work by the minute]
10 Ronia:		*diwaktuin?*
		[they time all your work?]
11 Aya:		*ya, terus rumahnya cukup besar (2.0) dalam rumah itu terdiri*
12		*tujuh orang (2.0) tingkat empat, mobil tujuh, yang bekerja*
13		*diri saya sendiri (1.5) terus kalau salah minta maaf saya*
14		*malah dipukul, itu yang menyebabkan saya nggak betah disitu*
15		*dan akhirnya kabur (0.5) lapor polisi [. . .] ada dua anak yang*
16		*kecil (3.0) tapi saya nggak pernah nyentuh anaknya, nggak*
17		*boleh, katanya kotor saya*
		[yes, their house is quite big (2.0) there are seven people in that house (2.0) there are four floors, seven cars, the only domestic helper there is me (1.5) if I made a mistake and apologized I'll get beaten instead, that's why I cannot stand working there and finally I ran away (0.5) reported to the police [. . .] there are two children in the house (3.0) but I never touched them, they forbid me to touch them, they said I'm dirty]

(Ladegaard, 2012, pp. 470–472)

According to Ladegaard (2012), this excerpt was a typical example of the way Indonesians help construct each other's stories in the sharing sessions. Speakers tended to give less elaborate verbal feedback, but, as the excerpt above illustrates, they still provided essential support in the form of single words, exclamations, or minimal response as shown in the transcript. Conversation analysis pays careful attention to length of pauses and other features of spoken interactions such as length of utterance, loudness, and the functions and applications of discourse features. Details are emphasized in the analysis and qualitative observations and interpretations from the researcher are always supported by transcribed texts. Below is Ladegaard's narrative briefly interpreting linguistic items such as laughter and loudness in Text Sample A1.1:

> In line 3, Nadia shows her support through a loud ironic exclamation: "**seven only**," followed by laughter from the other participants. She echoes Aya's words in line 2, but the loudness of the utterance and the laughter suggest that it is ironic and an expression of indignation that anyone would ask a helper to clean seven cars every day. The laughter in line 7 seems somewhat inappropriate, but is probably also meant to be supportive. Aya tells them that her employers demand that she smiles after they hit her, and the laughter indicates that the women think this is outrageous, even hilarious. (p. 472)

A1.5 Quantitative Approaches in Sociolinguistics

Quantitative research in sociolinguistics refers to the systematic data collection and analysis involving the application of mathematical and statistical techniques in further describing the nature of linguistic variation within a particular research setting. Data collection in quantitative sociolinguistics follows statistical sampling procedures to guarantee that a particular sample of participants (or texts) represents a target population. In quantitative studies, research questions are clearly defined, often specifying a statistical test such as test of significance and test of relationships to be used in establishing numerical points of comparison. Macaulay (2009) summarizes the three primary considerations in conducting quantitative research in sociolinguistics:

- defining the nature of datasets and exploring methods of collecting evidence of language variation;
- focusing on statistical methodology (how have data been collected and analyzed quantitatively);
- tabulating frequencies and conducting statistical analysis.

Variationist sociolinguistics benefits from quantitative approaches because these approaches provide a more comprehensive and definitive description of variation and relationships across social and linguistic variables. If qualitative (QUAL) studies focus primarily on description of patterns and emerging themes of language usage, quantitative (QUANT) studies are able to employ **inferential techniques** that show whether or not these patterns are **statistically** accounted for by a certain variable or combinations of variables. In addition, these inferential techniques (e.g., test of significance, correlations, predictions, and factor/cluster analysis) are also able to show that these variations did not occur by chance. For example, a measure indicating statistical significance (often through a probability value or a p-value) can support a conclusion as to whether or not the gender or age of participants can account for variations in the use egocentric sequences such as *I believe* or *I think* in unedited online writing samples.

Clearly, the approach to data collection in sociolinguistics, whether QUAL or QUANT, relies on the researcher's **research questions** motivating the study. These research approaches are not competing approaches and one is not necessarily better than the other. Qualitative, descriptive studies provide an in-depth set of data that explores highly specific details (e.g., the transcription of loudness and laughter in Ladegaard's study) and captures multimodal social and paralinguistic contexts. Quantitative, statistical studies, on the other hand, allow for inferential tests and comparisons from sampled participants (or texts) representing a certain population. Both will provide extensive datasets that will then have to be comprehensively analyzed within scientific and empirical perspectives in order to determine implications and potential applications of the research findings.

QUAL and QUANT researchers will have to be technically proficient in their approaches, and they must know the nature of linguistic data they are collecting. Further, these researchers will have to clearly document the study from the start of data collection, coding observations, and counting of frequencies through various analyses and resulting interpretations. As Macaulay (2009) prefaced in his book, *Quantitative Methods in Sociolinguistics*, "If linguistics is, as is often claimed, the scientific study of language, then it is reasonable to expect linguists to behave like other scientists" (p. ix). Methodological considerations and supporting details in sociolinguistic research will have to be presented in the study to show how a linguistic phenomenon can be accurately described by means of empirical observations or tests. Ultimately, QUAL and QUANT approaches are often combined in many sociolinguistic studies. QUANT approaches are followed in data collection and statistical analysis and QUAL interpretive techniques are utilized to explain the nature of variation in the dataset. Ethnographic and case-study descriptions of settings and participants are also typically used to contextualize the study. The combination of QUAL and QUANT approaches in research is called **mixed-methods approach**.

A1.5.1 Some Examples of Quantitative Sociolinguistic Studies

The application of statistical techniques in sociolinguistics has produced interesting inferential data that can directly explain the influence of social variables upon the use of linguistic features across various settings. The data collection in these studies often involves participant responses to questions and tests, a careful sampling of respondents, and running statistical tests. Experiments and testing of behaviors or attitudes can also be conducted to obtain comparable sets of data. The three sample studies below investigated how ethnicity and religious orientation influenced the pronunciation of certain vowel sounds (McCafferty, 2001), attitudes toward a cultural group and perceptions of success or failure in task-based communication (Lindemann, 2002), and regional/geographic origin in the United States and grammaticality judgments of selected sentence structures (Benson, 2009). These studies merged various QUANT approaches with QUAL descriptions of settings and contexts.

Kevin McCafferty (2001), *Ethnicity and Language Change: English in (London) Derry, Northern Ireland*

Research focus: the social aspect of language variation, particularly in the pronunciation of six phonological variables by Catholics and Protestants in (London) Derry, Northern Ireland, in 1994–1995. In addition to quantitative analysis, this study also focused extensively on ethnographic accounts of linguistic use from McCafferty's fieldwork (audio recorded interviews) and on how political turmoil and regional security affected ethnic differences or loyalties.

Linguistic variables: six phonological variables focusing primarily on the vowels of London Derry English; the study compared the pronunciation of the vowels in "fleece," "near," and "face" or the [I] and [e] sounds, which also distinguished formal and informal pronunciation.

Social variables/participants: McCafferty conducted a total of 187 interviews with Catholics and Protestants at community centers, first establishing personal relationships with informants before asking them to grant interviews. Among these interviews, 107 were used for actual sociolinguistic analysis. Additional social variables included gender, class (middle and working classes), and age (teenagers and adults). Questions about ethnic differences, solidarity, and identities were avoided during the interview.

Analyses and results: A significant difference in the pronunciation of the "face" vowel sound was found between Catholics and Protestants using chi-square statistical test of significance. In more informal speech for Catholic participants, [I] was significantly more frequent. The same was true for working class participants. For the other vowels in the study, interesting patterns of use were observed, but the differences were negligible. The innovative form was a diphthong [eI] in the pronunciation of "face," which was used more frequently by Protestants, particularly middle-class speakers. McCafferty contended that this study was the first to clearly establish the influence of ethnicity and religion in the pronunciation of some vowel sounds.

Stephanie Lindemann (2002), *Listening with an Attitude: A Model of Native-Speaker Comprehension of Non-Native Speakers in the United States*

Research focus: This study investigated how attitudes about nonnative English accents influenced listeners' comprehension of the speech of nonnative speakers (NNSs) of English. Specifically, Lindemann explored whether there was a relationship between negative attitudes toward nonnative speakers and the level of comprehension of those speakers. Twelve native English speakers whose attitudes toward Koreans had been assessed (positive or negative) were asked to complete an interactional map task paired with native Korean speakers. This study also analyzed the relationships between attitude, collaborative behavior, and perceived and actual comprehension using a combination of quantitative and qualitative data.

Linguistic variables: speech comprehension and accuracy of information (giving directions) from a map exercise; native English speakers' perception of the success or failure of their interaction with NNSs.

Social variables/participants: A subset of 12 study participants (native speakers of English) were assessed by an attitude measure as having either relatively positive or relatively negative attitudes toward Koreans. These participants were asked to complete an interactive map task, first with other native speakers of English and then with Korean NNSs. The study participants' interactions with NNSs were analyzed and compared with their interactions with other native speakers of English to determine if attitude was related to their level of collaborative behavior. Participants' perception of the success of the interaction and its actual success measured by the map exercise were compared.

Analyses and results: Lindemann's quantitative data included all participants' ratings of the success of each of their interactions as well as map accuracy data for interactions between study participants and their Korean partners. The accuracy of map replication was assessed by measuring the area of the difference between the route on the original map and the route drawn by study participants. This was accomplished by tracing both the intended route and the participant's route onto a sheet of graph paper, and counting the number of 1-cm squares falling between these two lines.

Results showed that participants who had been assessed as having negative attitudes toward Koreans rated their interactions with Koreans as "far less successful" than did those with more positive attitudes. An independent t-test showed this difference to be significant [$t(10)527.059, p = .001$]. In contrast, participants with positive attitudes toward Koreans rated their interactions with Koreans and with other native speakers as equally successful. In sum, this experimental study reported that people's own attitudes appear to be related to how they perceive the success (or failure) of their task-based interactions.

Erica J. Benson (2009), *Everyone Wants In: Want + Prepositional Adverb in the Midland and Beyond*

Research focus: This study explored **grammaticality judgments** from different informants representing dialect regions of the United States. Participant responses to a grammaticality judgment test were collected in 2002 and 2003 with 1,255 ratings of sentences containing forms of want + prepositional adverb by 163 lifelong residents of three dialect areas east of the Mississippi River—the Midland (95), the North (41), and the South (27). Benson's sentences were rated by respondents from a questionnaire with a "forced-choice," five-point scale adapted from Albanyan and Preston (1998). This questionnaire looked at two distinct judgments: (1) acceptability and use and (2) stylistic differentiation. For example:

> Choose **a** if you would never use this sentence.
> Choose **b** if you would use this sentence only in writing or in very formal speech situations such as a job interview or in court.

Linguistic variables: syntactic structures—want by/down/in/off/out—representing a subset of possible forms of want + prepositional adverb:

- The dog *wants fed*.
- Mark *wants by*, but he is too shy to ask people to move.
- When the dog scratches at the back door, he *wants in*.
- The child was scared on the swing and said she *wanted off*.

The constructions *want out/ in/off/down* were selected for the study based on previous literature. Midland respondents (58% of total participants) were the original focus because the use of *want* + prepositional adverb was common in spoken interactions by Midlanders.

Social variables/participants: Of the 163 respondents, 148 were university and technical college students, and the remaining 15 were residents recruited through local churches and a "friend-of-a-friend method." Respondents representing the North (25%) and South (17%) were used for comparison. Other social variables included residence (29% rural, 71% nonrural), gender (67% male, 33% female), age (67% 18- to 24-year-olds, 12% 25- to 34-year-olds, 11% 35- to 54-year-olds, and 11% 55-year-olds and older), and socioeconomic status (upper middle, middle middle, lower middle, upper working, and lower working). Socioeconomic data was based on the occupation of the primary wage-earner in the family.

Analysis and results: Results showed that Midlanders dominated the acceptability of *want* + prepositional adverb compared to residents of the North and South. Benson noted, however, that the rate of acceptability in the North and the South was much greater than she originally anticipated. The self-reported use of *want* +prepositional adverb in the Midland (84%), the North (68%), and the South (69%) was statistically significant across dialect regions using Pearson chi-square (Pearson χ^2 = 41, df = 2, p = .000). Overall, the same pattern was observed with the individual forms of *want* + prepositional adverb across the dialect regions and most of the social variables analyzed in the study.

Reflective Break

- Can you mention some limitations of the three sample quantitative studies? Both Lindemann (2002) and Benson (2009) used "self-reported" data within an experimental or testing context; McCafferty (2001), on the other hand, analyzed pronunciation samples from recorded interviews. What are the advantages and disadvantages in using these types of data from respondents/ participants?

- Following Benson's study, how would you "judge" the statements below? Do you think your responses are influenced by your regional origin or your first language background?

    - Gas is so *expensive anymore*.
    - That's *all the further* I'm going.
    - The clothes *need ironed*.

A1.6 Summary of Research Approaches in Sociolinguistics

In sum, meaningful analysis and functional interpretation of data, whether qualitative or quantitative, are primary considerations in conducting research in sociolinguistics. **Why then have we introduced these research approaches to you in the first section of this book?** The primary reason for this is to properly situate what we do in corpus linguistics in relation to the wider-ranging field— the context, if you will—of sociolinguistics. This merging of approaches positions corpus linguistics as a very good model in studying sociolinguistic variation. Corpora can provide a range of frequency distributions of linguistic features that could be "tagged" and counted using computational programs. These quantitative distributions are then analyzed and interpreted using qualitative techniques. Text samples from corpora can be provided for additional qualitative coding and more in-depth discourse analysis. We introduce corpus linguistics in the following sections, including its limitations in sociolinguistics, and future directions.

A2

CORPUS-BASED SOCIOLINGUISTICS

A2.1 Corpus Linguistics

As a research approach in the study of languages, corpus linguistics (CL) has developed and evolved over several decades to support empirical investigations of language variation and use. As emphasized by Biber, Reppen, and Friginal (2010), corpus linguistics is not, in itself, a model of language (unlike sociolinguistics). This implies a potential misnomer in how the term *corpus linguistics* has been used and applied in many research studies over the years. What is clear to us, and also the basic premise of this book, is that corpus linguistics is primarily a methodological approach that can be summarized according to the following considerations from Biber, Conrad, and Reppen (1998):

- It is empirical, analyzing the actual patterns of use in natural texts.
- It utilizes a large and principled collection of natural texts, known as a *corpus* (pl. *corpora*), as the basis for analysis.
- It makes extensive use of computers for analysis, employing both automatic and interactive techniques.
- It relies on the combination of quantitative and qualitative analytical techniques.

With the CL approach then, it is argued that research findings about variation in language have much greater generalizability and validity than would otherwise be feasible and/or justifiable. CL research in general offers strong support for the view that language variation is systematic and can be described using empirical, quantitative, and frequency-based methods (Biber, 1988).

It is important to remember that, although corpora offer measurable descriptions of texts and social groups, the researcher and subsequent consumers of these studies must still **interpret** these corpus-based findings (e.g., answer the question, *So what?*). There is little importance to knowing, for example, that one gender group uses more passive voice constructions than another without being able to explore the functional reasons behind that difference in a particular context (e.g., in an academic or professional setting; in narrative vs. expository texts). Hence, corpus methodologies can often be used in tandem with register-based methods, and corpora and quantitative data can be explored to answer questions related to social variation in language. Corpus data will then have to be functionally interpreted accurately and truthfully. In an interview with Friginal (2013a), Biber emphasized the importance of functional interpretation of corpus-based data:

> Quantitative patterns discovered through corpus analysis should always be subsequently interpreted in functional terms. In some corpus studies, quantitative findings are presented as the end of the story. I find this unsatisfactory. For me, quantitative patterns of linguistic variation exist because they reflect underlying functional differences, and a necessary final step in any corpus analysis should be the functional. (Friginal, 2013a, p. 148)

A2.2 What is a Corpus?

From the Latin word for "body," the word *corpus* has been used by researchers to refer to their datasets (i.e., their body of data). However, in linguistics, the term is even more narrowly defined. Instead of just being used to describe any collection of information, *corpora* are now seen as systematically collected, naturally occurring categories of *texts*. Note, also, that in this book, when we refer to text, we are not limited to describing language that was initially written. In addition, a text can also be a transcription of speech. Before the age of computers, such collection was completed by hand and was extremely labor-intensive.

In this day and age, however, with the advent of the personal computers and the digitization of much of our everyday language, CL has become a much more widely practiced, accessible field of investigation. In fact, for many, a linguistic corpus is, by definition, computerized or searchable by computer programs. Anyone with a computer and perhaps an Internet connection can begin to create a corpus, as long as it follows a logical and linguistically principled design. There are also dozens of publicly available corpora, which researchers around the world can study and analyze, almost like crowdsourcing the research completed on such data. Below are definitions of *corpus* as provided by corpus linguists:

> A corpus is a large and principled collection of natural texts. (Biber et al., 1998, p. 12)
>
> A corpus is a collection of pieces of language text in electronic form, selected according to external criteria to represent, as far as possible, a language or language variety as a source of data for linguistic research. (Sinclair, 2005)
>
> A corpus is a collection of (1) *machine readable* (2) *authentic* texts (including transcripts of spoken data) which is (3) *sampled* to be (4) *representative* of a particular language or language variety. (McEnery, Xiao, & Tono, 2006, p. 5)

For many, corpora and corpus-based tools offer relevant options to research a wide variety of questions in several branches of linguistics. For example, a lexicographer, or someone who designs dictionaries, may be interested in compiling and analyzing a large, representative corpus in order to get a sense of word frequencies as well as contexts in which words are found. A sociolinguist may want to use corpora of the speech and/or writing of a particular group to better understand it. These objectives and others like them are most often associated with, and are best served by, a **corpus-based approach**. Corpus-based analysis is "a methodology that uses corpus evidence mainly as a repository of examples to expound, test or exemplify given theoretical statements" (Tognini-Bonelli, 2001, p. 10). In other words, corpora can be used to answer preexisting questions about preexisting suppositions in frameworks that have already been accepted by scholars in the field. Such analysis has also been described as being *top-down* because of the nature of categories are known and chosen before going down to explore the lower levels of individual texts.

Some researchers have recognized the value of corpus linguistics as its own theory-generating branch in the field of linguistics. This perspective is seen more in **corpus-driven** approaches to research. This form of research is more inductive, or bottom-up, in that the linguistic features that are investigated come directly from analyses of the corpus, not from preestablished categories by the researcher. Biber (2009, p. 276) describes how such research tries to minimize the number of assumptions of linguistic constructs the researcher might have. Instead, the data is expected to speak for itself, in a way:

> In a corpus-driven approach the commitment of the linguist is to the integrity of the data as a whole, and descriptions aim to be comprehensive with respect to corpus evidence. The corpus, therefore, is seen as more than a repository of examples to back pre-existing theories or a probabilistic extension to an already well-defined system. The theoretical statements are fully consistent

> with, and reflect directly, the evidence provided by the corpus. . . . Examples
> are normally taken verbatim, in other words they are not adjusted in any way
> to fit the predefined categories of the analyst. (Tognini-Bonelli, 2001, p. 84)

Although **corpus-based** and **corpus-driven** approaches can be thought of as dichotomous, they are more like two poles on either end of a continuum. There are areas of research in which corpora are used purely to find examples of predefined linguistic features (e.g., most common stance words), and, at the same time, there are truly corpus-driven studies, such as allowing computer programs to determine the likelihood of multiple words being used together (e.g., the concept of lexical bundles or formulaic sequences). However, according to Biber (2009, p. 279) such corpus-driven research often includes some corpus-based techniques and can thus be considered "hybrids."

The similarity of these approaches is that both involve the collection and analysis of corpora of **natural language**. Many researchers are even interested in similar constructs. Compilation and analysis, however, are influenced by the ultimate goals: if one wants to study a preestablished construct, he or she might simply search for that construct in a corpus. If, on the other hand, the researcher is curious and does not want to come to the analysis with preconceptions, a large corpus may be collected and analyzed using corpus analysis that does not include a priori decisions of what to search for.

A2.3 Exploring Linguistic Variation with Corpora

As we noted in Section A1, sociolinguistic variation typically involves complex patterns consisting of the interaction among several different linguistic parameters and societal contexts. Ultimately, this variation in language is said to be systematic (Biber, 1988). One of the major contributions of CL is to document the existence of linguistic constructs that are not recognized by current sociolinguistic theories and to provide broad supporting documents and data for extensive functional analysis and interpretation. In a way, this is the essence of corpus-based sociolinguistics. We use well-developed corpora and employ a range of corpus tools to help us extract quantitative patterns of variation. We then use interpretive techniques, often supported by statistical tests as we attempt to generalize our results to our target population.

For example, the interaction of the use of personal pronouns: first person (*I, we, our*), second person (*you, your, yours*), and third person (*he, she, they*) across gender (men, women) and age groups (over 30 and under 30 years old) of bloggers is presented in Figure A2.1 below (Friginal, 2009a). In this comparison, CL allows for the extraction of data such as the frequency distribution of these personal pronouns from a corpus of blogs collected online from 2006 to 2008. The corpus is coded for gender and age of bloggers, together with related information such as the topics of blog entries, the geographical region in the United States where the blogger was based, and the primary textual characteristics (e.g., informational or personal/involved focus) of each blog text.

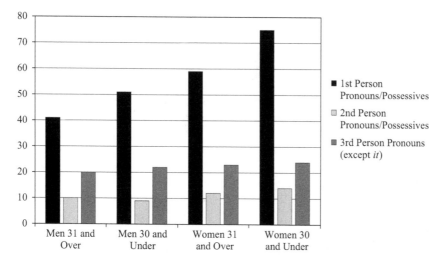

FIGURE A2.1 Personal pronouns by gender and age; data normalized per 1,000 words; first person pronouns/possessives gender (F=63.004, p<.0001), age (F=30.52, p<.0001); gender*age (F=10.23, p<.001); second and third person pronouns/possessives not significant

Source: adapted from Friginal, 2009a, p. 25

The figure above illustrates a pattern of increasing use of (all) personal pronouns from older male authors to younger female authors of blogs. In this study, the major source of variation was found to be with the use of first person personal pronouns, particularly in the use of the first person pronoun *I* by females under 30 and males over 30. Statistically significant differences across gender, age, and the interaction between gender and age of bloggers were observed in the frequency of first person pronouns (including possessives: *my, mine, our*) in the corpus. The differences in the distributions of second and third person pronouns were not significant. The use of first person pronouns (*I, me, my, our, we*) in blogs generally support many previous sociolinguistic studies of gender and use of personal pronouns suggesting that females "personalize" their spoken or written discourse more than males. We discuss gender-based distinctions identified in corpora further in Section B2.

In the case of blogs, personalization is exemplified by the use of the first person singular in explicitly referring to the actions and state of mind of the blogger. Overall, the use of first person (singular and plural) pronouns means that the writer refers directly to himself or herself in conveying information and communicating feelings, reactions, and ideas, while at the same time involving or drawing the reader into the discourse. This construction is shown in the short excerpt from the corpus:

> **I** will have to share **my** own personal feelings here. **I** was not very happy with the way **me** and **my** peeps were shouted at and ridiculed at the game. **My**

impressions have changed and **I** will not be attending that game with {school} anymore. Peace out. (Blogger: Female, 18 years old, high school student)

The availability of quantitative, frequency data from a corpus provides clear, visual comparisons as shown in Figure A2.1 that are common in CL-based research on linguistic variation. Another advantage of CL-based research is the easy access to text samples or text excerpts that can be used to support functional analyses of variations. In the two short excerpts below, the presence of many first person pronouns in a blog written by a 17-year-old female contrasts considerably with the tone and focus of blog writing by a 67-year-old male. The two excerpts seem to address personal topics and were both directed to readers who were mostly familiar with the bloggers. Although there are many contextual differences in these two samples, corpus data clearly help in potentially accounting for sources of linguistic variation in the use of first person pronouns/possessives. For group differences in this study, many blogs by older males differed substantially in linguistic composition, formality, and style from blogs written by younger females.

Text Sample A2.1. Comparison of Blog Texts

Female, 17 years old, high school student
Oh, thank you God. Band camp really sucks. **I** am so tired of all of it! **It** doesn't matter, tomorrow is the last day. **I** don't really feel like updating much. Go figure. **We** have the 1st, 2nd, and up to set 15 of the 3rd song completed, but just as last year, **our** drill writer is stupid and is falling behind. **We** have no more drill to work on. Hopefully **we** will have more tomorrow. Mr. C was pretty much a big idiot to get the same one as last year, because last year **we** like only got the 1st and half of the second song during camp. Ha. Ah, **my** eye is so itchy right now **you** wouldn't believe because **I** had to carry **my** cat outside and **I** must have gotten some of **her** hair or something in my face. **I** am very allergic to cats. **I** get itchy and sneezy. **I** am itching my eye too much, **it**'s starting to hurt.

Male, 67 years old, retired professor
Table talk for the Sunday brunch crowd was the Senior Prom at the Golden Age Center last night. Retired biology teacher Denver Zygote and Granny Garbanzo double-dated with Judge and Mrs. Halfthrottle. The big excitement came about half-way through the festivities when Granny attempted to Watusi with her cane in her hand. The elderly jurist was a little too close and the wildly waving walking stick caught him in a most sensitive part of his anatomy. While the ambulance crew carted Judge H. off to the emergency room, Denver and Granny disappeared. Arnie said he didn't know where the duo spent the rest of the night, but

it wasn't at home. Walter elbowed Arnie and quipped that the way things were going between his mother and Denver they'd soon be planning a honeymoon.

The gender and age of authors in the two excerpts arguably contributed to the differences in how these texts were written and presented to readers. Younger female bloggers exhibited a tendency to use more involved and conversational discourse features in their blogs than older males. Aside from the obvious biological factors affecting this result, possible contributing facets of writing in blogs involve topic choice, experience, and occupation, educational background, and intended or perceived readers.

Qualitatively, the topics, message, and intended audience in these two excerpts from the corpus were very similar. The texts were informal, personal, and specific to a particular event. In this case, the intended readers were close friends familiar with events and people mentioned by the bloggers. However, the linguistic features chosen by the authors in presenting the information and producing the texts were very different. The female, 17-year-old blogger used a greater number of personal pronouns, especially the first person *I*; present tense verbs ("*our drill writer is stupid and is falling behind; Band camp really sucks. I am so tired of all of it!*"), general emphatics, and contractions. In the second text sample, the male blogger did not refer to himself although he was primarily recounting his observations about the event. He used more nouns (and proper nouns) and had more long words based on average number of letters per word (male = 6.7 vs. female = 5.1 letters per word) in the texts. Aside from these features, it was clear that the texts differed in the level of engagement the authors intended with their readers. The female student was involving her readers ("*Ha. Ah, my eye is so itchy right now you wouldn't believe.*"), while the male author presented a narration of events without referring to himself or his readers.

As a written register, most Internet blogs are comparable to personal letters showing high engagement with readers and more informal features of language. The differences between blogs and personal letters are interesting subjects for extensive, empirical corpus investigations. Evidently, authors regard audiences in blogs, unseen and mostly unspecified, as very similar to the targeted reader of personal letters. Blogs and micro blogs are further discussed in Section B6.

A2.4 Register as a Sociolinguistic Variable

The term *register* has often been used interchangeably with *genre*. Although there is little consensus as to the meaning and/or use of these terms in applied linguistics, Biber and Conrad (2009) explain that such a distinction is a matter of focus. Both concepts refer to text categories that have been *situationally* defined and have shared general communicative purposes; the difference between the two is determined more by how those texts are studied or used. A genre perspective is more interested in the conventional structures that are used to create an entire text, or a section of a text, such as research article introductions or the abstract from a research article. On the other hand, a register perspective looks at the most common linguistic features across spoken and written texts. These linguistic features, from a register perspective, are thought to be pervasive, and thus a sample of a text can be analyzed. A genre analysis, however, would require the text to remain intact.

Although many corpus-based studies take a register perspective, they may also use or be supplemented with other methods to become more in line with genre-based approaches (Flowerdew, 2005). Wherever they land theoretically, however, corpus-based methodologies lend themselves well to answering the questions relevant to disciplinary specificity. Literacy practices, even those of the linguists studying such practices, may be entrenched and not noticed. Intuitive conclusions as to what is frequent or infrequent are not always accurate, and corpora offer measurable ways to describe what happens in the discourse empirically. Another benefit of corpus-based methods is that they allow for more objective studies. This is especially useful for researchers who view their role as descriptive, rather than prescriptive. Topics that can be investigated include but are not limited to, vocabulary, phraseological units, grammatical features, and rhetorical functions.

We consider the term *register*, therefore, as a sociolinguistic variable that categorizes the situational contexts of speaking and writing. A register distinction of spoken texts, for example, can cover subregisters such as face-to-face interaction, telephone interaction, and video calls (e.g., Skype calls or mobile "face-time" calls). Corpora representing these three subregisters could be collected and transcribed. These subregisters are differentiated by the medium and contexts, which can certainly influence the use of a range of linguistic features. Register variation in sociolinguistics, therefore, is primarily based on these contextual differences.

A2.5 Corpus Linguistics: A Brief Historical Overview

The focus on the collection of naturally occurring texts has been essential in corpus linguistics and certainly recognized as an important approach in earlier sociolinguistic research. It would not be surprising for a novice student of linguistics or sociolinguistics to imagine that CL emerged only in the 1980s and 1990s, concurrent with developments in computer science and desktop computing technology. This, however, is not exactly the case (Biber et al., 1998).

In fact, the standard practice in language research up until the 1950s was to base language descriptions on analyses of collections of natural texts from those collected by ethnographers and field linguists. Many of these collected text samples have been used to describe the structure of languages and produce dictionaries. Dictionaries have been primarily based on the analysis of word use in natural sentences taken from interviews with speakers representing a particular dialect region. For example, the *Oxford English Dictionary*, which was published in 1928, was based on around 5,000,000 citations from natural texts (totaling approximately 50 million words), compiled by over

2,000 volunteers for more than a 70-year period. Much earlier, Samuel Johnson's *Dictionary of the English Language*, published in 1755, was developed from a collection of 150,000 natural sentences written on slips of papers to illustrate the natural usage of words (Biber et al., 2010).

Precomputer or preelectronic corpora of texts such as newspaper writing, short stories, and scholarly essays were collected to study vocabulary use empirically and also to inform grammar studies and grammar teaching in English. Influential grammar books including those published before the 1950s such as Jespersen's (1952) grammars of English (1909–1949) used actual sentences taken from novels and newspapers to show various structures of formal, grammatically correct sentences, and syntactic items such as verb phrases and clauses. An even more notable example of this approach is the work of C. C. Fries, who wrote two corpus-based grammars of American English. The first, published in 1940, focused on usage and social variation based on a corpus of letters written to government agencies. This was followed by a second work, published in 1952, which was essentially a grammar of conversation, based on a 250,000-word corpus of telephone conversations, including grammatical features particular to conversation, such as discourse markers *well*, *oh*, *now*, and *why* when these markers initiate a "response utterance unit."

In the 1960s and 1970s, most research in linguistics moved to what Biber (1988) referred to as *intuition-based methods* (i.e., intuition vs. empirical analysis in research), which adamantly maintained that language was a mental construct and that empirical analyses of corpora were not relevant for describing language competence. This philosophical shift in linguistics also deeply influenced many sociolinguists' reactions to corpora and CL-based methodologies in studying linguistic variation at the time and, to some extent, continues to do so.

Nevertheless, some linguists continued to believe in the utility and validity of empirical linguistic analysis. In the early 1960s, for example, Randolph Quirk began a precomputer collection of 200 spoken and written texts, each approximating 5,000 words, dubbed the Survey of English Usage, which he subsequently used to compile descriptive grammars of English (e.g., Quirk, Greenbaum, Leech, & Svartvik, 1972). This descriptive tradition also had the continuing support of such functional linguists as Prince and Thompson, who argued that analysis of (still noncomputerized at this point) collections of natural texts was useful in the identification of systematic functional differences in linguistic variants. Thompson has been especially interested in the study of grammatical variation in spoken interactions and has analyzed factors that occur in conversation which influence the retention versus omission of features such as complementizers. In 1990, Fox and Thompson studied variation in the realization of relative clauses in conversation (Biber et al., 2010).

Work on large electronic corpora had actually begun in the 1960s with Kučera and Francis's (1967) compilation of the **Brown Corpus**, a one million–word corpus of published American English written texts. The Brown Corpus (or in full, the Brown University Standard Corpus of Present-Day American English) was collected to catalogue a wide variety of types American English, all of which were written in 1961. A total of 500 samples of approximately 2,000 words each were collected for this project, coming from 15 different genres. News, religious texts, biographies, official documents, academic prose, humor, and various styles of fiction were included (see Kučera & Francis, 1967). A parallel corpus of British English written texts, the **LOB Corpus** (London-Oslo-Bergen also *Lancaster*-Oslo-Bergen), followed in the 1970s.

Major studies of language use based on large electronic corpora did not begin to appear, however, until the 1980s, when these corpora became more accessible, as a result of the increasing availability of computational tools to facilitate linguistic analysis. For example, in 1982, Francis and Kučera provided a frequency analysis of the words and grammatical part-of-speech categories found in the Brown Corpus. Johansson and Hofland (1989) followed with a similar analysis of the LOB Corpus. Also during this period, book-length descriptive studies of linguistic features began to appear; for example, Granger (1983) on passives; de Haan (1989) on nominal postmodifiers; and the first multidimensional studies of register variation—for example, Biber (1988). This period also saw the emergence of English language learner dictionaries such as the *Collins CoBuild English Language Dictionary* (1987) and the *Longman Dictionary of Contemporary English* (1987), which were based on the analysis of large electronic corpora. Since the 1980s, most descriptive studies of linguistic variation in and usage of English have utilized analyses of electronic corpora, either a large, standard corpus such as the British National Corpus (BNC) (see Section B1) or a smaller, study-specific corpus such as a corpus of 20 biology research articles constructed for a genre analysis. Within applied linguistics, corpus research has been particularly influential and useful in such subfields as English for Specific Purposes (ESP) (see Section B4 on workplace discourse studies) and English for Academic Purposes (EOP); nearly all published articles in these subfields utilize some application of corpus analysis.

A2.6 Corpus Linguistics from a Social Perspective

In 2005, Wolfgang Teubert, who was then the editor of the *International Journal of Corpus Linguistics* published an essay entitled "My Version of Corpus Linguistics," which revisited ideas that, collectively, constitute corpus linguistics as an important theoretical approach to the broader study of language. Teubert argues that the corpus is now considered the default resource for almost anyone working in linguistics. He added that no introspection on linguistic change or linguistic variation can claim credibility without verification through real language data such as those provided by corpora. Indeed, corpus research has become a key element of almost all language study.

We agree with Teubert that corpus linguistics considers the nature of language not from a psychological but from a social perspective. This position supports and justifies the corpus approach in exploring variation in language from identifiable social groups of speakers and writers. Verbal interaction is what allows human social groups to be infinitely more complex than even groups of apes, our closest relatives. Humans are unique in that we can negotiate content collectively and form identities as we move further in the interaction. Without verbal interactions, we would be largely debilitated. "Without an audience, imagined or real, it would not make sense to formulate our thoughts" (p. 8).

In this same essay, Teubert listed 25 theses of corpus linguistics, synthesizing ideas that define the principles and goals of this still-developing discipline. He mirrored insights from European corpus linguists such as Michael Stubbs, John Sinclair, and Elena Tognini Bonelli in defining and widening the scope and applications of CL research. Provided below are summaries of some of Teubert's theses, which are directly related to research in corpus-based sociolinguistics (pp. 2–5):

- Corpus linguistics is the study of permanent records of language. Whether originally written or transcribed from spoken language, corpora allow language samples to be copied and analyzed continually.
- Corpus linguistics is based on observation of real language. The empirical nature of this area of study is based on the understanding that all of the texts (written and spoken) by a speech or discourse community constitute the potential target of investigation. However, only texts that have been recorded, saved, and organized can be used in such empirical observations. As researchers, corpus linguists must operationalize and restrict the sample and constructs that are investigated because to study every individual, every group, and every register is not possible.
- There is a diachronic aspect to discourse. Language that is used in the present relates to language of the past, present, and future. Although corpora appear to be static, the language represented in such databases was used in temporal context.
- Frequency and semantic relation, rather than statistical significance, are important parameters for detecting and analyzing recurrent patterns defined by the co-occurrence of words.

A3

CORPORA AND CORPUS TOOLS

A3.1 Types of Corpora

In this section, we describe the types of corpora that can be used in socio-linguistics. The beauty of corpora is that they can be created with a purpose. Researchers compile corpora and search for existing constructs or patterns that some have posited to be relevant or significant. A corpus allows for measurements of tendencies to verify such hypotheses. For example, if a lexicographer is interested in the use of respect markers (e.g., use of *sir* or *ma'am*, use of titles—*Mr. Johnson, Dr. Smith*) in task-based interaction by a particular group of people, he or she may construct a corpus of naturally occurring speech from speakers of the target group. If the corpus is **representative** of that group, her or she can find the distributions of these respect markers and describe the tendencies of those patterns.

Almost anyone interested in studying a language can utilize corpora and corpus-based methods to help uncover and begin to understand it. We have even found such methods traditionally reserved for impersonal grammatical studies to supplement qualitative analyses of such constructs as politeness and intercultural awareness. For example, Temples and Nelson (2013) utilized corpus-based analysis to explore the distribution of personal pronouns and modals of native English and native Spanish speakers interacting through computer-mediated communication (CMC). They found that distributions of personal pronouns, especially *we*, suggested that Spanish speakers used the plural first person to express awareness of themselves as forming a community, and they postulated that the use of this feature may have contributed to group cohesion in CMC interactions.

A3.2 Specialized and Reference Corpora

The first distinction between corpora is the number of groups and types of language that they are designed to represent. One researcher might be interested in studying a very specific group of language users, perhaps even a single individual. At the opposite end of the spectrum, another research might be interested in the language as a whole.

We can construct a corpus that reflects the language use of very large, diverse groups of people, or we can focus on a particular type of language user or situation. Whereas cultural anthropologists, for example, might gravitate toward the former, the latter situation is much more common in sociolinguistic research. For the most part, sociolinguists and other linguists who are interested in social and cultural relationships with language prefer their data to come from a single source whose context is as important to describe as the language itself. Data that has been collected in this way allows the researcher to more clearly understand the discourse domain and target group (or groups) of speakers and writers. In corpus linguistics, we call such a dataset a **specialized corpus**.

A specialized corpus allows the researcher to control for many more variables. It is designed to represent a particular register, domain, or variety of the language. This is useful especially when moving from the analysis of results to the discussion of generalizing toward a bigger population. For the most part, this is a question of scope. What is being investigated? Perhaps a researcher is interested in the talk of teenagers. What kind of language do they use? Do they use a lot of slang? These are interesting questions, but they are very difficult to answer because it would be problematic to collect a corpus that includes an equal **representation** of teenager talk from multiple geographic areas, ethnic groups, and socioeconomic levels. Not only would such a corpus be difficult to collect, if those variables are not represented in the corpus, the researcher would be unable to validly make connections from his results to discussion of the population as a whole. Instead, one can narrow his or her scope to ask a question about how teenagers in a particular region speak. This specification, narrowing down and controlling for independent variables, is important in the field of sociolinguistics, which is often concerned with particular speech communities.

One of the great things about corpora, however, is that some of those big picture questions can be answered if you have a large, well-designed corpus. While the linguist above may have wanted to study a particular group of teenagers, for example, another researcher might be interested in knowing how the data from such a localized study compared to the language at large. Continuing from the above example, maybe this second researcher is interested in exploring the linguistic aspects that differentiate this particular group from the larger speech or discourse community as a whole. In order to make such comparisons, we need to introduce another type of corpus: a **reference corpus**.

Sometimes called **general corpora**, reference corpora can be thought of as "super" corpora. They have been designed to represent the language-at-large. Multiple registers are included, giving a comparative, proportional view of how language is used. In the early days of corpus linguistics, a corpus of one million words was seen large (e.g., Brown and LOB corpora both had one million total words). Now, however, there are corpora of hundreds of millions of words. Thus, the size of the corpus does not, necessarily, make it a reference corpus. Instead, the inclusion and distribution of multiple registers does. While the Brown and LOB included many registers of English, they crucially lacked spoken language. If the goal of a corpus is to attempt to represent the language as a whole, it must also necessarily include samples of texts transcribed from speech. Newer generations of reference corpora have done just that. Not only are there now reference corpora that include many registers of both written and spoken language, they have also grown a lot larger. As computational power and memory increases, these large corpora are easier to compile and can be analyzed faster than ever before.

One of the larger, well-studied reference corpora is the British National Corpus (BNC). The latest edition of this corpus is made up of nearly 97 million orthographic words (The British National Corpus version 3 [BNC XML Edition], 2007). Because we usually speak more than we write, a representative reference corpus would reasonably contain a higher proportion of spoken language than written language. The creators of the BNC, however, decided to collect only about 10 percent of their corpus from spoken data, not because they believed that writing is nine times more prevalent or important than speaking but, rather, because of the enormous time and manpower resources needed to record and transcribe naturally occurring speech. A variety of forms of written language such as books, newspapers, and advertisements were included to give the sample breadth across genres. The process of selecting for multiple genres was extended to the collection of the speech data. The BNC includes multiple types of speaking from education, business, public life, and leisure from three geographical regions in the Great Britain (2.64% of the spoken texts came from speakers of unknown location).

Although the BNC is a very large corpus that is comprised of dozens of variables, one can conduct very specific sociolinguistic studies of it. McEnery and Xiao (2004), for example, used the BNC to explore the distribution patterns of the expletive *fuck* across sociolinguistic variables of age, gender, and social class. However, the authors are quick to admit that results from a corpus can only describe tendencies. Such results cannot explain the findings. Instead, other methods of investigation, such as the qualitative research more associated with sociolinguistics, offer complementary or triangulated understandings.

Another useful reference corpus is the Corpus of Contemporary American English (COCA). This is a corpus of more than 450 million words that is easily available online. Created at and maintained by Mark Davies of Brigham Young University, COCA is a very large and well-balanced corpus. The corpus consists of much copyrighted material, however, so most of the research that is done using COCA is on queries of the database. In other words, the creators can avoid legal problems because, under the United States Fair Use Law, none of the texts may be provided in full to any outside user. When you do a search in COCA, you can see several words on either side of your targeted word or feature. This gives limited linguistic context that is generally enough to understand how the feature is being used. COCA is only one of the corpora that have been created by Davies, and in many sections of this book, we also discuss his other collections including COHA (Corpus of Historical American English) and the 1.9 billion word GloWbE (Corpus of Web-Based Global English). We will revisit the BNC and COCA in Section B1 as we take an in-depth look at corpora that represent different varieties of English.

A3.3 Written Corpora

Corpora of written texts (e.g., newspaper articles, academic reports, fiction, and business memos) are more common than corpora of texts of spoken language. For obvious reasons, written corpora are much easier to collect. The sampling model used in the Brown Corpus has been used by other corpora of written language, allowing for comparisons across varieties of English and across time. As we previously mentioned, the LOB Corpus used the same sampling scheme to create a corpus that represented British English written in 1961. Other written corpora based on this model include, but are not limited to, American English from 1991 (the Friedburg-Brown Corpus of American English, **FROWN**), British English from 1991 (the Friedburg-LOB Corpus of British English, **FLOB**), Australian English starting from 1986 (the Australian Corpus of English, **ACE**), and Chinese (the Lancaster Corpus of Mandarin Chinese, **LCMC**).

We synthesize studies using specialized written corpora in diachronic comparisons (Section B5) and Web-based registers (B6). Corpus-based studies of academic writing, especially for learners of English, are very commonly done, and various corpora such as the Michigan Corpus of Upper-Level Student Papers (MICUSP) and the British Academic Written English (BAWE) have been collected and freely distributed online.

A3.4 Spoken Corpora

A leader in the collection of corpora intended for sociolinguistics is Sali A. Tagliamonte from the University of Toronto. She works in the variationist, Labovian tradition of recording and transcribing spoken data from large numbers of participants. Comfortable, unmonitored speech is the target recording because such researchers hope to capture real language in use, the kind of language style that speakers use when paying minimal attention to how they are speaking. This type of language, known as the **vernacular**, is important because it offers insight into the baseline of style for speakers. Also, because written language is not naturally acquired the way that speech is, most linguists and sociolinguists are concerned with how people speak.

One way to gain access to the vernacular is to use what has been called the **sociolinguistic interview** (see Section C1.3). This method of data collection is not what one might think of as a traditional interview. Instead, researchers use this method to get participants to provide narratives of their own experiences (Labov, 1984a). As participants are asked impersonal and general topics, the researcher slowly moves toward the more personal and more specific. It is at this point, Labov claims, that participants are more likely to produce the vernacular features the researcher is interested in. For a variationist sociolinguist interested in speech, such as Tagliamonte, for example, a corpus of data is thus a little different than one comprised of written data only. There are, in contrast, many more components defining the spoken corpus. The components of Tagliamonte's variationist research are included in the list below (Tagliamonte, 2006, p. 50):

- recording media, audiotapes (analogue, digital, or other formats)
- interview reports (hard copies) and signed consent forms
- transcription files (ASCII, Word, .txt)
- a transcription protocol (hard copy and soft copy)
- a database of information (FileMaker, Excel, etc.)
- analysis files (Goldvarb files, token, cel, cnd and res).

From this list, we can see that there are multiple data points for each participant. An important aspect of a corpus system used in sociolinguistics is, therefore, having carefully defined and efficient system for retrieving and connecting data. One can work with the transcripts, but the researcher will also need to be able to return to the audio files to confirm observations or make correlations with demographic information about individual or multiple participants. After such a corpus of spoken language has been compiled, the researcher may then identify and analyze linguistic variables. For example, using a corpus of speech from the English city of York, Tagliamonte and Roeder (2009) examined how the definite article, *the*, was used. In northern England, there is a form of the definite article that omits the vowel or otherwise does not follow the standard form of a voiced interdental fricative followed by a vowel, which is described as Definite Article Reduction (DAR). Orthographically, this form is usually written as *t'* instead of *the*. To further complicate matters, this dialect of English also allows for the complete omission of a definite article in places where it would be required in Standard English. In other words, there were three forms that the researchers investigated: full form *the*, DAR, and zero. Tagliamonte and Roeder's spoken corpus of 1.2 million words (from 92 York natives) gave the researchers many opportunities to explore how the speakers pronounced definite articles under differing phonetic and pragmatic situations.

While Tagliamonte is most associated with speech corpora that contain transcripts of sociolinguistic interviews, there are other spoken corpora that use different types of speech. The Santa Barbara Corpus of Spoken American English (SBCSAE) is a spoken corpus that consists of various speech events, some of which include face-to-face conversation, telephone conversations, sermons, and descriptions from tour guides. Containing almost a quarter-million words, this is a relatively large corpus of spoken language. Like the SBCSAE, the Wellington Corpus of Spoken New Zealand English (WSC) contains multiple types of speech events. With one million words, the WSC is large and well balanced, consisting of news monologues, sports commentary, judicial summaries, lectures, conversations, telephone conversations, interviews, radio conversations, political debate, and meetings. This corpus was also annotated for variables frequently studied in sociolinguistics. For example, gender, ethnicity, and age are variables included in the corpus. Other corpora are much more specialized. The Michigan Corpus of Academic Spoken English (MICASE), for example, is a 1.8 million–word corpus of transcribed speech from many different speech events in a college setting. These events include course lectures, discussions, seminars, and office hour sessions.

Reflective Break

- In Section C1, we offer ideas for collecting your own sociolinguistic corpus representing the vernacular form of language and also various considerations in setting-up sociolinguistic interviews. What subregisters of oral communication would you be interested in collecting?
- Are there ways to ensure that participants in oral interviews or spoken narratives will not monitor their speech? Note that audio or video recording of participants in a research study without their consent or permission is unethical and often not allowed in scholarly contexts.

A3.5 Analysis of Corpora

How do we study—process or analyze—corpora? Although a corpus is a collection of texts that has been systematically compiled and organized, a group of texts does not analyze itself. Instead, we use software tools to access and process data from corpora. Many forms of analysis of corpora can be accomplished using relatively simple, yet powerful, programs. These programs include concordancers such as *AntConc 3.2.4* (Anthony, 2012), *WordSmith Tools 6* (Scott, 2012), and *MonoConc Pro* (Barlow, 2012). Concordancers are programs that can extract words (or keywords) as they appear in the corpus. Their frequencies can be easily obtained and the contexts within which these words are used can also be collected by taking words that appear before and after these keywords in the corpus. This is an automated process called Key Word in Context or **KWIC**. Advanced researchers and computational linguists may need to use very specialized computer programs designed to extract particularly unique patterns that are not provided by concordancers.

AntConc is a concordancer that works with Windows, Mac, and Linux operating systems. Created and maintained by Laurence Anthony at Waseda University in Japan, two of the biggest benefits of this software are the availability across platforms and the cost: It's free. With a relatively easy-to-use interface, *AntConc* is a good tool for beginners. Also, there are many video tutorials on how to use the various functions of the program. Anthony also curates a Google group of *AntConc* users. This international digital community helps one another with troubleshooting and can ask Anthony questions directly about the software. Software packages like *AntConc* generally do not house a corpus. Instead, you have to upload your own files into the program to be analyzed. *AntConc* can process files that have been saved as text files (.txt). The program is able to read Unicode and thus can work for many orthographic systems used around the world. Figure A3.1 shows a screenshot of *AntConc*'s interface. The image presents the word list for the corpus that was uploaded into the program. In this case, we uploaded the text files from MICUSP.

The word list provides us with a list of the most frequent orthographic words in the corpus. You might notice that for this corpus of written academic English, all of the 18 most frequent items shown are function words. This is not uncommon in language. The finite number of function words which help give meaning

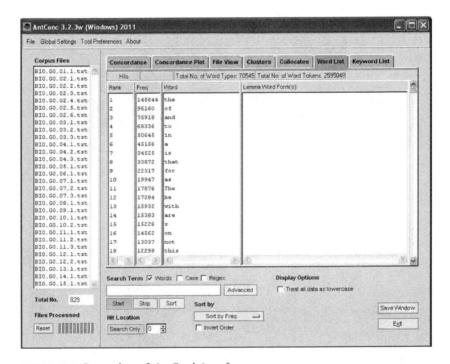

FIGURE A3.1 Screenshot of *AntConc*'s interface

to and connect content words are often repeated many times. Also, you may notice that *AntConc* provides information about how many words there are in the corpus. In this case, our sample had just fewer than 2.6 million words with 57,034 tokens. Using these numbers, we can calculate the type-token ratio (TTR), which is 0.022, or 2.2 percent. This means that many of the words are evidently not frequently repeated in the corpus. A text that has a very high TTR would be one that uses the same words over and over following this model of computation. For example, the song "You Oughta Know" by Alanis Morissette has 384 tokens and 130 types. That makes for a TTR of 0.339, or 33.9 percent. In other words, the lyrics to the pop song are much more repetitive than the writing of upper-level student writers across disciplines.

Reflective Break

- Comparing the type-token ratio (TTR) of 829 texts from MICUSP against one pop song is like comparing apples and oranges. How about face-to-face conversation compared to university lectures? They are both spoken, but one is more planned. Which do you think would have a higher TTR (more repetition)?

- How do you think TTR can relate to first language acquisition? Do you expect native speakers of English to have higher TTR than nonnative speakers in academic essays written in U.S. universities? What about second language acquisition? Reflect on your own experiences learning another language.

- ***WordSmith Tools 6***: *WordSmith Tools*, another concordancing software package, was developed by Mike Scott. It runs on Windows operating systems, and at the time of writing, cost $80 for a single license. Like *AntConc*, users of *WordSmith Tools* can also join a Google group to get help with the program or to run ideas by other corpus linguists, including Scott.

A3.6 Linguistic Constructs Investigated with Corpus Tools

In the following subsections, we focus on common linguistic constructs investigated using corpora, software tools, and corpus-based techniques. These constructs can all be applied to sociolinguistic analyses, especially when comparing a range of variables from well-designed corpora.

A3.6.1 Frequency

One of the most basic types of analysis that corpora offer researchers is the ability to determine the frequency of linguistic items. What words are the most frequently used words in a language? What about across different varieties and registers? For example, although many function words like determiners (e.g., *the*, *a*) and prepositions (e.g., *to*, *of*) consistently top frequency lists across varieties and registers of English, there is great diversity when one looks more closely.

Frequency is important in both the description of language varieties and also in determining what to focus on when considering language education. For example, it has been shown that even language specialists cannot accurately estimate relative frequencies of words (Alderson, 2007). This is a paradox because many of our intuitions of existence and frequency for words, word types, and grammatical constructions are influenced by what stands out to the observer as different. Thus, users and casual observers of language are more likely to perceive infrequent linguistic features as frequent.

The construct of frequency in CL, however, needs to be further described. How is it measured? The frequency of a linguistic feature is relevant when compared with other features or across groups. In order to make such comparisons, we need to discuss **normalized frequency (nf)**. Relative frequency can be determined by calculating the frequency of the construct per *x* number of words. Depending on the item being investigated and the convention in the literature, one might choose to measure the number of instances per 100; 1,000; or 1,000,000 words. This is also called normalizing.

In his analyses of grammatical constructions, for example, Biber (e.g., 1988, 2006b) uses the number of instances per 1,000 words to normalize. This is done using a simple calculation:

$$nf = \frac{\text{number of instances}}{\text{total number of words}} \times 1,000$$

Normalization not only allows for researchers to compare linguistic features with one another, it also, more importantly, allows us to compare texts and corpora of differing lengths. In sociolinguistics as in other areas of corpus-based linguistics, studies often involve the comparison of multiple subcorpora. When comparing the speech patterns of teenage men and women, the interviews of those participants would understandably have texts of varying lengths.

We searched for the word *dude* in the Corpus of Contemporary American English (COCA). COCA can be searched based on genre: spoken, fiction, magazine, newspaper, academic. When we searched for *dude* in the spoken subcorpus, we found that it occurred 502 times. The same search in the spoken subcorpus of the BNC resulted in 25 hits. However, that does not mean, necessarily, that this target word is used 20 times more in American speech than in British speech. Instead, to compare these two groups, we would need to calculate normalized frequency.

The spoken portion of COCA contains approximately 95 million words while the spoken section of the BNC contains about 10 million words. The two normalized frequencies are calculated below:

$$nf \text{ for } dude \text{ (COCA : spoken)} = \frac{502}{95,000,000} \times 1,000 = 0.0053$$

$$nf \text{ for } dude \text{ (BNC: Spoken)} = \frac{25}{10,000,000} \times 1,000 = 0.0025$$

Using this formula, we can see that *dude* appears to be more common in spoken American English than British English. However, the difference does not appear to be quite as marked when those frequencies are normalized.

For most corpus-based studies there are many texts involved. For some researchers who use corpora, the corpus is investigated as a whole. This practice differs from sociolinguistic investigation because sociolinguists are concerned about individual speakers. However, there is a way for the two groups to merge. Individual texts can also be treated as observations, often of separate individuals' language production. Thus, standardized scores can also be calculated for all of the texts individually and then averaged.

For many research questions, especially those asked by sociolinguists, separating the texts is preferable to averaging from the corpus as a whole. One advantage of doing so is that it enables the researcher to study variation across individuals. It also offers the researcher the ability to find possible outliers—that is, texts (or participants)—that do not "behave" like the others. It is important to remember, however, that texts cannot actually "behave." Instead, those texts are instances of a person's language production, and that *person* may not perform like the others. One can then revisit the text and/or the participant to explore possible reasons for the deviance. Had all of the texts been lumped together, no such analysis would be possible.

A3.6.2 Concordances and Key Word in Context (KWIC)

Sociolinguists are often interested in the context in which their participants use language. In addition to that outside context, CL offers ways to investigate the composition of linear strings of language. A concordancer, as we introduced earlier, is our default corpus tool. The central function of such programs is to provide the user with the organized contexts of items that are searched. Often, one might be interested in exploring the words before and after a given word. For example, perhaps one was curious about multiword verb combinations involving the verb *pick*. Using a concordancer, he or she can search a corpus for *pick*, and all of its instances will be shown, organizable by words on the left and right—that is, **KWIC** lines (Text Sample A3.1).

It is important to note, however, that KWIC searches are not, necessarily, of orthographic words. On the contrary, one can search for letters, morphemes, and even multiple words. In languages like Chinese and Korean, one might even use such a program to search for characters.

Reflective Break

- Words can also have affective meaning (known as "semantic prosody"). This means that emotions can be connected. For example, the words *war, hate, anger,* and *boredom* will probably have negative emotions associated with them. On the other hand, words like *peace, love, happiness,* and *excitement* may evoke

---

Text Sample A3.1. KWIC Lines for *Pick* in a Conversation Corpus

point is they thought they could	**pick**	someone whose accent was
too subtly different for him to	**pick**	up on all of it from listening to rap
don't think it's necessary to	**pick**	one thing and exclude every-thing else.
over there hoping it would uh,	**pick**	up some of you and not all of that
I got to get Nancy in so she can	**pick**	up the car and get into Ann Arbor
because we could not um	**pick**	up the recorder from Kristie.
We can call up and	**pick**	off your CD ROM. Yeah
Yeah. Okay then or you	**pick**	up the phone and say look this up for me.
the brunch cause I can, can	**pick**	out things that I want.
a good freeze before you	**pick**	them. That's when they turn sweet.
I got gas when I went to her and	**pick**	up Nancy the first time.
I can definitely go and then I	**pick**	them up there together
there and then to the two	**pick**	so that it can change
Sharon can them do to the right	**pick**	to the boy up there
all the books have been there	**pick**	up is for tonight

---

positive emotions. These examples are clearly negative or positive. But what about a word like *cause*?

- **Now try this**: Using an online corpus (e.g., BNC, COCA), search for a word. Some examples that you can try are *cause*, *reaction*, and *juvenile*.
  - For each search, pull up a KWIC list and randomly select 20 contexts of about 10 words on the left and the right.
  - For each context, consider whether the words around the word you searched for are positive, negative, or neutral. Compare your findings with a classmate.
  - What are your assessments about the semantic prosody of each word?

A3.6.3 Collocations

Although much can be studied using KWIC searches and browsing concordance lines, we might start to notice that particular words attract other words. Firth (1957) revolutionized the way that discrete linguistic elements such as words are understood by modern linguists. Instead of seeing these units as independent from rules and other words, Firth famously wrote, "You shall know a word by the context it keeps" (p. 11).

Incorporating the ideas of Firth and advances in computational power, we are now able to determine the statistical significance of combinations of words. In the *pick* concordance lines above, take a look at the words that followed *pick*. What did you notice? Another example, when we searched for the word *macaroni* in COCA, we found a very strong collocate of *cheese* and, to a lesser extent, *elbow*. We can use the collocation search in COCA, as in other concordancing packages, to filter the results to describe the frequent combinations to the left or to the right of the target word. Continuing with our example of *macaroni*, we know that it is a noun, and can thus take premodifiers, which are often adjectives or nouns. If we wanted to explore what most typically premodified the target word, we can select for one word to the left. Doing this shows the most common premodifier is *elbow*.

Collocations can also be found using more objective measurements from statistical results obtained from reference corpora. Prediction models of what might follow or precede a word, a noun, or a verb can be measured based on their expected frequencies.

A3.6.4 Multi-Word Units (MWU)

Related to the concept of collocation is that of multi-word units (MWUs). If, as Firth claims, words are connected to and often derive their meaning totally or partially from each other words in the unit, one might expect that some words frequently occur as linear strings, like a prefabricated "chunk" of language. Although most sociolinguistic studies and even most corpus-based studies focus on discrete linguistic forms (e.g., sounds, morphemes, words), there is a lot to learn about language use by investigating extended strings of language such as MWUs. Group preferences to use more-or-less prefabricated sequences are essentially social phenomena. Research on MWUs has shown that discourse communities and speech communities use such chunks differently.

There are various ways to explore this construct of formulaic language using corpus tools. Here, we will introduce three of the commonly used approaches: n-grams, lexical bundles, and p-frames.

- **N-grams**: The most basic construct associated with MWUs is that of the **n-gram**. The "n" in its name stands for any number variable. For example, we can have bi-grams (two words in order), tri-grams (three words), four-grams, and so on. N-grams can also be extracted using most basic corpus packages—both *AntConc* and *WordSmith Tools 6* have commands for n-gram extraction.
- **Lexical bundles**: Another often-investigated MWU construct is that of **lexical bundles**. Lexical bundles are a type of n-grams, but there are more limitations on how they are extracted. Traditionally, lexical bundles consist

of at least three words (tri-grams) that occur frequently across a corpus of at least one million words. This is determined by a count per one million words. The frequency, however, can be determined by the researcher. For example, we might be interested in only the absolute most frequent lexical bundles and set a high cutoff score. Many studies have used the number of 40 per million words when investigating lexical bundles, while others have been interested in examining more bundles, especially if the minimum cutoff does not yield enough instances to be investigated. Another important criterion for labeling MWUs as lexical bundles is that they surface in at least five different texts in the corpus. This is necessary to avoid any idiosyncratic language usages. A sociolinguistic study interested in features that are more pervasive across even more members of the population can set this cutoff even higher.

The extraction of lexical bundles is only the first step toward analysis. Because lexical bundles are often phrasal constructions, such as *because of the* and *the most of the*, they are usually described functionally. Taxonomies of lexical bundles in academic writing, for example, have shown that these bundles have particular discourse functions and syntactic structures.

- **P-frames**: An interesting development in MWUs has evolved as researchers have moved beyond looking only at uninterrupted strings of language to also examine frequent patterned constructions. We can also use computer programs to analyze large amounts of data to find these phraseological structures that allow for variability in one position. These are called phrase frames, or **p-frames**, for short.

An example of a p-frame, found by Römer (2010), is *it would be ★ to*, in which the asterisk represents an open slot. Grammatically, any number of nouns might go into the blank slot in this example. Römer used computer programs to create lists of different numbers of n-grams, and from those lists, the program then found n-grams between two and seven words, then found patterns that differed only by a single word, creating lists of p-frames in book reviews from applied linguistic journals. Römer found that the most frequent words in that fill blank slot were *interesting, useful, nice*, and *better*, accounting for 77 percent of all the variants in the corpus. Such research can provide insight into language teaching, but it can also show language variation across registers and varieties.

Other methods for extracting phraseological patterns with variable slots are also available. For example, in addition to p-frames, academic language has also been studied using lexical frames (Gray & Biber, 2013) and concgrams (Cheng, 2007).

The study of formulaic language is an exciting area of research that is only possible with the advent of computers. Most of the research that has been done in this area, however, has focused on academic writing. Because of the size of a corpus required to extract lexical bundles, for example, fewer studies have been conducted on the formulaic language of speech and even fewer from a sociolinguistic perspective.

A3.6.5 Keyness and Keywords

Keyness is related to word frequency, but instead of providing descriptive statistics as in numerical frequencies or averages, **inferential statistics** can also be used to determine if a word is more or less likely to occur in one corpus versus another. **Keywords** can be extracted using *AntConc* and *WordSmith Tools*.

Keyword analysis involves the use of a statistical procedure in order to identify significant differences in the distribution of words used by speakers or writers between two groups of texts or two corpora. Scott (1997) defines a keyword as "a word which occurs with unusual frequency in a given text" (p. 236). This "unusual frequency" is based on the likelihood of occurrence of the word in a target corpus from a process called cross-tabulation. To identify keywords, it is necessary to compare the distributional data from one corpus with data from a reference (or target) corpus that is logically representing similar linguistic and contextual characteristics or qualities. These comparisons provide an interesting look at the unique features of one type of discourse, language variety, or register compared to another. Other related applications of a keyword analysis of societal variables such as gender, social status, or nationality could be further explored with the right parallel corpora.

In Section C4 we provide step-by-step instructions for running a keyword analysis using *AntConc*.

A3.6.6 Linguistic Co-Occurrence and Multidimensional Analysis

The vast majority of quantitative studies in sociolinguistics focuses on the frequencies of a small number of variables. For example, you might be curious as to how different groups of people refer to carbonated beverages across different geographical areas in the United States (e.g., *soda, soft drink, "coke," cola*) evident in a corpus of spoken texts. Your study would be fairly straightforward—you could simply divide your corpus into regional groups then conduct a KWIC search for the frequency of these words used to refer to carbonated beverages. Your results will show distributions of these words across U.S. regions (the South will probably have more frequencies of "*coke*," while *soda* might be more popular in the West and the Northeast). Similarly, if you do not have a corpus, perhaps you could conduct an online survey asking participants from all over the United States to send you their response to this question together with their demographic information (e.g., gender, age, occupation). There are, in fact, several Web sites that have featured **isoglosses** of "*coke*" versus *soda* regional distributions, which are easy to search through Google.

However, as you already know by now, language use is often influenced by multiple variables and linguistic variation may be more clearly explicated by how combinations of discourse features are distributed in a corpus. Registers within communicative contexts may influence the way speakers and writers use structures of a language. How we write is clearly different from how we speak, and the purposes and audiences for such language production also affect the form of language we use. For example, although the traditional sociolinguistic interview attempts to get participants to speak in a way that is most natural for them, those same participants are likely to adjust their language use when situations change. We may speak differently with our peers than we do with our employers or researchers such as William Labov or Sali Tagliamonte who may be recording our responses. In order to further investigate linguistic variations—for example, in the broader registers of speaking and writing—a single variable or feature may not be enough to give us the big picture. Hence, a *"coke"* versus *soda* distinction can also be supplemented by other linguistic features that are used together or that co-occur with these words across registers and groups of speakers.

The concept of **linguistic co-occurrence** explains that the linguistic composition of a subregister; for instance, face-to-face interaction may have higher frequencies of questions and responses, inserts, dysfluent markers (e.g., filled pauses—*uh, um*), and backchannels (e.g., *uh-huh*) used often by speakers in the corpus. Conversely, these features may not be common in written texts (unless they come from character dialogues in fiction). Linguistic features such as pronouns, past tense verbs, and nouns often go together whenever speakers engage in everyday conversations or talk about their previous experiences and recent events. These same features could also appear together with very high frequency in written, first person narratives or soliloquies about past events. In order to capture and document these co-occurring features from corpora, a simple KWIC search will no longer be sufficient. A more advanced statistical framework is necessary to identify the composition of features that are frequently found together within a corpus.

You will read about **multidimensional (MD) analysis**, which is the corpus-based approach that explores the construct of linguistic co-occurrence in Section B6. In Section C2, we provide an extensive discussion of MD studies, and we also introduce the statistical procedures and steps necessary in running this analysis.

A3.7 Corpus Annotation and Markup

The previous subsections described ways that corpora can be investigated in which the texts include simply the words as they were originally spoken or written. However, other computer programs can also be used to annotate the corpus. **Annotation**, also known as "tagging," involves the labeling of linguistic features onto the text. For example, one program might attach a part-of-speech (POS) label to every word in the text (i.e., **POS-tagging**). By doing this, when the researcher wants to count how many nouns or verbs were used, he or she can simply search for the number of the labels. Fortunately, most such programs also produce "tag counts." In addition to tagging, linguistic **parsing** can also be done by computer programs in order to segment or separate parts of a sentence or paragraph. A parser may be able to identify and separate verb phrases and clauses and also extract long versus short sentences (depending on the number of words) from a corpus. We describe several programs below that can be used to annotate corpora.

A3.7.1 POS-Tagging Using the Biber Tagger

The Biber tagger is a computer program developed by Douglas Biber (2006b) to provide a grammatical tag for each word in a text file. POS-tags follow every word or punctuation mark in the text output. The tag symbols and tag fields represent the grammatical and semantic annotation identified by this tagger. For example, the first word in the Text Sample A3.1, *Even*, has a "^rb++++= Even" tag. That means that *Even* is used as an adverb ("rb") in this context. Tagged texts allow easy and immediate processing and counting of the rates of occurrence of linguistic/grammatical features. A complementary "tag-count" program can be used to extract actual frequency counts of POS features occurring in a corpus.

Using the Biber Tagger, the short excerpt below from the International Corpus of English (India) is transformed into the following tagged version.

Text Sample A3.1

Text Input

> <ICE-IND:S1A-001#21:1:B>
> Even in Madras also we have <indig> na </indig><,> uh
> sea-shore <,> and after three <w> O'clock </w><,> uh in the afternoon
> we
> have a very cool breeze and we enjoy that <,> sea breeze like anything
> <&>
> clears throat </&>

Tagged Output

> Even ^rb++++= Even
> in ^in++++= prep
> Madras ^np+++??+= noun
> also ^rb++++= also
> we ^pp1a+pp1+++= pron
> have ^vb+hv+vrb++= have
> na ^fw++not++= foreign word
> uh ^uh++++= uh
> sea ^nn++++= sea-shore = noun
> - ^-++++= EXTRAWORD
> shore ^nn++++= noun
> and ^cc++++= conj
> after ^in++++= prep
> three ^cd++++= three
> O'clock ^rb++++= O'clock = adv
> uh ^uh++++= uh
> in ^in++++= prep
> the ^ati++++= the

```
afternoon ^nn++++= noun
we ^pp1a+pp1+++= pron
have ^vb+hv+vrb++= have
a ^at++++= art
very ^ql+amp+++= ql
cool ^adj++++= adj
breeze ^nn++++= noun
and ^cc++++= conj
we ^pp1a+pp1+++= pron
enjoy ^vb++++= verb
that ^dt+dem+++= that
sea ^nn++++= noun
breeze ^nn++++= noun
like ^vb++++= like
anything ^pn++++= pn
clears ^vbz++++= vrb
throat ^nn++++= noun
```

The Biber Tagger combines computerized dictionaries with the identification of word sequences as instances of a linguistic feature (e.g., noun + WH pronoun and not preceded by the verb *tell* or *say* = "relative clause") (Biber, 1988). There are over 150 POS-tagged categories in the output, which includes grammatical and some syntactic elements. Tag accuracy is around 95 percent for written texts. Accuracy goes down a little bit for spoken text, especially that which is not consistently transcribed. Unfortunately, access is an issue with this tool, since the Biber Tagger is not commercially available or accessible online. However, researchers may contact The Corpus Linguistics Research Program at Northern Arizona University for information about corpus tagging and analysis using the Biber Tagger.

A3.7.2 CLAWS, LIWC, and Other Taggers/Parsers

Below are POS-taggers and linguistic parsers that you can purchase or access online:

- The Constituent Likelihood Automatic Word-tagging System (**CLAWS**) is a POS-tagger that was used to tag the BNC and is available for user licenses as well as copies for single sites. CLAWS has over 160 different POS- and semantic tags (current version: CLAWS7) developed by the University Centre for Computer Corpus Research on Language (UCREL). Not only can it be used as a downloaded program on an individual computer, but it can also be accessed directly online. The CLAWS team from Lancaster University offers tagging services, and charges depending on the amount of text being tagged (http://ucrel.lancs.ac.uk/claws/). This program has consistently achieved 96 to 97 percent accuracy which may vary based on the type of text or transcription convention.

- A program designed to grammatically and semantically tag corpora is **Wmatrix**, a corpus comparison tool also from Lancaster University (Rayson, 2003, 2008) (http://ucrel.lancs.ac.uk/wmatrix/). This tool combines the CLAWS tagger and a semantic annotation system. Many recent studies have been conducted using this program because of its extensive tagset and its accessibility. For example, Xiao and McEnery (2005) and Xiao (2009) used Wmatrix to replicate the methodology of Biber's (1988) MD analysis.
- **The Stanford Parser** and the **Stanford Tagger** (http://nlp.stanford.edu/software/lex-parser.shtml) may also be used to obtain POS-tagged data, although the current tagsets for these tools are limited to primary POS counts of 30 to 40 linguistic features (e.g., nouns, verbs, modal verbs, prepositions). Another available Web-based tagger is **Go Tagger** (http://web4u.setsunan.ac.jp/Website/GoTagger.htm), which offers free tagging services asynchronously.
- The **Coh-Metrix** tagset is generally similar to the Biber Tagger with additional features focusing on lexical diversity and specificity markers. Data and related research from Coh-Metrix, including contact information for potential tagging requests, are located at http://cohmetrix.memphis.edu/cohmetrixpr/index.html.
- **The Linguistic Inquiry and Word Count** (LIWC, pronounced *Luke*). **The current version of this program** was developed by Pennebaker, Chung, Ireland, Gonzales, and Booth (2007), employing a different form of corpus tagging technique. LIWC utilizes a dictionary with 80 preset categories in order to analyze the linguistic composition of texts. The output includes linguistic dimensions (e.g., percentage of words in the text that are pronouns, articles, auxiliary verbs, etc.), word categories tapping psychological constructs (e.g., affect, cognition, biological processes), personal concern categories (e.g., work, home, leisure activities), paralinguistic dimensions (e.g., assents, fillers, nonfluencies), and punctuation categories (periods, commas, etc.). LIWC is available for purchase (http://www.liwc.net/). See Section C4.3 for a sample LIWC study.

A3.7.3 Manual Tagging Software

Finally, many additional constructs from corpora that sociolinguists are interested in are not easily tagged or parsed automatically. For example, a researcher might be interested in investigating the **themes** (e.g., social or linguistic themes) that emerge in interviews with participants. Although there is not a way to automatically label such qualitatively determined features, there are software and tools available that can help in keeping track of such items. Manual coding and annotations may be required, but once these are completed, the software tools are able to automate the extraction of these coded themes or categories together with text samples. ATLAS.ti (http://www.atlasti.com/index.html) and NVivo (http://www.nvivo10.com/) are two coding software packages that incorporate corpus technology for qualitative research.

A4
CORPUS DESIGN AND REPRESENTATIVENESS

A4.1 Corpus Design

Although there are several potential benefits to using corpus-based methods in many areas of linguistics, including sociolinguistics, we need to be careful about how we design and collect corpora. This is because the texts act as our sample in the same way that human volunteers may participate in a psychological or medical study. In order to answer questions about a particular language variety, we need to *sample* appropriately to answer the questions we want to ask. For example, if a new medication were to be offered to the public at large, we would hope that it had been tested on groups of participants that represent the entire population: not only a certain age or gender. Just as other social scientists would want to have appropriate numbers of participants and purposeful sampling, so also do corpus linguists. In order to answer questions about tendencies in a dialect or register, a corpus needs to be created with these requirements in mind. This section describes the essential requisites for corpus design and representativeness.

A4.1.1 What Is the Purpose of a Corpus?

Corpora are generally not created without particular research questions in mind. Corpora are usually planned, collected, organized, and analyzed in ways that the researcher has thought of studying from the inception of the idea to create them. Although it has been traditional for some researchers to utilize publicly available corpora for their own research, this methodology limits the extent to which the researcher can be familiar with the data and its context. It also narrows the focus of the types of subsequent questions a researcher can ask. For example, if someone were interested in differences in writing by men and women, the corpus being used would have had to include that variable to be separated. The same would be true for any variable commonly associated with sociolinguistic research (e.g., age, geographic location, social class).

It is thus important to understand how an existing corpus is able to provide information about the particular characteristics or variables in the subject area or population that you want to research. At this juncture, as is the case with a growing number of corpus-based sociolinguistic studies, it may be more appropriate to design and collect texts based on established research questions first than to utilize already-existing or available corpora. With the now ever-present personal computer and the digitization of so much language in the last few decades, corpus creation is increasingly feasible to individual researchers. This is an important development in the field, which allows an individual's curiosity and time to determine the direction a study goes. Although we later discuss in detail the specifics in designing your own sociolinguistic corpus (Section C1), the information in the following subsections will give you some general background understanding of some of the principles behind systematically designed corpora.

A4.2 Corpus Representativeness

One of the key elements in Sinclair's (2005) definition of a corpus in Section A2.2 is that the collection of texts is **used to represent a language or language variety**. In other words, corpora are created for the purpose of better understanding a particular type of language. Thus, a sample of texts that together can serve as a *characteristic example* of the target variety or target domain is needed. This description brings to light the concept of **representativeness**.

Biber (1993) defines representativeness as "the extent to which a sample includes the full range of variability in a population" (p. 243). In more general sense beyond corpus linguistics, representativeness refers to the idea that one can collect a smaller sample than the population as a whole but that that smaller sample could show as much variability in the subset as in the overall population. Because a corpus should represent a particular language or variety of that language, corpus designers must be aware of the kinds of questions they would like to answer or think that others who use their corpora might ask. According to Biber, the representativeness of a corpus can be considered both contextually and linguistically. *Contextually*, a corpus of the target language or variety should include the full range of various registers or text types used. In other words, because the different situations in which a language is used affect the way that language is actually utilized across contexts, those different registers need to be included in order to fully understand the variety as a whole. *Linguistically*, a corpus can be said to be representative if it includes the full range of different lexical and grammatical features present in that language or variety.

A4.2.1 Sampling

If the primary purpose of a corpus-based sociolinguistic research is to describe a language or a particular variety of a language, a systematic sampling of data from participants, texts, and observations is essential. Because of the impossibility of collecting and analyzing all language instances, we have to limit ourselves to small samples of all the language that have occurred. Much like a medical study could not possibly examine every human being but instead studies a group that is representative of the target population, linguistic data collection requires us to sample from the language as a whole.

We can think of our target language or language variety as being our *population*. Instead of people, however, there is a set of language acts that we are interested in. For example, we might be interested in studying the spoken interactions of female teenagers from a particular neighborhood of New York. Our population would thus be all of the conversations these young women have with each other. Understandably, we could not collect samples of our entire population. What we could do is take a sample of those interactions, which could act as a smaller, more manageable subset of the population. How that subset is chosen is thus very important because it will potentially be used to make generalizations about the population as a whole.

Perhaps you have heard of **random sampling**. Random sampling refers to the idea that in a study, every member of a population (in corpus linguistics, that would be every text or instance of the speech act) has an equal likelihood of being chosen. The sample would thus not be skewed by any of the researchers' subjective criteria. Most linguistic studies do not use true random sampling. Instead, we tend to limit our sampling to what is most convenient for us. For many of us, literate college students are easily accessible, but they might not represent the general population reflected by our research questions. In consideration of convenience, therefore, we may have to narrow our research question depending on the amount of access we are able to obtain from potential participants. But, if we have a question about a specific population, we need to be sure that our sampling reflects the variety of that population. Because of the difficulty of achieving perfect representation in sampling, many corpus linguists tend to hedge their findings. This means that they often will emphasize that their findings represent only tendencies found in their corpora, which may have potential sampling issues and might not apply exactly the same way to the population at large.

Determining which registers or text types we collect in our sample is also important. In doing so, researchers must be sure that they are using externally defined criteria when they include a text in a corpus. This is important to avoid having any subjective interpretations of the language influencing selection. In the previous example of female teenagers in New York, we would want to base our selection of those participants and their language on the situation—that is, all of the conversation of females in the particular neighborhood in New York—not on how we perceive them speaking. If we "cherry-pick" the samples that we notice are different, the results have the possibility of not being representative of the population as a whole. Instead, we should include a random, or as random as possible, sample of all the interactions we can, not only those that have a feature we are looking for.

Another consideration in sampling is the amount of a given text that is included in a corpus. For registers with texts of few words such as *Facebook updates* or *e-mails*, it may be easy and convenient to include whole texts in the corpus. However, what if you wanted to study fiction? Or how about the speech of sportscasters during a five-day-long cricket match? Some registers are simply too long to include entire texts. There are also legal and ethical questions when it comes to data collection of whole texts (these are further discussed in Section C1). Finally, sampling strategies can also be applied to the collection of corpus data that comes from registers of long texts, such as books or movie screenplays. While it would be ideal to understand the language of texts as a whole, there are situations where it is appropriate and necessary to sample only sections of texts.

A4.2.2 Balance and Proportion

Related to sampling is the concept of *balance*. Not only must we choose our texts using appropriate sampling techniques, we also need to think about how sampling of different types of texts, or registers, could affect the corpus. A corpus is said to be balanced if the full range of registers associated with the target population is represented in the sample. One way that balance is achieved is by proportional sampling. That is, sampling that is done relative to the frequency of register use in the population.

For example, if we were interested in examining all language used by accountants in offices in North America, we might want first to better understand the ways this population uses language. Perhaps such a setting involves mostly speech (e.g., face-to-face conversation, telephone interactions with clients) and e-mail. A smaller percentage of the language used may be through intraoffice memos or written letters for the mail. If we were to create a corpus that overall represents the language used by these accountants, we might want to make our text collection proportional to the frequency of these various forms of language usage in offices. Thus, we would have more texts from conversations and e-mails than from the less-frequent registers like memos. On the other hand, a researcher might be equally interested in all of the important registers used by the target population, regardless of their relative frequency. In this case, the corpus collection might include equally large numbers of texts from the various participants or text categories.

Although these two options for achieving balance—based on relative frequency or based on registers being equally represented—are ideal, even the most balanced of corpora can only approximate complete and perfect balance. For example, the BNC and COCA are often described as balanced corpora. These reference corpora both consist of millions of words from a variety of registers. However, both of these corpora include much more written language than spoken language. COCA, which continues to expand, is constructed using the system of balancing registers by representing them as equal. Thus, although more American English is spoken than written, the spoken samples for the corpus that are added annually equal the numbers of words added from the other four registers included: fiction, magazine, newspaper, and academic writing.

Table A4.1, which comes from COCA's Web site (Davies, 2008) shows the balance of COCA. As you can see, each year involves an addition of around 20 million words to the corpus. These additions are split across the five registers chosen by the corpus creators.

There is no formula or measurement to determine whether or not a corpus is balanced after the fact, and thus we can only work to plan the corpus before collection. In CL, it is common for researchers to create a corpus matrix before collecting data. A corpus matrix is a useful tool to help the researcher set goals for the amount and sources of data that would be ideal to answer her research questions. This matrix then becomes a sampling plan for the researchers to collect data.

Below is the corpus matrix for the British Academic Written English (BAWE) corpus (Nesi, 2008, 2011). As you can see from Table A4.2, the researchers were interested in different disciplines. The goal of this project was to create a corpus that contained a balanced number of writing samples from various disciplinary groups across university systems in Great Britain. Notice that they have equal numbers of subjects for each of the four disciplinary groups. They also wanted to balance their corpus for the number of texts per year. This ensures that their sample would include equal representation of the levels of students in each subject. Some subjects (e.g., archaeology, medical science), however, are not taken at all levels of study, so fewer papers were expected. For medical science, for example, the corpus planned to include only upper-level students (16 in their final year of undergraduate and 48 at the graduate level). Although the primary topic here is not directly related to sociolinguistics ("academic writing"), we used this example to provide an illustration of a corpus matrix and how you might develop your own when you design your corpus.

The BAWE's corpus matrix is a good example of how to set out to create a balanced corpus, one that can help researchers answer questions associated with the target population. The matrix for the BAWE corpus does not show balance in terms of how much writing is done in each of these disciplines. In other words, a discipline like history or philosophy might involve a lot more writing of prose than some of the applied subjects (e.g., hospitality, health and social care). The corpus creators were not interested in asking questions of relative balance of writing. Instead, they thought it would be best to give each subject equal representation, avoiding any idiosyncrasies that might be associated with a particular subject that might involve a lot more writing.

TABLE A4.1 Distributions of words from five registers of COCA from 1990 to 2012

Year	Spoken	Fiction	Magazine	Newspaper	Academic	Total
1990–1991	8,608,624	8,329,476	8,231,081	8,148,208	7,955,110	41,272,499
1992–1993	8,943,068	7,799,864	8,678,040	8,177,512	8,098,507	41,696,991
1994–1995	8,922,686	8,053,812	8,715,580	8,202,970	7,986,918	41,881,966
1996–1997	7,935,768	7,688,998	8,678,456	8,177,130	8,448,501	40,928,853
1998–1999	8,842,871	7,885,318	8,706,416	8,176,755	8,054,653	41,666,013
2000–2001	8,402,286	7,795,121	8,615,552	8,101,406	7,978,602	40,892,967
2002–2003	8,734,834	7,840,717	8,575,498	8,108,011	8,022,422	41,281,482
2004–2005	8,726,048	8,151,672	8,629,377	8,173,752	7,864,771	41,545,620
2006–2007	8,187,099	8,110,285	8,464,204	8,061,231	8,296,072	41,118,891
2008–2009	7,605,209	8,299,112	8,061,292	8,003,376	8,159,609	40,128,598
2010–2011	8,129,020	8,095,189	8,005,389	8,240,932	7,880,955	40,351,485
2012	2,348,159	2,294,570	2,203,821	2,109,683	2,298,658	11,254,891★
Total	95,385,672	90,344,134	95,564,706	91,680,966	91,044,778	464,020,256

Source: adapted from Davies, 2012

★ The latest update for 2012 was in summer 2012, and includes texts from Jan.–June 2012.

TABLE A4.2 Corpus matrix for planning the British Academic Written English (BAWE) corpus

Group	Discipline	Ideal: Papers Per Year	Ideal: Total
Arts and Humanities	Applied Linguistics/Applied English Language Studies	32	128
	Archaeology	16	64
	Classics	32	128
	Comparative American Studies	32	128
	English Studies	32	128
	History	32	128
	Philosophy	32	128
Life Sciences	Agriculture	32	128
	Biological Sciences/Biochemistry	32	128
	Food Science and Technology	32	128
	Health and Social Care	32	128
	Medical Science	16, 48★	128
	Plant Biosciences	32	128
	Psychology	32	64
Physical Sciences	Architecture	32	128
	Chemistry	32	128
	Computer Science	32	128
	Cybernetics and Electric Engineering	32	128
	Engineering	64	256
	Mathematics	16	128
	Physics	32	128
Social Sciences	Anthropology	32	128
	Business	32	128
	Economics	32	128
	Hospitality, Leisure and Tourism Management	32	128
	Law	32	128
	Publishing	16	64
	Sociology	32	64
Other	Other	43	172
Total			**3500**

Source: adapted from Nesi, 2008, pp. 216–217
★ More papers were thought to be available from graduate students. In the final BAWE corpus, 80 papers were collected from medical science, and all were from masters' level students.

Because the BAWE project was interested in exploring disciplinary variation, those involved wanted to balance the amount of writing collected from each subject. However, another researcher might be interested in studying how language is used across registers while putting more importance on the registers that are most frequently used. For example, if we were to propose a study that investigated all the language experienced (either produced or consumed) by college students, we would have to include other registers. Lectures, lecture notes, readings, conversations with peers, office hour interactions, exams, student papers, and so on would need to be included in our corpus. If the students in our study only went to office hours once a semester, we might not want to attach as much weight to those texts as, say, course lectures, which are heard for several hours every week.

This system is called **proportional sampling**. This type of sampling is related to balance because for some studies there is a desire to create a sample that reflects most salient characteristics of the target population. Consider our previously proposed study of teenager speech by young women in New York. We may want to check how we could create a balanced corpus through proportional sampling. If our research question were along the lines of How do female teenagers from New York speak? We would then have to better understand the context.

Perhaps using ethnographic methods, we could begin to understand how and with whom our participants communicate in various settings. We might find that they spend around 70 percent talking to other female teenagers, 20 percent talking with male teenagers, and 10 percent talking with adults. If we only wanted to answer questions about how they speak with each other, our corpus data would not need to include their other interactions. However, if our research question was more general, we might want to include those other types of interactions because of the possibility that with different types of interlocutors, they speak differently. Using proportional sampling in this case would help us understand their discourse as a whole, avoiding the error of overgeneralizing from only one type of interaction.

A4.2.3 Register Variation in Corpus Design

Corpus-based research on register variation has shown that the lexical and grammatical findings from one register of a language cannot be generalized to other registers or to the language as a whole (Biber, Conrad, & Reppen, 1998). In other words, if findings are made for texts that come from one situational context, those findings may not apply to language that is used in other contexts. For example, the way that we speak to an employer would differ from the way a sports announcer calls the action in a basketball game.

Biber and colleagues (1998) explored this idea by investigating how the lemma *deal* was used in two written registers (academic prose and fiction) from the Longman-Lancaster Corpus. Each of these subcorpora consisted of two million words. The researchers were interested in seeing how often *deal* was used as a noun or as a verb. Out of the four million–word sample of the corpus, the difference between nouns and verbs was not that great. *Deal* as a noun was used 366 total times and as a verb, 482 times. However, when looking at the differences between registers, they found that the distribution of the nominal and verbal forms was quite different. In fiction, *deal* was more likely to be used as a noun, and in academic prose, it was much more likely to be used as a verb.

A much more extensive description of register variation in English can be found in the *Longman Grammar of Spoken and Written English* (LGSWE) (Biber, Johansson, Leech, Conrad, & Finegan, 1999). Over 1,200 pages, this book covers many lexical and grammatical topics in British and American English. One of its unique characteristics, however, is that it is corpus-based. Descriptions of grammatical features and constructions were analyzed and presented to the reader based on four registers: conversation, fiction, newspaper writing, and academic writing. It is important to consider register variation when conducting sociolinguistic studies. Although one might find that a rich and complete description of his or her participants can contextualize their language use, it is also important to realize that these participants would use language quite differently depending on the context of and purposes for that language use.

Reflective Break

- In Section A3.2, you read about **reference** (or general) and **specialized** corpora. What are some issues of sampling and balance that would come up for each type? How do you think collecting these two different types of corpora are different?
- Imagine the following: Your group has been asked to investigate how teenagers interact with each other on social media message boards. You are curious about how the variable of gender influences such interaction. With your group, determine how you will sample your data, considering how much and from which types of interactions you will collect. Create a corpus matrix showing how your data will be balanced.

A4.2.4 Determining Representativeness

Representativeness is not easily planned and verifiable at the onset of a study. Instead, it is an iterative process that can only begin after data has been collected. While a corpus collector can plan his or her corpus to be balanced and appropriately sampled, there is no way of knowing if that plan will work until the corpus begins to be built. We can recall Biber's (1993) definition of representativeness as how a sample, such as a corpus, includes contextual and linguistic variability in the population as a whole. This is no small task because, if you think about it, how can we know what the variability of a population is if we have not studied it yet? Tagliamonte (2006) describes how ethnographic methods of qualitatively investigating a population can be useful in understanding the population, getting to know how language is used. Often in corpus-based research, the size of the corpus is described. Some might think "the bigger, the better" when it comes to corpus size. However, as discussed earlier in this section, corpus creation should consider where the data comes from and not just how much data can be collected. Defining the population being focused on and describing how samples will systematically be taken from that group as a whole are more important.

A5

EXPANSION, LIMITATIONS, AND FUTURE DIRECTIONS OF CORPUS WORK IN SOCIOLINGUISTICS

A5.1 Expansion of Corpus Work

The LGSWE (Biber, Johansson, Leech, Conrad, & Finegan, 1999) helped tremendously in introducing corpus-based data to "mainstream" applied linguists as well as the general audience composed of English language teachers and language learners. As we briefly mentioned in the previous section, the LGSWE provides extensive distributional data of the lexico/syntactic features of written and spoken registers of British and American English. The LGSWE also presents corpus findings that explain the functional parameters of two national English varieties based on frequencies and comparative patterns of usage. The analysis and presentation of corpora from the LGSWE have contributed an assortment of frequency distributions to many language/grammar classrooms with potential applications in register and cross-linguistic comparisons. Such comparisons of British and American English are directly related to linguistic dialectology (see Section B1) and sociolinguistic studies of geographic variation.

There have also been many recent updates in the structure of reference corpora that coincide with methodological changes in CL research. Sociolinguistic metadata (e.g., speaker/writer demographic information—gender, age, region, social class, occupation) have actually been added to the updated BNC since 2007. There are now many collections of parallel registers of spoken and written texts representing dialect varieties of global Englishes, and the number of multilingual corpora continues to increase. The creation of **mega corpora** such as Google Lab's Google Books Ngram Viewer and the Corpus of Global Web-Based English (GloWbe) (Davies, 2013), which provide information suitable for temporal studies (both synchronic and diachronic), contributes to the growing number of research studies describing sociolinguistic variation and change across registers and contexts. These mega corpora have at least 450 million words, with Google Books and GloWbe in the billions of words and still increasing. Corpus availability and access have improved immensely, at least in the past five years, as computational technology and online resources converge to provide easy platforms for CL researchers to share texts and data.

The increasing number of master's and doctoral-level classes in CL in many universities in Europe and North America has also started to underscore the need for strict discipline in corpus-based research that is supported by data, meaningful analyses, and reliable claims. Also contributing to the many applications of the CL approach in academia is the presence of publishing platforms that provide opportunities for book treatments of specialized CL topics. Major book publishers such as Cambridge University Press, Routledge, Longman, John Benjamins, University of Michigan Press, Rodopi, and Continuum have actively supported research in CL. For example, John Benjamin's *Studies in Corpus Linguistics Series* has now published over 60 volumes. In addition, influential CL-only international academic journals (e.g., *International Journal of Corpus Linguistics* and *Corpora*) continue to publish peer-reviewed CL studies that have gone through a strict refereeing process. And finally, CL-only international conferences such as the American Association for Corpus Linguistics Conference, the Corpus Linguistics Conference in the United Kingdom, and the International Computer Archive of Modern and Medieval English (ICAME) Conference have all included strands exclusively for corpus-based sociolinguistics topics.

A5.2 Trends in Corpus-Based Sociolinguistic Research

In this book, we survey the growing number of studies that merge corpora and qualitative and quantitative approaches in the field of sociolinguistics (Section B). We also provide ideas and suggestions for designing and developing corpus-based sociolinguistics studies (Section C). Our approach is grounded on a clear definition and scope of CL within sociolinguistics to highlight best practices and sound analytical procedures in this growing area of research. *Corpus-Based Sociolinguistics* has not yet been fully integrated into the larger field of sociolinguistics, but there is no denying its important contribution and increasing influence. The following themes illustrate the expansion of corpus work in sociolinguistics.

Corpus-Based Analysis of Regional Variation in English

Sociolinguists have typically employed ethnographic and survey methodologies in their analysis of social and regional dialect variation. However, a number of studies in the past two decades have investigated regional dialect variation from a corpus perspective. Many of these research projects have been developed in European universities (e.g., Freiburg, Helsinki, Newcastle) and have focused on British

English dialects, resulting in the collection of the Newcastle Electronic Corpus of Tyneside English, the Helsinki Corpus of British English Dialects (Ihalainen, 1990), and the Freiburg English Dialect Corpus (FRED) (Kortmann & Wagner, 2005). Corpus analysis of dialect variation in American English has been largely influenced by the Linguistic Atlas Projects and many of its interrelated spin-offs, including the *Dictionary of Regional American English* (DARE). Grieve's (2009) study of regional variation from a corpus of letters to the editor collected from over 70 cities from across the United States shows how corpus-based methodologies can be directly applied to dialectology. Grieve carefully designed his corpus (written texts) to account for geographic regions in the United States and their influence on variations across a range of linguistic usage. We discuss Grieve's work and other related studies on regional dialectology in Section B1.

Sociolinguistic Study of Global Varieties of English

Related to regional variation, the corpus approach in the study of World Englishes focuses on emerging varieties of English as they adapt to changing circumstances of use and contact with local languages and cultures (Breiteneder, 2009). World Englishes has been operationalized to show the expanding nature of English used by English as a second or foreign language (ESL/EFL) speakers in various contexts. Studies of World Englishes have focused on two major subareas: (1) indigenous varieties of English, and (2) the study of English as a Lingua Franca (ELF). Corpus development efforts in representing indigenous varieties of English are best represented by the International Corpus of English (ICE). The ICE project is an attempt to construct comparable corpora for all varieties of English spoken around the world (Greenbaum, 1996). Each corpus in ICE (e.g., ICE India or ICE Jamaica) ideally has the same corpus design: a total size of 1 million words, with 500 texts of approximately 2,000 words, each from the same registers (news, lectures, parliamentary debates, etc.). The authors and speakers are aged 18 or over, are educated through the medium of English in their respective countries, and are either born in the target country or moved there at an early age. The texts in the corpus date from 1990 or later (Nelson, 1996).

According to Seidlhofer (2007), the most widespread contemporary use of English throughout the world is that of English as a Lingua Franca. ELF is the variety of English used as a common means of communication among speakers from different first-language backgrounds. The Vienna-Oxford International Corpus of English (VOICE) is a structured collection of texts representing spoken ELF interactions. The VOICE project features a large-scale and in-depth linguistic description of spoken ELF interactions accessible online. Another related project focusing on English as a lingua franca is the Corpus of English as Lingua Franca in Academic Settings (ELFA) (Mauranen, 2007) representing texts collected from academia.

Sociolinguistic Analysis of Web Registers: Blogs and Microblogs

The exponential growth of Internet technology in the last decade has definitely influenced corpus-based research. Collecting Web registers such as online newspaper articles, academic papers, opinion columns, reader comments, and Weblogs has become easily accomplished, while more and more types of specialized texts have been developed and freely distributed online. The Internet as a corpus (Crystal, 2006, 2011) not only covers English texts but also, increasingly, other languages used online by multimillions of users worldwide. Automated transcriptions of Web-based audio and video clips and translation services have also been developed, and these services have promising applications that could help with the collection of spoken texts online.

Blogging and microblogging in social media (e.g., Facebook and Twitter status updates) have been the subject of many large-scale studies, many of them directly addressing a range of sociolinguistic research questions. Because social media produces a new variety of language that continues to evolve, this book's discussion of research issues and constructs in Section B6 could help inform the design of future synchronic and diachronic investigations of this register. In addition, the study of linguistic variation in blogging, including online posts and tweets, has functional applications in other domains such as big data analytics and media and marketing research.

Using Spoken Corpora in Sociolinguistics

The study and analysis of accents, pronunciation, and especially socio-phonetic features of speech may not yet be completely possible in corpus-based sociolinguistics, given obvious procedural and technical limitations. However, multimodal annotations of spoken texts that incorporate speech patterns such as prosody have been developed, potentially paving the way for more descriptive, phonetically driven transcriptions in the future. In Section B4, we highlight the creation and applications of the Hong Kong Corpus of Spoken English (HKCSE) *prosodic* (Cheng, Greaves, & Warren, 2005) and its corpus design and manual prosodic transcription, as well as its practical uses in workplace communication studies.

Many corpus-based analyses of spoken discourse have also offered directions for empirical investigations of linguistic features in various types of formal and informal conversations. Work in this area has incorporated corpus-based methods in analyzing television talk shows, job interviews, and professional interactions. Friginal (2009b), for example, analyzed the discourse characteristics of outsourced telephone interactions, while Rayson, Leech, and Hodges (1997) conducted a corpus-based analysis of speech that is differentiated socially and contextually. Several studies have utilized corpora in discourse analysis and in describing the lexis and grammar of conversation. Among these studies is McCarthy and Handford's (2004) work on defining the structure of spoken business English using the Cambridge and Nottingham Corpus of Business English (CANBEC). They explored the different dimensions of business talk in relation to everyday casual conversation.

Multidimensional Analysis of Spoken and Written Registers

Douglas Biber developed the framework for multidimensional (MD) analysis using POS-tagged data, and this approach continues to be applied in the study of linguistic variation in spoken/written texts. MD studies have covered a wide range of sociolinguistic variables including cross-cultural interaction, gender, and world Englishes. Also, MD analysis has been used to document historical patterns of register variation and in the study of historical change in fictional dialogues. We discuss MD studies in-depth and provide step-by-step instructions for running MD statistical analysis in Section C2.

A5.3 Limitations and Objections to Corpora

In general, sociolinguistics has been resistant to the application of corpus-based analyses, and so most studies of social and regional dialect variation continue to employ traditional methodologies. (Biber, Reppen, & Friginal, 2010, p. 562)

A corpus of naturally occurring texts does not, in itself, give information about the context from which it came. Thus, we would argue against and agree with others who object to the use of decontextualized corpora in studying languages. The nature of decontextualized language from electronic texts and the ways they are often used in research typically overlook or contradict outright many important themes and constructs that are central to the studies of sociolinguists. Quantitative data, when presented in isolation can be misleading and ineffective in fully capturing the essence of language across communication contexts.

To some extent, many objections to the use of corpora in the wider field of applied linguistics and in sociolinguistics in particular have resulted from the negative reactions to how CL researchers have, at times, overgeneralized their claims. Sociolinguistic theory can certainly be operationalized in corpus linguistics within appropriate datasets, but there have been studies that have *exaggerated* the meaning of frequency distributions in relation to social variables such as gender or nationality. Clearly, observations and patterns of variation, even from a corpus of over 10 million words, cannot be carelessly or offhandedly attributed to a single social variable. Careful and detailed data analyses are necessary to show direct and valid societal connections that may have motivated or influenced unique patterns of variation in language in a given context.

Henry Widdowson (2000) describes how finding and describing usage patterns that language users themselves are not consciously aware of using is also a limitation of corpus linguistics. He claims that, because corpus findings can contradict intuition, those findings do not reflect the users' awareness. In other words, purely textual analyses of corpora do not offer researchers the ability to explore and better understand the beliefs and self-perceptions (i.e., attitudes and prejudices) of speakers and writers. Language, in this case, is complicated and extremely complex and may not have to be quantified. Corpora are limited because they cannot fully capture language and what it represents, particularly with respect to the users' perspective. Widdowson's observations are not necessarily objections to corpus-based sociolinguistics per se but are focused more specifically on the application of corpus data in the broader discipline of applied linguistics relative to the way CL has attempted to *systematize* variations over a more holistic synthesis of intuitions and sociocultural experiences. Scholars who share the same perspectives also point out that corpora are only able to represent lexical and grammatical features of language within a "surface-structure" level, leaving behind deeper connotations, multimodal manifestations of behavior, and more meaningful experiences.

A5.3.1 Shifting Research Perspectives

The theoretical arguments over what can and cannot be fully captured in corpora and how to best conduct research and interpret the results raise important considerations that should further define corpus linguistics and its research applications. As succinctly articulated by Yumana Kachru (2008),

> Corpus-based linguistic research is as good as the corpora on which it is based, and grammatical or lexical analyses of corpora are as good as the analytical tools, such as grammatical tags or concordances, which are developed to analyze them (Knowles, Wichmann, & Alderson, 1996). Furthermore, only limited attempts have been made to carry out semantic and pragmatic analyses and analyses that take into account sociolinguistic factors. There is plenty of scope for interaction between theoretical linguistics, grammatical description, applied research, and corpus linguistic research. (2008, pp. 6–7)

Y. Kachru, in fact, believes that corpora and corpus linguistics deserve serious attention from linguists and applied linguists, as they are very relevant to linguistic description, language variation, lexicography, and language education. She recognized that corpus-based research has produced various expected and unexpected yet revealing results in the areas of variation focusing on grammatical and lexical devices. The overarching theme here is the need for more studies that clearly define the merging of approaches and modeling of what corpora can represent in analyzing linguistic variation. For sociolinguists, the message is to also explore what is *behind* textual quantities and grammatical co-occurrences; to the extent possible, capture awareness and subjectivities of speakers and writers; and consider corpora as a dataset, not as a *language*.

McEnery and Wilson (2001) noted that while sociolinguistics has traditionally been based upon empirical data, the use of standard corpora in this field has been limited, thus far. By "standard corpora," they were referring to reference corpora that represent a variety of language such as the British National Corpus, the American National Corpus, or any large corpora of other languages. They added that expansion of corpus work in sociolinguistics appears to have been hampered by three problems (p. 108):

- the operationalization of sociolinguistic theory into measurable categories suitable for corpus research;
- the lack of sociolinguistic metadata encoded in currently available corpora; and
- the lack of sociolinguistically rigorous sampling in corpus construction.

In the past 10 years, however, there have been many positive developments in CL research that have emphasized mixed-methods approaches and sensibly constructed protocols for qualitatively interpreting frequency data from corpora. These advances can be expected to continue as CL practitioners further refine and improve corpus design and collection, utilize statistics even more extensively and consistently in corpus-based studies, and improve the overall quality of interpretive techniques in corpus analysis. Many researchers involved in the study of linguistic variation (e.g., Douglas Biber, Paul Baker, Mark Davies, William Kretzschmar, Yueguo Gu, to name only a few), studying diverse groups of speakers/writers and registers, have developed models of corpus design that argue for representativeness and generalizability of data. They also support the operationalization of sociolinguistic theories from corpora. Multimodal annotations for domain-specific texts have also been slowly implemented to capture many features of discourse not originally explored during earlier collections of corpora.

Reflective Break

- **Further Reading**: We briefly referenced above Widdowson's (2000) reservations about the use of corpus data in linguistic research, which was taken from an essay he wrote for the journal *Applied Linguistics*. We recommend that you read this article as well as a response in favor of corpus-based approaches by Stubbs (2001), which is from the same journal.
- Y. Kachru (2008) also discussed the need to consider subjective language in corpus-based research. "Subjectivity" in this context refers to aspects of language used to express opinions, evaluations, and speculations across spoken and written contexts. How can corpora also explicitly represent subjective language? What linguistic features can you search using a simple concordance

program that can provide data on subjective language? How accurate are corpus-based data in capturing subjectivity when it is obviously harder to capture behaviors such as sarcasm or figurative language in transcribed texts?
• Do you think you can capture humor from corpora? How?

A5.3.2 Genuine Limitations and Difficult Areas

One strength of corpus-based methods is that the quantitative collection and analysis of language allows for linguistic features in use that would otherwise remain hidden or undetected by speaker's/writer's perceptions to be found and disclosed. Macro analyses to address groups of people, various demographics, registers, or situational contexts can be conducted, producing a range of numerical data for interpretation and potential application in practical contexts. Although we believe that corpora and corpus-based methodologies can be effectively used to answer many sociolinguistic research questions, we also recognize that there are important topics and constructs that are not particularly well-suited to be answered in this way or do not yield readily to this research methodology.

Perhaps the most notable area of sociolinguistics that is difficult to study using corpora and corpus-based methods also happens to be the area that many sociolinguists are primarily interested in: **sociophonetic features of speech**. **Segmental** (e.g., various vowel and consonant sounds) and **suprasegmental** (e.g., intonation, rhythm, pith and volume, word stress and sentence stress) pronunciation of words and discourse have been extensively analyzed in sociolinguistics across societal categories, especially gender and regional background. **Accent** and **pronunciation** studies differentiate American versus British English or dialects of American English, and these sound patterns are also used to trace the presence of linguistic attitudes and prejudice in the way speakers project themselves in various communicative contexts. A New Yorker speaks differently from an Alabama Southerner, and listeners can form their perceptions about these speakers based on the subtleties of what they hear. Some might say that the speaker from New York is arrogant, brash, or educated/smart, while the Alabama speaker is lazy and ignorant or friendly and kind.

Diglossia refers to the situation in which members of a single speech community use two distinct languages for different functions. In some situations, interlocutors may choose to use one language with each other and another in a different context or for a different purpose. Corpora, which are static representations of language, are not the best tool for exploring under which circumstances those decisions are made (i.e., choice or conscious shift in form). Related to diglossia are phenomena that influence speakers and listeners to intentionally vary their speech and paralinguistic behaviors. **Power dynamics** of language use and interaction, contextual or environmental factors, and psychosocial behaviors can all affect the forms and functions of utterances employed by speakers. Without sufficient context, a *thank you* simply becomes a (potentially) polite response; within power structures, this response suggests hierarchies or ranks. Construction of identity, solidarity, and togetherness are also difficult to capture from transcribed texts as well as multilingualism and **style** and **linguistic repertoire**.

American sociolinguistics includes extensive research of African American Vernacular English (AAVE), which is also referred to as *Ebonics* or Black English. Similar research of other cultural groups includes Native Americans and their language varieties (including topics on the *death* of many Native American languages) and code-switching from Hispanic American speakers or Spanish/English–speaking immigrants in the United States (i.e., *Spanglish*). To date, there are no expansive corpora specifically collected to represent these groups, and with the clear and somewhat daunting challenges in designing and collecting these sociolinguistic corpora of racial and social classes, it may be more appropriate to leave the study of these groups to interactional sociolinguists and ethnographers. The same is true for studies of **pidgins** and **creoles**, especially their historical shifts, **dialect leveling** (i.e., change or shift in pronunciation based on contact between speakers of different dialects), and descriptions of **social persona** and the process of **gendering**—all of which are not, at least at this point, suitable topics in corpus-based sociolinguistics.

Finally, sociolinguistic areas in which corpora may not be needed include the **sociology of language**, **language policy** and **language planning**, and **standardization in language** (although it may be possible to compare the linguistic characteristics of "standard vs. nonstandard" varieties from corpora when these are defined clearly). Studies of **linguistic discrimination** need spoken and written evidence, but these do not necessarily require corpus collection and corpus processing.

A5.4 Future Directions

We mentioned earlier that the study of accent and pronunciation is difficult to accomplish with corpus-based approaches. This, however, may already be changing. The annotation of spoken corpora for prosody with the Hong Kong Corpus of Spoken English (HKCSE) (see Section B4.2.3) and more detailed contextual transcriptions and annotations of spoken texts paint a promising future for capturing some sociophonetic features of speech in orthographic transcripts. Although not necessarily considered corpora in the traditional sense, available databases of speech that are designed to be analyzed phonetically, phonologically, or acoustically point to a possible framework for developing a phonetically annotated corpus.

The *Speech Accent Archive* (http://accent.gmu.edu/) (Weinberger, 2013), currently with 1,720 speech samples, is an online database of speakers from around the world. By using crowdsourcing techniques, various speakers can also send submissions of their speech patterns and accents digitally. All of these speakers are asked to read aloud a single paragraph:

> Please call Stella. Ask her to bring these things with her from the store: Six spoons of fresh snow peas, five thick slabs of blue cheese, and maybe a snack for her brother Bob. We also need a small plastic snake and a big toy frog for the kids. She can scoop these things into three red bags, and we will go meet her Wednesday at the train station.

This paragraph was designed to elicit many of the possible sounds and sound combinations occurring in English. The audio samples are then transcribed phonetically using the International Phonetic Alphabet (IPA), forming a "corpus" of IPA-transcribed texts. Nearing 2,000 participants, this project offers views into English variation, both native and nonnative, across the world. Although the sample is read and not naturally occurring, the *Speech Accent Archive* offers the beginning of what could be possible in phonetically transcribing a corpus. In terms of sociolinguistics and contexts of the participants, the *Speech Accent Archive* also includes demographic questions for each speaker. Every entry in the archive is thus tagged for birthplace, native language, other language known, age, age when first learning English, method of English learning (in school or not), length of time having lived in an English-speaking country (and which country, if that is the case). All of these variables are also searchable on the Web site. That makes it easy for a teacher, phonetician, speech pathologist, or anyone interested in accents to search for a group of speakers to explore phonetic and phonological processes. Another useful feature of the *Speech Accent Archive* is that its Web site allows users to search for audio and transcripts by categories of phonetic characteristics as they differ from General American English (GAE). Phonetic generalizations for the samples can be searched by vowel, consonantal, and syllabic differences from the GAE.

Also related to phonetic analyses of corpora, the C-ORAL-ROM project (Cresti & Moneglia, 2005) was developed to acoustically analyze spoken texts of Italian, French, Spanish, and Portuguese (no English samples have yet been analyzed using this model). For American English, Clopper and Pisoni (2006) have developed the Nationwide Speech Project corpus which contains nearly 60 hours of recorded speech from 60 informants, 5 males and 5 females from 6 dialect regions in the United States: New England, the North, the Mid-Atlantic, the South, and the West. What is now becoming increasingly common is the multimodal annotation of spoken interactions (see, e.g., Gu, 2002, 2007). Together with enhanced prosodic and acoustic markups of spoken corpora, multimodal transcripts linking video recordings to nonlinguistic features that play a crucial role in communication, such as facial expressions, hand gestures, and body position, are highlighted and can be automatically extracted. Studies like these indicate that the strengths of corpus analysis can be extended to include aspects of communication and sociolinguistic variables beyond the analysis of the lexico-grammatical fabric of spoken and written texts (Biber et al., 2010).

And finally, a future direction for corpus-based research in sociolinguistics is the more prominent use and application of Critical Discourse Analysis (CDA). CDA is defined by Fairclough (1993) and Gee (2011) as follows:

Discourse analysis which aims to systematically explore often opaque relationships of causality and determination between (a) discursive practices, events, and texts, and (b) wider social and cultural structures, relations and processes; to investigate how such practices, events and texts arise out of and are ideologically shaped by relations of power and struggles over power; and to explore how the opacity of these relationships between discourse and society is itself a factor securing power and hegemony. (Fairclough, 1993, p. 135)

Any form of discourse analysis that seeks to engage with politics . . . Critical discourse analysis deals with whose "interests" are represented, helped, or harmed as people speak and write. When "critical discourse analysis" is spelled as "CDA" it often refers to the work of Norman Fairclough and his associates. (Gee, 2011, p. 204)

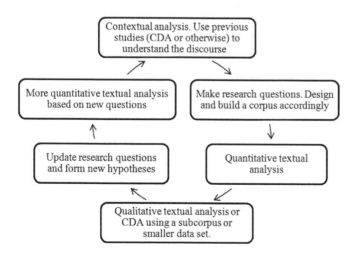

FIGURE A5.1. Potential stage cycle for critical discourse analysis supported by corpus linguistics

Source: adapted from Baker et al., 2008, p. 295

One key figure in corpus-based CDA is Paul Baker, who has applied corpus approaches in studying discursive practices across cultural structures and dimensions of gender and sexuality. Baker argues that the use of corpora makes CDA more objective. With his colleagues, Baker has proposed an iterative cycle when combining critical approaches to corpus linguistics (or corpus approaches to CDA) (Baker et al., 2008). They suggest a progression of stages from quantitative to qualitative data collection and analyses. A truncated version of this series of questions, corpus creation, quantitative analysis, qualitative analysis, and more questions is shown below in Figure A5.1. Although linearly ordered, Baker and colleagues noted that a person can enter the structure at any given stage. When applied to sociolinguistic topics such as power and role relationships, perceptions of equality and civil rights, and manifestations of hate and ideology in language this model may produce more meaningful, objective results.

SECTION B

Survey of Corpus-Based Sociolinguistic Studies

B1

CORPORA AND THE STUDY OF LANGUAGES AND DIALECTS

B1.1 Languages, Dialects, and Varieties

There are various definitions of **language** and **dialect** in the interrelated fields of linguistics, sociology, and anthropology. Most of these definitions overlap and scholars may sometimes use these two terms interchangeably. In general, there are no commonly accepted criteria distinguishing a language from a dialect, and subjective definitions are largely based on scholars' particular field or research focus. For example, it is common for Chinese speakers to refer to Mandarin and Cantonese as two distinct *dialects* although Mandarin and Cantonese are not **mutually intelligible** and are spoken by people representing diverse regions and cultural traditions in China. In other contexts, Mandarin and Cantonese are identified as two independent languages. The complication here is intensified by the fact that Mandarin and Cantonese can be written using the same classical or standard "Chinese" scripts. Dialects have also been categorized according to social judgments by speakers (e.g., what is proper or standard form against informal, nonstandard) and level of prestige or usage (e.g., not written or not codified, speakers are few).

In sociolinguistics, it is important to *operationalize* these two terms, as a clear distinction helps identify the meanings and contexts of variation in speakers'/ writers' use of words, sentences, and discourse. In this book, we define language and dialect as follows:

- **Language**: a collection of words, meaningful sounds, and gestures that form a system for their common use by groups of individuals belonging to the same **speech community**. A speech community may cover a geographical region, a nation, or people with same cultural tradition, norms, and identities (*French* language, *English* language in the United States, *Kinyarwanda* in Rwanda).

- **Dialect**: a variety of a language that can clearly be distinguished from other varieties of the same language. These dialects are typically mutually intelligible but with clear differences in features such as accent and pronunciation (phonology), sentence structures (syntax), and use of vocabulary (lexis). Dialect speakers may be separated from other dialect speakers geographically or socially.

The *English* language in the United States has been classified into regional dialects in many ways by linguists. For example, the most detailed dialect distinction in American English based on pronunciation lists the following groups: (1) Northern New England, (2) the North, (3) Greater New York City, (4) the Midland, (5) the South, (6) North Central, and (7) the West. We discuss some of these dialect groups in this section.

B1.2 The Study of Regional Dialectology

In this section, we focus first on regional dialectology research and how this tradition has influenced the use of corpora in sociolinguistic studies of languages and dialects. Taken together, linguistic variation in this context is attributed primarily to geography and regional differences. The study of regional variation in language has been one of the most important foci of sociolinguistic research, with many pioneering projects originating in Europe in the early nineteenth century. The primary goal of these dialectology studies was to interview older speakers in order to list common vocabulary and local terms and phrases unique to speakers of a particular village or region. In France, for example, the *Atlas Linguistique de la France* was a product of extensive fieldwork by Jules Gillieron and Edmond Edmont using standard questionnaires, note-taking techniques, and a systematic transcription of how locals pronounced different words or phrases. Over the years, the works of Gillieron and Edmont have inspired various atlas projects in European countries including Italy, Spain, Germany, Switzerland, and the United Kingdom. These studies have produced dialect maps and translation dictionaries that illustrate regional variation in speakers' vocabulary use and pronunciation of speech sounds.

In the United States, a project to develop the *Linguistic Atlas of the United States and Canada* was begun in 1931 by Hans Kurath. Kurath (1891–1992) studied German linguistics at the University of Chicago and his original research allowed him to travel to various remote areas of the eastern United States tracking migration movements of German speakers and collecting a variety of spoken and written data. This experience in data gathering and geographically tracking dialect distinctions helped Kurath to identify and map distinctive dialects and speech and pronunciation patterns, as well as the structure and evolution of American English. Kurath's interests in historical linguistics and the study of English brought about by European settlers inspired a groundbreaking set of projects that eventually produced the *Linguistic Atlas of the United States*. He introduced a systematic data-gathering approach while interviewing speakers of dialect groups particularly of the New England region and plotting similarities and differences on maps. In the 1930s, supported by the Modern Language Association, Kurath directed and completed the *Linguistic Atlas of New England*. The first volume of this atlas was published in 1939. The primary result of Kurath's work suggested that there are three major dialect areas in the eastern United States: the North, the Midland, and the South (see Figure B1.1). This atlas became the model for succeeding regional atlases that have been initiated by teams of American linguists.

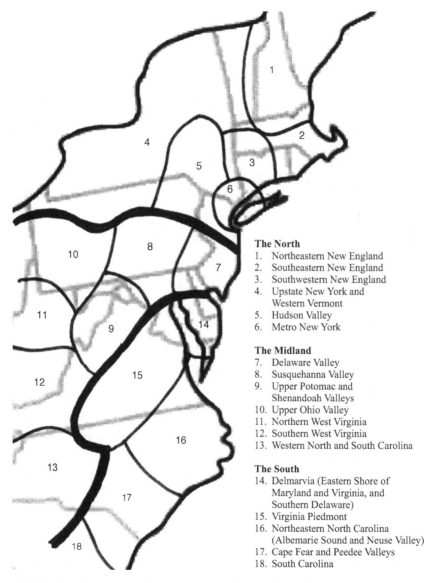

The North
1. Northeastern New England
2. Southeastern New England
3. Southwestern New England
4. Upstate New York and
   Western Vermont
5. Hudson Valley
6. Metro New York

The Midland
7. Delaware Valley
8. Susquehanna Valley
9. Upper Potomac and
   Shenandoah Valleys
10. Upper Ohio Valley
11. Northern West Virginia
12. Southern West Virginia
13. Western North and South Carolina

The South
14. Delmarvia (Eastern Shore of
    Maryland and Virginia, and
    Southern Delaware)
15. Virginia Piedmont
16. Northeastern North Carolina
    (Albemarie Sound and Neuse Valley)
17. Cape Fear and Peedee Valleys
18. South Carolina

FIGURE B1.1. Three major dialect areas of the Eastern United States

Source: adapted from Kurath, 1949, p. 91

In the United Kingdom, the *Linguistic Atlas of England*, edited by Orton, Sanderson, and Widdowson (1978), mapped regional linguistic variation in British English—including lexical, phonological, morphological, and syntactic features—based on the data gathered for the Survey of English Dialects. Isoglosses were also plotted midway between adjacent locations with contrastive forms. Nine primary regions—Southwest, Southeast, London, East, West Midlands, East Midlands, Yorkshire and Humber, Northwest, and Northeast—now often referred to as the dialect regions of present-day England, have been identified based on this atlas.

Over 1,300 questions designed to elicit 730 lexical items, 387 phonological items, 128 morphological items, and 77 syntactic items were used, primarily focusing on the oldest and most conservative forms of vernacular English. Data collection occurred primarily in rural and farming areas, and most questions considered topics about the countryside and farming as well as universal subjects such as numbers, time, and the human body. The field investigators were instructed to interview older residents who had been born and raised in the area they represented and whose parents were also likely to be native to the area, as well. Moreover, because it was assumed that males would be more likely to speak traditional dialects than females, the investigators were told to favor male over female informants. In addition to the focus on rural England, the settings for interviews were based on location and population, with the overall objective of sampling one community in England every 15 miles. The survey was conducted from 1950 to 1961, facilitated by recording technology that was developed after 1953. A total of 11 field investigators collected data in 313 locations across England during this period. Overall, several findings of these interviews were not as consistent or as clear-cut as the American surveys directed by Kurath; however, this may be more attributable to the potentially conservative approach adopted by the British dialectologists compared to their American counterparts than with the nature of British dialect regions (Grieve, 2009).

B1.3 Linguistic Atlases in the United States

Who uses *skeeter hawk, snake doctor,* and *dragonfly* to refer to the same insect?

Who says **gum band** instead of *rubber band*? (Kretzschmar, McDavin, Lerud, & Johnson, 1993)

Subsequent to Kurath, linguistic atlases in the United States have been produced by scholars mostly affiliated with the *Linguistic Atlas of the United States and Canada*. In addition, other groups of linguists collected data that focused on specific subareas in the eastern United States. The first three primary categorizations of dialect groups in the Eastern Seaboard (the North, the Midland, and the South) were further divided into subcategories (e.g., the North was further divided into northeastern, southeastern, and southwestern New England). New York, with its ever-growing number of immigrant communities and traditional European settlers, has also been further divided into groups such as Upstate, Hudson Valley, and Metropolitan Area.

Regional Linguistic Atlas projects have produced dictionaries, various publications, and digital archives, and they continue to be maintained in U.S. universities. These projects include the *Linguistic Atlas of the Middle and South Atlantic States* (LAMSAS), *Linguistic Atlas of the Western States* (LAWS), *Digital Archive of the Southern Speech* (DASS), *Linguistic Atlas of the Gulf States* (LAGS), and *Linguistic Atlas of the North-Central States* (LANCS).

- *Linguistic Atlas of the Middle and South Atlantic States* (**LAMSAS**)
  LAMSAS came directly from Kurath's framework of extensive interviews with 1,200 informants from the state of New York to Florida (northern Florida only) and from the Atlantic coast to the borders of Kentucky and Ohio. Interviews were collected from the 1930s to the 1940s. Regional variations in word use, grammar, and pronunciation were mapped in LAMSAS during the time when migration movements were more limited than they are today. Hence, data from these interviews allow for correlations between language patterns and settlement or migration movements in the United States. LAMSAS is considered as the largest single survey of regional and social differences in spoken American English (Preston, 1993).
- *Linguistic Atlas of the Western States* (**LAWS**)
  It took a while before U.S. linguists started covering the Western States, with more concentrated efforts dedicated to the Eastern Seaboard and its population's slow migration movements to the Midwest and the West. LAWS is still a work in progress, but fieldwork has been completed in Colorado, Utah, and Wyoming. Additional interviews in Texas and California began in the 1990s. The primary goal of LAWS is to provide recorded data on the speech of the American West by creating an inventory of regional and social markers characterizing Western culture and traditions. Also highlighted are influences from Mexico and the Spanish language (e.g., prevalence of Spanish words, proper nouns, and code-switched terms). Preston (1993) noted that work with LAWS extends beyond traditional atlas dialectology, as all interviews are recorded, which allows linguists the ability to explore all features of discourse.
- *Digital Archive of the Southern Speech* (**DASS**) and the *Linguistic Atlas of the Gulf States* (**LAGS**)
  LAGS benefits from available digitized versions of interviews that feature Southern English that are now accessible through computer-based files (e.g., .wav or .mp3 files). LAGS covers Florida, Georgia, Tennessee, Alabama, Mississippi, Louisiana, Arkansas, and Texas. Interviews were sampled across the LAGS region to cover older residents and a range of topics. In addition, one African American speaker for each of the 16 LAGS areas is included in the database. The presence of subcategories of speakers, especially African

American speakers of southern English, makes LAGS an important atlas that directly addresses sociolinguistic regional and racial variation.

• *Linguistic Atlas of the North-Central States* **(LANCS)**
The states of Wisconsin, Michigan, Illinois, Indiana, Ohio, and Kentucky are the primary focus of LANCS, but this group also includes speech and interview samples from Ontario, Canada. Most of the questions used to interview participants followed the traditional Linguistic Atlas model, but data collection has taken an extended period, starting from as early as 1933 through 1978. A total of 564 interviews with 154 audio tapes has been collected for LANCS (Preston, 1993).

B1.4 The Dictionary of American Regional English (DARE)

The *Dictionary of American Regional English* (DARE) resulted from dialect surveys in the United States created by Fred Cassidy from the 1960s to the early 1970s. Although it is not directly a product of the Linguistic Atlas projects, DARE follows the same research tradition. Data from DARE came from responses to questionnaires from local residents of over 1,000 locations systematically sampled from states that have clearly defined migration patterns and historical developments in the United States. More than 1,600 questions focusing on weather patterns, agricultural practices, flora and fauna, insect, religious beliefs, and everyday life were created for Cassidy's surveys. Over 80 fieldworkers were sent out to target communities to interview residents who had lived there all their lives. About 66 percent of DARE informants were age 60 or older; 24 percent were between 40 and 59; and 10 percent were under 39 (Cassidy, 1985). Audio recorded samples with informants reading different passages are available at the DARE Web site together with many sample entries (see below). A multivolume book is available for purchase.

DARE as a source of lexical usage across regions in the United States has been extremely useful to linguists, teachers, historians, journalists, and writers for movies or plays. Although DARE is not as popular as traditional home dictionaries, phrasebooks, or thesauri, there are many applications of DARE entries for pedagogy and sociolinguistic research. In addition, idiosyncratic regional words and phrases have been utilized by forensic investigators and the police in tracing clues that can help identify a criminal. Folk medicines and names of medicinal plants and their traditional applications are documented in many of DARE's entries related to science, together with names associated with indigenous plants and animals. DARE data resemble various corpora in how lexicon and interview materials are coded and compiled, and its focus on frequency distributions actually relates to important corpus-based approaches such as wordlists, word clouds, and keywords. Below is a sample DARE entry for "dropped egg" with a map showing locations in the United States where this phrase has been used.

Text Sample B1.1. An entry from DARE:

*dropped egg*n Also *drop egg*[Prob from Scots dial; cf SND drap v. 5. (2) (b) 1824->]*chiefly NEng*somewhat old-fash
*A poached egg.
*1884*Harper's New Mth. Mag.69.306/1 *MA, Martha was . . eating her toast and a dropped egg. **1896** (c1973) Farmer Orig. Cook Book 93, Dropped Eggs (Poached). **1933**Hanley DisksneMA, Dropped egg—take and put a pan of milk on the stove and boil and drop the egg in and let it cook. **1941**LANE Map 295 (Poached Eggs), **throughout NEng**, Dropped eggs . . . 1 inf, **ceVT**, Drop eggs. **1948** Peattie Berkshires 323 **wMA**, In Berkshire . . you could not get a poached egg, but you could get a "dropped" egg, which was the same thing. **1965**PADS 43.24 **seMA**, 6 [infs] poached eggs, 4 [infs] dropped eggs, 1 [inf] dropped egg on toast. **1965–70**DARE (Qu. H35, *When eggs are taken out of the shell and cooked in boiling water, you call them _____ eggs) 40 Infs, *chiefly NEng, Dropped;*NH15, Dropped egg on toast. *[33 of 41 Infs old]1975 Gould ME Lingo 82, Dropped egg—Maine for poached egg, usually on toast. **1977**Yankee Jan 73 **Isleboro ME**, The people on Isleboro eat dropped eggs instead of poached.
Common in the Northeast United States

(*Source*: DARE Web site—http://dare.wisc.edu/)

B1.5 William Labov and the Study of Regional Variation

William Labov is considered to be one of the most influential American linguists who singlehandedly founded the discipline of variationist sociolinguistics in the United States. Labov's work in the late 1960s introduced a systematic way of conducting sociolinguistic interviews and obtaining scientific demographic data from various informants representing dialect groups in the eastern United States. His methodologies have improved over a series of interrelated studies in the 1960s, mostly focusing on phonological variation across regional dialects in the United States. His research approaches were easily replicated and triangulated to produce more meaningful data and technical linguistic analyses.

Labov's many contributions in the earlier stages of sociolinguistic research include the groundbreaking Martha's Vineyard study, which he started in 1961 (1962, 1972b); investigation of varieties of English speech in New York City, which is described in a book entitled *The Social Stratification of English in New York City* (1966); and various studies on the linguistic characteristics of African American Vernacular English (AAVE) and nonstandard dialects in the 1970s and 1980s. His recent major work, with Sharon Ash and Charles Boberg, *The Atlas of North American English*, published in 2006, collects speech samples (audio) from over 400 speakers of American English across U.S. dialect maps. Vowel sounds are mapped to show regional distributions of phonetic variables from speakers identified within grouping categories that include gender, age, and education, among other variables. This work also focuses extensively on language change (sound change) in pronunciation and the increasing divergence of English in the United States

Labov is affiliated with the University of Pennsylvania where he continues to teach and research topics in language change and dialectology. Many of his students have also become word-famous linguists themselves (e.g., Penelope Eckert, who studies adolescent languages and gender; John Rickford, who has focused on African and Afro-American studies; and Geoffrey Nunberg, who works with semantics, pragmatics, and text classification), and his approach on social dialectology research has influenced corpus-based sociolinguistics.

B1.5.1 Labov's Martha's Vineyard Study

Labov's Martha's Vineyard study (1962, 1972b) was the first to study phonological variation focusing on a specific linguistic feature (the diphthongs: /au/ and /aI/ in words such as *mouse* and *mice*). Martha's Vineyard is an island on the south of Cape Cod in Massachusetts known to be a favorite summer vacation destination for the region's affluent crowd. Labov's goal was to identify the influence of social factors such as occupation (fishermen vs. other occupational groups), age (29 and younger, 30–60, 61 and older), and where informants lived on the island (Up-Islanders—rural, original inhabitants; Down-Islanders—more populated areas frequented by summer vacationers) on variations in the pronunciation of these diphthongs.

Labov's study differentiated the islanders' ways of pronouncing words such as *bout* or *sound* that distinguished centralized pronunciation from a more traditional form typical of the English variety spoken in New England. To Labov, it appeared that younger residents of Martha's Vineyard sounded "older" and were speaking with the traditional forms more than the previous generation. This observation informed his research questions that explored specific social factors as the primary cause of linguistic variation (i.e., more than just geography). Now, *attitude* and behavioral norms are clearly accepted as important sources of linguistic variation, but before Labov, these were not well-established variables in research. In fact, before this study, the notion of **free variation** was the accepted norm. Free variation suggests that variants are interchangeable across speakers and contexts, implying that variation happens within an unsystematic or untraceable set of sequences.

Another innovation introduced by Labov in his Martha's Vineyard study was to record his interviews with informants talking about their lives, living on the island, and what Martha's Vineyard meant to them, instead of the more traditional interview with predetermined questions and target items for pronunciation.

After listening to the recordings and establishing pronunciation patterns from his coding schemes, Labov came up with the following generalizations:

- **Gender, age, and identity**: Young men who identified themselves as natives of Martha's Vineyard prominently used the centralized pronunciation of diphthongs suggesting that they did not conform to the norms and speech style of the mainland.
- **Occupation**: Island fishermen were not accommodating of the wealthy summer visitors, regarding the influx of seasonal visitors as an intrusion infringing on traditional island life. This attitude encouraged most fishermen to establish a nonstandard dialect to maintain their social identity.

The marked pronunciation of diphthongs for many Islanders was an innovation that, to the locals, epitomized desirable values. The linguistic divide of *us* versus *them* allowed many speakers to maintain a linguistic identity, which gradually became a dialect norm.

> The 50th Anniversary of Labov's study was celebrated on Martha's Vineyard in the summer of 2011 as a groundbreaking sociolinguistic study that has significantly influenced modern linguistics. A collection of oral history recordings of generations of Vineyarders is available at Martha's Vineyard Museum. (Kendall, 2011)

Reflective Break

The contributions of these seminal studies on U.S. dialectology research can not be minimized or underestimated; however, there are limitations in their data collection and analyses. These limitations have been addressed in more recent studies, especially with the use of sophisticated audio recorders and sound processors, and additional data sources. Reflect on the following items and think about the contribution of corpora and corpus-based approaches in offering improvements in dialectology research.

- **Problems with traditional interview data**: Although the traditional research methodology of interviewing individuals is an efficient and effective approach for gathering data on lexical and phonological variation, this approach has limitations when utilized in the investigation of some other areas of linguistic variation—notably, grammatical variation. Grammatical features are usually abstract, as well as rare, and are, therefore, unlikely to be elicited by the interviewer or expressed spontaneously by the informant during the interview (Grieve, 2009).
- **The corpus-based approach to dialectology**: Grieve (2009) also noted that in contrast to lexical and phonological features with single, particular identifiers, there may be a variety of forms of a single grammatical feature—for

example, contracted and full forms of auxiliary verbs—requiring the dialectologist to track many tokens of a particular grammatical feature in discourse in order to determine its relative frequency in all its forms. Analyzing a **large amount of natural language** is the only way to overcome these challenges inherent in the study of grammatical variation, and, therefore, a corpus-based rather than interview approach is a more appropriate and effective research methodology in the study of regional grammatical variation.

- **Reliability and validation**: An additional shortcoming of many American dialect surveys appears during the data analysis of these studies, often characterized by an overreliance on the dialectologist's subjective opinions and procedures rather than objective statistical techniques to identify regional linguistic patterns and plot **isoglosses**, the borders between dialect regions. In many cases, such subjective procedures are not even replicable. Kurath, for example, relied solely upon his own judgment to define the distribution of a particular feature across a region. Labov's Martha's Vineyard study was also largely based on his analysis and interpretations of what he heard from audio recordings and was not validated by other analysts or raters.

B1.6 Newer Ways to Conduct Dialect Surveys

Before we move on to corpora and dialectology research, let's take a quick look at a more recent online approach to collect data for dialectology studies. Online surveys can be easily conducted, and they can focus primarily on vocabulary and grammatical questions. However, questions about pronunciation using recorded sound files or video excerpts could also be incorporated into online questionnaires. The *Dialect Survey* conducted at Harvard between 2000 and 2005 (Vaux, 2005) used a series of questions such as rhyming word pairs, vocabulary words, and phrasal units to explore lexis, grammar, and phonology commonly used by speakers of American English. The questions (and the dedicated online site) were developed by Bert Vaux. There are no expected right or wrong answers when responding to the questionnaire. Vaux structured each question to extract a response to "**what one really says**" and not "**what one thinks is right**." Sample questions include the following:

Text Sample B1.2. Sample dialect survey questions from the *Dialect Survey* (Vaux, 2005)

- What word(s) do you use to address a group of two or more people?
- Would you say "Are you coming with?" as a full sentence, to mean "Are you coming with us?"
- Would you say "where are you at?" to mean "where are you?"
- Which of these terms do you prefer for a sale of unwanted items on your porch, in your yard, etc.?
- What do you call the game wherein the participants see who can throw a knife closest to the other person (or alternately, get a jackknife to stick into the ground or a piece of wood)?

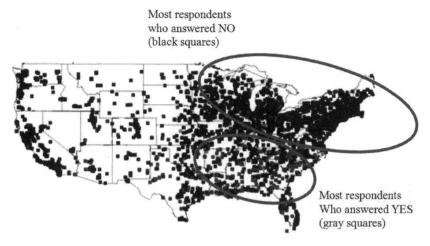

Most respondents
who answered NO
(black squares)

Most respondents
Who answered YES
(gray squares)

FIGURE B1.2. Breakdown of responses to the "might could" question from the *Dialect Survey*

Source: adapted from Vaux, 2005

Sample question and result: The question below considers the use of modal verbs in grammatical combinations such as "might could" or "used to could."

Modals are words such as "can," "could," "might," "ought to," and so on. Can you use more than one modal at a time? (e.g., "I might could do that" to mean "I might be able to do that"; or "I used to could do that" to mean "I used to be able to do that").

Online results show that there were 10,739 people who responded to this question with the following breakdown: Yes (11.51%), No (87.68%), and Other (0.81%). Figure B1.2 shows that a majority of respondents who answered **No** to this question were located in the northeastern part of the country (black little squares). Most respondents who answered **Yes** (only 11.51%) were located in the south (gray little squares).

Reflective Break

• Below are some more survey questions from the *Dialect Survey* (Vaux, 2005). Are your responses to these questions influenced by your regional back-ground? If you are not from the United States, what similar words or phrases can you use to explore lexical and grammatical variation in the dialects of your native language?

    • Do you use the word *cruller*?
    • Do you use the term "*bear claw*" for a kind of pastry?
    • What do you call someone who is the opposite of *pigeon-toed* (i.e., when they walk their feet point outwards)?
    • What do you call the box you bury a dead person in?

B1.7 Corpora in Dialectology Research

Dialectologists have paved the way for the extensive collection of transcribed interview texts and responses to survey questionnaires. Although there are similarities between these texts and an actual corpus, there are, at the same time, important differences. Many dialectologists have often referred to their collections of transcribed and/or recorded interviews as "corpora," but these fall short, as such, because they (1) are not naturalistic and (2) do not represent a common register of natural spoken language (i.e., conversation, tasked-based interaction, job interview). In other words, according to Grieve (2009), true corpus linguistic methodology has rarely been employed in such studies. Additionally, since the informants were aware that their language was being recorded for a study, these collections might well be "contaminated" due to the Observer's Paradox (Labov, 1972b), a problem avoided by the use of true corpus-based linguistics methodology.

Most, but not all, dialect surveys fail to base their research on true natural language corpora. One of the earliest, and probably most important, of this relatively small number of true dialect corpora is The Helsinki Corpus of British English Dialects (Ihalainen, 1990), based on recordings of spontaneous speech. As a dialect corpus, the primary objective in this corpus collection was to compile running, spontaneous speech within which forms of continuous grammatical variation could be observed. Although compilation of the corpus is still underway, this corpus already comprises over one million words and a total of 210 hours of speech.

With the obvious limitations in conducting corpus-based dialectology that considers variation in geographic speech patterns, corpora have been used to analyze varieties of language based on lexical and grammatical distributions. National English and international English corpora have been developed to represent a particular region of English relative to contexts such as native versus nonnative variety; spoken versus written transcripts; or medium, such as technology-mediated communication and Internet-based discourses. In the following sections, we describe reference corpora (e.g., British National Corpus and the American National Corpus) and specialized international corpora of English that can be used to extract linguistic data for cross-linguistic comparisons. We also highlight two innovative research studies on American English dialectology, Grieve (2009) and Eisenstein, O'Connor, Smith, and Xing (2010), which provide replicable frameworks that can influence the future of corpus-based dialectology studies.

B1.8 National and Global Englishes

Corpora intended to represent national and international varieties of English have been compiled over the years, generating large-scale reference corpora such as the British National Corpus (BNC) and the American National Corpus (ANC), representing two national varieties of English. The International Corpus of English (ICE) and the Vienna-Oxford International Corpus of English (VOICE) denote international/global varieties of educated English. Many other corpora collected by groups of scholars and individual researchers to represent a language variety are available online. Mark Davies has spearheaded an extensive compilation of English and non-English corpora which could all be used for research in dialectology and cross-linguistic comparisons. For example, Davies's Corpus of Contemporary American English (COCA) matches the BNC and ANC in depth and breadth and is presented in a user-friendly online interface. A recent massive collection of Internet-based global English, **GloWbE**, was released by Davies online in early 2013. A short profile of Mark Davies, including his corpus work, can be found in Section B5.

The collection of corpora representing national and international Englishes is deeply rooted in the original design of Brown and LOB, enabling comparisons between American and British English. Brown and LOB have been complemented by more recent collections with the same design (FROWN and FLOB), which also provide opportunities for studies of historical change (see Section B5) and dialect variation. Several linguistic comparisons of American and British English have been based on these corpora, with more recent studies making use of the BNC, ANC, and COCA. The Kolhapur Corpus of Indian English (Shastri, Patilkulkarni, & Shastri, 1986) also matches the Brown and LOB for cross-register and cross-linguistic comparisons. Finally, in addition to the BNC and the ANC, large corpora have been constructed to represent Australian English (Collins & Peters, 1988) and New Zealand English (Bauer, 1994).

B1.8.1 The British National Corpus (BNC)

The 100 million–word British National Corpus has consistently been used in many corpus-related studies more than any other corpus of English since its release in the early 1990s. The BNC was a result of a collaborative project among two universities in the United Kingdom (the University of Oxford and Lancaster University), the British Library, and three publishers (Oxford University Press, Longman, and W. & R. Chambers). Overall, the BNC was designed as a *general*, *monolingual*, and *synchronic* corpus of British English.

The BNC comprises a collection of over 4,000 written and spoken texts from a wide range of sources, originally developed to represent a cross-section of modern British English from the later part of the twentieth century up to the 1990s. Written registers of the BNC include newspaper articles, specialist periodical and journal articles, published academic texts, popular fiction, published and unpublished letters and memoranda, student essays, and nonacademic prose and biography, among others. Spoken registers include transcriptions of unscripted informal conversations and other types of spoken language collected in different contexts such as formal business meetings, radio shows, and parliamentary discussions. In total, 90 percent of all texts in the BNC are dedicated to written registers with only 10 percent for spoken registers. These texts were sampled for a wider coverage of registers around the 100 million–word target. Many written texts have a total of 45,000 words that were taken from different parts of a single-authored source for longer registers such as fiction and biographies. This process was used to limit the overrepresentation of idiosyncratic parts of texts, including those from extended bibliographies or indexes. Shorter texts (e.g., newspaper, interviews, and journal articles) were included in full.

Data collection for the BNC was completed in 1994 with no new categories of texts added as of 2013. Davies (2009), who also developed an online BNC interface, pointed out that, valuable as it is, the BNC "is beginning to show its age in some respects" (p. 159). Although texts files and demographic information on some registers have been corrected or updated in 2001 and 2007, it appears that there is no currently planned expansion to the BNC, which means that it may become increasingly out of date in consideration of recent changes in English and the need to represent additional registers (e.g., texting language/short message service [SMS], online language—social media, blogging, etc.).

However, since its original release, the BNC has become very accessible to many researchers, especially online. The complete corpus can still be purchased in two versions on CD-ROMs, BNC World (2001), which was a second edition release, and its most recent XML version, BNC XML Edition (2007). Other previous versions of the BNC available for purchase include a comparative and parallel collection of one million written and spoken texts (BNC Sampler) and a four million–word sampler from four different comparative registers (BNC Baby). BNC XML Edition is completely POS-tagged using CLAWS. This version is encoded following the Guidelines of the Text Encoding Initiative (TEI) to match many text processing protocols used in many corpus and computational tools. Various contextual and bibliographic information is also included with each text from well-defined TEI-conformant header information.

Currently, many components of the BNC can be accessed through the following online sites as part of the BNC consortium of universities in the United Kingdom (Oxford, Lancaster, and Leeds) and those that are developed by unaffiliated individuals or groups:

- **BNCWeb at Lancaster University**: an online interface of the BNC XML Edition (2007) with interactive options for unique searches, concordance outputs, and various features and functions. This interface also features user-specific applications (e.g., categorized queries and an option to upload an external data file), frequency lists and keywords, and the capability to explore labels and text headings. A BNCWeb book *Corpus Linguistics with BNCweb—a Practical Guide* was published in 2008 (Hoffmann, Evert, Smith, Lee, & Berglund-Prytz, 2008). Account registration (free) is required to access the interface (http://bncweb. lancs.ac.uk/cgi-binbncXML/, or search "BNC web Lancaster University").
- **Intellitext**: "Intelligent Tools for Creating and Analysing Electronic Text Corpora for Humanities Research" was developed by the Center for Translation Studies at the University of Leeds and is an excellent resource that allows access to various online, multilingual corpora including the complete version of the BNC. Concordance searches and advanced features such as "multivariate analysis," which project BNC distributional data along functional dimensions

developed by Douglas Biber ("Biber dimensions" and "Biber POS features),
are also provided (http://smlc09.leeds.ac.uk/itb/htdocs/Query.html, or
search "Center for Translation Studies University of Leeds").

- **BNCWeb at Oxford**: complete BNC texts housed in Oxford University
  and is accessible primarily by Oxford university users (requiring registration
  and password) (http://www.natcorp.ox.ac.uk/, or search "BNC Oxford").
- **Phrases in English (PIE) and the BNC**: a database developed using BNC
  World Edition (2001) that allows for search options of words and phrases
  including n-grams, phrase-frames, PoS-grams, and char-grams in the corpus.
  PIE provides querying with regular expressions and downloading of resulting
  datasets (http://phrasesinenglish.org/, or search phrases in English BNC).
- **BYU-BNC (Brigham Young University)**: Davies's BYU-BNC interface
  allows users to conduct concordance searches and visual and frequency comparisons across categorized written and spoken texts of the BNC. An easy-
  to-use chart function provides normalized frequency outputs. Other features
  include collocations and frequency/POS lists (http://corpus.byu.edu/bnc/,
  or search "BYU-BNC").

B1.8.1.1 Using the BNC Web (Lancaster University) for Sociolinguistic Research

The BNCweb at Lancaster University ("BNCweb, CQP-Edition") provides a client
program for searching and retrieving lexico/syntactic frequencies directly from online
Web browsers. A standard querying option can be filtered from available writer/
speaker metadata annotations encoded on BNC texts. As a result, this interface can
address a range of corpus-based sociolinguistic research questions across written and
spoken registers. The structure and functionality of the BNCweb allow researchers
to organize quick queries that can compare linguistic distributions across geographic,
situational, and social variables. Registers (including domain and text type) can be
clearly identified and compared, and specific and specialized speaker demographics
(e.g., age brackets, social class identifiers, speaker dialect/accent, intended audience)
are also provided. Figure B1.3 shows the BNCweb's standard query page.

For corpus-based sociolinguistic research, the BNCweb can be explored using
its built-in searchable domains and demographics. KWIC results can be viewed
or complete sentences can be retrieved from the BNC database. In addition, all
searches can be saved and results are easily downloadable. Frequency lists can be
sorted and are linked to the larger contexts, which also provide the bibliographical
and speaker information of each text, when available. Standard queries for written
and spoken registers can be "restricted" according to the following fixed categories:

Written Registers

> **Publication date**: 1960–1974, 1975–1984, 1985–1993
> **Medium of text**: book, periodical, miscellaneous; published, miscellaneous;
> unpublished, to-be-spoken

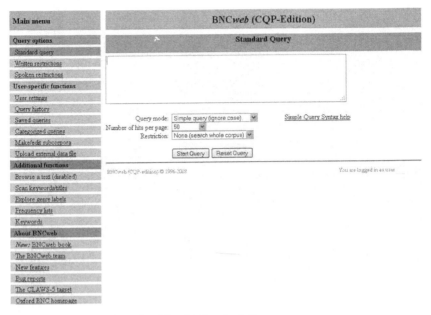

FIGURE B1.3. Screenshot of BNCweb's Standard Query page

Text sample: whole text, beginning sample, middle sample, end sample, composite

Domain: imaginative prose, informative (e.g., natural and pure sciences, applied science, social science, world affairs, arts, etc.)

Derived text type: academic prose, fiction and verse, nonacademic prose and biography, newspapers, other published written material, unpublished written material

Estimated circulation size: low, medium, high

Perceived level of difficulty: low, medium, high

Domicile of author: United Kingdom and Ireland, Commonwealth, Continental Europe, United States, "Elsewhere"

Age of author: 0–14, 15–24, 25–34, 35–44, 45–59, 60+

Sex of author: male, female, mixed

Type of author: corporate, multiple, sole

Target audience age: child, teenager, adult, "any"

Target audience sex: male, female, mixed

Genre: (multiple, e.g., academic, fiction, newspaper)

Spoken Registers

Overall: demographically sampled, context-governed

Interaction type: monologue, dialogue

U.K. region where spoken text was captured: South, Midlands, North

Genre: (multiple, e.g., broadcast, parliamentary debates, classroom discussions, interviews)

Age: 0–14, 15–24, 25–34, 35–44, 45–59, 60+, "unknown"

Sex: male, female, "unknown"

Social class: AB, C1, C2, DE, "unknown"

Education: still in education, left school 14 or under, left school 15/16, left school 17/18, education continued until 19 or over, "information not available"

First language: British English, North American English, unknown Indian language, German, French, unknown

Dialect/accent: Canada, German, East Anglia, French, Home Counties, Humberside, Irish, Indian subcontinent, Lancashire, London, Central Midlands, Merseyside, North-East Midlands, Midlands, South Midlands, North-West Midlands, Central northern England, North-East England, Northern England, Scottish, Lower South-West England, Central South-West England, Upper South-West England, European, American (United States), Welsh, West Indian, other or unidentifiable

Domain: Educational/Informative, Business, Public/Institutional, Leisure

Age of respondent: (not of speaker): 0–14, 15–24, 25–34, 35–44, 45–59, 60+

Social class of respondent: AB, C1, C2, DE

Sex of respondent: male, female

Reflective Break

- Develop sociolinguistic research questions using demographic information from spoken and written registers of the BNC. What social demographics are you interested in using?
- The BNC includes four social classes categorized according to a person's occupation: AB, C1, C2, and DE. According to Burnard (2000), AB denotes "top or middle management, administrative or professional," C1 is "junior management, supervisory or professional," C2 is "skilled manual," and DE means "semi-skilled or unskilled." There were many texts in the BNC that are "unspecified" for the social class of speakers. What additional information would you like to know about the social class categories of the BNC? Is occupation a good marker of social class? Explore text samples from these social class categories and search for immediate identifiable markers of variation. What are the strengths and limitations associated with social class-coded texts?

B1.8.2 The American National Corpus (ANC)

The BNC served as the model for the creation of the American English parallel corpus, ANC (http://americannationalcorpus.org/), which has released two versions of component subcorpora totaling over 22 million words, so far. Work on the ANC is still ongoing (although at a very slow pace), and there is currently no user-friendly client program available for automatic database online searches, except for

TABLE B1.1 Categories of the ANC (second release) 2013

Spoken Registers

Corpora	Domain	No. Files	No. Words
Call Home: 24 unscripted telephone conversations between native speakers of American English covering a contiguous 10 minute segment of each call. Call Home transcripts are time-stamped by speaker turn for alignment with the speech signal included in the corpus.	Telephone	24	52,532
Charlotte: The Charlotte Narrative and Conversation Collection (CNCC) in the ANC contains 93 narratives, conversations, and interviews representative of the residents of Mecklenburg County, North Carolina, and surrounding North Carolina communities. Information on speaker age and gender is included in the header for each transcript.	Face-to-Face	93	198,295
MICASE: 50 transcripts from the Michigan Corpus of Academic Spoken English are included in the ANC with information on speaker age, gender, and role (e.g., teacher or student).	Academic Discourse	50	593,288
Switchboard: 2,307 texts of spontaneous conversations averaging 6 minutes in length and comprising about 3 million words of text, spoken by over 500 speakers of both sexes from every major dialect of American English (see Section B3.5.2 for additional information on the Switchboard corpus).	Telephone	2,307	3,019,477
Spoken Totals		2,474	3,863,592

Written Registers

Corpora	Domain	No. Files	No. Words
911 Reports: full text of reports released on July 22, 2004, by The National Commission on Terrorist Attacks Upon the United States.	Government, Technical	17	281,093
Berlitz Travel Guides: collection of 179 travel guides written by and for Americans, split into separate files by country/city and section.	Travel Guides	179	1,012,496
Biomed: technical articles by American authors obtained from BioMed Central, which publishes open access, peer-reviewed biomedical research articles.	Technical	837	3,349,714
Buffy the Vampire Slayer Blogs: contains slightly over three million words from the Buffistas.org web forums (blog), written between March 2003 and May 2004.	Blog	143	3,093,075

Written Registers

Corpora	Domain	No. Files	No. Words
Hargraves: collection of fiction writing which includes *Dead Man's Effects*, a novel set mainly in London's Docklands in the 1990s, includes some dialogue in British dialect; *The Old Windrow Place*, a contemporary novel of spiritual growth and reckoning with the past; and *Morocco Pentagraph*, five stories of varying length, set in Morocco.	Fiction	106	405,195
Eggan: Ferd Eggans *The Story Continues*, an online serial novel.	Fiction	1	61,746
ICIC: The Indiana Center for Intercultural Communication corpus of Philanthropic Fundraising Discourse consists of fundraising texts, including case statements, annual reports, grant proposals, and direct mail letters.	Letters	245	91,318
NY Times: *The New York Times* component of the ANC consists of over 4,000 articles from the *New York Times* newswire, for each of the odd-numbered days in July 2002.	Newspaper	4,148	3,625,687
OUP: The OUP contains a quarter of a million words of nonfiction drawn from five Oxford University Press publications authored by Americans.	Non-fiction	45	330,524
PLoS: The Public Library of Science is an online, public domain journal consisting of scientific and medical literature. Texts include articles written by American authors taken from PLoS Medicine (2004–2005) and PLoS Biology (2003–2005). In addition to technical articles, PLoS journals include editorials, commentaries, book reviews, and essays.	Technical	252	409,280
Slate: *Slate Magazine* is an online publication that features short articles on topics of current interest, including news and politics, arts, business, sports, technology, travel, food, and so on.	Journal	4,531	4,238,808
Verbatim: *Verbatim* is a "magazine of language and linguistics for a person without a Ph.D.," containing articles about linguistics and language use from 1990 to 1996.	Journal	32	582,384
Web Data Materials: Web Data Materials was drawn from public domain government Web sites, including reports, speeches, letters, and press releases from the Environmental Protection Agency, the General Accounting Office, the Japan U.S. Friendship Commission, the Legal Services Corporation, the National Center for Injury Prevention and Control, and the Postal Rate Commission.	Government	285	1,048,792
Written Totals		10,821	18,530,112
Corpus Totals		13,295	22,393,704

one that is designated for an n-gram search. However, the ANC has downloadable text files (totaling over 15 million words) and the annotated versions of the corpus also include grammatically tagged data using the Biber Tagger and other XML annotations. Just like the BNC, the ANC's collection of texts reflects work done from early to mid-2000s with no continuing contributions that allow for diachronic comparisons across registers. Table B1.1 briefly describes the spoken and written texts comprising the most recent release (second release) of the ANC.

B1.8.3 Davies's Corpus of Contemporary American English (COCA) and the Corpus of Web-Based Global English (GloWbE)

The Corpus of Contemporary American English (COCA), developed and published online by Davies, was released in early 2008. It covers a diverse collection of American English texts totaling more than 450 million words from 1990 to 2008 (20 million words each year) across registers grouped into the following categories: spoken, fiction, popular magazines, newspapers, and academic journals. COCA's online interface has been widely used by researchers, teachers, and students since its release for various purposes including materials production in teaching lexico/syntactic features of English, collocations, and synchronic word frequency changes across registers. COCA is comparable to the BNC/ANC in terms of text types, with deviations especially with texts included in its spoken data component. COCA's spoken texts (20% of the corpus) come from television news and interview programs, for the most part, and not from the types of conversation data (e.g., face-to-face conversation, service encounters, and telephone interactions) available in the BNC or other corpora such as the Longman Corpus. Davies (2009), however, maintains that COCA's overall balanced composition means that researchers can compare data across registers and achieve relatively accurate results that show patterns of change in the language from the 1990s to the present. Related to COCA are the Corpus of Historical American English (COHA), also from Davies, and the Google Books Ngram Viewer or Google Books Corpus collected by Google, which are both time-stamped from the 1800s to the present. We discuss these two corpora in Section B5 (diachronic studies of change in language).

The Corpus of Global Web-Based English (GloWbE, pronounced *globe*) (Davies, 2013) has a staggering 1.9 billion words from 1.8 million Web sources in 20 different English-speaking countries. Texts are grouped according to where they came from online (e.g., Web sites, Web pages, or blogs) and the English dialects they represent. The 20 countries currently in GloWbE include: (native varieties) United States, Canada, United Kingdom, Ireland, Australia, and New Zealand; (nonnative varieties) India, Sri Lanka, Pakistan, Bangladesh, Singapore, Malaysia, the Philippines, Hong Kong, South Africa, Nigeria, Ghana, Kenya, Tanzania, and Jamaica. Davies released the corpus and its online interface in April 2013. Comparing corpus size, GloWbE is more than 4 times as large as COCA and nearly 20 times as large as the BNC. Dialect studies with GloWbE can cover international varieties of English, as they appear online, with cross-comparisons

TABLE B1.2 Spoken and written registers of the International Corpus of English

Spoken Texts (300 2,000-word samples)	Written Texts (200 2,000-word samples)
Dialogues (180)	Student exams (10)
Spontaneous conversations (90)	Student essays (10)
Telephone conversations (10)	Social letters (15)
Class lessons (20)	Business letters (15)
Broadcast discussions (20)	Learned humanistic (10)
Broadcast interviews (10)	Learned social sciences (10)
Political debates (10)	Learned natural sciences (10)
Legal cross-examinations (10)	Learned technology (10)
Business transactions (10)	Popular humanistic (10)
Monologues (120)	Popular social sciences (10)
Spontaneous commentaries (20)	Popular natural sciences (10)
Unscripted speeches (30)	Popular technology (10)
Demonstrations (10)	Press reportage (20)
Legal presentations (10)	Administrative/regulatory directives (10)
Broadcast news (20)	Instructional skills/hobbies (10)
Broadcast talks (20)	Press editorials (10)
Scripted speeches (10)	Fiction (20)

focusing on British and American English texts (in more than 775 million words of text for just these two dialects).

B1.8.4 The International Corpus of English (ICE)

The International Corpus of English (ICE) consists of one million words per spoken and written variety of English produced by over 20 research teams worldwide (http://ice-corpora.net/ice/). For most participating countries, the ICE project serves as the first systematic investigation of the national, "educated" English variety (Nelson, 1996). Each component corpus follows a common corpus design and a similar scheme for grammatical annotation. The ICE was primarily intended for comparative studies of emerging Englishes all over the world. For example, Asian varieties of English available for free download from the ICE Web site include subcorpora from countries/territories such as Hong Kong, the Philippines, India, and Singapore, where English has been used extensively as the language of business and education. Table B1.2 lists the spoken and written texts collected for the ICE by its research teams.

B1.8.5 The Vienna-Oxford International Corpus of English (VOICE)

VOICE, the Vienna-Oxford International Corpus of English, is a structured collection of spoken registers focusing exclusively on **English as a lingua franca** (ELF).

ELF is the most widespread contemporary use of English throughout the world, used by speakers from different first-language backgrounds to communicate with each other. ELF interactions may include business negotiations between Japanese and Swedish businessmen, classroom interactions between a Saudi Arabian and Korean student in a biology class, or a French tourist in Bali, Indonesia, asking a local travel guide in English how to get to the airport. These interactions in English with nonnative speakers across varying levels of proficiency in the language are actually much more common globally than English native interactions. The pervasiveness of this variety of English certainly creates more opportunities to further study how global communications continue to evolve. A corpus collection of texts representing ELF usage across contexts certainly has important pedagogical applications.

VOICE was compiled by the department of English at the University of Vienna in Vienna, Austria, under its project director Barbara Seidlhofer. VOICE in 2013 has over one million words of transcribed spoken ELF from domains such as professional, educational, and leisure interactions. Transcribed texts of naturally occurring, nonscripted face-to-face interactions in English came from 120 hours of audio-recorded conversations from experienced ELF speakers from a wide range of first language backgrounds. The current version of VOICE in 2013 includes over 1,250 different speakers representing 50 different first languages but mostly those of European countries. In addition to domains, VOICE also covers speech functions (e.g., exchanging information, enacting social relationships), participant roles and relationships (acquainted vs. unacquainted, symmetrical vs. asymmetrical), and speech events (e.g., interviews, press conferences, service encounters, seminar discussions, working group discussions, workshop discussions, meetings, panels, question-answer sessions, conversations). These functional categories are very valuable in using VOICE for sociolinguistic research. Published VOICE studies include the analysis of ELF in international business (Pitzl, 2010), Anglophone-centric attitudes and English for globalized communication (Seidlhofer, 2012), and the exploration of correctness versus effectiveness in ELF interactions (Hülmbauer, 2009).

B1.9 Corpus-Based Studies of English Dialects

As we have previously mentioned, corpus-based dialect studies in English, although still few in number, have been conducted for British English using the Helsinki Dialect Corpus (Ihalainen, 1985, 1991). This corpus has been used, for example, to investigate regional differences in the expression of tense in Southwestern England. Ihalainen (1991), cited in Grieve (2009), compared the frequency of the periphrastic expression of tense (e.g., *they do change* _____) relative to the inflectional expression of tense (e.g., *they change* _____) in east and west Somerset. He found periphrastic expression of tense more commonly in the east and inflectional expression of tense more commonly in the west; however, he also found that, in some cases, speakers used both forms, supporting his conclusion that there is, in reality, a dialect continuum from east to west in Somerset. Clearly this result would only be possible by using corpus data, which provides a more reliable picture of continuous language variation.

The BNC, which is coded with some regional dialect information, has been used for numerous studies of regional grammatical variation in British English. The *Comparative Grammar of British English Dialects* (Kortmann, Herrmann, Pietsch, & Wagner, 2005) is based on the BNC, together with additional texts from the Helsinki Dialect Corpus. Other dialect studies of English have also been based on FRED or the Freiburg English Dialect Corpus (Hernández, 2006). The FRED corpus is created from oral histories representing the face-to-face story-telling tradition of the English language, although the storytellers were aware that their speech was being recorded. The oral histories comprising this corpus were obtained during interviews from 1968 to 2000 with informants from England, Wales, Scotland, the Hebrides, and the Isle of Man who were selected so as to cover the nine traditional dialect areas of the United Kingdom. FRED contains 2.5 million words and 300 hours of recorded speech produced by 372 informants at 163 different locations (Grieve, 2009). The Linguistic Innovators Corpus or LIC (Kerswill, Cheshire, Fox, & Torgersen, 2008) utilized sociolinguistic interviews collected from 100 working-class adolescents (who were college students) and 18 elderly speakers in two English boroughs, Hackney and Havering. The LIC corpus has been used to test whether or not London is the center of linguistic innovation in southeastern England. A related sociolinguistic objective for the LIC corpus focuses on the role of ethnicity and social networks (or "friendship networks") in the analysis of language change. Gabrielatos, Torgersen, Hoffman, and Fox (2010) analyzed the use of indefinite article forms in spoken London English using LIC, and they found a relatively high frequency of the indefinite article *a* before words that begin with a vowel (in contrast to the standard form that often used *an*). They found place of residence as one of the primary predictors of this pattern, together with social factors such as speakers' age and ethnicity.

B1.10 Regional Dialect Survey of Written American English, Grieve (2009)

Grieve's (2009) study of grammatical variation in written American English is groundbreaking research that applied a corpus approach to analyze the regional dialects of "Standard American English." There are not very many extensive dia-lectology studies of this type, especially in written American English. Grieve has created a framework for corpus collection in regional dialectology research, com-plemented by technical approaches in extracting patterns of grammatical varia-tion—for example, on adverb position (Grieve, 2012) and contraction rate (Grieve, 2011). Grieve (2009) created a framework for corpus collection in regional dia-lectology research, complemented by technical approaches in extracting patterns of grammatical variation from corpora. The corpus used in this study has over 25 million words of **letters to the editor** published by city and statewide newspa-pers (e.g., *Atlanta Journal Constitution* in Atlanta, Georgia, or *Houston Chronicle* in Houston, Texas) collected from 200 cities from across the United States. In his study, Grieve used the term "Standard American English" consistently, perhaps suggesting that written, Standard English in this context is more formal, prepared, and edited, and based on editorial conventions, compared to informal and spontaneous writing in registers such as blogs, e-mails, or mobile short message services (SMS). We provide a summary of this study below, followed by a brief interview with Grieve focusing on his motivations and challenges in conducting this research.

Research goals: This study focused on a regional dialect survey of grammatical variation in written Standard American English, based on a unique statistical and corpus-based approach to the analysis of regional linguistic variation. Grieve's (2009) dialect survey is only the third complete dialect survey of American English and the first dialect survey to focus on grammatical variation in American English and regional variation in written Standard American English. The first major goal of this survey was to determine if individual grammatical features were **regionally patterned** in written Standard American English. In order to answer this question, the values of 45 grammatical features (e.g., pronoun replacements, forms of negation, various modal verbs, demonstrative pronouns, prepositions, and relativizers) were analyzed across a 25 million–word corpus of letters to the editor using **spatial autocorrelation statistics**. The second major goal of this survey was to map the regional dialects of American English based on the values of the set of grammatical features. The values of a series of grammatical features were analyzed using multivariate statistics to identify general patterns of regional linguistic variation in American English.

Register (letter to the editor register of Standard English): Grieve (2009) noted that this register was selected because it is a variety of written Standard English that is very well-suited to the analysis of regional linguistic variation: letters to the editor are published frequently, which allows for data to be collected from a relatively short time span; distributed freely online in machine readable form, which allows for data to be collected quickly and economically; and annotated for an author's current place of residence, which allows the data to be easily sorted by geographical location. It should also be noted that the length of time that an author has lived at his or her current place of residence is rarely indicated anywhere in the letter. The inclusion of a letter to the editor in the corpus can therefore only be based on the current place of residence of its author, as listed in the byline of the letter.

Corpus: The entire corpus contains 25,794,656 words. The mean subcorpus size is 128,973 words. The size of the city subcorpora ranges from 26,885 words (Omaha) to 317,592 words (Nashville). In addition to Omaha, the smallest city subcorpora are Seaford (27,458 words), Ardmore (32,237 words), Marquette (34,980 words), and Lubbock (36,826 words). Aside from Nashville, the largest city subcorpora are Los Angeles (295,967 words), Santa Fe (279,536 words), San Diego (258,650 words) and Springfield, Illinois (247,402 words).

Establishing American dialect regions: American dialect regions were established by Grieve using a combination of statistical tests: Principal Component Analysis (PCA) and Hierarchical Cluster Analysis (HCA). These tests identified

FIGURE B1.4. American regional grammatical dialects (1 to 12)

Source: adapted from Grieve, 2009, p. 266

the set of grammatical variables that were found to exhibit a significant degree of spatial correlations across letters to the editors representing various U.S. cities. A clustering algorithm helped Grieve to statistically organize dialect groups based on their common grammatical clusters. This analysis yielded the following 12 American dialect regions (Figure B1.4):

1 *Pacific Northwest*, which consists primarily of Washington, Oregon, and Idaho;
2 *Pacific Southwest*, which consists primarily of California and Nevada;
3 *Mountain West*, which encompasses most of Arizona, Utah, New Mexico, Colorado, Wyoming, and Montana, as well as Bismarck, North Dakota, and presumably the entire Great Plains region, which is underrepresented in the survey;
4 *West Texas*, which includes San Antonio and the other cities of western Texas, as well as Carlsbad, New Mexico;
5 *Western Midwest*, which consists primarily of Minnesota, South Dakota, Nebraska, and Kansas, as well as western Iowa and the Upper Peninsula of Michigan;
6 *Eastern Midwest*, which consists primarily of Illinois, Wisconsin, and the Lower Peninsula of Michigan, as well as St. Louis, Missouri, and northern Indiana and Ohio;
7 *New England*, which consists primarily of the Maine, Massachusetts, Rhode Island, New Hampshire, Vermont, and Connecticut;

8 *Mid Atlantic*, which consists primarily of New York, New Jersey, Pennsylvania, Maryland, Delaware, Washington, D.C., and northern Virginia;

9 *South Atlantic*, which consists of most of Florida, as well as Savannah, Georgia, and Charleston and Bluffton, South Carolina;

10 *Upper South*, which includes most of South Carolina and Tennessee, all of North Carolina, West Virginia, and Kentucky, and the southern parts of Virginia, Indiana, and Ohio;

11 *Deep South*, which consists of Alabama, eastern Georgia, including Atlanta, and Pensacola, Florida; and, finally,

12 *South Central*, which consists primarily of eastern Texas, Oklahoma, Louisiana, Mississippi, and Arkansas.

Grammatical variation: Overall, 35 grammatical variables were found to exhibit significant patterns of use that contributed to salient regional variation in the corpus. Grieve reported that general patterns of regional grammatical variation included the following: (1) Northeast versus Southeast pattern, (2) an East versus West pattern, (3) a Midwest versus West Coast pattern, and (4) a Southwest versus Northwest pattern. In addition, he also found two patterns that distinguished the (5) Midwest and the (6) South Central states from the rest of the United States.

The grammatical variables found to exhibit the highest levels of influence in regional variation include *pronoun replacement* (pronouns were found to be relatively common in the Southeast and the Central states and relatively uncommon in the Northeast), *be going to* (which was found to be relatively common in the Central states and California and relatively uncommon in the Northeast), and *do not contraction* (which was found to be relatively common in the West and relatively uncommon in the East). Other variables found to exhibit a significant degree of influence on regional variation include *sentence negation, by passives*, and *modal splitting*, as well as various other measures based on *contractions, word positions*, and *function word alternations*. Based on these statistical results, Grieve (2009) was convinced that a clear regional grammatical variation existed in American English and that regional linguistic variation could be statistically established in written Standard American English.

Figure B1.5 shows a sample result illustrating clusters in the distribution of *do not contraction* (i.e., use of *don't, didn't, doesn't*) in letters to the editor. Low values of *do not contraction* were found to cluster in the Northeast (dark dots), indicating that *do not contraction* is relatively uncommon in this region. High values were found to cluster on the West Coast (lighter dots), especially the Northwest and in the western Midwest, indicating that *do not contraction* is relatively common in these regions. The South Central states and the western Midwest were identified by Grieve as regions of variability.

Additional findings: Aside from statistically establishing the dialect regions of Standard American English, a secondary goal of Grieve's survey was to compare the linguistic characteristics of his resulting regional dialects with the traditional

FIGURE B1.5 Distribution of *do not contraction* clusters

Source: adapted from Grieve, 2009, p. 180

dialect regions identified by previous American dialect surveys (such as those in the Linguistic Atlas projects). This comparison can help determine if regional grammatical variation from written texts is similar (or not) to lexical and phonological variation. Grieve concluded that, overall, his dialect regions corresponded quite closely to the dialect regions identified by previous surveys with respect to how primary dialect areas are distinguished (e.g., distinction between the North and South; the North and the West). However, they also differed in numerous, important ways. Grieve's dialect regions corresponded closely to modern American cultural areas. In other words, people from different cultural regions in the United States seemed to use different varieties of language. This cultural explanation of regional dialect variation can also account for the dialect regions identified by previous dialect surveys, which differed slightly from the dialect regions identified by Grieve's survey (2009, p. 293). Additional patterns of change in this study may also reflect regional dialect change resulting from changing American cultural areas.

Reflective Break

- Grieve claimed that letters to the editors represent Standard American English. Do you agree with this description? What is Standard English and how does it differ from nonstandard varieties?
- Can letters to the editors accurately represent residents of a particular U.S. city or state? What do you think are the primary group characteristics of people who write letters to newspaper editors in terms of gender,

age, occupation, and social class? Have you written to your city newspaper's editor for publication? What were your main reasons for doing so?

• Most letters to the editor are edited for format and style before they are published. Do you think this is a research issue in Grieve's corpus collection?

B1.10.1 Corpus-Based Dialectology: An Interview with Jack Grieve

Jack Grieve is a lecturer in forensic linguistics in the School of Languages and Social Sciences at Aston University in Birmingham, England. His research involves the quantitative analysis of language variation and change. Grieve is especially interested in regional grammatical and lexical variation in American English and the development of new methods for collecting and analyzing dialect data. He also conducts research on functional and sociolinguistic variation and on quantitative authorship attribution. Grieve responds to our questions about his model of corpus-based dialectology below.

What motivated you to conduct a U.S. dialectology study using corpora? What observations and results have been surprising or most important to you?

Grieve: The main reason I decided to use a corpus-based approach was that I was interested in analyzing regional variation in writing. It therefore made sense to gather texts that were already available online rather than to collect data through elicitation. I also took this approach because I was interested in analyzing quantitative grammatical variation. It is very difficult to elicit that type of data. The corpus-based approach is also much more efficient than interviewing informants. By adopting a corpus-based approach, I was able to collect large amounts of data from across the United States over a relatively short period of time, sampling hundreds of informants at each location.

I think the most important finding of my study is that regional variation exists in writing. For me, this really shows that regional linguistic variation is much more pervasive than is generally assumed. I also think the regional patterns I identified were surprising. They look a lot more like modern American cultural regions than traditional American dialect regions. I think this is evidence of regional linguistic change in American English, with the traditional Northern and Midland dialect regions being replaced by modern Northeastern and Midwestern dialect regions.

Were there criticisms of your data collection and your primary research design? How have you addressed these criticisms? Do you see further areas for improvement of this approach?

Grieve: The most common criticism I receive from dialectologists is that my corpus is not controlled for length of residence. In general, when dialectologists collect data, they only sample informants who have lived in that region for their entire lives. Originally, this was because dialectologists were interested in identifying historic dialect patterns and because they were only able to interview a few informants at each location. This approach has since become the standard in dialectology, and it is now generally taken for granted that you must control for length of residence. But I think people have forgotten the original motivations for this methodological choice, and in many situations I don't believe it is necessary or even desirable to control for length of residence at all. In particular, I think that if you are interested in mapping modern regional linguistic variation across the general population, then you should ignore length of residence. Every current resident of a city should have an equal chance of being sampled, regardless of how long they have lived in that city because they are all members of that speech community at that point in time. Ignoring length of residence does make it harder to identify regional patterns, but it also leads to more generalizable results.

That said, I would still like to have access to information about length of residence, so that I could directly factor this into my analyses. That would enable me to compare the language of short- and long-term residents, which would be especially useful for identifying patterns of regional linguistic change. I would also like to have access to more information on the demographic background of each informant so that I could directly factor social variation into my analyses as well.

What are future directions and applications of corpora and corpus-based approaches in dialectology studies?

Grieve: In general, one of the main limitations of the corpus-based approach is that it is still relatively difficult to compile large spoken corpora. In dialectology, this is especially problematic because most dialectologists are primarily interested in speech. However, technology for processing spoken language is quickly improving, and it will soon be possible to build large corpora of automatically transcribed speech harvested online from social networking and video-sharing Web sites. When we reach that stage, I really think the corpus-based approach will become the standard in dialectology.

I also think one of the main advantages of the corpus-based approach is that it allows for the careful comparison of regional linguistic variation across different registers. Aside from research on attention paid to speech, we currently know very little about how regional linguistic variation, and sociolinguistic variation in general, varies across different communicative situations or vice versa. I think that the relationship between social and situational variation is under-researched and that the complexity and significance of this relationship has been underestimated. A corpus-based approach is perhaps the only way to study this relationship in a systematic way.

B1.11 Conducting Regional Dialectology Research with Twitter, Eisenstein and Colleagues (2010)

Eisenstein and colleagues (2010) used computational models to identify regional markers from user postings on the microblogging site Twitter. These postings, also known as "tweets," form the corpus used for this study. (In Section B6, we explore blogs and microblogs in sociolinguistic research under the umbrella of Web registers.) Eisenstein and his colleagues from the School of Computer Science at Carnegie Mellon University acknowledged the rapid growth of social media in paving the way for their extensive data collection and computational models in analyzing various language patterns. Although this line of research is primarily intended for computational modeling of large sets of data, there are clear applications of this approach to corpus-based dialectology research. The important link here is how Internet and mobile technology can code for variables such as **location**. As it is, Twitter and many other microblogging Web sites can access users' geographical coordinates (e.g., from mobile devices that are enabled by Global Positioning Systems or GPS). This feature produces "geotagged" text data that researchers can obtain from online logs. Most users' tweets are geotagged, which means that analysts are able to identify the users' location, especially if they tweeted from their mobile phones. Posts from desktop computers or permanent computer terminals may be identified from their Internet access addresses or universal resource locators (URL). There are more and more studies that mine geotagged data online, mostly focusing on trends and Internet-user traffic. These types of information are useful to marketing analysts and survey companies that collect quantitative tracking data of user behavior from the Internet.

Research goals: This research primarily focused on the tracking of words/slang and expressions that were evident in tweets as they were in everyday conversations. These tracked words and expressions were then modeled to identify the U.S. geographical region that can statistically account for their unique distributions. Eisenstein and colleagues' model incorporated two sources of lexical variation: topic and region. They considered tweets and their locations as outputs from a generative process—at the base level of the model were "pure" topics (e.g., sports, weather), and these topics were rendered differently in each region (they called this modeling approach a "cascading topic model").

Like Grieve (2009), Eisenstein and colleagues (2010) noted that their interest in dialectology from written data reflects the move to newer analytical frameworks that make use of naturally occurring texts. Geotagged tweets already have their locations/regions coded, making corpus collection of this sort more manageable. Grieve manually identified newspapers from various cities in the United States for his corpus collection, which combined automatic crawling and manual cut-and-paste approaches. Unlike Grieve's register, tweets may not necessarily represent Standard English. Twitter posts offer a new way of studying regional lexicon because tweets are often informal and more conversational or interactive, potentially closer in structure and form to spoken discourse. The 140-character limit of Twitter posts also makes messaging abbreviated and directly concerned with delivering information and explicit reactions. Most tweets are spontaneous and unedited and also not read by editors before they are posted.

Corpus: The research team collected a week's worth of Twitter posts in March 2010 and selected geotagged messages from Twitter users who wrote at least 20 messages. That collection formed a corpus of tweets from 9,500 users and 380,000 messages. Although users' locations with geotags were clearly established, other variables such as gender and age in the tweets were not coded. Eisenstein and colleagues noted that it was reasonable to assume that people sending lots of tweets from mobile phones were younger than the average Twitter user and the topics discussed by these users (e.g., school, popular media) seemed to reflect that (Spice, 2011).

Summary of findings: Eisenstein and colleagues (2010) concluded that their automated method for analyzing geographic variation in Twitter posts shows that words and topics can be identified with high affinity to a particular U.S. region or state. Although the present research did not use an established U.S. dialect map such as Labov's or Kurath's to plot the results, clear differences were observed in how words or expressions were used in—for example, Northeastern versus Western states. The model jointly identified words with high regional affinity, geographically coherent linguistic regions, and the relationship between regional and topic variation. Eisenstein and colleagues also emphasized that regional dialects appear to be evolving within social media, with the tracking of unique expressions, including foreign words and newer lexical innovations, present in geotagged datasets. The list below provides a short summary of this study's linguistic findings (Spice, 2011):

- Tweets reflect some well-known regionalisms, such as Southerners' *y'all*, and Pittsburghers' *yinz*, and the usual regional divides in references to soda, pop, and Coke.
- In Northern California, something that is cool is often tweeted as *koo*, while in southern California, it is *coo*. In many cities in the United States, something is *sumthin*, but tweets in New York City favor *suttin*.
- While many might complain in tweets of being "very" tired, people in Northern California tend to be *hella* tired, New Yorkers are *deadass* tired, and Angelenos are simply tired *af*.
- The *af* is an acronym that, like many others on Twitter, stands for a vulgarity. *LOL* is a commonly used acronym for *laughing out loud*, but Twitterers in Washington, D.C., seem to have an affinity for the "cruder" *LLS* (or *laughing like shit*).

In addition to the short summary of linguistic results above, Table B1.3 from Eisenstein and colleagues (2010) shows a comparison of the keywords/expressions from five base topics (basketball, popular music, daily life, emoticons, and chitchat) across five locations (Boston, Northern California, New York, Los Angeles, and Lake Eerie).

In addition to these word distributions, the influence of geography was also apparent in the corpus. Reversing the analysis, the statistical model was found to likewise predict the location of a microblogger in the United States with a median error of about 300 miles. In other words, Eisenstein and colleagues (2010) can validate a user's location by distinguishing regional and topical variation from their dataset. They saw this as a first step toward an unsupervised methodology

TABLE B1.3 Twitter topics and regional variants

	Basketball	Popular Music	Daily Life	Emoticons	Chit Chat
U.S. State or Particular Location	PISTONS KOBE LAKERS *game* DUKE NBA CAVS STUCKEY JETS KNICKS	*album music beats artist video* #LAKERS ITUNES *tour produced vol*	*tonight shop weekend getting going chilling ready discount waiting iam*	:) *haha* :d :(;) :p xd : / *hahah ahahah*	*Lolsmhjk yea wyd coo imawassupsomthinjp*
Boston	CELTICS *victory* BOSTON CHARLOTTE	*playing daughter* PEARL *alive war comp*	BOSTON	;pgnaloveee	ese exam suttinsippin
Northern California	THUNDER KINGS GIANTS *pimp trees clap*	SIMON *dl mountain seee*	6 am OAKLAND	*pueshellakoo* SAN fckn	hella flirt hut iono OAKLAND
New York Los Angeles	NETS KNICKS #KOBE #LAKERS AUSTIN	BRONX #LAKERS *load* HOLLYWOOD *imm* MICKEY TUPAC	*iam cab omw tacos hr* HOLLYWOOD	oww *afpapi raining th bomb coo* HOLLYWOOD	wassup nm wyd coo afnadatacos messinfasho bomb
Lake Erie	CAVS CLEVELAND OHIO BUCS *od* COLUMBUS	*premier prod joint* TORONTO *onto designer* CANADA *village brr*	*stink* CHIPOTLE *tipsy*	;d *blvd* BIEBER *hve* OHIO	foul WIZ salty excuses lames officer lastnight

Source: adapted from Eisenstein et al., 2010, p. 8

Note: For the base topics, words and phrases are ranked, while regional variants show keywords per sample region. Foreign words are shown in italics, while terms that are usually in proper nouns are shown in small capital letters.

for modeling linguistic variation using raw text. This predictive model was related to an earlier study of morphosyntactic variation by Szmrecsanyi (2010), which reported that geographical factors account for only 33 percent of the observed variation. Twitter data shows a more promising prediction model, which could be further developed. Eisenstein and colleagues indicated that their analysis might improve if nongeographical factors were considered, including age, race, gender, and income and whether a tweet location was urban or rural. Estimates of many of these factors, although difficult to obtain and potentially unethical, may be obtained by cross-referencing geography with demographic data.

Reflective Break

- Eisenstein and colleagues argued that "it might be a mistake to assume that the greater interconnectivity afforded by computer networks and sites such as Twitter will necessarily result in more homogeneity in language. The social circles maintained by social networks such as Twitter often are geographically focused. Also, many people use the Internet to seek out like-minded people with similar interests, rather than expose themselves to a broader range of ideas and experiences" (Eisenstein et al., 2010, p. 9). Do you agree or disagree with Eisenstein and colleagues? Does this observation apply to various celebrities with global followers?
- What are the primary limitations of this Twitter-based study? What areas for improvement or future research applications do you want to see in similar studies? Do you think Twitter (or Facebook) data are subject to noticeable lexical changes within three to four year span? (Note that Eisenstein et al.'s tweets were collected in 2010.)

B1.12 Non-English Corpora

There is an increasing number of non-English corpora available online. International groups of linguists continue to collect corpora of specialized (national) language varieties and also parallel texts to match already existing databases. Popular corpora of Chinese, Spanish, and Arabic languages have been completed and analyzed, with historical/diachronic studies and cross-linguistic comparisons as common research topics. Some of these established non-English corpora are listed below.

Chinese

- **The Project LIVAC—Linguistic Variations in Chinese Speech Communities Synchronous Corpus** (http://livac.org) has collected and analyzed more that 450 million Chinese characters of media texts from major Chinese speech communities such as Beijing, Hong Kong, Macau, Shanghai, Singapore, and Taiwan. The LIVAC is primarily a *monitor* corpus (i.e., corpus that is regularly updated) that also features POS-tagged texts from a very large database of over 1.6 million word types. LIVAC word types can be compared with English and other Western alphabetic languages. The LIVAC research team has conducted several cross-linguistic comparisons, diachronic studies, and many sentiment analyses of global events such as the Chinese press coverage of U.S. presidential elections. In 2012, the "LIVAC Pan-Chinese Celebrity Roster" listed Taiwanese American professional basketball player **Jeremy Lin** as the international celebrity with the highest exposure in Chinese media.

- **The Chinese Internet Corpus** has approximately 280 million words, and the **Chinese Business Corpus** (30 million words) was compiled by Serge Sharoff from various online sources in February 2005. Sharoff has also collected online English, German, and Russian texts.
- **The Lancaster Corpus of Mandarin Chinese** was created by Richard Xiao and Tony McEnery from Lancaster University.
- **The UCLA Written Chinese Corpus** has over one million words of written modern Chinese also collected online from 2000 to 2012. Text categories are primarily based on the FLOB and FROWN corpora of British and American English, with some additional texts (e.g., adventure fictions) to accommodate Chinese characters.

Spanish

- **Corpus del Español Actual (CEA)** (the Corpus of Contemporary Spanish) has over 540 million words (lemmatized and POS-tagged). The CEA is made up of the following texts: (1) the Spanish part of the 11-language parallel corpus Europarl: European Parliament Proceedings Parallel Corpus, volume 6 (1996–2010); (2) the Spanish portion of the trilingual Wikicorpus, which was obtained from Wikipedia (2006); and (3) the Spanish part of the 7-language parallel corpus MultiUN: Multilingual UN Parallel Text 2000–2009. The MultiUN corpus features texts of United Nations resolutions. The CEA provides a dedicated online search interface, the CQPweb, which can be used to search for words, lemmas, or sentence constructions.
- **Davies's Corpus del Español** is a 100 million–word diachronic corpus of Spanish (1200s–1900s) compiled by Davies, funded by the U.S. National Endowment for the Humanities. The corpus interface (similar to COCA and COHA) allows users to search frequency data and use of words, phrases, and grammatical constructions in different historical periods. Registers of Modern Spanish (e.g., fiction, news) are also categorized.

Arabic

- **The International Corpus of Arabic (ICA)** is a representative corpus of the Arabic language collected from different Arab countries. Texts include newspapers, magazines (general and specialized), electronic press, and "subgenres" in literature (prose, poetry, and studies of linguistics and literature).

Arabic novels, short stories, children's stories, and plays are categorized under prose. **The Corpus of Contemporary Arabic or CCA** (Al-Sulaiti & Atwell, 2006) represents contemporary texts of the Arabic language.

- The **Quranic Arabic Corpus** exclusively focuses on Arabic grammar, syntax, and morphology for each word in the Quran. Scholars have used this corpus primarily for morphological annotation and semantic ontology of Quranic words and sentences.

Other Non-English Corpora

- Davies's **Corpus of Portuguese** has over 45 million words of written and spoken Portuguese from the 1300s to the 1900s; it's similar in corpus design and structure to the Corpus del Español. The **Indian Languages Corpora Initiative** is a collaborative project that aims to collect parallel corpora of 12 Indian languages (including English) in similar domains (health and tourism). Indian texts for Hindi, Marathi, Telugu, and Bangala as part of this initiative can be found online. The **Base de Français Médiéval Database (BFM)** comprises Old and Middle French texts of over 3 million words. The **Russian National Corpus** is a large, annotated corpus that includes both written and spoken registers. Regional dialects are marked in a subcorpus of this corpus, enabling exploration of morphological and syntactic dialectal variation. The Russian National Corpus also includes parallel subcorpora of translations in English, German, Ukrainian, and Belorussian.

B2

CORPUS-BASED STUDIES OF GENDER, SEXUALITY, AND AGE

B2.1 Speaker Demographics: Gender, Sexuality, and Age

In this section, we overview social variables that are often studied in sociolinguistics: *gender* and *age*. We also briefly discuss research on a less-studied social variable, *sexual orientation* through corpora. Although these three variables may seem relatively clear-cut, according to "traditional" thinking, they are actually complex. For example, a person's gender, age, and sexual orientation may be pretty straightforward to him or her. In fact, even in using the pronouns *him* and *her*, we (as speakers of English) are assuming that there are two groups (i.e., two genders) or types of people who can be differentiated solely by their biological makeup. However, not all languages and cultures make such clear distinctions. This section introduces the constructs of gender, age, and sexual orientation, providing summaries of sociolinguistic research that has explored how these variables interact with language.

Corpus-based research offers another perspective on language practices of different social demographics, which most often are studied qualitatively. We do not argue that quantitative methods should replace qualitative methods, especially for gender, which is viewed as a very personal, situation-dependent, and performed construct. However, we view quantitative analyses as complementary to contextual gender studies of limited breadth. By combining small-scale case studies with tendencies of language use on a bigger scale, corpus-based studies may be able to provide a better understanding of how gender groups use language. For example, one important approach to sociolinguistic research on language and gender is to study individuals who do not use language in ways that are expected of them based on their actual or perceived gender. Such research is understandably *local* and qualitative, as researchers would study the participants' communities of practice rather than the speech community at large. However, it is also useful to understand the speech community as a whole in order to better document or quantify how speakers are using language differently.

Introduced by Lave and Wenger (1991) as a way to explain how people learn socially, the concept of communities of practice has since been incorporated into the area of language learning, teacher education, and also sociolinguistics. For example, Eckert and McConnell-Ginet (1992) have called for sociolinguistic research to be more local, admonishing researchers of gender to check their assumptions and critically challenge the misconceptions "that gender can be isolated from other aspects of social identity and relations, that gender has the same meaning across communities, and that the linguistic manifestations of that meaning are also the same across communities" (p. 462). Because, gender, as viewed today, develops and emerges socially, researchers who blindly compare groups of males and females (or more accurately, perceived males and females) are oversimplifying a complex phenomenon. By studying local communities of practice, Eckert and McConnell claim, the nuances obscured by the sharp XX/XY divide can be explored in greater depth and more accurately.

B2.2 Operationalizing Gender, Sexuality, and Age

Just as it was important for us to operationalize the terms *language* and *dialect* in the previous section, we find it useful to provide clear descriptions of what we mean by the constructs of gender, age, and sexual orientation. Although each will be further elaborated upon, briefly we define the words as follows:

- **Gender**: the personal and social identity of a speaker. Unlike *sex*, gender is not necessarily determined by physiology. Instead, speakers may self-identify as a member of a particular group. Such identification may be associated with physical and/or behavioral traits.

  Gender in this research context is not to be confused with **grammatical gender**, which is the classification of nouns into various categories. For example, Spanish nouns are assigned a gender: *la puerta* (the door; feminine) versus *el puerto* (the port; masculine). Grammatical gender is not limited to masculine and feminine, however.

- **Age**: the measure of a person's length of life. For adults, this is often measured in years after birth. However, other cultures may use measurements based on years after conception, or even from the beginning of the year of birth. Also, note that in child development, we speak of *chronological age* and *developmental age*, to muddy things further. The grouping of people according to age is socially constructed. For example, in the United States, we group people into categories such as *teenagers* (13–19 years). Although there are associated physiological changes, this grouping is based primarily on the numbers that the language uses: thirTEEN to nineTEEN. Similarly, grouping people by decades (e.g., 30s, 40s, 50s) is equally culturally subjective.

- **Sexuality or sexual orientation**: the personal romantic attraction to a particular sex. Traditional categories include heterosexual (attraction to the opposite sex), homosexual (attraction to the same sex), and bisexual (attraction to both sexes).

B2.3 Gender

Whereas the study of regional dialectology can explore people in and from different, clearly defined physical locations, studying a social variable like gender requires different types of questions and sampling techniques. Gender variation is an important and ever-growing area of research in sociolinguistics, and much of this research has focused on how men and women use language in conversation. It is relatively easy in many cultures and also in many research settings to simply divide a sample into men and women. Note, however, that such divides are rarely done according to biological sex. It would be much more likely for participants to either self-identify their gender identity or for the researcher to judge using his or her own gendered beliefs to categorize participants. To prove biological sex would not only be inconvenient but incredibly intrusive.

It is clear that for many social scientists, however, there is a need for an operationalized difference between *sex* and *gender*. The former, sex, is often reserved to describe a biological or physiological category. In humans, one's visible body parts have traditionally determined this category. With the advent of genetic testing, we now know that most people are either born with one of two chromosome patterns: XY (male) or XX (female). Gender, on the other hand, is often viewed as a **social construct**, one of the most basic ways to organize populations socially. Unlike one's sex, gender is acquired through cultural norms (i.e., the process of *gendering*), being exposed to and interacting with other members of a society, who exhibit, teach, and reinforce "gender appropriate behavior." In other words, this argument means that we are born with our sex, but we acquire our gender.

Different cultures and languages have shown that people can be categorized other than according to the binary categories familiar to English speakers in the Western world. In the traditional Diné culture (more commonly known as Navajo) in the American Southwest, for example, men and women are not always divided into those two biologically determined groups. Instead, some Diné believe that there is a spectrum of gender. In this sense, people may be categorized according to their respective biological sex as well as how they present themselves. Another example of a culture that differs from the dual gender system can be found in Oaxaca, Mexico. Based on her study of Juchitán de Zarragoza in Oaxaca, Stephen (2002) describes how Zapotec communities in this area have three genders: men, women, and *muxes*. Stephen writes how muxe men in this culture are not considered homosexual, nor are they viewed as having the gender of women. Instead, these are people who are seen as having male physical bodies but having "different aesthetic, work, and social skills" compared to most males in their communities (p. 43).

We briefly presented these examples to underscore that the construct of gender is complex and often problematic in research. In a corpus-based sociolinguistic study involving gender as a variable, therefore, one may decide to take cultural norms such as interpretations of gender roles into consideration when asking research questions, designing a study, collecting a corpus, and interpreting data. Because corpora and corpus-based methods of analysis are often relatively static, and the analyst may lack qualitative understanding of his or her participants, it is important to carefully synthesize, describe, and interpret data. In many settings, it would probably be best to simply report descriptive results in distinguishing linguistic patterns across gender groups. In order to simplify these categorizations, Baker (2006) suggested using **sex** as a grouping category (instead of gender) in corpus-based research.

B2.3.1 Gender in Conversation

Early sociolinguistic research asked questions about what aspects of language use were different between men and women in conversation. For example, in some languages, there may be words or sounds that are exclusively used by one group and not the other. Such linguistic characteristics that directly correlate to gender are very rare and possibly nonexistent in many languages. Instead, it is much more likely that certain linguistic features are used with greater or less frequency by one group or the other. These are called **preferential differences**. Such differences would not directly mark a language user as a member of a particular group, but that group may have a greater or less of a tendency to use that feature with the same function or frequency as another socially constructed group.

An early researcher in preferential differences of language use according to gender is Robin Lakoff. Lakoff's *Language and Woman's Place* (1975) ushered in a rich area for future investigations. Gender is an oft-studied independent variable in sociolinguistics, and it thus finds itself being investigated in relation to many dependent variables (i.e., linguistic distributions across gender groups). For example, Lakoff and others have described women's speech as being more polite than men's speech (see Section B3, Politeness and Stance). In this line of research, women's speech has been compared to the normative **masculine speech** associated with men, who were more likely to be in positions of power. The unavoidable and unfortunate implication might be that women's language was (and to some extent still is) described *in terms of* men's language—as if the former is somehow deviant or of less worth. More descriptive comparisons, however, have less risk of implying such unintended default status designations.

Below, we provide some of the generalizations derived from research in the area of gender and language variation. Labov (1990, 2001) has described that for stable linguistic features, for which there are distinct choices for standard and nonstandard forms, women use the standard more often than men. In seeming contradiction to this generalization, however, women are also characterized as more likely than men to include novel, nonstandard aspects into the language. In other words, women are more likely to use the standard forms but the nonstandard aspects of language that they do include in their speech are more likely to feature new changes (i.e., innovations) than their male counterparts.

In their review of sociolinguistic studies of gender, Biber and Burges (2000, 2001) summarize generalizations about language use according to speakers' gender:

- Women speak less than men in mixed-gender settings (Crawford, 1995; James & Drakich, 1993).
- There are differences in focus: women tend to focus on interactional and personal aspects of conversation while men are more concerned with transmitting information (Holmes, 1995; Lakoff, 1990). This has also been found in the writing styles of the two groups (Argamon, Koppel, Fine, & Shimoni, 2003).
- Women are more likely to be tentative in conversation than men (Coates, 1996, 2004). Women tend to use more linguistic features associated with hesitation, including hedges and egocentric sequences such as *I think* or *I guess* (Rubin & Greene, 1992).
- Men tend to use more persuasive strategies in their language while women are more likely to use narration (Fleishman, 1998; Rubin & Greene, 1992).

We want to emphasize that these are generalizations of gender differences. Many studies on these constructs have been conducted using qualitative methods with relatively small sample sizes. Also, such research usually does not purport to generalize to all members of a given gender. We also must remember that such practices are socially constructed; thus, different societies and speech communities may vary in the extent to which such generalizations are valid. Because there are speech communities for which such generalizations do not apply, we know that one's gender does not cause or determine the extent to which one displays any of the linguistic characteristics described but that any such differences are attributable to social or gender determinants of the speech community.

In sum, more research across different languages and speech communities will create greater understanding of gender roles and gender influences in language use. In addition, quantitative methods, such as those that use a large sampling of a population and are supported by data from corpora, can also complement the qualitative findings of previous research. We highlight related corpus-based studies on gender in different sections of this book. Below is a summary list of sections that describe results of gender studies in conversation using corpora:

- Section B3.3.1: A study by Ishikawa (2011) explored the distribution of *thanks* and *thank you* in British dialogues from the BNC across gender and social class categories of speakers. Results showed that male speakers in the BNC used more of these politeness responses than their female counterparts in dialogues. Overall, a statistical significance test using chi-square showed that gender of speakers significantly influenced the distribution of *thanks* and *thank you* (p<.001) in BNC dialogues. This quantitative data from the BNC contradicted results from most seminal descriptive studies of gender and politeness features in speech, especially Lakoff's (1975) and Holmes's (1995)—that females tended to give *thanks* and show explicit appreciation in their speech more than males.

- Section B3.3.2.1: Contrary to Ishikawa's results from the BNC, female American speakers in task-based telephone interactions had a consistently greater frequency of *thanks, please, sorry,* and *sir/ma'am* than males (Friginal, 2009b). The distribution of these markers in the discourse of American male and female callers supported generalizations from previous research of gender and politeness in formal or business settings (e.g., Beeching, 2002; Coates, 1996; Mills, 2003). American female speakers used relatively more polite speech-act formulae and apologies than males.

- Section B3.5.3: A study by Precht (2008) investigated the distributions of stance expressions used by men and women in conversations by comparing three groups of stance markers: affect, evidentials, and quantifiers from the spoken subcorpora of the Longman Corpus of Spoken and Written English (LCSWE). In general, qualitative studies of gender and affect have shown that men use more expletives, insults, and explicit expressions of anger than women. Precht's corpus-based data supported these studies—men had significantly higher frequencies of words such as *stupid, damn, fuck, hell,* and *shit* than women in the LCSWE. Overall, men's stance expressions were also interpreted to be more negative than women's.

- Section B5.3.2: Biber and Burges (2001) used dramatic dialogues from a diachronic corpus (ARCHER) to study the historical shifts in the language of males and females in speech-based registers. Speech in this context was represented by dialogues from plays. The gender of speakers (characters) in these historical plays, as well as the gender of authors, were coded and used as independent study variables. Biber and Burges reported that the central determining factor influencing "involved" speech (e.g., use of personal pronouns, private verbs, and emphatics in speech) has become the distinction between cross-gender or same-gender dyads.

Reflective Break

- In interactional sociolinguistics, especially studies of conversations between men and women, it is relatively easy to track behavioral patterns, paralinguistic markers, use of specific linguistic features, and contexts to describe gender-based patterns in speech. What, then, are the primary advantages and disadvantages of corpora and using corpus-based approaches in studying interactional patterns between men and women? What do you see are major limitations of corpora in studying gender as a sociolinguistic variable?

- Think about the best way to collect a "gender-specific corpus." What registers would be best to consider in collecting gender-coded texts? How will you collect your corpus?
- **Suggested readings**: American linguist Deborah Tannen is globally recognized as an authority in gender in conversation research. Most of Tannen's works combine discourse analysis with interpersonal communication and qualitative observations of recorded speech events. Her book *Conversational Style: Analyzing Talk Among Friends* has often been used as a model in collecting and analyzing sociolinguistic data from talk in interaction. Her many publications regularly include topics on gender and discourse analysis: *Gender and Discourse*; *Talking Voices: Repetition, Dialogue and Imagery in Conversational Discourse*; and *The Handbook of Discourse Analysis*.

  In addition to these primarily academic texts, Tannen has also written popular or general-audience books such as *You Just Don't Understand—Women and Men in Conversation*; *That's Not What I Meant!: How Conversational Style Makes or Breaks Relationships*; *Talking from 9 to 5: Women and Men at Work*; *The Argument Culture: Stopping America' War of Words*; *I Only Say This Because I Love You: Talking to Your Parents, Partner, Sibs, and Kids When You're All Adults*; and *You're Wearing THAT?: Understanding Mothers and Daughters in Conversation*.

  Although Tannen does not extensively cover corpus-based data, her books can give student researchers ideas about what to investigate and what to collect for an exploratory corpus that may be used to study gender or role/relationships.

B2.3.2 Gender in Writing

The combination of gender and writing research in sociolinguistics is still relatively limited, unlike studies of male-female interactions in many subregisters of face-to-face conversation. Traditionally, some scholars have even emphasized that except for personal correspondence, where there is a clearly identified receiver (i.e., target reader), there has been no measurable difference in the qualitative analysis of male and female writing structure and style (see, e.g., Berryman-Fink & Wilcox, 1983; Palander-Collin, 1999; Simkins-Bullock & Wildman, 1991). For example, in formal, edited texts, it has been argued that gender markers are stripped in favor of style sheets or formatting conventions from publishers. The typical "unseen" audience of formal written texts such as academic articles, news reports, and textbooks affects the linguistic choices of writers, thus reducing the influence of gender and relationships between the writer and the reader. Editing/proofreading and delayed production also potentially diminish the influence of the writer's gender in the final written output. In sum, for formal written texts, it is argued that many of the linguistic universals observed in the analysis of speech do not play a major role, either in determining authorship or distinguishing specific linguistic characteristics of male or female writers.

The utilization of corpora and computational tools, however, might disprove these earlier assertions related to gender and writing. In fact, Argamon and colleagues (2003) found *extraordinary gender-based variations* in the personalization of texts from selected formal written registers of the British National Corpus. They reported that across register categories (e.g., academic writing, books, periodicals), women writers used significantly more personal pronouns (first, second, and third person) than men. In the case of third person, singular personal pronouns, they found that women used more *he* or *she* in their writing, specifying the gender of the antecedent more than men did. In their comparison of third person, singular pronouns, men showed a tendency to use more generic pronouns (*they*) or avoid a direct reference. Argamon and colleagues also looked at the frequency counts of determiners (e.g., *a, the, that, these*) and quantifiers (e.g., *one, two, more, some*), which were all used more by men than women in their subcorpus. The contrast between personal pronouns and determiners/quantifiers suggested that women emphasized relationships in their texts whereas men wrote more about objects (or proper nouns), even in formal written texts. Related to these results, you can also find corpus-based studies of gender and writing (both in blogs) in these two sections:

- Section A2.3: A study by Friginal (2009a) focusing on the interaction between gender and age groups on the use of personal pronouns: first person (*I, we, our*), second person (*you, your, yours*), and third person (*he, she, they*) in personal blogs. A comparative figure (Figure A2.1) illustrated a pattern of increasing use of (all) personal pronouns from older male authors to younger female authors of blogs. Friginal found that the use of first person personal pronouns, particularly the use of the first person pronoun *I* by females under 30 against males over 30, was the primary source of significant variation between gender and age groups.
- Section B6.2.2.1: This section provides a summary of studies of gender differences in blogs. Pedersen and Macafee (2007) analyzed blogs in the United Kingdom compared to blogs in the United States to investigate gender differences in themes and blogging behavior and also to measure the extent of gender inequalities in online communications. Studies on gender and age in blogging by Friginal (2009a), Argamon and colleagues (2003), and Argamon, Koppel, Pennebaker, and Schler (2007) are also discussed in this section.

B2.3.2.1 Identifying the Gender of Written Texts

Gender Genie (http://bookblog.net/gender/genie.php or search for: bookblog + gender genie) is a Web site developed by Moshe Koppel of Bar-Ilan University in Israel and Shlomo Argamon of Illinois Institute of Technology that attempts to identify the gender of the author of written texts. You can paste in a text sample, select one of three registers—fiction, nonfiction, or blog entry—and the *Gender Genie* tabulates weighted frequencies of "male" and "female" grammatical function words. The author's gender is assigned according to whichever category scores the highest.

While the *Gender Genie* may be viewed as not intended for sociolinguistic or purely scholarly applications, it is actually based on serious research: a machine-learning algorithm to identify author gender in literary and nonliterary texts (Herring & Paolillo, 2006). It is noteworthy that Koppel and Argamon's research both take gender and subregisters of writing into account. That is, the connection between language use (in this case, personal pronouns, determiners, prepositions, quantifiers, conjunctions, etc.) and broadly defined writer gender is mediated by the classification of texts into conventional types (i.e., registers). In Koppel and Argamon's computational research, word frequencies alone are insufficient to predict author gender; some context must be supplied. The choice of written register is also interesting, especially the inclusion of fiction and blogs in the *Gender Genie*.

The motivation to publish the *Gender Genie* online was an article from the *New York Times* entitled "Sexed Texts" written by Charles McGrath (2003) together with a gender and writing preference test also previously published in the *New York Times*. Koppel and Argamon's gender-identifying algorithm picks up linguistic trends in men's and women's written discourse. For example, as noted in this section, women are far more likely than men to use personal pronouns. The algorithm finds that men, in contrast, use determiners (e.g., *a*, *the*, *that*) more often. Quantifiers and numbers are also more present in men's writing than women's. These findings, similar to Tannen's (1996), are based on the idea that women use more "involved" words and men use more "informational" words.

Reflective Break

- **Use *Gender Genie* to Analyze a Writing Sample**
  In using *Gender Genie*, you can collect a text file, preferably with over 500 words, to be pasted on the site's "text box." For a blog sample, choose "Blog Entry" as the genre, then click "submit." *Gender Genie* returns a female and male score and a decision point indicating the computed author's gender. An analysis of feminine and masculine keywords is also provided showing distributions and specific scoring mechanisms.

  Below is a text excerpt from a blog written by an 18-year-old male from Atlanta, Georgia.

Text Sample B2.1. Blog Entry for *Gender Genie* Analysis

i actually dont expect you to read that. but just do it. its really cool. i guess. its an old song. 4'th grade(ish).

So today i really have done absolutely NOTHING. i cleaned my room. i guess. because my mom was like "your room has gotta be SPOTLESS for the cleaning people". and i was like uuh think about what u just said. and

The Gender Genie

Attention: The Genie needs your help. In order to continue improvements to the site, please take a few minutes to complete our demographic survey. Your participation is much appreciated. Thanks!

Inspired by an article and a test in *The New York Times Magazine*, the Gender Genie uses a simplified version of an algorithm developed by Moshe Koppel, Bar-Ilan University in Israel, and Shlomo Argamon, Illinois Institute of Technology, to predict the gender of an author. Read more at BookBlog; *The New York Times*; and *The Guardian*.

Scroll down for your results...

Original:	Keywords:
i actually dont expect you to read that. but just do it. its really cool. i guess. its an old song. 4th grade(ish). So today i really have done absolutely NOTHING: i cleaned my room. i guess. because my mom was like "your room has gotta be SPOTLESS for the cleaning people". and i was like uuh think about what u just said. and she got mad. whatever. so. peace up a town down. i listened to a loveline today. with ishe from the contender. not trying to get u hooked on the show. just showing it off. as i frequently make refferences to it that no one else gets. haha now im listening to a nappy roots re-mix. jimmy crack corn cross the county line with marry jane. its like a rock re-mix with POD of that country boys song. i think ill change the artist. yea how about something from meteoria. thats a great CD. by the way so i've been doing a lot of programming recently. some pretty cool stuff. and reading and my mommie is supposed to come home at like 4 to take me swimming. and then out to dinner! my last friday here. im leaving for europe on sunday im me, and say "i want a postcard" and ill send u one. yea. rock on haha ciao for niao trebor posted by gherkinfiesta at 12:20 PM	2 comments My family, plus Maeve. Minus me. And Campbell. After we learned that our neighbors would be moving. The Dodges. Do you know them? I think so. Graham Dodge got expelled. from DA. He beat up my other neighbor. And walks around the neighborhood. Wit a hatchet. We are excited. Congrats to Josh zoffer. His cast gets off today. No more worrying about ingrown pinky toenails. Yup! Yup! http://serials.com "the ultimate site for the Geek Squad. Its a real company. For Serious. Look! over the ridge! Its BECKYS GIRAFFE! MerMaid wOMAN. To the rescue! cas posted by Casi <3 at 12:16 PM	0 comments Thursday, June 23, 2005 I am finally back	i actually dont expect you [to] read that but just do [it] its really cool i.guess its an old song 4th gradeish so today i really have done absolutly nothing i cleaned my room i guess because my mom [was] like [your] room has gotta [be] spotless for [the] cleaning people [and] [i] [was] like uuh think about [what] u just [and] [she] [got] mad whatever so peace up [a] town down i listened [to] [a] loveline today [with] ishe from [the] contender [and] trying [to] get u hooked on [the] show just showing [it] off [as] i frequently make refferences [to] [it] that no one else gets haha now im listening [to] [a] nappy roots re-mix jimmy crack corn [i] county line [with] marry jane its like [a] rock re-mix [with] pod of that country boys song i think ill change [and] artist yea how about something from meteoria thats [a] great cd by [the] way so i have been doing [a] lot of programming recently some pretty cool stuff [and] reading [and] my mommie is supposed [to] come home [as] like 4 [to] take [me] swimming [and] then out [to] dinner my last friday here im leaving for europe on sunday im [me] [and] say i want [a] postcard [and] ill send u one yea rock on haha ciao for niao trebor posted by gherkinfiesta [at] 1220 pm	2 comments my family plus maeve minus [me] [and] campbell after [and] learned that our neighbors would [be] moving [and] dodges do you know them i think so graham dodge got expelled from da he beat up my other neighbor [and] walks [around] the neighborhood wit [a] hatchet [we] [are] excited congrats [to] josh zofter his cast gets off today no [more] worrying about ingrown pinky toenails yup yup http//serialscom [is] ultimate site for [and] geek squad its [a] real company for serious look over [and] ridge its berkys giraffe mermaid woman [tn] rescue cas posted by casi

FIGURE B2.1 Screenshot of results from *Gender Genie* with highlighted masculine and feminine keywords

she got mad. whatever. so. peace up a town down. i listened to a loveline today. with ishe from the contender. not trying to get u hooked on the show. just showing it off. as i frequently make refferences to it that no one else gets.

haha now im listening to a nappy roots re-mix. jimmy crack corn cross the county line with marry jane. its like a rock re-mix with POD of that country boys song. i think ill change the artist. yea how about something from meteoria. thats a great CD. by the way so i've been doing a lot of programming recently. some pretty cool stuff. and reading and my mommie is supposed to come home at like 4 to take me swimming. and then out to dinner! my last friday here. im leaving for europe on Sunday im me, and say "i want a postcard" and ill send u one. yea. rock on

haha

ciao for niao

The excerpt above shows only the first 200 words of the test file. A total of 515 words were used in this activity. Figure B2.1 shows a screenshot of *Gender Genie*'s results.

Gender Genie provides a **Female Score of 306** and a **Male Score of 363** for this blog entry (including the rest of the file with 515 words) and a result indicating that "***Gender Genie* thinks that the author of this passage is male.**"

- **Discussion questions**: How reliable are these author-gender predictors and algorithms? Do these types of predictive findings support generalizations on gender and writing in general? Are these author-gender algorithms **useful** in sociolinguistic studies?

- Could an algorithm identifying other social variables (e.g., age, race, regional background, married vs. single) be successfully modeled? If you are interested in computational modeling topics, we suggest that you look for publications on **author attribution research**.

- The inherent problem when using an algorithm to analyze and predict authors' gender in written texts is the nature of writing itself. As previously mentioned, Deborah Tannen speaks of the differences between "rapport" (i.e., using language to establish connections) and "report" (i.e., language that deals with facts) in distinguishing the styles of speech that men and women use and that these distinctions also tend to characterize written language as "male" language. Tannen's observations may account for many of the differences in writing but only within certain contexts and perhaps only in registers that require self-disclosure.

B.2.4 Language and Sexuality

As with the frequent attribution of a person's gender to his or her biological sex, so too is sexuality viewed from the perspective of the most frequent type—that is, heterosexuality. The concept of heteronormativity (Warner, 1991) can help explain this phenomenon. Heteronormativity refers to the prevailing perspective from which sexuality is viewed. Because heterosexuality is the norm, individuals and aspects of the culture will be compared and understood relative to this standard (Chambers, 2003). A person whose sexuality differs from the heterosexual norm will often be compared or measured based on this expectation. On the other hand, those who conform to these norms will not be automatically described in contrast to homosexuals. Lakoff (1975) described how some men, for example, deviate from the masculine norms: hippies, academics, and homosexual men. She suggested that these men who use fewer "masculine" features of normative male speech, thus speak more "feminine." While this may be the case, there is also the possibility of multiple variables being factored: just because one does not speak like a masculine man does not, necessarily, mean that he speaks like a feminine woman.

How, then, do we study sexuality and language? Many sociolinguistic studies select their participants using demographic sampling criteria, meaning that data is collected from different social groups for representative purposes. However, for many studies, sexuality is not an independent variable that is considered when collecting demographic information (unlike gender/sex). Although many sociolinguistic studies have either ignored sexuality in their sampling, or have assumed heterosexuality, there has also been research conducted on speakers of other sexualities. Leap (e.g., 1995, 1996), for example, has extensively studied the speech of gay American men. However, much of that research has been limited to small, relatively homogeneous samples of convenience. Large-scale, corpus-based analyses across gender and sexuality, clearly still very limited, can help us better understand how such groups compare.

B.2.4.1 Sexuality and Corpus-Based Data

To show the potential for corpus-based studies on gender and sexuality, we briefly discuss an ambitious study that compares the language of men and women, gay and straight. In an effort to avoid these researcher-developed classifications, Caskey (2011) created a corpus of spontaneous conversation that sampled speakers based on their self-identified gender (female or male) and sexuality (queer or non-queer). From 185 participants from across the United States and of various socio-economic and ethnic backgrounds, Caskey collected a corpus of nearly 300,000 words. The size of his corpus was rather large, considering all of the recording and transcription required. He organized his corpus according to the interlocutors of the conversations: (1) heterosexual females; (2) heterosexual males; (3) queer males; (4) mixed, hetero-females and hetero-males; and (5) mixed, hetero-males and queer males. The first three of these groups were homogeneous, while the latter two included interlocutors of differing sex (group 4) and differing sexual orientation (group 5). For each of these groups, Caskey recorded 10 conversations and transcribed over 10 hours of speech.

The design and results of Caskey's (2011) study show a wide variety of ways to use corpus linguistics in exploring sociolinguistic variation in gender and sexuality. These included topics discussed, manners in which one's ideas were conveyed, interruptions, laughter, and use of expletives. Table B2.1 provides a summary of some of Caskey's findings for the homogeneous groups and is further described below.

What did Caskey's (2011) participants talk about? To answer this question, he used a discourse analytic approach, rather than automated, more corpus-driven techniques. Reading his transcriptions, themes or groups of topics emerged from the data. This list included topics such as work, family, gossip, and so on. Once he had a system of themes, he then coded the conversations for instances of those themes. He found, for example, that women are much less likely than their male counterparts of either sexual orientation to talk about relationships, dating, and sex. However, they were much more likely to talk about familial topics and gossip. Using a similar system but relying on categories determined by previous research, Caskey also explored how his participants spoke to each other: By what means did they convey their discourse? An interesting finding was that his queer male participants used jokes much more than females and heterosexual males. Overall, the queer male group was much more likely to interrupt interlocutors, and heterosexual and queer males used flirtation in their discourse more frequently than females. In studying the use of expletives in the corpus, Caskey (2011) organized these words into four categories based on the type of person they are meant to insult: misogynistic (women, e.g., *whore*), misandric (men, e.g., *bastard*), homophobic

TABLE B2.1 Sexuality and corpus-based data, from Caskey (2011)

	Females (F)	Heterosexual Males (HM)	Queer Males (QM)
Themes discussed	Had high levels of talking about people (gossiping or not). They talked about family more than HM and QM. Less likely than HM and QM to use flirtatious language.	Broad range of thematic topics. They were more similar to F than QM in discussing gossip and work.	Shared more in common with HM than with females (e.g., relationships, suggestive, and partying). The theme they shared with females (and not HM) was about clothing.
How discourse is conveyed	Used stories more than HM and QM. They also used more repetition in their speech	Used twice as many jokes as F. They also provided less advice than F and QM	Used nearly four times as many jokes as F. Used the least amount of repetition.
How speakers interrupted their interlocutors	Used much more back channels than HM and QM.	Along with QM, HM were 13 times more likely to interrupt using flirtation than F.	Interrupted much more than F and HM. Ways included, for clarification, providing answers, and joking.
Instances of laughter loud enough to halt conversation	1,528	993	110
Types of expletives (all three groups had similar amounts of expletives per one million words)	With QM, used more misogynistic and misandric expletives than HM.	Used more homophobic expletives than F, but fewer than QM.	Used much more gendered (misogynistic, misandric, and homophobic) expletives than F and HM.

(queers, e.g., *homo*), and gender neutral (e.g., *shit*). Overall, he found that females, heterosexual males, and queer males used a relatively similar number of expletives in their utterances. However, they differed in their distribution across categories. Interestingly, females included the highest number of misogynistic expletives, and queer males included the highest number of homophobic expletives.

One of the most important findings from Caskey's work is that the language of queer males may constitute its own variety. Some may assume that because such speakers deviated from the hegemonic masculine norms, they deferred to the language of females. However, Caskey showed that in many ways, the language practices of queer males were more like their heterosexual male counterparts.

Reflective Break

- Caskey (2011) collected a spoken corpus that coded participants' self-identified gender and sexuality. Describe how you would analyze this corpus across demographics and settings. What potential complex or problematic issues do you see from this corpus?
- Look at the findings from Caskey's study in Table B2.1. For each category described, discuss how heterosexual females, heterosexual males, and queer males compared. Are any of his findings surprising to you? Why?
- Caskey explored thematic topics, how discourse is conveyed, how speakers interrupt their interlocutors, frequency of laughter, and the use and distribution of expletives. How do these constructs capture variation across social groups? What do you think are the limitations in studying such constructs?
- What other linguistic variables would you be interested in exploring with regards to gender and sexuality? Develop your research questions and describe your ideal gender or sexuality-coded corpus.

B2.5 Age

It is clearly difficult to follow groups of speakers extensively in a life span or in **real-time** to document various linguistic patterns or changes. There are also challenges in grouping speakers or writers based on their ages, and, so far, studies that attempt to create age groups follow different, somewhat arbitrary models and justifications. However, comparing the language of different age groups based on observations of a number of informants is clearly important in tracking language change, especially in vocabulary trend studies. Although contextual differences among these informants preclude many researchers to produce well-structured generalizations about the actual influence of age in linguistic variation, the age stratification of many lexico/syntactic features in a cross-sectional grouping of younger versus older speakers can be used to illustrate language change especially as they happen in **apparent-time**. In sociolinguistics, apparent-time has been defined as change in progress based on a comparison of groups of speakers representing broader age categories (Bailey, 2002). For example, a group of 80-year-old speakers in New York against 30-year-olds from the same setting may show patterns of change that have occurred in American English, specifically in New York, in the past 50 years. A well-developed apparent-time study will have to represent the population of speakers, the same vernacular speech, and similar contextual variables (e.g., education, overseas travel, racial background).

The majority of age-based research in sociolinguistics is done on the language of adolescents. This is where glimpses of possible future language changes are also investigated, looking into how younger speakers on the periphery of speech communities adjust or change the mode through which they communicate with other members. Adolescence is appealing to sociolinguists as it is regarded as a stage when linguistic changes and innovations from below are advanced (Eckert, 2004). Accordingly, sound change, slang, the use of quotative markers (especially *like*), and expletives have been four of the most intensely studied linguistic phenomena related to youth language. These linguistic innovations by adolescents, which also include expressive pronunciation of words, coinage, and syntactic deviations, have been explored and documented across many cultures, especially in the Western world. Penelope Eckert (2004) has done extensive research on the language of adolescents, and she emphasizes the importance of studying this age group as a major linguistic contributor in our society:

> Adolescence is not a natural life stage. It is peculiar to industrialized nations, where people approaching adulthood are segregated from the adult world and confined to schools where they are expected to interact and identify primarily with those their own age. In many ways, adolescents' position in society is similar to that of the aged. One could say that they are an institutionalized population, and much of their care is left to professionals who have come to constitute a major industry in our society. (Eckert, 2004, p. 362)

In recent years, various researchers focusing on adolescent language have also investigated the distribution of linguistic variables such as intensifiers, discourse markers, information structure, and nonstandard grammar. The distribution of **taboo language** in many recent corpus-based studies has also been explored through corpora collected from conversations between adolescents. The Linguistic Innovators Corpus (Kerswill, Cheshire, Fox, & Torgersen, 2008) was collected from sociolinguistic interviews with 100 working-class adolescents in London, in part to document linguistic patterns that could be compared with other speaker groups. Adolescent communities and contexts have been clearly defined, from schools and playgrounds to adolescent speech represented in movies and television programs. School subcultures (e.g., Eckert's distinctions between nerds, jocks, burnouts, and adolescent gang members) have also been considered as integral part of this speech community. Interestingly, Barbieri (2008) noted that this inordinate amount of research on youth language has very few counterparts in other age groups. For example, we know very little details about the language of the elderly.

B2.5.1 Age and Corpora

Working in the areas of health sciences and social psychology, Pennebaker and Stone (2003) used a computer program, the Linguistic Inquiry and Word Count (LWIC), to analyze spoken transcripts and written essays of more than 3,000 participants focusing specifically on the variable of age. The current version of the LWIC measures about 80 different features from four different categories: (1) linguistic processes (e.g., word count, parts of speech, past tense), (2) psychological processes (e.g., words about family, friends, positive emotions, causation, hearing, sex, motion), (3) personal concerns (e.g., words about work, leisure, home), and (4) spoken categories (e.g., assent, fillers). (In Section C4.3, we provided a sample activity that makes use of data from LIWC.)

Most previous research in the area of changes to cognition by age had been measured using tasks or self-reported answers. Just as many corpus linguists prefer to work with corpora because they include examples of natural language without the effects of participants' self-perceptions and intuitions, Pennebaker and Stone wanted to see if natural language would exhibit psychological and linguistic differences across various age groups. They anticipated, as with research conducted using different methods found, that complex linguistic patterns would peak in middle-age. Pennebaker and Stone (2003) compiled data (over 3.8 million words) from 45 different studies to conduct their analysis of age. Of those 45 studies, 32 of them involved participants who were asked to write on one of two types of topics: (1) emotional or traumatic, or (2) superficial. This accounted for more than half of the sample. Twelve more of the studies had participants who only wrote about traumatic events. The other three studies used interviews instead of writing.

LWIC was used to examine each text. Counts for all of the dependent variables were made and averaged across the groups. Pennebaker and Stone's (2003) findings showed that with age, emotion words changed. More positive and fewer negative words were used. With age, writers also included fewer references (to themselves and to others). They were also more likely to write using modals associated with future time while decreasing the number of verbs in the past tense. This might be contrary to a person's intuition. One might expect that the older a person is, the more likely he or she would be to talk about the past. Also, as predicted, the researchers found that the older age groups included more characteristics of cognitive complexity in their language (e.g., big words, words that show causation, words that refer to insights). Another surprising finding made was that the much older participants (70+) used many more positive words than even their counterparts between 55 and 69 years of age.

A keyword analysis conducted by Barbieri (2008) compared two subcorpora from an American Conversation corpus, a large corpus of casual, everyday conversation that was part of the Longman Corpus of Spoken and Written English. A keyword is "a word which occurs with unusual frequency in a given text" (Scott, 1997, p. 236). A determination of an unusually high frequency occurrence of words from a corpus is based upon a comparison with a target corpus and computed statistically from a measure of likelihood of occurrence. In Section C4.2, we provide instructions in running a keyword analysis using the software *AntConc 3.2.4* (Anthony, 2012).

The two subcorpora were of similar sizes: the Younger Corpus had 195,400 words, while the Older Corpus has a total of 204,200 words. These subcorpora comprised conversations from 139 speakers: 85 speakers aged 15 to 25 (46 males and 39 females) and 54 speakers aged 35 to 60 (17 males and 37 females) from approximately 57 hours of conversation.

Barbieri analyzed up to 450 words from two keyword lists: one generated using the Younger Corpus as main corpus and the Older Corpus as comparison corpus, and vice versa. Listed below are the first 25 keywords from the Younger Corpus compared to the Older Corpus:

1. likes	14. cool
2. unclear*	15. Wayne
3. you	16. shit
4. fucking	17. right
5. um	18. no
6. mhm	19. fucked
7. Ayesha	20. totally
8. man	21. Chomsky
9. dude	22. everyone
10. fuck	23. interview
11. m	24. ah
12. really	25. wine
13. I	

***unclear** refers to the use of words in the transcript that was undecipherable. Barbieri implied that, based on this outstanding number of words which were unclear to the transcribers, younger speakers' talk may be faster or more "dysfluent" than older speakers' speech.

The list of keywords from the two groups was then used as a springboard for more detailed qualitative comparisons of lexical features of age-based variation. In summary, Barbieri's (2008) qualitative analyses showed that, based on outstanding keywords, younger speakers favored the adverbs *totally*, *really*, and *seriously*, all of which were adverbs of degree that intensified intended meanings. This finding suggested that intensifier use varied across age groups. Other significant age-based differences were found to include the use of personal pronouns, modal verbs, quotative verbs, attitudinal adjectives, stance adverbs, inserts and discourse markers, and slang. The results of this study revealed that younger speakers made a dramatically more frequent use of a range of slang and swearwords, inserts, attitudinal or personal affect adjectives, intensifiers, discourse markers, first and second person singular reference, and particular quotative verbs (e.g., *like*).

Reflective Break

• Did you notice something potentially problematic in this list of first 25 keywords from Barbieri (2008)? If you thought *Ayesha*, *Wayne*, and *Chomsky* were questionable, highly topic-based results, you are probably right. Here's how Barbieri addressed this observation:

   One caveat of the reliance on *outstandingness* of frequency in the identification of keywords is that it might yield meaningless or uninterpretable results, such as common and proper nouns (e.g., *Ayesha, Wayne, Chomsky, wine, Joey, Jamaica*, etc.). Common and proper nouns are highly dependent on local context and topic, and as such are likely to be confined to particular conversations (and texts) (cf. Baker 2004). The present study does not take into account the distribution of keywords across texts. Thus, though they were not excluded from the output of the keyword analysis, common and proper nouns were ignored in the actual interpretation of patterns of keywords. (pp. 63–64)

- What other age-based comparisons can you investigate? Think about your options in grouping adults according to age categories (e.g., 21 to 31; 32 to 41, 42 to 51, and so on). How can you justify these age categories? What linguistic features will you compare from these groups?
- **Real time change:** *The Up Series* (Granada Television, 1964–2012) is a continuing documentary film from director Michael Apted that focuses on the lives of 14 British children from 1964 to the present. Starting with **7 Up** (or Seven Up), when these children were only seven years old, this series now has eight episodes from over 49 years of recorded interviews and extensive footage of England as viewed through the lens of participants, who represent different socioeconomic backgrounds. In 2012, *56 Up* premiered on British television; the film version was released in the United States in early 2013.

What diachronic/age-based sociolinguistic studies can be developed using data from *The Up Series*?

B3

POLITENESS AND STANCE

B3.1 Politeness as a Sociolinguistic Variable

This section focuses on lexical and grammatical politeness, stance and hedging, vague words, modality, and related speech acts investigated using corpora and corpus-based approaches. Politeness (or impoliteness) and the use of vague reference words or phrases (e.g., *stuff*, *all that*, and *all sort of things*) have been widely studied in sociolinguistics, especially in the context of speech and face-to-face communication. These linguistic variables have been explored across unique settings such as dinner conversations, telephone-based transactions, and workplace interactions. For example, stance and hedging, together with other paralinguistic markers of speech, have been analyzed to account for the influence of hierarchies and status of participants in office talk or job interviews. Written manifestations of politeness and vagueness have been studied, especially in e-mails, business memos, or announcements and advertising texts. These evaluative discourse features of speech and writing have been compared across cultures and languages, with emphasis on cross-cultural interactions (and also cross-cultural pragmatics).

The study of polite discourse features is closely related to interactional pragmatics and more detailed analyses of speech acts (Austin, 1975; Searle, 1969). **Speech acts** are generally utterances or statements that are categorized based on their structure and intent. We can be making requests, asking questions, or offering apologies, but what we say when delivering these utterances may not directly reflect these intentions, and our listeners may also interpret them very differently from our original purpose. The theory of speech acts includes the evaluation of the relative success or failure of these utterances. What we say has literal and direct meanings from a linguistic sense, of course. For example, the statement, "*It's chilly in here!*" might be interpreted literally to focus on the room's cold temperature.

However, it could also be indirectly interpreted as a request or command, depending on the intention of the speaker and the unique speaking context or tone (i.e., *"Please turn the heater on"* or *"Shut down the windows!"*). Hence, the study of politeness and speech acts emphasizes the interaction between the literal, linguistic meaning of utterances and the deeper-level or subjective meaning and interpretation of the speaker's intent. A primary focus, therefore, in analyzing these discourse features is how to best identify and account for the effects of functional variables and the speaker intentions that influence the success or failure of talk in terms of its intended outcome.

Corpora and corpus approaches have been used in the study of politeness and speech acts with some interesting results and clear limitations. Most corpus-based studies of politeness, stance, and speech acts are primarily **descriptive** and are limited to researcher interpretations of linguistic distributions from corpora. In this sense, it is hard to construe indirect meanings and listener/audience interpretations of an utterance, as most corpora are not coded or annotated for behaviors that are typically documented in many qualitative studies. In addition, sarcasm and many figurative expressions (including humor, skepticism, irony, or "mockery," for example) are clearly not easily captured in transcribed texts.

B3.2 Lexical and Grammatical Politeness

Politeness in conversation is generally perceived as a manifestation of proper social decorum, good manners, sensitivity, courtesy, and respect. Politeness finds expression in a variety of ways through language, gestures, and other nonverbal signals. All of these modes of expression are affected and defined to varying degrees by the contextual factors characterizing the interaction, as well as the particular culture within which the interactions are occurring.

Politeness in spoken interaction, covering a range of contexts and speaker demographics, has been enthusiastically and extensively explored by linguists over the past several decades. For example, some studies (e.g., Beeching, 2002; Lakoff, 1975; Locher, 2004; Mills, 2003; Tannen, 1986) have shown that women are more likely to use politeness markers and speech-act formulae than men. Other demographic factors such as age and educational background of speakers are also found to influence the use of politeness markers in formal interactions such as job interviews (White, 1994). In addition, cross-cultural relationships based upon factors such as nationality and race potentially determine the use of politeness markers in communications between and among multicultural speakers.

The variations in the frequency of use of politeness and respect markers are found to be influenced by social variables such as social distance and imposition within national cultures (see e.g., Economidou-Kogetsidis, 2005, on Greek politeness terms in service encounters). Emphasizing cross-cultural differences in politeness studies has become a popular focus, as extensive research from countries such as Japan, South Korea, China, and Saudi Arabia have provided many important insights into the description and interpretation of polite/impolite behaviors in business negotiations, tourism, and education.

The most influential work on linguistic politeness was conducted by Penelope Brown and Stephen Levinson, producing what is commonly referred to as "Brown and Levinson's Politeness Theory" (1987). Brown and Levinson's framework differentiates two types of politeness: **positive** and **negative** politeness. Positive and negative politeness are directly related to the notion of "face," first introduced in the field of sociology by Erving Goffman. Face refers to a personal quality or attribute (i.e., our social persona) that each individual wants to protect, enhance, or improve within a particular community. Positive face, for example, includes desirable traits such as friendliness, openness, and solidarity that are mutually understood and agreed upon by community members. Brown and Levinson's framework identifies strategies that avoid offence, or "face-threatening acts," by showing deference and respecting private space (and privacy) as **negative politeness**. Communicative strategies that highlight pleasantness, cooperation, and kindness are identified as **positive politeness**. A very important component of this theoretical framework is the attention a speaker pays to his or her interlocutor's "**face wants**."

Most English expressions that are intended to be polite in everyday speech can be categorized as negative politeness. Showing respect or deference to the interlocutor and explicitly referring to social distance or privacy between interactants are typical of English conversations (and the Western culture) in many contexts. Evidently, it is harder to capture linguistic manifestations of negative politeness in transcribed conversations than to identify and capture explicit lexical expressions of positive politeness; *thanks, thank you, you're welcome, good morning*—expressions of appreciation and greetings representing friendliness can be easily counted and normalized across sociolinguistic corpora.

Many sociolinguistic studies of polite discourse have extensively examined the use of politeness markers in professional, cross-cultural interaction. The analysis of polite discourse in the cross-cultural workplace continues to illustrate how speakers make linguistic adjustments in using and understanding a range of politeness formulae. Hierarchies and asymmetries in the workplace, especially those involving different cultural backgrounds, are perceived to influence the extent and nature of polite language and behavior of interactants in these situations. Specific politeness techniques such as using euphemisms and tag questions (e.g., "*It's a very problematic issue, isn't it?*") add to the common lexical devices and specialized morphology (e.g., using verb forms for polite discourse) employed by speakers across cultures in showing deference, respect, and recognition of roles and social status (Beeching, 2002).

The use of positive and negative politeness in conversation may also come from the recognition of roles or power relationships between speakers. When power structures are involved, politeness markers are used to make sure that parties acknowledge certain standards of order and decorum. A study of parliamentary discourse in the United Kingdom examined apologies as politeness strategies employed by British lawmakers in heated parliamentary debates (Christie, 2002). Formal debates, which are often televised or open to the public, employ procedural language that include respect markers and polite discourse markers to interrupt, interject, or transition to the next speaker. The primary intent of these apologies may not necessarily reflect the default functional interpretation of phrases such as *I'm sorry* or *I apologize* as polite utterances. In contentious exchanges, apologies directed to an opposing parliamentarian may be used by the speaker more to emphasize or create the impression (or maybe an illusion) among others of a speaker's positive behavior, evidence of integrity and respect for norms and so on rather than to convey genuine sympathy for or consideration of the opponent. Also in the arena of political discourse, televised political interviews are status and power-influenced, during which interviewers often combine polite forms of questioning and conventionally respectful tone when discussing problematic issues with guests. The television as a medium generally restricts the use of "rapid-fire" direct questioning more than is the case in parliamentary or congressional debates. Political interviewers often rarely employ apologies for personal benefit or advantage. In the United States, most television interviews with politicians are handled with expected question-answer sequences, with lawmakers, as the primary sources of information or opinion, accorded a certain amount of deferential respect.

In the business world, which is highly dependent upon building positive relationships between and among parties, politeness is used as an integral part of communication strategies that allow participants to gain trust and respect with the ultimate, if not entirely altruistic, goal of selling products and/or services. Common linguistic expressions of politeness are often utilized to make all the parties relaxed and comfortable with one another. In selling products and services or requesting information in service encounters, politeness is an important part of the interaction and a critical determinant of the outcome and, ideally, often characterizes the prevailing tone of the interaction. The specific objectives of the participants generally require them to use polite language and paralanguage in order to successfully engage the other party in the conversation and achieve their respective goals.

And finally, in all these settings, various polite expressions are both culturally and contextually defined. Speakers coming from different cultural backgrounds may not immediately share similar understanding and expectations of polite markers and gestures. It often happens that cultural standards in one society defining the expression of politeness are considered unusual, strange, or even rude in another. Hence, it takes some level of familiarity with the cultural norms and practices of people from different backgrounds in order to use appropriate polite markers and correctly interpret speakers' meaning or intentions during communication. Social status, education, and related social variables such as types of job across cultures (e.g., doctors, teachers, lawyers, and elected officials are often highly respected) may also define the use of politeness formula and respect markers in conversation.

B3.2.1. Exploring Politeness Features in Service Encounters

Do you recall our responses to *thank you* discussion at the beginning of this book? Politeness and respect markers are common in face-to-face service encounters from both the server and the servee. These markers are used together with appropriate suprasegmental features of speech to express appreciation for service (from servees) and patronage (from servers). In face-to-face service encounters such as in a coffee shop, it is very common for customers to order coffee using polite request markers and phrases such as *please* or *can I have . . .* and then give polite acknowledgement of service afterwards (e.g., *thanks* or *thank you*) as shown in Text Sample B3.1. Servers also often match these markers with polite responses (e.g., *no problem, you're welcome*) during the transaction. In these types of face-to-face service encounters, the roles of the server and the servee are clearly established, affecting the linguistic choices of these participants.

Text Sample B3.1. Politeness Markers in a Service Encounter

1   Server: Yes, hi, can I help you?
2   Servee: Sure, **can I have**, uh **please**, hazelnut mocha? Uh, large, that one . . . **please**
3   Server: Definitely . . . uh, nice day today right?
4   Servee: Yes it is, oh **please** extra . . . yeah, um, extra hot **please**
5   Server: Oh **sorry** about that, sure, extra hot
6   Servee: **Thanks**
7   Server: [long pause] Here you go, hazelnut mocha, **thanks**
8   Servee: **Thanks, thanks**
9   Server: **Welcome, thank you, no problem**, have a good day
10   Servee: You too, **thanks**

The nature of service transactions defines the social roles of customers and servers and, in turn, perceptions and impositions related to the use of polite terms in maintaining the transaction. Most servers are "coached" about the value of maintaining customer patronage or loyalty by providing efficient service and establishing rapport during service interactions. In the process, servers employ positive politeness strategies that they perceive will satisfy most customers (note the response by the server in line 9: "*Welcome, thank you, no problem . . .*"). The communicative purpose of participants is also very clear in these interactions: customers purchase products or request service, while servers are expected to provide the necessary product, action, or solution.

Another layer of power relationship and negotiation between customers and servers arises in transactions that originate as a result of faulty products or services. Customers have higher service expectations and often demand immediate solutions for problematic products or services that they have purchased. In this context, customer complaints may add tension and may affect the tenor of the interaction and the use of language by both participants. It is up to the servers to use positive and negative politeness strategies that refocus the purpose of the interaction and lead to successful resolution of the specific problem. To accomplish this, an effective server is able to maintain a problem-solving focus throughout the interaction and gain the customer's trust or patience by using polite and respectful language, focused on the particular and specific need(s) of the customer.

B3.3 Politeness in Corpus-Based Studies

The comparison of various politeness features in discourses across corpora has become the focus of research questions in corpus-based sociolinguistics. Politeness has been operationalized differently from basic frequency distributions of *please* or *thank you* in gender-coded texts to the contrasts between lexico/syntactic markers of directness and indirectness in speech along a formal-informal register continuum. The raw frequency counts of politeness features from corpora are easy to obtain and these distributions are interpreted on a macrolevel in several studies. For example, Holmes (1995) explored a corpus of conversations in New Zealand to quantify compliments and apologies given by male and female speakers. She reported that females accounted for 68 percent of all the compliments and 75 percent of all the apologies in the corpus. A quantitative analysis showed that gender significantly influenced the use of compliments and apologies in naturally occurring verbal interactions in this study.

Note that some studies of basic distributional data from corpora have been criticized because of unsupported generalizations. Clearly, there are other contextual variables in naturally occurring conversations that may in fact have influenced these distributions more than just, for example, the gender of speakers (e.g., gender of interlocutors/hearer, task categories, or speaker roles). The addition of subregisters to process as well as clearly situating the analysis into a specific context are certainly very important in making sure that corpus-based information accurately represents variation in the discourse and the potential variables influencing it.

The three corpus-based studies featured in the following sections look at (1) the distribution of *thanks* and *thank you* across gender and social class from spoken texts of the BNC; (2) the comparisons of lexical politeness markers in telephone-based, cross-cultural customer service interactions; and (3) the study of impolite utterances from a corpus of political interviews in the United Kingdom. These studies utilized corpora collected to represent interrelated variables such as gender, social class, tasks, and contexts.

B3.3.1 Uses of Thanks in British Dialogues (Ishikawa, 2011)

The distribution of lexical expressions of gratitude (e.g., *thanks*, *appreciate*) and polite request (e.g., *please*) across corpora have been frequently investigated from a range of perspectives. Specialized domains such as workplace interactions and wider cross-cultural comparisons from reference corpora have produced distributional data that can be interpreted sociolinguistically. Biber, Johansson, Leech,

Conrad, and Finegan (1999) compared normalized frequencies of *thanks* and *thank you* from British and American conversations. They reported that American speakers significantly make greater use of these two features in their utterances than British speakers do. Overall, conversational data from parallel corpora of face-to-face interactions, tasked-based conversations, and telephone talk show that American speakers generally say *thanks* or *thank you* in these domains more than their British counterparts. In contrast, British speakers have higher frequencies of *please* used as an insert in speech than Americans do. Biber and colleagues' primary suggestion was to study these two groups of politeness features separately and contextually to further identify culture-specific features of politeness.

A more granular level of analysis in the distribution of *thanks* and *thank you* in British dialogues from the BNC was conducted by Ishikawa (2011) to revisit previously reported data on these features used by males and females in conversation. Most seminal descriptive studies of politeness features, especially Lakoff (1975) and Holmes (1995), have reported that females, in general, tend to give thanks and show explicit appreciation in their speech more than males. As we noted in Section B2, similar results from qualitative studies of gender and speech have produced related stereotypes.

Ishikawa analyzed spoken registers of the BNC across gender and social groups (AB, C1, C2, and DE) as identified by speakers' occupation (see Section B1.8.1.1. for a description of these categories). A total of 721,299 dialogues were extracted from the spoken texts of the BNC, with 287,944 made by male speakers and 298,069 by female speakers (other dialogues from unspecified speakers were not included in the analysis). Contrary to stereotypes and results from Lakoff (1975) and Holmes (1995), Ishikawa reported that male speakers in the BNC used more *thank you* and *thanks* more than their female counterparts in dialogues. Overall, a statistical significance test using the chi-square showed that gender of speakers significantly influenced the distribution of *thanks* and *thank you* ($p<.001$) in BNC dialogues. Male speakers used these utterances more frequently than female speakers (Figure B3.1). Across social groups, male speakers in AB, C1, and DE also have more of these features than female speakers. These differences also yielded statistical significance especially the contrast between AB and the three other social groups.

Males and females in the AB group were very likely to use *thanks* and *thank you* more than speakers in the three other social groups. Specifically, male speakers from AB had the most *thanks* and *thank you*, while male speakers in C2 and female speakers in DE used these utterances relatively less frequently. In this study, the focus on gender and social groups and the distributions of expressions of gratitude and appreciation in dialogues may show how corpus-based data can support (or not support) previously established stereotypes. Ishikawa's functional analysis of these distributions did not provide definitive explanations of the overall likelihood of educated and professional males to use more *thanks* and *thank you* in dialogues than females across most social groups. This study also did not consider the gender of the hearer, and specific tasks or topics of the conversational dialogues were not investigated as well. However, it is quite surprising to see how consistent

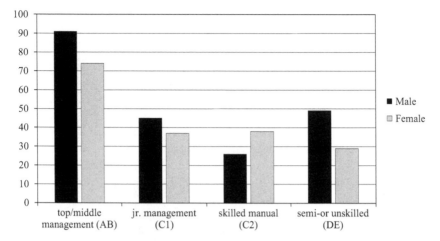

FIGURE B3.1 Gender differences in the use of *thanks* and *thank you*

Source: adapted from Ishikawa, 2011, p. 388

data from British male speakers on the use of *thanks/thank you* compare with females in parallel spoken extracts from the BNC. Higher educational attainment and a high-paying profession (AB group) may have exposed speakers in this group to a more formal context of speech where proper decorum is more frequently the norm. In addition, *thanks* and *thank you* in these conversational dialogues may also involve negative politeness of deference.

Reflective Break

- Try to explain further the distributions in Figure B3.1. What other factors may have influenced the use of these features by males (especially C2 vs. AB and DE groups)?
- What do you think will be the distributions of *please* across gender and social groups of spoken dialogues in the BNC following Ishikawa's datasets? Will you expect the overall patterns to be the same (e.g., AB males and females will have more polite requests than the other groups)?
- You can conduct your own search of politeness features by using the BNC-web. What other forms of lexical or grammatical politeness or speech acts are you interested in searching?

B3.3.2 Lexical Politeness in Outsourced Call Center Interactions (Friginal, 2009b)

To investigate expressions of gratitude, respect, apologies, and polite requests in *outsourced* customer service call centers based in the Philippines (and serving American callers), Friginal extracted distributions of lexical politeness and respect markers (e.g., *please, thank you, apologize, sir/ma'am*) across roles, gender, and other social demographics of interactants. The setting here is telephone-based customer service in the United States that has been outsourced overseas to countries like India and the Philippines due to business demands to trim expenses incurred in maintaining these call centers on the mainland. "Outsourcing" is defined by the World Bank as the contracting of a service provider overseas to manage, deliver, and operate a client's functions (e.g., data centers and customer service call centers). Developments in telecommunications and international business practices in the last decade paved the way for various services to be more transportable and fragmented, thereby simplifying logistics and allowing them to be easily relocated. The considerable increase in the number of American companies employing offshore call center agents based in the Philippines (and India) has affected the structure and quality of spoken interactions in telephone-based customer service in the United States as well as the outcomes and satisfaction levels of customers utilizing these services.

As one would expect, there is a very high frequency of these politeness and respect markers used by customer service agents in service transactions. An initial survey of *please, thank you*, and the use of titles and the respect markers *sir/ma'am* indicated that Filipino call-takers ("agents") preferred to structure their questions and requests with the constant use of these features. It is not very clear whether American customers do or do not prefer frequent use of politeness and respect markers in call center transactions. Friginal's data, however, showed that the use of these features served other purposes in the interactions as discussed below. This study looked at distributions of politeness and respect markers that were grouped into four subcategories:

- **Polite speech–act formulae**: Polite speech-act formulae include the use of *thank you, thanks*, and *appreciate* (e.g., "*I appreciate your help*") by customers and agents. *Thanks/thank you/appreciate* in interactions are generally used to express appreciation or gratitude for service, favor, or another person's kindness or particular action.
- **Polite requests**: Polite requests make use of *please* in speaker turns. All occurrences of *please* were counted in the analysis of requests coming from agents and callers. Polite requests expressed through modal verbs (e.g., "... **may** I get your phone number?" "... **could** you give me ...," or "... **can** I have your ...") were not included in this particular analysis. Speakers use *please* in requests to lessen the impact of an imposition, recognize the value of another person's help, or maintain good relationships during interactions (Economidou-Kogetsidis, 2005).
- **Apologies**: The class of apologies in Friginal's study includes *sorry* (e.g., "*I'm **sorry** for the inconvenience, sir*"), *apologize* (e.g., "*I **apologize** for the delay*"), *pardon* (e.g., "***Pardon** me, could you repeat that*"), and *excuse* (e.g., "***Excuse** me, I did not hear you*"). These markers of apologies are commonly used for various purposes by both the agents and callers in transactions. Aside from actual apologies (e.g., "*I'm **sorry**, that was the wrong number*"), agents often apologize on behalf of the company for defective products or faulty service.
- **Respect markers**: Respect markers include the use of *sir* or *ma'am* and titles such as *Mr.* or *Ms.* (or *Dr.* for doctor whenever the caller explicitly referred to

him or herself as such during the transaction). American callers also use respect markers in the transactions, and there are certainly regional differences in their usage. Americans coming from the Southeastern United States are known to use more *ma'am* or *sir* in spoken discourse than those from Western states.

B3.3.2.1 Distributions of Politeness Markers in the Call Center Corpus

Friginal's sociolinguistic Call Center Corpus (2009b) was provided by a U.S.-owned call center company based in the Philippines. The corpus was carefully collected to represent various speaker categories obtained from Filipino agents and American callers. Situational subregisters such as task categories (e.g., trouble-shooting service calls vs. product purchase) or level of transactional pressure (e.g., high-pressure calls from complaint-oriented transactions vs. low-pressure calls from product questions or inquiries about service) were also coded. There were 500 complete call transactions in the corpus with 553,765 total number of words.

There was a consistent pattern in the frequencies of politeness and respect markers across roles and gender in the Call Center Corpus as shown in Figure B3.2. Agents had more of the four classes of markers than callers, while female agents and female callers had more frequencies of these markers than their male counterparts. The single exception in this pattern was in the use of *sir* or *ma'am* by male and female agents. Filipino male agents had more frequencies of *sir* or *ma'am* than female agents.

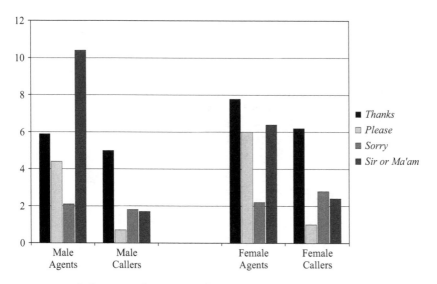

FIGURE B3.2 Politeness and respect markers across role and gender, normalized per 1,000 words

Source: adapted from Friginal, 2009b, p. 183

Unlike Ishikawa's results from the BNC, female Americans had a consistently greater frequency of *thanks, please, sorry,* and *sir/ma'am* than males. The distribution of these markers in the discourse of American male and female callers supported generalizations from previous research in gender and politeness in formal or business settings (e.g., Beeching, 2002; Coates, 1996; Mills, 2003). In communicating with the agents, American female callers used relatively more polite speech-act formulae and apologies than males. The use of more apologies by females perhaps implied that these callers were more respectful of the agents and showed explicit recognition of agents' efforts during the transactions. These apologies in callers' turns also suggested that female callers were more overt in acknowledging their mistakes in following instructions or possible limitations in understanding the agents.

Friginal noted that there were different factors that could potentially explain the distribution of respect markers between male and female Filipino agents. The *military* style (e.g., "*yes, Mr. Johnson,* **sir** . . .") use of respect markers by Filipino males may have come from their perceptions of power relationships showing great respect for females and greater, more explicit respect for males in professional settings. This observation was consistent especially in transactions between male agents and older-sounding male American callers in high-pressure or difficult transactions. In these situations, male agents noticeably used very high frequencies of *sir* in their turns. Another possible factor affecting the use of respect markers by Filipino male and female agents was the use of vocatives (e.g., *Mr. Johnson, Ms. Smith*) in which female agents were able to use callers' first or last name more consistently without using additional respect markers in their turns.

Aside from satisfying the common purposes of these polite and respect markers, it appeared that many agents in call center transactions had developed speech mannerisms that often included the use of *thanks* or *thank you* whenever they received a response from their callers. In addition, most of the calls in the corpus started with "***Thank you** for calling* . . ." as agents' greeting sequence in the calls. These instances of *thanks* or *thank you* significantly increased the frequencies of politeness markers in the Call Center Corpus. The repetitive use of *thanks* or *thank you* as agents' acknowledgement of callers' response to questions or requests was common in all task categories (e.g., troubleshooting or inquiry calls). Aside from a possible mannerism acquired through months or years of work in the industry, Filipino agents potentially used these repetitive speech-act formulae to ensure a continuous flow of response in the transactions to avoid pauses or dead air. In some instances, *thanks* or *thank you* appeared to act as discourse markers to introduce the agents' next question or main response to the callers. Text Sample B3.2 shows the constant use (perhaps *overuse*) of *thank you* by the agent as part of her response after the caller's turns.

Text Sample B3.2. Agent's Use of *Thank You* (from Friginal, 2009b)

1 Agent: **Thank you** for calling [XX Company]; my name is Melanie. Can I have your phone number starting with the area code please?
2 Caller: Yes it's [x-x-x].

3   Agent: **Thank you**, is there an extension number?
4   Caller: No.
5   Agent: Let me bring up your account here, and can I have your first and last name please?
6   Caller: Yes, it's [x-x-x].
7   Agent: **Thank you** [x-x-x].
8   Caller: The name on the account should be Mark, uhh Mark [x-x-x].
9   Agent: **Thank you**, and while I'm bringing up the account information, how can I help you today?
10   Caller: Uhm our, the uhh the print on our postage machine is uhh, there's a lot of gaps and missing uhm characters on the when we print it out, and I've run the uhh the print function, the printer function key.
11   Agent: Uh-huh?
12   Caller: The clean uhh maintenance key many times, and it's still not clearing up.
13   Agent: **Sorry to hear that, but don't worry; I'll be glad to help you with your concern and** [interruption] . . .
14   Caller: **Thank you**.
15   Agent: It will take a few minutes of your time. **You're welcome**.

For callers, the frequency of these markers was potentially influenced by the primary type of issue they had in making the call. Customers ordering or inquiring about a product had higher frequencies of these polite markers than those complaining about service or asking assistance to troubleshoot a machine. American callers used a relatively high frequency of *thanks/thank you/appreciate* compared to the three other classes of markers in this study. These were used to show appreciation for service or recognition of agents' assistance. Most of the occurrences of *thanks/thank you/appreciate* appeared at the end of the transactions. *Please, sorry*, and respect markers *ma'am* or *sir* were used sparingly by callers, but these markers typically achieved their specific communicative purposes in callers' turns.

Reflective Break

- There was a major difference between the frequencies of *please* by callers versus agents in the transactions as shown in Figure B3.2. Considering that the callers were asking for service or information when they initiated the calls, polite requests, as in face-to-face service encounters, would usually be expected from them more than from the agents. What do you think were the reasons for this result? If the call center agents were Americans, instead of Filipinos, do you think distributions and patterns would be different?
- **Power relationships**: What other manifestations of power differences between the caller and agent in call centers can we observe here? How does language proficiency (from foreign call center agents) play a part in these interactions? Could we also study linguistic discrimination from this type of cross-cultural interaction?

B3.4 Negative Politeness and Impoliteness in Institutional Discourse (Taylor, 2011)

Speaker 1: *Minister, with the greatest possible respect . . .*
Speaker 2: *Oh, are you going to insult me again?* (Taylor, 2011)

Taylor (2011) identified *impolite* events from a corpus of parliamentary discourse in the United Kingdom, with additional texts from political interviews and a public inquiry. These three discourse domains were used because they all show instances of public, institutional discourse, which features a restrictive turn-taking format. Taylor noted that conversations in these formal contexts are known to sanction aggressive negotiations and "facework." In addition, speakers in these three contexts hold relatively similar status and power, as the interactions involved politicians. Power is heavily involved but roles, unlike in the call center study, are not clearly delineated.

Within these discourse domains, polite phraseologies are expressed to perform a variety of overlapping functions such as showing awareness of the discourse norms (e.g., *"with all due respect"*), allowing other speakers to aggressively defend an issue in an acceptable way and demonstrating that the speaker can handle the pressures of contentious interactions. "Mock politeness" or an impolite move can also be one of the primary functions of polite political phraseologies to superficially express distance and deference.

Taylor (2011) proposed that occurrences of impolite phraseologies often analyzed through qualitative discourse approaches can be captured using corpora and corpus-based tools. Specifically, the following categories can be used to start a KWIC search across corpora in order to extract identifiable expressions of impoliteness: (1) meta-pragmatic comment on the discourse norms, (2) reception/judgments of impoliteness from an addressee, (3) reception/judgments of impoliteness from third parties, and (4) shifts from transactional to interactional mode. Taylor also noted that the choice of any of these approaches depends on the theory of (im)politeness central to the study's unique context. Political discourse, including its goals and intentions, is certainly different from business or casual conversations in how disagreement or disrespect is conveyed. Intuitively, a speaker's intention seems to be crucial to the perception of impoliteness, but it is difficult to see how an intention-dependent definition from corpora can be operationalized or automatically extracted using computational tools. A search for meta-pragmatic phrases such as *"don't mean to be rude . . ."* from Taylor's specialized corpus provided the following text samples:

Text Sample B3.3. Concordance Lines for *I Don't Mean to Be Rude/Impolite*

| A0F | I don't | **mean to be rude,** | but how on earth are you going to |

CA3	I'm sorry, dear boy, I don't	**mean to be rude**	
F9C	He didn't	**mean to be rude.**	
G0P	I'm sorry, I don't	**mean to be rude.**	
G0X	He doesn't	**mean to be rude,**	explained Betty.
GY7	You see you see I don't	**mean to be** erm **rude**	or anything but as I'm sure
H8X	said breathlessly, I didn't	**mean to be impolite**	

Taylor also suggested that aggressive behavior as a form of impoliteness can be captured using concordance data. An analysis of search terms such as *confront, feisty, belligerent,* and similar words from a corpus of newspaper articles could show how a politician may be interpreted as showing aggressive behavior in an interview or a parliamentary discussion. These lexical search terms could directly relate to an individual's aggressive facework when analyzed within a certain context. For example, British prime minister Tony Blair was identified as aggressive in an interview with political talk show host David Frost on BBC1's *Breakfast with Frost* on September 28, 2003, based on the following extracts:

Text Sample B3.4. Reactions to Blair's Television Interview (from Taylor, 2011)

1   This is what Mr Blair is certain to do in his speech tomorrow—saying, as he did in his *unusually feisty performance* on *Breakfast with Frost* yesterday—that what really motivates him is crime, asylum, health, and education. (*Scotsman* 29/09/2003)

2   Mr Blair used a *combative interview* on BBC1's *Breakfast with Frost* to *confront* his critics and tell them he was in no mood to back down. (*Telegraph* 29/09/2003)

3   Mr Blair again showed his resilience yesterday in a *combative performance* on the BBC One show *Breakfast with Frost*. (*Times* 29/09/2003)

4   Mr Blair gave a *combative performance* on BBC's *Breakfast with Frost* programme. (*Independent* 29/09/2003)

5   It wasn't just a *belligerent performance* he gave on *Breakfast with Frost*, it was *arrogant*. (*Mirror* 29/09/2003)

Five different major papers referred to Blair's interview as combative or arrogant. In addition, referring to the interview, many other observers described Blair as having been "astonishingly direct." The text excerpts above do not necessarily indicate impoliteness per se, but these reactions from journalists and observers are what Taylor suggested as the effect of a shift from established norms on the hearer or audience. The implication here is that keyword searches in corpus-based studies can provide sufficient evidence that can support identification of (im)polite features of speech or aggressive behavior.

From these excerpts, Taylor conducted further analysis of keywords from the Blair-Frost interview such as Blair's use of second person *you* to directly refer to Frost. A keyword comparison of the Blair-Frost interview with a reference conversation corpus showed that second person *you* (2.16 in the Blair-Frost interview compared to 1.31 occurrences per 1,000 words) was one of the top keywords. Taylor interpreted this data as manifestations of Blair's directness following a scan of text excerpts focusing on KWICs of *you* in Blair's utterances. A large proportion of the uses of *you* were made up of Blair's characteristic discourse marker, *you know* as an utterance launcher or a feature marking invitations for consensus. However, Taylor noted that 10 out of 81 occurrences of Blair's *you* were directly addressing Frost (e.g., ". . . then I just tell **you** the economic insecurity that will result from" or ". . . let me just tell **you** and tell the public the other side of the . . .").

B3.5 Stance

Stance is defined as the linguistic mechanisms used by speakers/writers to convey their personal feelings and assessments or evaluations (Biber et al., 1999). Stance expressions in speech suggest a range of personal attitudes that speakers have about a specific item of information and how certain they are about its veracity (Biber, 2006b). Precht (2008) also pointed out that stance is the expression of a personal point of view that is relatively easy to identify. For example, in the text excerpt below, the italicized words in the passage were clearly used to express a personal point of view during a conversation between a male/female couple who were looking to buy a house. To describe one's experience or impressions, stance expressions are used in speech and writing.

Text Sample B3.5. Conversation between a Couple Looking at Houses (Precht, 2008)

1. F: Was this a neighborhood we *liked*?
2. M: *I don't think we ever seriously* really looked out here.
3. F: *Too* expensive?
4. M: No . . . *I don't know* . . . *I mean*, I, first of all, *I don't think* there was much out here.
5. F: Oh . . . These are *decent* sized houses.
6. M: Yeah, they're /?/.
7. F: *Some of* them aren't *too bad*.
8. M: The trees are *a little more* established over here too.
9. F: Well, *I don't know* about that.
10. M: *I don't think* this is a *terrible* place.
11. F: Mohawk? I've never *heard* of this.
12. M: That's *strange*.
13. F: Oh, this is *very interesting*, Mark.
14. M: We've drove through here a number of times. *I don't think* there was anything

15 on the market back then. There's not that *much* on here right now . . . It's
16 *probably* a *pretty desirable* place.
17 F: Yeah.
18 M: They *probably* sell *pretty* quickly.
19 F: Some of them are *pretty bad*. But, *a lot* of these are *very nice*.

In spoken registers, the expression of stance is evident both in the lexico/syntactic patterns of speech and also the prosodic features and other paralinguistic devices speakers utilize to directly and accurately express their feelings and opinions. These various linguistic and paralinguistic markers affect the flow of talk and influence the way participants engage each other during the conversation. The use of stance markers also reflects the relationships existing between speakers in conversation. This relationship may include power and the recognition of roles as well as the level of familiarity speakers have with each other. It is clear that an effective understanding of speaker roles or power relationships positively contributes to achieving success in the conversation, thus, avoiding misinterpretation of meaning and information and facilitating a smooth flow of communication. This understanding of relationships, speakers' intentions, and the context of conversation influence the use of stance markers characterizing the interaction.

The study of linguistic variation on the expression of stance and modality has been popular in corpus-based research. A few of these studies compared the ways in which stance is articulated in spoken versus written registers. For example, Conrad and Biber (2000) examined adverbial markers of stance in speech and writing, while Biber and Finegan (1989) and Biber and colleagues (1999) surveyed variations in the use of numerous grammatical stance devices (e.g., modal verbs, stance adverbials, and stance complement clause constructions, etc.) and also compared their patterns of usage in spoken versus written registers. Keck and Biber (2004) analyzed stance patterns from university spoken and written texts. Other studies focus exclusively on stance and modality in written registers, often with academic writing texts. Among these studies, Charles (2006, 2007) compared stance markers across different disciplines, while Hyland (1994, 1998) looked at hedging in academic written texts. Additional studies have framed stance within the rubric of "evaluation" or "assessment" in academic writing (e.g., Hyland & Tse, 2005; Römer, 2005).

Several qualitative approaches to the investigation of stance have extensively explored a limited number of texts (or lines in transcribed texts) or speech events for discourse analysis. Seminal studies from Labov (1984b), Chafe (1986), and Biber and Finegan (1989) analyzed a few episodes of conversations focusing on how interlocutors construct and interpret stance expressions. In these earlier studies, the term *stance* has also been referred to as *hedge*, *affect*, *intensity*, or *evaluation*. The investigation of specific stance or evaluative features of conversation was established and interpreted by these influential linguists to fully describe the structures and functions of stance in language (Biber, 2006b).

The Longman Grammar of Spoken and Written English (LGSWE) (Biber et al., 1999) provides a more specific description of grammatical stance features across spoken and written registers of British and American English that are not commonly achieved in the studies of stance using qualitative discourse analysis. Corpus-based techniques and corpus tools have allowed researchers to automatically extract multiple stance markers across groups of texts. However, because stance in spoken discourse also relies on phonological and prosodic features of speech representing stance expressions, most corpus-based analyses of stance in have clear limitations. Biber (2006b) noted that some features, for example *intensity* in speech, would not be captured in corpora unless text transcriptions included phonological tags or additional annotations. In conversations, stance can be explicitly expressed through *value-laden word choice* or paralinguistic devices (Biber et al., 1999) that may have more immediate effects on speaker-hearer's feelings than grammatically marked stance features extracted corpora.

B3.5.1 Categorizing Lexico/Syntactic Features of Stance

Biber's (2006b) framework of stance attribution incorporates three major categories of lexico/syntactic features: (1) modal and semimodal verbs, (2) stance adverbs, and (3) complement clauses controlled by stance verbs, adjectives, and nouns. These groups of stance features were developed primarily to automatize stance searches from corpora. As part of the Biber Tagger (1988, 2006b), Biber has developed an automated stance tagging system that can immediately extract the normalized counts of these categories. Table B3.1 lists the composition of these groups of grammatical stance features.

Modal and Semi-Modal Verbs

The semantic classes of modal verbs include possibility/permission, necessity/obligation, and prediction/volition modals expressing a variety of purposes following their explicit meanings. These modal verbs are used to give directives (e.g., "*You **can** now proceed*"), ask questions (e.g., "*Did you say I **could** ask them to replace it for me?*"), or outline steps of procedures in conversations (e.g., "*What we **will** do is, we **will** start by replacing this wallpaper*"). The frequency of modal verbs used for requests and clarifications (possibility/permission modals: *can, could, may*) is very high in spoken texts compared to written texts.

Stance Adverbs

Stance adverbs are divided into four major semantic classes: certainty, likelihood (epistemic stance adverbs), attitude, and style. These stance adverbs are found to be more common in spoken registers than in written registers, except for style adverbs (e.g., *generally, typically*) that are more frequently used by writers in academic disciplines, especially in textbooks (Biber, 2006a, 2006b; Biber et al., 1999). Stance adverbs in conversations may be used to indicate events that are likely to occur (e.g., "*This **probably** will be returned to you with no charge*"), to identify or underscore the veracity of information (e.g., "***Obviously**, I'm not going there right now and **clearly** there's something wrong with your phone*"), or to suggest options that might solve a problem (e.g., "*Let's remove the filter, the blue filter, this **possibly** will fix it*").

TABLE B3.1 Lexico/syntactic features used for stance analyses

I. Modals and Semi-Modals
- *can, could, may, might*
- *must, should, (had) better,* [have] *to, got to, ought to*
- *will, would, shall,* [be] *going to*

II. Adverbs of Stance
- Epistemic
  - Levels of Certainty or Doubt: e.g., *actually, certainly, never*
  - Likelihood: e.g., *apparently, perhaps, possibly*
- Attitude: e.g., *amazingly, importantly, surprisingly*
- Style/Perspective: e.g., *according to, generally, typically*

III. Complement Clauses That Follow Stance Verbs, Adjectives, or Nouns
i. Stance Complement Clauses That Follow Verbs
Stance Verb + *that*-Clause
- Epistemic Verbs
  - Certainty: e.g., *conclude, determine, know*
  - Likelihood: e.g., *believe, doubt, think*
- Attitude Verbs: e.g., *expect, hope, worry*
- Speech-Act and Other Communication Verbs (Non-Factual): e.g., *argue, claim, report, say*

Stance Verb + *to*-Clause
- Probability (Likelihood) Verbs: e.g., *appear, happen, seem*
- Mental (Cognition/Perception) Verbs: e.g., *consider, believe*
- Desire/Intention/Decision Verbs: e.g., *intend, need, want*
- Speech-Act and Other Communication Verbs: e.g., *advise, remind, request*

ii. Stance Complement Clauses that Follow Adjectives
Stance Adjective + *that*-Clause (often extraposed constructions)
- Epistemic Adjectives
  - Certainty: e.g., *certain, clear, obvious*
  - Likelihood: e.g., *(un)likely, possible, probable*
- Attitude/Emotion Adjectives: e.g., *amazed, shocked, surprised*
- Evaluation Adjectives: e.g., *essential, interesting, noteworthy*

Stance Adjective + *to*-Clause (often extraposed constructions)
- Epistemic (Certainty/Likelihood) Adjectives: e.g., *certain, likely, sure*
- Attitude/Emotion Adjectives: e.g., *happy, pleased, surprised*
- Evaluation Adjectives: e.g., *essential, important, necessary*
- Ability or Willingness Adjectives: e.g., *able, eager, willing*
- Ease or Difficulty Adjectives: e.g., *difficult, easy, hard*

iii. Stance Complement Clauses That Follow Nouns
Stance Noun + *that*-Clause
- Epistemic Nouns
- Certainty: e.g., *conclusion, fact, observation*
- Likelihood: e.g., *assumption, claim, hypothesis*
- Attitude/Perspective Nouns: e.g., *hope, view*
- Communication (Non-Factual) Nouns: e.g., *comment, proposal, report*

Stance Noun + *to*-Clause: e.g., *failure, obligation, tendency*

Source: adapted from Biber, 2006b, pp. 92–93

Stance Complement Clauses

Stance complement clauses comprise structures controlled by verbs, adjectives, and nouns followed by *that* or *to* clauses. These verb, adjective, and noun-controlled *that* or *to* clauses illustrate the functions of the semantic categories of the three part-of-speech classes (e.g., for verbs—certainty, likelihood, attitudinal, and communication) followed by clauses that complete the speaker's expression of personal feelings and evaluations (e.g., "*I* **think that** *it's going to be cheaper*" or "*I* **think** *Θ* *it's fine*"). Biber found that stance verb + *that* clause constructions are much more common in spoken university registers than in written registers. Certainty (e.g., *conclude, know*) and likelihood (e.g., *believe, think*) verbs were found to be the two most common semantic categories of verbs controlling *that* clauses.

B3.5.2 Expressing Stance in Spoken Corpora

Expressions of personal feelings, value judgments, and assessments are prevalent in many task-based interactions (e.g., service encounters, business meetings). Participants in the performance of tasks are not hesitant to express their personal feelings, especially in reaction to problematic instructions or suggestions. In reference to Friginal's (2009b) study of call center interactions in this subsection, it is clear, for example, that value judgments about offshore agents' provision of service and sometimes their use of language do occur. Within the subregisters of call center discourse, transactions that involve angry callers have resulted in higher frequencies of grammatical stance features than the number occurring in simple inquiry-type transactions, which are more often characterized by typical question-answer sequences. Conflicts and miscommunications in difficult transactions lead to an increase in the number of callers' personal assessments and value judgments. In addition, some grammatical stance features identified in previous research—for example, possibility and obligation modal verbs—are perhaps more common in call center interactions than in other spoken registers. The agents' directives while troubleshooting sequences or addressee-focused responses to questions typically involve modal verb phrasings to articulate a specific instruction or detail. Detailed explanations, expressions of possibility, and explicit cause-result statements commonly make use of these modal verb constructions to provide sufficient information to customers (e.g., "*. . . and you* **can** *restart the system after the uh application is installed . . . this* **can** *improve your machine's performance*"). Polite requests, which are very common in the transactions, are also expressed by using these modal verbs (e.g., "***May** I have your name and address, please?*").

Friginal (2009b) conducted a register comparison of stance categories in call center interactions, American Conversation, and Switchboard discussions. The American Conversation subcorpus, with over four million words, was obtained from the Longman Corpus of Spoken and Written English (LCSWE). This corpus was designed to be a representative corpus of American conversation covering a wide range of speech types (e.g., casual conversation, service encounters, task-related interaction), locations or settings (e.g., home, classroom), geographic regions in the United States, and speaker characteristics (e.g., age, gender, occupation). The **Switchboard Corpus** was collected by Texas Instruments and funded by the Defense Advanced Research Projects Agency (DARPA). This corpus is comprised of spontaneous conversations of "telephone bandwidth speech" between American speakers. The topics for conversation (e.g., *"What do you think about dress codes at work?"* or *"How do you feel about sending an elderly family member into a nursing home?"*) were randomly identified by the system. A complete set of Switchboard CD-ROMs available from the Linguistic Data Consortium includes about 2,430 conversations averaging six minutes in length (with over 240 hours of recorded speech) and about three million words of text, spoken by over 500 speakers of both sexes from every major dialect of American English ("Switchboard: A Users' Manual," 2004). The distribution of the major structural categories of stance features from Biber (2006b) across three spoken registers is shown in Figure B3.3.

Figure B3.3 shows that modal verbs are used more frequently in the Call Center and American Conversation Corpora compared to stance adverbs and stance complement clauses. This result, showing the frequent use of modal verbs as stance markers in conversation, mirrors the findings from Biber's (2006b) study of spoken university registers and relates to the distinction between modality and more specific stance meanings in the interpretation of the functions of these modal verbs in spoken discourse. For Switchboard, stance complement clauses are used more frequently than modal verbs and stance adverbs. It is likely that exchanges in Switchboard that use more certainty and likelihood verbs controlling *that* or *to* clauses (especially in expressing personal opinions, e.g., *"I **think that** we should consider message from other religions and not be afraid*

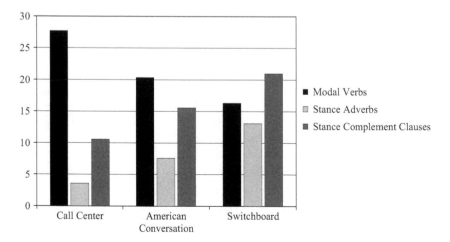

FIGURE B3.3 Major stance features across thee spoken registers, normalized per 1,000 words

Source: adapted from Friginal, 2009b, p. 151

of them when they are against, you know, western beliefs . . . that's what I think") greatly influence this distribution of stance markers across registers. Speakers in call center interactions have significantly more modal verbs and less stance adverbs and stance complement clauses than speakers in the other two registers of conversation in this study.

The spontaneous discussions of a wide range of topics in Switchboard call for more personal opinions and elaboration of ideas from speakers. These telephone-based discussions often sound academic rather than casual primarily because of distance as well as the level of formality and personal familiarity between the participants. There seems to be a need to further express epistemic stance through certainty and likelihood adverbs in supporting personal ideas or opinions as speakers discuss their assigned prompts. The short excerpts below illustrate the use of these stance adverbs in the Switchboard Corpus.

Text Sample B3.6. Common Use of Stance Adverbs in the Switchboard Corpus

<xces:u>0043: when you **certainly** can speak their language uh and there are problems with you know the wet back problem you know for everyone **certainly** knows what we're talking about when say wet back problem and then we should somehow</xces:u>
<xces:u>0044: yes, **obviously** that's the case, I agree with that, uh, **obviously** they know what it is although I wondered what **exactly** it was when I heard about it</xces:u>
<xces:u>0043: yes, uh-huh?

<xces945>just so **amazingly** intelligent and educated people. I mean they uh were **amazingly** empowered by that system. In my mind I mean.
<xces946> that is right. Perhaps we can say that we can also be empowered by a similar system, although<xces:u>
<xcess945>yeah, although, I don't know, **possibly**, uh<xces:u>
<xcess946>it it is possible I'm pretty sure
<xcess945>**possibly**

Reflective Break

- **More on the Switchboard Corpus**
  Data for Switchboard were collected under computer control and without human intervention. Interaction with the switchboard system was conducted via touchtones and recorded instructions given to the participants. The two speakers, once connected, were allowed by the system to "warm-up" before recording began. The speakers did not know each other personally and have no previous information about each other's personal background before the

warm-up conversation. The collection of speakers' sound files was transcribed following a documented transcription convention (see Switchboard Manual, available at http://www.ldc.upenn.edu/Catalog/readme_files/switchboard. readme.html) and encoded with a time-alignment file to show the beginning time and duration of specific words and turns in the transcripts. Transcriptions were checked for formatting and accuracy by an automated scripting program. Information about the speakers, together with the dates, times, and other pertinent data about each phone call, was recorded in a database. This supplemental demographic information was provided in the accompanying corpus files.

- Do you consider Switchboard as a corpus of "**naturally occurring telephone conversation**"? Why or why not?
- Aside from register comparison, what sociolinguistic research questions can you investigate using the Switchboard Corpus?

B3.5.3 Gender and Stance Expressions in Conversation

Precht (2008) investigated the distributions of stance expressions used by men and women in conversations by comparing three groups of stance markers: *affect*, *evidentials*, and *quantifiers* (Table B3.2). These three groups are divided into subcategories including *expletives, factuality*, and *hedges*. As with Biber's (2006b) categories, these makers can be tagged and searched easily from a corpus.

Related studies on gender and **affect** show that men use more expletives, insults, and explicit expressions of anger than women. On the other hand, women

TABLE B3.2 Stance expressions by category

Affect
  Opinion, attitude, lexical backchannels
    love, like, hate, interesting, good, bad, beautiful, ugly
  Expletives, exclamations
    boy, damn, dude, fuck, gee, god, gosh, hell, shit
  Disposition
    would like, need (to), want (to), feared (that)
Evidentiality
  Certainty, doubt, factuality
    definitely, seem, actually, true, look, right, seem, show, sure, told, true
  Mental verbs
    know, think, believe
Quantifier
  Emphatics
    always, especially, much, never, a lot, such a, totally, very
  Hedges
    probably, sometimes, a bit, almost, sort of, usually

Source: adapted from Precht, 2008, p. 92

tend to express less vulgarity and softer criticisms. **Evidentials** suggest speakers' degree of certainty or doubt and studies focusing on gender and certainty and factuality have focused on the use of mental verbs and egocentric sequences (e.g., *I think, I believe*). As Precht (2008) stated, a hedge or evidential marker could be used to show a range of emotions from modesty, insecurity, and camaraderie to sarcasm. Research on gender and quantifiers has examined how hedges and emphatics could be interpreted by prevailing norms.

Precht's (2008) data also came from the LCSWE. From this corpus, three contexts of conversation were chosen: adult-only, family, and work. Adult-only texts included conversations among related and unrelated adults where no children were present, while family included related adults and children. Work texts included any conversations involving people in a variety of work contexts. There are relatively equal proportions by gender, context, and age in Precht's final database for comparison, with about 7,000 words per text from 127 hours of conversation. Table B3.3 shows a summary of stance expressions with significant differences between men and women in conversations.

Precht (2008) found a total of 34 statistically significant expressions (out of 180) from men and women in conversations highlighted in Table B3.3. In **affect**, men had significantly higher frequencies than women for three stance expressions: *third person + like, problem, stupid*, while women had significantly higher frequencies of *better, glad, okay/backchannel, thank*. Men's stance expressions seemed to be more negative than women's, in general.

TABLE B3.3 Stance expressions with significant differences between men and women

Stance Expression Categories	Men Higher	Women Higher
Affect		
General	*they like*	*better*
opinion	*problem*	*glad*
attitude	*stupid*	*okay* (backchannel)
emotion		*thank*
Expletives/	*damn*	*gosh*
exclamations	*dude*	
fuck		
hell		
shit		
Disposition	*I need to*	*I dont want to*
Evidentials		
General	*actually*	
definitely		
sure		

(*Continued*)

TABLE B3.3 (*Continued*)

Mental verbs	*guess* + 0	*I know* + clause
you think + 0		
I thought		
I wonder		
Quantifiers		
Hedges	*about*	*almost*
basically	*maybe*	
like+ adj or noun	*well*/hedge	
pretty		
Emphatics	*even* + verb	*so* + adj
a lot		
totally		

Source: adapted from Precht, 2008, p. 99

B3.6 Hedges and Nouns of Vague Reference

Finally in this section, we look at the distribution of hedges and nouns of vague reference in American English conversations. Spoken discourse makes use of devices with vague reference (e.g., *stuff*, *thing*, or *things*), coordination tags (e.g., *and stuff like that*, *or something like that*), and hedges (e.g., *kind of*, *sort of*) because speakers often share similar and familiar contexts and have the same pressure of immediate online production. Nouns of vague reference and hedges are very common in casual interactions between participants who are not "required" to provide actual and more specific subjects to complete a turn. The use of these devices in casual conversation presupposes a common understanding of topics and issues between speakers so that the failure to complete a thought unit is often tolerated and compensated for by continued turn-taking, responses, or immediate topic shifts.

In most instances, these linguistic features are also used to mitigate potential threat to face created by an overly direct statement (Quaglio, 2009). However, for formal and performance-based interactions such as job interviews, broadcast talks, and lectures, these hedges and vague conversational devices may not be acceptable or preferred by listeners and may also affect subjective impressions about a speaker's ability to express clear and complete ideas and/or their knowledge and competence. Figure B3.4 shows the distribution of hedges, nouns of vague reference, and coordination tags from American conversation texts of the LCSWE.

The need for speakers in purposeful, focused interactions such as job interviews or clinical discussions between doctors and patients to be more specific in communicating ideas and information to the listener potentially limits the use of these conversational devices. Because of the more formal level of talk in these contexts, participants may need to provide complete information and thoughts and not opt to

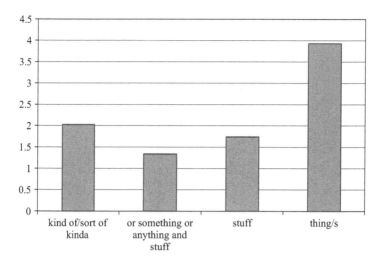

FIGURE B3.4 Distribution of hedges and nouns of vague reference in conversation from the LCSWE, normalized per 1,000 words

utilize shortcuts in their turns as they might in casual conversation. Nouns of vague reference (*stuff* and *thing/s*) are more common in face-to-face conversations than in other spoken registers. The text sample below shows repetitive vague references and hedges (e.g., "*yeah, good* **stuff**"; "*usual* **stuff**"; "*that* **thing**"; "*that particular* **thing**").

Text Sample B3.7. Hedges and Nouns of Vague Reference in American Conversation from the LCSWE

<1309> a lot of it or anything but I think they bought some good **stuff**

<1308> Wednesday and doing a lot of **stuff** usual **stuff** you worry about in large crowds <unclear> so I keep how they do and **stuff** and then realized she didn't see her mother has this **stuff** appear on your screen, but if you have a printer put my **stuff** on

<1310> No we're getting a lot of **stuff** for our software, we're from the Land's End Outlet? . . . any particular, I mean the **stuff**

<1310> A lot of computer-assisted **stuff** allergies because it's **stuff** that's sucked through the water up my **stuff** before I want to move up . . . well I guess I could move

<1309> And then you would bring the **stuff** up <unclear>

<1311> And then we'd bring the rest of the **stuff** <unclear> that

<1309> because most of the **stuff** I can actually fit in my car ours, we'll take the extra seats out and just **stuff** 'em in <unclear> move her **stuff** her **stuff** up and spend a day or so there, then <unclear> written up some **stuff** that we'd do in Tucson and just cave **stuff** and, and cool imagery and symbols and it . . .

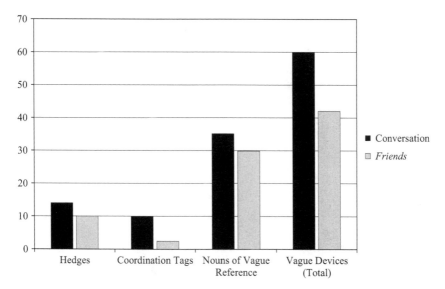

FIGURE B3.5 Comparison of vague devices in conversation and *Friends*, data normalized per 1,000 words

Source: adapted from Quaglio, 2009, p. 74

Reflective Break

- Quaglio (2009) and Overstreet and Yule (1997) noted that vague language is stigmatized because of its apparent ambiguity and also its potential lack of fluency. However, the use of vague expressions has been shown to serve important functions in conversations. For instance, vague expressions can minimize the impact of overly direct statements. In this context, vague language also functions as a politeness marker. Have you used these expressions to specifically address face threatening situations? Did you accomplish your communicative goals? Do you think women use more vague references than men in casual conversations? Why or why not?
- A study by Quaglio (2009) compared the distributions of hedges, coordination tags, and nouns of vague reference from face-to-face American conversation (also a subset of the LCSWE) and sitcom dialogues from the TV show *Friends*. Quaglio collected TV scripts of *Friends* episodes online in order to compare similarities and differences between a scripted comedy and real-world interaction. Figure B3.5 shows Quaglio's comparative results.
  - Analyze and try to explain the distributions in this figure. What do think are the primary reasons for these variations? To what extent do scripted TV comedies represent real-world conversations?
  - As an application of Quaglio's data, do you think we can use TV shows as accurate examples of American English conversation, especially for ESL or EFL teaching purposes? Provide supporting details to your answer.

B4

WORKPLACE DISCOURSE

B4.1 Spoken and Written Professional Discourse

Research studies focusing on spoken and written professional discourse are directly related to the subfields of English for Specific Purposes (ESP) or English for Occupational Purposes (EOP). Over the past 20 years, ESP and EOP have both become highly corpus-based with respect to how linguistic data are collected and analyzed. A survey of articles from many recent issues of the *English for Specific Purposes Journal*, for example, shows that linguistic descriptions of special or occupational varieties of English are almost always based on corpus analysis (Biber, Reppen, & Friginal, 2010).

Despite obvious limitations (e.g., in capturing accent or suprasegmental features of speech), corpus linguistics has made it possible to investigate salient linguistic features of spoken professional discourse and compare their distributions across internal and external categories of transcribed text. Results from comparative analyses and interpretations of linguistic patterns of spoken texts have led to conclusions about the functional parameters influencing the linguistic choices of professionals. Overall, corpus-based methodologies still remain underexploited in the analysis of spoken discourse, but a growing number of CL studies has examined the frequency distribution and statistical co-occurrence patterns of professional, spoken registers within ESP/EOP. Results from studies that merged corpora and discourse analyses have offered new directions for the empirical investigations of spoken discourse in the workplace. For example, Sinclair's (2000) study of the interaction of lexis and grammar in association patterns of speech, Rayson, Leech, and Hodges's (1997) corpus-based analysis of language usage that is differentiated socially and contextually, and Rühlemann's (2007) corpus-driven approach in the study of conversation in context all provided in-depth descriptions of the characteristic features of lexis and grammar in professional or business conversations.

McCarthy and Handford (2004) investigated the structure of spoken business English using the Cambridge and Nottingham Corpus of Business English (CANBEC). They presented the different dimensions of business talk in relation to everyday casual conversation. CANBEC and the Cambridge Business Corpus (CBC) have both been used in the production of business training textbooks (e.g., the "Business Advantage" series of Cambridge University Press). The CBC has 200 million words of spoken and written texts from, or relating to, business interactions. CANBEC features a collection of spoken business English texts transcribed from recorded interactions from various multinational companies to smaller firms. Texts include meetings, business presentations, telephone interactions, and conversations in informal settings.

The study of written professional discourse has covered topics and subregisters such as written legal language, grant proposals, fundraising letters (especially mailed letters), business letters and memos, and business/financial news articles. Professional, written texts from the CBC and also from the Wolverhampton Corpus of Written Business English (WBE) have been tagged and analyzed to directly produce linguistic distributions for various ESP/EOP applications. For example, Fuentes-Olivera (2007) examined the distributions of lexical gender (e.g., *Mr.*, *Mrs.*, *Miss* or *Ms.*) in the WBE, investigating whether or not the "male-as-norm" principle in business contributed to reinforcing typical gender stereotypes. Results showed that for each "woman" referred to in the WBE Corpus, there were more than 100 occurrences for "man." However, patterns of "non-sexist English" were found to influence written business English in some contexts. "*Ms.*" was used more than nine times as frequently as "*Mrs.*" and "*Miss*," suggesting that "*Ms.*" had been accepted as the norm in professional settings.

The WBE Corpus is a specialized corpus of business English collected online from a total of 23 Web sites. This corpus has over 10 million words of written business texts that were posted on the Internet during a six-month period from 1999 to 2000. Texts from the WBE comprise product descriptions, company press releases, and annual financial reports, business journals, academic research papers, political speeches, and government reports. Additional transcripts of speeches during business meetings amount to about 0.7 percent of the total corpus. Several texts were obtained from organizations such as the World Trade Organization, and official documents (with 123 files and 765,005 words) were collected from press releases, research and analysis reports, trade policy reviews, ministerial conferences, and public domain speeches. This ingenious collection to create a specialized corpus from publicly available materials online illustrates the importance of the Internet in CL. As noted by Fuentes-Olivera (2007), the WBE Corpus could also be used to explore variations in business English from different countries (e.g., Hong Kong English, WTO English, British English, American English). These cross-cultural comparisons in the context of business

English could provide further information about the similarities and differences of global written Business English varieties and practices. Considering the authors and intended audience of business documents and also other coded variables such as gender and tasks would certainly be relevant research foci for WBE and other similar specialized corpora.

B4.2 Studying Workplace Discourse

Over the years, large-scale, longitudinal collection of workplace corpora has been initiated to also include many sociolinguistic categories such as gender/age, occupation, power relationships, and workers with disabilities. ESP and EOP studies on workplace discourses often focus specifically on practical and pragmatic applications of communication patterns (see, e.g., Bargiela-Chiappini & Harris, 1997; Handford, 2010; Warren, 2004). Audio and video recordings of workplace interactions have been used to identify the characteristics of effective communication or diagnose potential causes of miscommunication. Cross-cultural contexts using English in global business communication have also been investigated, especially within ESP/EOP and World Englishes. The Wellington Language in the Workplace Project (LWP), the AAC and Non-AAC Workplace Corpus (ANAWC), and the Hong Kong Corpus of Spoken English (HKCSE) are profiled in the following sections.

B4.2.1 The Wellington Language in the Workplace Project (LWP)

The Wellington Language in the Workplace Project (LWP) at Victoria University of Wellington, New Zealand (Holmes, 2000; Stubbe, 2001), has collected over 1,500 interactions from 450 people in 20 different government and private workplace settings. Work with the LWP has included the analysis of meetings, humor in the workplace, and gender and cultural issues. Various social demographics of speakers are encoded in the corpus (e.g., gender of speakers, ethnicity, and age, together with roles or particular occupations in New Zealand). The LWP also features interactions from small businesses and factories and organizations with workers with intellectual disabilities. Many qualitative analyses of workplace settings from the LWP have produced functional applications and comprehensive descriptions of unique contexts. For instance, Holmes (2003) and Holmes and Fillary (2000) followed workers with intellectual disabilities in order to investigate their participation in small talk (i.e., the discussion of topics that are unconnected with workplace tasks) and their use of formulaic responses with coworkers. These studies reported that workers with intellectual disabilities tended not to engage in social talk and often gave brief, monosyllabic answers when they were solicited to participate in social interactions.

Ongoing research on the LWP is conducted by a team of linguists under the supervision of sociolinguist **Janet Holmes**, who is also LWP's project director.

Aside from the LWP, over the years, Holmes has published seminal studies focusing on gender in conversation, gender in the workplace, pragmatic applications of gendered speech, and also on social dialect surveys of English in New Zealand. She has authored or coedited multiple sociolinguistics (text)books and readers (e.g., *An Introduction to Sociolinguistics*; *Gendered Talk at Work, Women, Men and Politeness*; the *Blackwell Handbook of Language and Gender*; and *Gendered Speech in Social Context*). Holmes's work with the LWP is supported by the government of New Zealand, and the project specifically explores the applications of various pragmalinguistic findings for New Zealand workplaces. The LWP team sets out to document the characteristics of effective communication in the workplace and also to diagnose possible causes of miscommunication in actual on-the-job conversations. Holmes (2005) has also studied mentoring and how gender may or may not influence the processes of mentoring within a leadership perspective. And finally, from 2006, the LWP team has studied the language of leadership in organizations specifically examining the similarities and differences in *Māori* (indigenous people of New Zealand) and *Pākehā* (New Zealanders who are of European descent) leadership styles. The research team continues to investigate how *Māori* leadership strategies and communication styles are being utilized (or underutilized) in mainstream business settings in New Zealand.

Corpus-based studies using the LWP corpus are relatively outnumbered by published qualitative case studies and discourse analyses using LWP texts. However, the distributional data of tagged linguistic features of the LWP has been produced, and some register comparisons have also been conducted. For example, Pickering, Friginal, Vine, Bouchard, and Clegg (2013) compared the distribution of modal verbs and stance markers from the LWP with the AAC and Non-AAC Workplace Corpus (ANAWC) from workplace settings in the United States. (We introduce this corpus in the section below.) Modal verbs *can, could, might, be able to* were the most commonly used modals to convey a low level of force and a high level of tentativeness and politeness in workplace settings, especially in the context of giving directions and instructions. Results from Pickering and colleagues (2013) showed that there was a clear difference in the use of modals and their functional groups between workplaces in New Zealand and the United States. Speakers from the United States used significantly fewer modals overall (see Figure B4.1) and also fewer modals of permission, possibility, and ability (e.g., *can, could, may*), and modals of obligation and necessity (e.g., *should, must*). In general, American workplaces used 40 percent fewer modals than those in New Zealand.

An LWP qualitative study conducted by Vine (2009) looked at the influence of contextual factors on the frequency and expression of directives given by three managers working in two New Zealand government departments. Various aspects of social context, including purpose of interaction, participant status (power), and social distance were found to clearly affect both directive frequency and expression. Daly, Holmes, Newton, and Stubbe (2004) adopted a *community of practice* (Lave & Wenger, 1991) framework to explore aspects of politeness within a

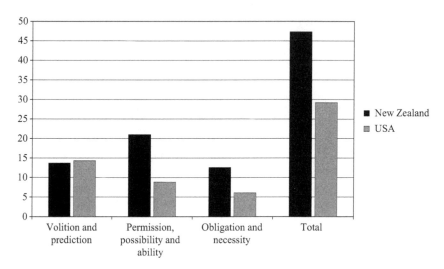

FIGURE B4.1 Comparison of modal verb categories in directives: New Zealand vs. United States, normalized per 1,000 words

Source: adapted from Pickering et al., 2013

work-team culture. The community of practice approach focuses on what members do within the work group. In this context, coworkers are observed by focusing on the activities and behavioral norms that they share and the extent to which they identify with other group members. This approach also accounts for collective beliefs, values, and relationships of members.

Daly and colleagues (2004) followed Wenger's (1998) model in analyzing community of practice based on patterns of interaction within shared ways of engaging and doing things together. Shared activities in the workplace encourage displaying group membership, such as common greetings and leave-takings, social and small talks, and the use of humor and figurative language. The researchers emphasize that over time, workplace communities construct a unique set of discursive practices from the resources available to them, compatible with other aspects of the way they work together. These shared practices, and the ways in which individuals conform to or challenge the group's norms, contribute to the construction of a particular community of practice (Daly et al., 2004, p. 947).

One manifestation of group membership and cohesiveness is the acknowledgement and common use of politeness markers and expletives in work settings. Daly and colleagues (2004) explored the range of expletives used by a group of factory workers, particularly *fuck*, which was repeated most frequently and consistently across different speech acts. *Fuck* has a range of meanings and functions especially as a more overtly attention-grabbing particle (e.g., *fuck! look at that*) and an intensifier (e.g., *that's fucking amazing*). The corpus frequency of *fuck* in the

LWP can be easily identified by concordances across settings, and Daly and colleagues looked at distributions of *fuck* that may serve to express positive politeness or solidarity and also potentially function as a mitigator of the strength of complaints or concerns from factory workers. They suggested that in certain contexts, forms of *fuck* may serve to express team identification—a "we know each [other] well thing" (p. 949).

A form of an indirect complaint (referred to as a *whinge*) indicated that the addressee was not held responsible for the perceived offence, and the whinge provided a means of off-loading negative feelings in a safe, collegial environment. These expressions may include *fuck* often to acknowledge camaraderie and team work. Text Sample B4.1 from Daly and colleagues (2004) illustrates whinges between two male factory workers who were close friends. Speaker "Russell" had done overtime work to earn extra money, and his colleagues had been teasing him about this. In this excerpt, Russell was whingeing that he did not receive the accurate payment the previous week.

Text Sample B4.1. Whinge with Expletive *Fuck* in Workplace Conversations from (Daly et al., 2004)

Context: Robert, a Samoan male aged 25 to 29, working as a manufacturer, is talking to Russell, a Samoan European male also aged 25 to 29, who is a packer.

1 Russell: *fuck* man I got a short pay last week again ++
2 eight ninety + that's only for three days ++
3 Robert: ( ) + eight ninety? + stick it up your *fucking* arse
4 you did overtime you *cunt* +
5 Russell: oh yeah too high
6 Robert: (yep) + you get that this week eh +
7 *fuck* I won't get mine till next week
8 Russell: oh yeah Sunday eh
9 Robert: I did yesterday
10 Russell: yeah +
11 Robert: Sunday Sunday

In this excerpt, Daly and colleagues (2004) suggested that Russell's attention-grabbing device in line 1 (*fuck man . . .*) followed by this expression of complaint was a whinge that was acknowledged humorously by Robert. Robert's response in line 3 challenged the information in Russell's whinge, which then turned the table for him to initiate his own complaint in line 7 (*fuck I won't get mine till next week*), matching Russell's whinge. The language and exchanging complaints in this excerpt showed clear solidarity and agreement even with the contradictory statements and use of expletives and hyperbolic vulgarities (e.g., *stick it up your fucking arse . . . you cunt*). As members of a community of practice, Robert and

Russell maintained a similar tone and style of language that mirrored each other's focus and attention to discourse.

What is the contribution of CL/corpora in this context? The frequency data from the LWP corpus helped direct the design of Daly and colleagues' research. Corpus-based information on a certain feature like expletives could be easily obtained from corpora to justify the point of sociolinguistic or pragmatic comparisons. There are then many options to pursue in analyzing linguistic patterns and how social constructs such as community of practice or power relationships influence communicative exchanges.

Reflective Break

- How common do you think expletives are in the workplace? What social contexts will have to be present among the participants for these expletives to become part of the conversational norms? Have you heard expletives in academic settings such as the classroom or during office hour interactions? What will be your reaction if your instructor uses the word *fuck* in class?
- What expletives have you used with your coworkers and in what situations have you used them?

B4.2.2 The AAC and Non-AAC Workplace Corpus (ANAWC)

A study by Friginal, Pearson, Di Ferrante, Pickering, and Bruce (2013) examined the linguistic co-occurrence features of workplace discourse of persons with *communication impairments* who use **augmentative and alternative communication** (AAC) devices (see Figure B4.2). Perhaps the most visible form of an AAC device is the one used by theoretical physicist **Stephen Hawking**. Hawking, who is almost completely paralyzed, relies on his Voice Output Communication Aid (VOCA) to deliver his lectures and communicate with colleagues and students in academia, as well as with family and personal acquaintances in nonprofessional settings. AAC devices are presumed to facilitate interaction and promote fuller participation for users in most social situations. Often, AAC users are primarily dependent on their equipment to perform basic communicative spoken or written tasks as they ask a range of questions and provide responses to people around them. Pickering and Bruce (2009) designed and collected the AAC and Non-AAC Workplace Corpus (ANAWC) from workplace settings in the United States. It features over 220 hours of spoken interaction involving 8 focal participants and more than 100 interlocutors in seven different work locations. The specialized nature of this type of spoken corpora requires well-defined procedures for recording and transcribing interactions. The ANAWC was collected based on procedures rather similar to those used in the LWP (Holmes, 2000, 2009). Participant-controlled speech samples were gathered over five consecutive workdays to ensure a wide range of routine and novel range of topics. Interactions were captured via wearable digital voice recorders.

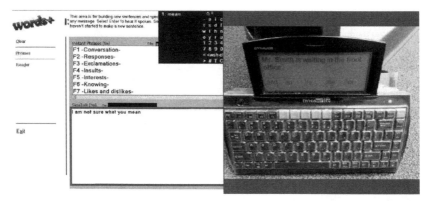

FIGURE B4.2 Sample display options from AAC devices ezKeys and Dynawrite

For corpus collection, the audio transcription for the ANAWC required an incredible amount of time for cleaning and annotating texts. Transcribed texts were subjected to random accuracy checks to promote reliability of transcription, and all personal identifiers (e.g., names, proper nouns, addresses, phone numbers, etc.) were meticulously replaced by generic proper nouns in the corpus. The transcripts were also partly annotated for nonverbal markers and other markups (e.g., length of pauses, number of filled pauses, and vocalizations). The ANAWC analyzed by Friginal and colleagues (2013) comprised approximately 464,000 words in two subcorpora—one with AAC users in the workplace (214,619 words) and one from their non-AAC counterparts (249,503 words). These subcorpora represented interactions of eight focal participants and their various interlocutors across a typical (40-hour) workweek. AAC users produced far less speech as measured by number of words (a range of 614 to 5,676 words) than their non-AAC, job-similar counterparts (a range of 18,057 to 45,312 words) in a typical workweek. This finding was not at all surprising, given reports of the labor-intensive nature of AAC devices and the limitations of preprogrammed pages (Wisenburn & Higginbotham, 2008). However, ANAWC transcripts indicate that AAC participants make use of vocalizations (e.g., sounds indicating short responses to yes/no questions), not counted as actual words, which often substituted for their linguistic responses or backchannels in interactions. Friginal and colleagues (2013) noted that there was no major difference between the total word counts of interlocutors (i.e., coworkers) of the eight target participants in the two subcorpora.

The majority of the turns by AAC participants included one-word or preprogrammed chunks such as *yeah, yes, no, I don't know, soon, tomorrow*, which reflected the way interlocutors addressed many of the communicative tasks when working with AAC users. Beyond the documented limitations of AAC devices for workplace communication, however, the linguistic limitations of AAC users appear to be manageable in the ANAWC dataset during a 40-hour workweek. Lengthy preprogrammed information might be necessary for the likes of Stephen Hawking and others who are engaged in giving lectures or training support to various listeners, as an improved device would provide longer, in-depth answers that could minimize wait times. For others in more conventional office settings, additional support for the use of specific key/common vocabulary (content words) and some office-based formulaic sequences may improve the flow of question-answer turns.

A sociolinguistic comparison of the two subcorpora of the ANAWC showed microscopic differences in AAC versus non-AAC interactions. For instance, most measures focusing on lexical variety/diversity and richness show that AAC texts have lower average counts for type-token ratio, length of turns, and word count (per hour/day) compared to their non-AAC counterparts. AAC users, however, have more content words—nouns and verbs—on average (normalized frequencies) in their turns (Figure B4.3). These key content words are often delivered as a one-word or part of a phrasal response to a question (e.g., *Atlanta, the kitchen, communicate*). AAC users relied on lexical verbs to indicate actions or procedures in their responses to interlocutors. These lexical verbs include very few mental/ private verbs compared to typical conversation corpora (Friginal, 2009b). More proper nouns (especially names of people, places, and events) were frequently distributed across AAC texts including the use of concrete nouns (e.g., *camera, computer*), animate nouns (e.g., *applicant, patient, child*), and nominalizations (e.g., *communication, interaction*).

There were limited AAC user-initiated topics and very few narratives and responses to small talk (Di Ferrante, 2012). Most AAC responses did not feature

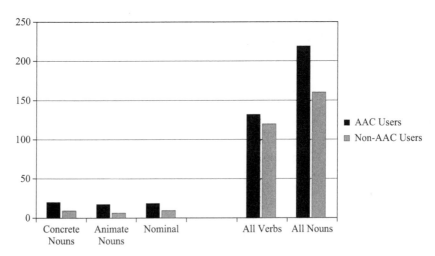

FIGURE B4.3 Comparison of AAC and non-AAC texts verbs, nouns, and semantic categories of nouns, normalized per 1,000 words

Source: adapted from Friginal et al., 2013, p. 290

personal pronouns and private verbs (e.g., *think, feel, believe*), although overall, AAC users had more normalized counts for all verbs than non-AAC users. In the text excerpt below, AAC user "Ron" was communicating with a coworker by providing short nominal responses (e.g., *city, address, truck*). Ron used vocalizations and nonverbal responses in complementing his speech-generated utterances. The coworker appeared to follow and comprehend Ron's turns completely and was able to introduce topic shifts that were not directly related to their primary conversational task. The excerpt illustrated that Ron was able to successfully provide direct responses or information needed by the coworker. However, the coworker's several clarifications and questions in this short excerpt were clearly triggered by Ron's limited speech production.

Text Sample B4.2. Sample AAC User Interaction (from Friginal et al., 2013)

1 *AAC-Ron: City*
2 Coworker: He wants me to do the epic route power out tomorrow morning
3 *AAC-Ron: And*
4 Coworker: They've got a bit swim meet he wants me to get up at three and check if it's snowing go in at four coz the rest of the crew comes in at six on Saturday so I'm gonna get a jump on it
5 *AAC-Ron: And*
6 Coworker: No just street address will be fine
7 *AAC-Ron: Address*
8 Coworker: But it's a good thing you asked. I'm listening where is this going in? On the side? On the bottom? You got these upside down sir
9 *AAC-Ron: Right address*
10 Coworker: You bragging, I'm leading
11 *AAC-Ron: [voc]*
12 Coworker: I getting ornery but
13 *AAC-Ron: Right*
14 Coworker: What? I just read yours? Told ya I'm gettin ornery. But see if I'm right, go ahead.
15 *AAC-Ron: No city*
16 Coworker: [laughing] I was right
17 *AAC-Ron: [voc] I can do a lot of things but reading lines is not one [voc]*
18 Coworker: [laughing] uh oh did I lose my ten dollar bill? I lost my ten dollar bill. You see a ten dollar bill floatin' around it's mine.
19 *AAC-Ron: Look in the truck*
20 Coworker: His should have been black ones
21 *AAC-Ron: Look in the truck*
22 Coworker: Huh?
23 *AAC-Ron: Look in the truck*
24 Coworker: Good thinking you're right. What truck?

Phrasal discourse markers and formulaic sequences in conversation (e.g., *you know, I mean, well, that's what I thought*) were not common in AAC turns nor were dysfluencies (e.g., filled pauses and repeats), which were therefore not present in the transcripts. AAC users also had very limited stance markers and hedges in their texts compared to non-AAC users. Workplace discourse is highly interactive and involved, often making use of narrative markers (e.g., past tense verbs and third person pronouns) and situation-dependent references (use of time and place adverbial markers). Non-AAC corpus data showed extensive use of communicative features such as discourse markers of participation (e.g., *you know*) and information management (e.g., *okay, well*), but these were not common in AAC interactions.

Reflective Break

- Detailed qualitative analyses of conversational features such as small talk, topic shifts, turn-taking, and interruptions in the ANAWC are being conducted to also focus on how AAC devices influence the way coworkers frame utterances or questions to AAC users. With regard to topic selection, an initial analysis of the ANAWC showed that common topics in general workplace settings (e.g., weather, health, family, appearance, professional life, sports, and people known by the participants) were also frequent in the corpus together with other topics such as food and drinks, technology/mass media, and (extended) greeting routines (Pearson et al., 2011). These identified topics and contexts potentially help in mapping the structure of workplace exchanges. Further analysis will account not only for the typologies and number of topics, functions, and distributions in ANAWC, but also for hierarchies and conflict mechanisms based on, for example, power or gender dynamics (Di Ferrante, 2012).
- What do you think are additional areas of sociolinguistic research that could be conducted using an expanded ANAWC? Do you think gender in the workplace with AAC users will influence the distribution of some linguistic features? What are these features?
- How do power relationships, age, and task-based contexts influence linguistic use in AAC-based interactions?

B4.2.3 The Hong Kong Corpus of Spoken English (HKCSE)

The Hong Kong Corpus of Spoken English includes over two million words of texts transcribed from 50 hours of recorded naturally occurring talk. The corpus is divided equally into four subcorpora: academic, conversation, business, and public. Collected in Hong Kong between 1997 and 2002, the HKCSE was recorded in different contexts of spoken discourse from academic lectures in lecture halls and conversation in university offices to interactions from churches and public utility centers. Two versions of this corpus exist: one orthographic and the other prosodically transcribed. The HKCSE has been described as an intercultural corpus featuring English interactions of various cultural groups based in Hong Kong's metropolitan areas. Most participants who contributed to the recordings were Hong Kong Chinese speakers of English and native English speakers in academic and business settings (see Cheng & Warren, 2005; Warren, 2004).

A book about the HKCSE entitled *A Corpus-Driven Study of Discourse Intonation: The Hong Kong Corpus of Spoken English (prosodic)* (Cheng, Greaves, & Warren, 2008) provides detailed description of the corpus collection and prosodic transcription for the HKCSE as well as information on a software program called the iConc Concordancing Program, which can be used to explore HKCSE texts. The main focus of both the book and the structure of the prosodic corpus was to apply David Brazil's Discourse Intonation model in the manual transcription of texts. About 53 percent of the HKCSE has been prosodically transcribed and made available in electronic format as part of the book. So far, the HKCSE is the largest prosodically transcribed corpus currently in existence, although it is not the first corpus to have included a prosodic transcription component. In fact, the London-Lund Corpus has some prosodic transcription indicating tone units, onsets, direction of nuclear tones, and some degrees of stress. The Survey of English Usage corpus (Svartnik, 1990) has a more complete marking of prosodic features, including degrees of loudness and tempo, modifications in voice quality, and other paralinguistic features. Also, the Lancaster/IBM Spoken English Corpus (SEC) (Knowles, Wichmann, & Alderson, 1996) marked tone groups, stressed and accented syllables, pitch direction, and simple and complex tones (Cheng et al., 2008).

Brazil's (1985, 1997) *Discourse Intonation Systems* argues that spontaneous speech is a purpose-driven talk that is directed by the choices speakers make in a context-dependent environment. Brazil emphasizes that speaker intonational choices include four systems: prominence, tone, key, and determination. These systems could be incorporated in the transcription of spoken texts to highlight particular intonation patterns within an annotated context (e.g., native English speaker and nonnative speaker distinctions). The HKCSE followed a prosodic transcription of Brazil's model that represented very impressive but highly time-consuming manual work, which sets the stage for future transcription models of spoken texts. Extensive training for transcribers of the prosodic component of the HKCSE was necessary and Cheng and colleagues (2008) have also documented problems and challenges they encountered while transcribing and annotating prosodic texts. These challenges would be very useful to consider, particularly for researchers who intend to work beyond verbatim or orthographic corpus transcriptions of spoken discourse. An intertranscriber reliability measure was utilized to ensure the quality and consistency of the transcription and these prosodic transcriptions were similarly subjected to cross-checking involving three individuals and an expert researcher/transcriptionist.

Discourse intonation combines a description of the grammatical and attitudinal functions of intonation in speech. Grammatical descriptions suggest that some tones are typically used within particular syntactic structures, such as a rising tone for *yes/no* questions and a falling tone with *wh* questions, statements, and commands. Attitudinal description of intonation on the other hand assigns meanings to certain tones depending on the function of the utterance. A rising tone, for example, maybe attributed to expressions of solidarity and friendliness in informal contexts; the same rising tone may indicate frustration in more formal business settings. Brazil's model of intonation in discourse has been applied in various settings of naturally occurring speech. Pickering (2001, 2004), for example, explored the role of tone choice and the structures and functions of intonational paragraphs from university teaching assistants who are not native speakers of English.

Detailed sociolinguistic studies focusing specifically on social demographics and situational categories of speech across these intonation systems could certainly be conducted and developed further. The HKCSE has been transcribed and annotated to match definite sociolinguistic research questions, and the subfield merging corpus-based approaches and representations of suprasegmental features of speech certainly benefits from more additional research using this corpus. Brazil's model, which also originated from interrelated practical and pragmatic systems (see, for example, Cauldwell, 1997; Coulthard & Brazil, 1981; Coulthard & Montgomery, 1981; Hewings, 1990; Sinclair & Brazil, 1982), is directly concerned with the functional and communicative value of English intonation. Hence, this model is relevant to studies in cross-cultural communication and cross-cultural pragmatics (Cheng & Warren, 2005).

The business subcorpus of the HKCSE contains audio-recorded interactions from various business and professional settings. Texts were obtained from hotel and airport reception desks, information kiosks, meeting rooms in business organizations, and administrative offices. Additional data were taken from existing Web sites of different organizations in Hong Kong. More than 29 hours of audio recorded interactions came from service encounters, meetings, interviews, presentations and announcements, conference call/video conferencing, informal office talk, and workplace telephone talk. Conversation texts (27 hours total) and public discourse (25 hours total) feature speeches, speeches followed by question and answer (Q&A), press briefings (also followed by Q&A), interviews (TV and radio), and discussion forums. The academic discourse subcorpus of the HKCSE consists of lectures, seminars, tutorials, and staff workshops collected from various departments of the Hong Kong Polytechnic University (Cheng et al., 2008).

B4.2.4 The Corpus of Spoken Professional American-English (CSPA)

The Corpus of Spoken Professional American-English (CSPA) was collected by Michael Barlow (1998) between 1994 and 1998. The two million–word CSPA includes interactions from about 400 different individuals focusing on professional academic and political topics. A copy of this corpus is available for purchase. CSPA registers are divided into academic discussions (faculty council meetings and committee meetings related to assessment) and political question-and-answer sessions

(White House press conferences). CSPA texts from the White House press corps during the presidency of Bill Clinton (the 42nd president of the United States) contain policy statements and official White House statements on various political issues. Interactions among speakers consist mainly of question-and-answer sessions with the White House press secretary and members of the White House press corps. Academic discussions from university faculty meetings and various committee meetings held at different locations around the United States focus on the creation of national assessment instruments. Interactions also include some questions, but for the most part, they involve extended discussion of issues and statements. Barlow provided a comparison of some features of these two groups of registers (Table B4.1) with each other and also with a one million–word newspaper corpus.

The small selection of linguistic measures from Barlow (1998) below provides a brief comparison of the two spoken registers with a written (newspaper) register. Question marks, and therefore, the number of questions, were extremely frequent—as would be expected in White House press briefings—but were relatively rare in newspaper texts. The frequency of the first person pronoun *I* in meetings (1.99%) and in the White House texts (1.20%) was higher than the newspaper paper corpus. The pronoun *it* (0.69%) was the most common pronoun in the newspaper corpus.

The CSPA includes transcription markups for paralinguistic features such as laughter and codes for speaker turns, which could be searched and counted using a concordance program. (Barlow is also the developer of a concordancing software called *MonoConc Pro* [Barlow, 2012], which is, likewise, available for sale.) A list of speakers with their genders could be used to explore the corpus as well. Names of popular politicians and university officials as speakers in the CSPA (e.g., Madeleine ALBRIGHT, Secretary of State, White House [F]; Al GORE, Vice President USA, White House [M]; Elena KAGAN, Deputy Assistant to the

TABLE B4.1 Comparison of CSPA registers and a newspaper corpus

	White House	*Newspaper*	*Meetings*
Approximate number of words	0.9 million	1.1 million	1.1 million
Number of question marks	10,644	649	6,579
Most common verbs	*think, know, said, say*	*said, …*	*think, know, get, say*
Most common pronouns	*I, we, you, it, he, they*	*it, he, they, I, we, us*	*I, we, you, it, they*
Words 14 characters or more	2965	4369	3646
Frequency of *why*	0.08%	0.02%	0.07%

Source: adapted from Barlow, 1998

President, White House [F]; and Gene SPERLING, National Economic Advisor, White House [M]) are provided on the CSPA Web site.

Waugh (2011) explored the distribution of lexical bundles from White House texts of the CSPA identifying all bundles of three to nine words with a minimum raw frequency of 10 and 3 for the *Podium* and *Press* conference subsections. The frequency for both sets was normalized per million words, and bundles with frequency under 20 per million words were eliminated. This resulted in 2,911 three-word and 810 four-word bundles, with 219 of at least five words or longer. For her functional analysis, Waugh eliminated bundles that were shorter than five words. The most common sequence of words in White House texts was a negative response: *I don't know the answer to that.* White House press secretaries (Dee Dee MYERS [F] and Mike MCCURRY [M]) used this sequence repeatedly in the corpus.

Biber, Johansson, Leech, Conrad, and Finegan (1999) provided a structural taxonomy of four-word lexical bundles in conversations, which included 14 major categories. This taxonomy has been used to identify the structure of formulaic patterns for comparison across corpora. In the CSPA-White House, Waugh (2011) also found a higher proportion of lexical bundles that included a lexical verb: 75 percent for *Podium* and 83 percent for *Press*. Conversation registers from a related study by Biber, Conrad, and Cortes (2004) showed that 90 percent of lexical bundles contained lexical verbs. The most common structural pattern in the *Podium* data was *personal pronoun + lexical verb phrase (+ complement clause)*, which accounted for 73 percent of lexical bundles in this set. This structure also appeared in 15 percent of the *Press* bundles. The most frequent pattern in *Press* was *yes/no* or *wh question fragments*; this was found in 63 percent of the bundles.

Reflective Break

- The annotation and prosodic transcription of spoken corpora are currently receiving increased attention in corpus-based research. As we noted earlier, the London-Lund Corpus actually included detailed coding to reflect pitch, length, and pausing features of transcribed speech (Svartnik, 1990). These additional features, however, have been mostly ignored in the linguistic analyses of that corpus. Why do you think linguists in the 1990s generally disregarded these coded features in the London-Lund Corpus?
- The HKCSE (Cheng, Greaves, & Warren, 2005, 2008) team adapted Brazil's Discourse Intonation Systems to manually code this corpus for prosodic features. How beneficial is this additional prosodic information? Do you see other applications of these features (e.g., pedagogical or business training applications)?
- How would you analyze data from the academic meetings and White House texts of the CSPA? What specific linguistic features of meetings and formal question-and-answer sequences could be investigated across identifiable social groups of this corpus?

B4.3. Written Professional Discourse

Aside from written business texts such as those collected for the CBC, CANBEC, and WBE, professional written discourse has also been investigated from many online databases that archive government and public documents. The Internet has provided easy access to professional documents under public domain which could be downloaded when collecting specialized, written corpora. Recently, some private, multinational companies in the United States have been required by the federal government to release internal (private and confidential) documents to the public, following litigation against these companies' practices that violated major U.S. laws. With these documents becoming publicly available, new corpora that include unique, originally confidential materials have been collected and shared online for free. The two most widely popular corpora of this nature are the Tobacco Industry Corpus or the University of Georgia Tobacco Documents Corpus (Kretzschmar, Darwin, Brown, Rubin, & Biber, 2004) and the ENRON e-mail corpus.

B4.3.1 The Tobacco Industry Corpus

Millions of internal documents from the tobacco industry were released to the public as a result of various state and federal litigation and legislative hearings on fraud and negligence cases, including the alleged industry cover-up of the health impacts of smoking. According to the Center for Disease Control (CDC), monetary fraud and the financial and personal impact of tobacco industry negligence and deception have caused the United States to lose over $150 billion per year in smoking-related economic damages (Brown, 2006; Center for Disease Control, 2002). Furthermore, smoking caused 264,087 male and 178,311 female deaths each year between 1995 and 1999 (Center for Disease Control, 2002). Tobacco companies in the United States settled an unprecedented lawsuit that, in part, required these companies to share all of their internal documents for public scrutiny (Brown & Rubin, 2005). Virtually all documents from seven major tobacco companies in the United States, together with documents from tobacco trade organizations, were released and have been stored in physical and electronic repositories at various universities. Documents from as early as the 1950s were also included in the release. The University of Georgia has developed the University of Georgia Tobacco Documents Corpus (of over four million individual texts), and the University of California at San Francisco hosts an electronic repository of over seven million documents available online (Brown, 2006).

These tobacco industry documents include everyday activities and sensitive materials such as confidential reports, meeting notes, and memos. Industry-sponsored research papers, procurement invoices, and letters from executives and lawyers were also made available. When these documents were first released to the public, most research and data-mining activities focused on finding the "smoking gun," which would further show legal accountabilities and major negligent practices of these major tobacco companies. Researchers searched for internal accounts of unethical and deceptive business practices and externally imposed restrictions and limits, as well as marketing strategies, product design, and possible deception. Brown and Rubin (2005) and Kretzschmar and colleagues (2004) explored the structure of deceptive and manipulative language strategies that may have been used by the tobacco industry in its efforts to allegedly cover up the extremely harmful effects of smoking upon public health. What became the Tobacco Industry Corpus was remarkably huge in size, and it provided one of the best samplings of naturally occurring written, professional discourse showing the distinctive nature of communication in this entire industry.

The Linguistic Analysis of Tobacco Documents Project at the University of Georgia (Brown & Rubin, 2005) features a sampling of texts representing various subregisters of the Tobacco Industry Corpus. A workbench of tools was made available online to enable researchers to conduct linguistic studies and corpus-based analyses on key distributional data. Their subcorpus of tobacco industry texts was also tagged for part-of-speech and other semantic categories using the Biber Tagger. The documents that are available for download in this interface were selected through a stratified random process (Kretzschmar et al., 2004). Texts were hand-keyed to show specific elements of the documents such as cross-outs and handwritten marginalia. The interface provides different tools to extract a keyword-in-context concordance, plot significant differences in the use of words or phrases, plot peak usage of words across time, or access a set of rhetorical document cases (Kretzschmar et al., 2004).

Brown and Rubin (2005) examined causal adverbs in tobacco industry texts in order to document and analyze the "pragmatics of responsibility" that could be captured in confidential documents. They searched for frequencies of causal constructions initiated by *because* to express strong causality and *whereas*, *since*, and *as* used to express causality and convey a weaker, disjunctive relation. Their results showed that statements framed with *because* constructions challenged the tobacco industry's responsibility for causing diseases or business losses. On the other hand, statements that incriminated the industry were more likely to use disjunctive (causal *since*) phrasing. A related study by Fellows and Rubin (2005) examined how industry marketers construed and targeted Asians, Asian Americans, and Pacific Islanders in the United States in tobacco advertising campaigns. They noted that strategies to appeal to these cultural groups were carefully orchestrated and employed, resulting from sophisticated analyses of social identities and the value systems of these groups.

Following a more typical corpus-based approach, Kretzschmar and colleagues (2004) analyzed trends across time, focusing on characteristic keyword features of tobacco industry documents. In the 1950s and 1960s, the tobacco industry was generally well-respected and globally dominant in marketing a product that was often associated with "relaxation and hardiness." However, changes in overall public sentiment in the last 50–plus years have projected the industry as increasingly deceptive and strategically misleading. In Kretzschmar and colleagues' study, keyword and sentiment analysis across time traced diachronic language patterns documenting how the industry responded to changing conditions and public perceptions. The names of tobacco companies, tobacco products and their components, and words for the act of using tobacco (*smoke, smoking*, and *smoker*) had positive meanings in the 1950s and 1960s. These words and clusters, however, turned negative from the 1970s. In the 1990s, brand names have become somewhat associated with positive meanings, but particular products (*carton, cigarette*) and references to the act of using this product (*smoking*) have turned negative. In Section B5, we discuss language change and diachronic studies of change using time-coded corpora.

B4.3.2 Workplace E-Mails: The ENRON Corpus

As was the case with the Tobacco Industry Corpus, the Enron E-Mail Corpus was a product of a groundbreaking legal decision to force Enron Corporation, an American energy, commodities, and services company, to release its private documents to the public. Thus, the Enron E-Mail Corpus became the first massive collection of workplace e-mails from employees and executives, including Enron's late CEO Kenneth Lay, Enron's CEO at the time of the scandal, from 1985 until his resignation in 2002. The widely reported Enron scandal led to the collapse of Enron Corporation and Kenneth Lay was sentenced to a maximum 5 to 10 years in prison for 11 counts of corporate abuse and accounting fraud. Lay died in 2006 before his official sentencing (Mulligan & Bustillo, 2006). During the criminal investigation of Enron's business activities, the preservation of e-mail messages, especially from corporate executives, was ordered; a collection 619,446 messages sent by 158 senior Enron executives was subsequently made available to the public. A threaded corpus with 517,431 messages sent by 151 employees from 1997 to 2002 was developed and freely distributed online (Klimt & Yang, 2004; Shetty & Adibi, 2004).

Internet versions of the Enron e-mail database were first posted on the Federal Energy Regulatory Commission Web site and the Cognitive Assistant that Learns and Organizes (CALO) Project. U.S. universities such as the University of Pennsylvania, Carnegie Mellon University, and University of California, Berkeley host database searches and visualization features for topics and sentiment labels (Cohen, 2009). Enron e-mails have been explored from various perspectives, ranging from an analysis of e-mail messages in corporate management audits, the spread of gossip in e-mails and computer-mediated communication, the examinations of e-mails' electronic structure, and the use of electronic data for machine learning and natural language processing. A document classification of the Enron e-mail dataset was completed by Bekkerman, McCallum, and Huang (2004) to establish a model of automatic e-mail foldering using a corpus of real-world e-mails.

Although corpus-based, sociolinguistic studies examining the lexico/syntactic features of Enron e-mails are still limited, the availability of this corpus provides linguists the opportunity to explore a range of frequency distributions in workplace e-mails. Sociolinguistic categories such as gender and role (e.g., mid-level employees vs. executives; junior vs. senior managers) are encoded in the raw e-mail texts and individual folders of this database. A register comparison of workplace e-mails with other online registers such as blogs and Facebook and Twitter posts has been conducted. (See Section B6 for a more detailed register comparison of online texts, including e-mails.)

Mitra and Gilbert (2012) analyzed the spread of *gossip* that could be identified and tracked from the Enron E-Mail Corpus. They defined gossip loosely, following Hannerz (1967) and Besnier (1988) as "conversations focusing on the discussion of someone who is currently not present" (Mitra & Gilbert, 2012, p. 1). In e-mail exchanges, these could be tracked simply by looking at personal references to a third party (not the sender or the receiver of the message) as shown in the two excerpts below:

Text Sample B4.3. Tracking Gossip from the Enron E-Mail Corpus

E-mail 1: hey—seems like we aren't the only ones that think kyle is an arrogant asshole anymore—susan told me that on saturday night she had it out with him and doesn't want him around—also, apparently he's been treating dana like shit and it's starting to get noticed by other people—just thought this was an interesting development.

E-mail 2: Here's the third party assessment of current western supply issues that we're most in agreement with. Sam Van Vactor's group publishes the daily energy market report that's widely read, and Pickel is with Tabors Caramanis, consultants that we have employed on several issues.

In general, gossip has received mostly negative connotation (E-mail 1), suggesting negative intent in the discussion of a third party. However, Feinberg, Willer, Stellar, and Keltner (2012) argue that gossip is essential in modern, healthy societies, especially in groups and organizations. Discussions of others in this professional context, when moderated by common standards of decency, can benefit group and organizations in maintaining both collegial and competitive foci in solving issues and concern. In Mitra and Gilbert's study, the focus was primarily to automatize the tracking of instances of gossip sent and received by various individuals. Sociolinguistic variables such as rank (coded 0 = employee to 6 = CEO) and position or job titles were also included (Table B4.2). However, they also wanted to conduct a sentiment analysis of instances of gossip to figure out if "negative gossip" was more frequent than "positive/neutral gossip" in workplace settings.

To answer the question *Who starts the gossip?* Mitra and Gilbert (2012) examined the percentages of gossip e-mail originating from each rank. After a filtering process to check for accuracy of data, they then restricted their dataset by keeping

TABLE B4.2 Relative ranks of job titles, from Mitra and Gilbert (2012)

Rank	Position or Job Title	
6	CEO	*President*
5	Vice President	*Director*
4	In-House Lawyer	
3	Manager	
2	Trader	
1	Specialist	*Analyst*
0	Employee	

only messages in which the recipient list contained at least one Enron employee. This process allowed them to track mixtures of ranks in the recipient list (e.g., a vice president mailing a trader or an executive assistant). After these initial filtering steps, a final corpus consisting of 49,393 messages was generated, with 7,206 identified as gossip e-mails. A summary of results shows that gossip was very common among every rank in the company, with Ranks 3 to 5 receiving the highest percentages. Additional observations included the following:

- Workplace gossip from the Enron E-Mail Corpus was common at all levels of the organizational hierarchy.
- Employees and executives mostly gossip with their peers (i.e., other employees belonging to the same rank).
- Employees with lower ranks play a major role in circulating gossip e-mails.
- The instances of gossip were largely similar across personal exchanges and formal business communication. However, the nature of these gossips in personal versus formal messages was different.
- It was more likely for an e-mail to contain gossip if it was targeted to a smaller audience.
- The sentiment analysis showed that gossip e-mails from the Enron corpus were often negative. Negative gossip e-mails were 2.7 times more frequent than positive/neutral ones.

Reflective Break

- What do you think about the overall research design of Mitra and Gilbert's (2012) study? How could their summary of results be further interpreted? Both Mitra and Gilbert are not sociolinguists, but their study explored clearly identifiably sociolinguistic variables (e.g., occupation and rank in the workplace). How can sociolinguists contribute to the growing research associated with data mining and natural language processing software?

• Sentiment analysis is very popular in the business fields of online marketing and "big-data" analytics—usually utilized in computational and Internet-based trend studies of enormous datasets and variables. Companies are very interested in understanding and profiling public sentiment (e.g., positive, negative, neutral) relative to their products from online posts, articles, and consumer reports and reviews. In Mitra and Gilbert's (2012) study, they employed an automated sentiment analysis to measure whether a gossip e-mail has negative or positive sentiment. What do you think are the advantages and disadvantages of these

---

Sara Palin's E-Mails and Memos

In June 2011, the state of Alaska released 24,000 pages of e-mails from Sarah Palin's tenure as governor. Palin was Alaska's governor from 2006 to 2009. She was also the Republican Party's vice presidential candidate under John McCain in the 2008 U.S. presidential election, which was won by Barack Obama. The public release of Palin's e-mails was requested by news organizations and local activists from a combination of legal cases that investigated Palin's administrative decisions as governor. Major newspaper outlets such as the *Los Angeles Times* have scanned these printed e-mails and have posted them in a searchable online archive. In addition to memos and her official state e-mail account, Palin's two Yahoo e-mail accounts have also been included in the release (Kellogg, 2011).

Immediate analyses of Palin's memos and e-mail messages were conducted by the media, focusing on the topics and subjects of her official and private messages. Some of the results include the following (Newton-Small, 2011):

• America Online (AOL) reported that Palin's writing skills reach an eighth-grade level, which was considered "excellent for a chief executive" according to two "writing experts." These writing experts also noted that Palin came off as a solid communicator. E-mails sent via Palin's mobile phone scored at grade 8.5 level.
• There were few "Alaskanisms," or instances of regional slang, in Palin's e-mails.
• Palin has circulated jokes and forwarded funny e-mail messages and also engaged in what Mitra and Gilbert (2012) consider to be gossip. She lamented, repeatedly, media reports and gossip about her family, especially her daughter Bristol's pregnancy.
• Clearly, Palin's official e-mails represent political and higher-level executive discourse that are not often available for public scrutiny. Politicians' private letters have been released, often posthumously, but a current politician's e-mails and memos shared because of litigation are still relatively rare. What do you think are the contributions and applications of Sara Palin's e-mails to sociolinguistics? What linguistic features would you analyze and explore using her e-mail messages?

automated sentiment analysis software programs? What problems or concerns do you see from these applications?

B4.4 Occupation: The Language of Nurses and Patients

Workplace discourse studies have also focused specifically on speakers' occupation and role instead of the broader context of the workplace. The discourse of doctors or patients, callers or call-takers, and teachers or students have been functionally analyzed to produce data that could be used to extensively describe communication contexts, specifically for training purposes. For example, Henry and Roseberry (2001) used a discourse-focused approach to analyze a spoken corpus of 20 academic professionals introducing guest speakers in public speaking events. They found that a core set of patterned moves (e.g., *giving background to talk*, *introducing the speakers*, *providing lighthearted/funny contexts*) was used to illustrate a specialized, yet routinely structured, discourse. Doctor-patient interaction has been investigated using discourse and conversation analysis, often with specialized corpora providing data. Medical specializations such as physiotherapists, pharmacists, occupational therapists, and a variety of alternative practitioners were subjects of previous research (Adolphs, Brown, Carter, Crawford, & Sahota, 2004).

Adolphs and colleagues (2004) analyzed a task-based corpus of 17 nurse-patient telephone consultations, and they came up with a list of consistent features characterizing this type of talk. These features include (1) deploying the authority of sources for directives and commands, (2) politeness strategies and concern for the hearer (patient), (3) range of linguistic patterns associated with directives and politeness strategies. Data for this study consisted of a series of *staged* telephone conversations between callers and advisers in the United Kingdom's "NHS Direct" health-advisory service in Nottingham. Nurses who were the health advisers were not aware that the calls they received were staged by the research team. The corpus collected for this study was relatively small, with only 17 completed calls addressed to NHS Direct staff from two male and two female researcher participants. The callers described health problems and symptoms from a broad range of illnesses and discussions centered on advice for medications and treatment. The callers also improvised their calls based on a prearranged script with essential features such as age, occupation, residence, and the nature of the complaint.

Among the many sets of results analyzed in this study by Adolphs and colleagues (2004) was the distribution of modal verbs used to mark courtesy and respect in nurses-patient discourse. As noted by Harris (2003), modalizers and mitigators are often used in asymmetric situations by professionals in order to minimize the threats to face inherent in directives and categorical statements given to patients or clients. Modal verbs *can* and *may* were found to introduce optionality into the discussion, giving patients alternatives or choices to make their own decisions—that is, whether or not to follow the advice that was given by the nurses. Concordance lines from the health professional corpus showing the use of the modal *may* are provided below:

Text Sample B4.4. Concordance Lines of *May* in the NHS Direct Recordings (from Adolphs et al., 2004)

1. And they also say cool baths	**may**	help itching and just gently
2. It may be that there	**may**	be some other course for it.
3. taking with this medication	**may**	cause flushing nausea vomiting
4. and diarrhea and rashes	**may**	also occur.
5. Tetracycline	**may**	discolour developing teeth
6. They	**may**	dry the skin out and they
7. stopping it tonight	**may**	not reduce your symptoms tonight
8. I think you	**may**	find useful and there is sort of sort
9. actually improving you	**may**	still need to have a course the

In these text samples, Adolphs and colleagues (2004) suggested that *may* was used primarily to soften the more or less categorical listing of side effects of certain treatments or conditions provided by the nurses. The nurses also suggested further action on the part of the patient by using *may* (e.g., *I think you* **may** *find useful and there is sort of one and a half*). *May* served a dual role in this context: as an epistemic softener of the message and possibly as a politeness device recognizing the relationship between the adviser and advisee.

The functional nature of studies examining the discourse of doctors and nurses adds to our understanding of health communication in general which potentially leads to generating guidelines for best communicative practice. The impact of certain styles of communication from health professionals on patients' responses or understanding of sensitive information would certainly be an important topic of future research. Adolphs and colleagues noted that there were considerable concerns in the health care industry about the low rates of patient compliance across a whole range of clinical specializations. Further corpus-based research suggested by Adolphs and colleagues (2004) highlighted the following issues:

- a more detailed analysis of linguistic patterning in the language of health care professionals relative to specific tasks or speech events;
- an analysis of the language of emergency calls where it may be inappropriate for the health professional to be vague and where politeness strategies may have to compete with concerns over efficiency and urgency of information transfer;
- an analysis of more complex encounters such as telephone calls related to mental health issues and other sensitive topics;

- an analysis of the effect of strategies of patient empowerment on issues of compliance and some level of accountability with a prescribed course of action given explicitly to the patient;
- an analysis and categorization of the types of questions asked by the health care professionals, as well as the types of answers they yield.

B4.5 Role: Revisiting Caller versus Agent Interactions

In Section B3, we looked at politeness in cross-cultural call center interactions from Friginal's (2009b) Call Center Corpus. We revisit caller and agent roles in this section to explore further how customer service agents compare with nurses-advisers in the study by Adolphs and colleagues (2004) as they provide information and instructions to callers/customers. Customer service is certainly very different from telephone medical consultations, especially in role relationships and interlocutor symmetry. Communications in outsourced call centers have clearly defined roles, power structures, and standards against which the satisfaction levels of customers during and after the transactions are often evaluated. Callers typically demand to be given the quality of service they expect or can ask to be transferred to an agent who will provide them the service they prefer. Offshore agents' "performance" in language and explicit manifestations of pragmatic skills naturally are scrutinized closely when defining "quality" during these outsourced call center interactions. In contrast, for a foreign businessman in many cross-cultural business meetings, or for the nurses-advisers in Adolphs and colleagues (2004), there is limited pressure to perform following a specific (i.e., native speaker) standard in language, as many business partners and health care patients are often willing to accommodate linguistic variations and cultural differences of their counterparts/advisers in negotiations and performance of tasks (Friginal, 2009b).

These transactions in outsourced call centers, therefore, have produced a relatively new register of cross-cultural communication involving a range of variables not present in other globalized business or international and interpersonal communication settings. In addition, the political and economic implications related to the outsourcing of American jobs and the public perceptions thereof have also saturated the media, and consequently, the realm of popular opinion in the United States, affecting callers' attitudes and prompting calls from some sectors for policy changes and possible restrictions in business outsourcing practices.

It is clear that cross-cultural communication in customer service has become an everyday phenomenon in the United States as callers come into direct contact with agents who do not share some of their basic assumptions and perspectives. Before the advent of outsourcing, Americans had a different view of customer service facilitated on the telephone. Calling help desks or the customer service departments of many businesses mostly involved call-takers who were able to provide a more localized service. Interactants shared typically the same "space and time" and awareness of current issues inside and outside of the interactions. Of course callers had common concerns about overall quality of service, comprehension of technical and specialized information, wait times, and the agents' content knowledge of procedures and service persona; however, there were minimal cultural divides and speakers were able to clarify or negotiate, often successfully, in their exchanges.

In contrast, for Indian and Filipino agents, successful communication requires (1) language proficiency in English, (2) cultural awareness related to customer contexts, (3) knowledge and skills in transferring and understanding technical and specialized information, and (4) pragmatic skills in localizing support and accommodating requests or complaints and potential performance limitations of speakers (e.g., in troubleshooting equipment) (Friginal, 2009b). Both agent and caller in this service encounter are constantly dealing with a combination of these factors and the interaction among them that generally affect the conduct and outcomes of the transactions.

Public sentiment about the quality of outsourced call center communications in the United States continues to shift to the negative, as revealed by national surveys and qualitative interviews with customers (Brockman, 2010). For example, Anton and Setting (2004) reported that most American consumers base their perception of companies directly on their call center experience; these consumers claim that communication issues with offshore call center agents have negatively impacted their customer service satisfaction levels and their future purchasing behavior. Based on a 2010 survey, customer satisfaction with calls perceived to be handled in the United States was more than one-fifth higher than with calls perceived to be handled outside the country. Furthermore, callers said that one of the biggest differences between "foreign and American call centers" was the ease of understanding the customer service agent (Brockman, 2010; Friginal, 2011, 2013b). Clearly, these additional contexts affect the way offshore agents attempt to connect and interact with their customers across various types of tasks. Employment in call centers in the Philippines and India has been very competitive, and agents receiving consistent caller complaints may be easily replaced.

B4.6 International Teaching Assistants

U.S. universities have increasingly employed international graduate students (especially doctoral students) as teaching assistants. These international teaching assistants (ITAs) typically assist professors in grading papers. They also manage study groups and hold regular office hours to meet with students regarding class projects and examinations. In mathematics, science, and engineering departments, ITAs commonly teach many introductory courses themselves. These ITAs know the contents of the class very well, but limitations in language and also with teaching strategies have been reported by students (Reinhardt, 2010). Several students have complained about the difficulty in understanding ITAs' pronunciation and have raised concerns about their overall proficiency in spoken English. Many universities have addressed these language-related issues by providing ITAs with additional intensive English training. Various studies on the language of ITAs in the classroom and during office hour interactions have been conducted, in part to produce training materials that address specific language issues. Although some studies (e.g., Pickering, 2006; Pickering & Wiltshire, 2000) have reported that student complaints about ITAs' use of language were motivated primarily by prejudicial behavior or the general complexity of the content of the class, continuing training and research are instituted in many graduate programs to help ITAs improve their use of English in the classroom.

A study by Reinhardt (2010) investigated spoken directives by ITAs in office-hour consultations from a corpus-based perspective. Two corpora were used in the study for comparison: the ITAcorp (Thorne, Reinhardt, & Golombek, 2008), which was a learner corpus that collected classroom activities from advanced ESL and ITA preparation courses, and MICASE, the Michigan Corpus of Academic Spoken English (Simpson, Briggs, Ovens, & Swales, 2002). ITAcorp represented the language of ITAs while MICASE was used for comparison, as it provided samples of spoken texts by academic professionals (e.g., full-time instructors and professors). The ITAcorp includes spoken academic English texts (e.g., lecture presentations, discussion leadings, and office hour role-plays). Spoken texts from MICASE include 152 academic speech events (e.g., advising, colloquia, discussion sections, lectures, office hours, and tutorials, from a balance of university academic disciplines [Simpson-Vlach & Leicher, 2006]). MICASE also features coded sociolinguistic variables such as speaker ages, gender, academic rank, and field of study.

The primary goal of Reinhardt's (2010) comparison was to inform ITA instruction in the context of ESP and cross-cultural pragmatics. In addition, a social-functional approach was conducted to analyze variables such as politeness in academic conversations involving directives. Summative corpus results showed that the ITAs made fewer statements marking independence and inclusion appeals than instructors and professors, but they used directive constructions more frequently. The use of "directive vocabulary constructions" (e.g., *I suggest that, I recommend that you*) by ITAs and professors illustrate ITAs' preference for these constructions much more than professors (or "experts"). Overall, ITAs had 73 total constructions in contrast to 10 from experts. Reinhardt, citing Blum-Kulka, House, and Kasper (1989) suggested that performatives such as *I suggest* or *I recommend* as used by ITAs had the effect of an indirect imperative used to soften the force of the instruction. Directive vocabulary constructions preferred by ITAs emanate from an institutional authority, but many ITAs have distanced themselves from the power source of the directive by invoking policies or rules (e.g., *it is required* or *the administration suggests*).

As a group, ITAs have shown a tendency to utilize more directive constructions that can restrict choice or promote dependence. Consequently, they used fewer constructions that promote inclusion. Reinhardt suggested that fewer constructions appealing toward inclusion (e.g., *you want to*, *I would*) and more frequent constructions that restrict choice (e.g., *you had better*, *I recommend*, *I suggest*) may be due to (lack of) instruction or exposure to typical academic norms in spoken interactions. These structures may have also been influenced by these ITAs' first language backgrounds.

Reflective Break

- As mentioned briefly above, Pickering (2006) argued that student complaints about ITAs' language in the classroom were more motivated by prejudicial behavior or the general complexity of the content of the class rather than proficiency or comprehensibility issues. Do you agree or not with this observation? Have you taken classes with ITAs or with foreign-born professors who are nonnative English speakers? How did you handle language factors such as pronunciation, accent, and clarity of instructions?
- What are the similarities and differences in power and role relationships between the three speaker groups (based on occupations) discussed above: (1) native English speaking nurses, (2) offshore call center agents, and (3) "inshore" ITAs? What particular linguistic features would you want to study across these three groups of speakers?

B5

LANGUAGE CHANGE: DIACHRONIC STUDIES OF CHANGE

B5.1 The Process of Language Change: Time as a Sociolinguistic Variable

It is not at all surprising that languages change. In fact, our language—our current use of vocabulary, idioms, and syntactic structures, including our pronunciation of words—is different from generations past in these and many other respects. Both denotative and connotative meanings of words and phrases change as well, and our perceptions of what is formal or informal in spoken and written language also evolve. Sociolinguists have used time (i.e., temporal change) as a variable that causes distinct transformations in language use. For example, there are many words and phrases that were popular in the 1920s that are no longer as common or used nowadays. The following words and phrases were popular from the 1920s to the 1940s and are clearly not as widespread these days:

> *All Wet*—describes an erroneous idea or individual, as in, "*He's all wet*"
> *Applesauce*—an expletive; same as *horsefeathers*, as in, "*Oh, applesauce!*"
> *Flat Tire*—a dull-witted, insipid, disappointing date; same as *pill, pickle, drag, rag,* or *oilcan*
> *Frame*—to give false evidence; to set up someone
> *Gams*—a woman's legs
> *Giggle Water*—an intoxicating beverage; alcohol
> *Hard Boiled*—a tough, strong guy
> *High-Hat*—to snub
> *Soitently*—Sure!
> *Spiffy*—an elegant appearance
>
> Daniels, n.d.

Many of us will find Shakespeare's sixteenth-century dialogues hard to understand and English poetry or literature before Shakespeare incomprehensible. While Shakespearean plays were performed for the general public in the 1600s, making use of popular, everyday lexicon, puns, and syntactic structures, Shakespeare at present is regarded as having a more formal, rigid, academic tone that is very distinct from popular and current English usage. There are now approximately 540,000 words in the English language ("official" dictionary words and some slang/street words), which is about five times more words than during Shakespeare's time. Based on its algorithmic methodologies, The Global Language Monitor, an Internet-based big-data aggregator, projects that there were over one million English words being utilized by various users online in 2012. This number is similar to projections from Google and also from a study on lexicography conducted by Harvard University in 2013.

The number of new words introduced by print media, at least in the last 50 years, and the Internet revolution from the mid-1990s have contributed to the continuing, exponential growth of the English vocabulary. Words such as *tweet*, *app*, and *hashtag*, three Internet-derived words, have each been adjudged a "Word of the Year" by the American Dialect Society—from 2009, 2010, and 2012 respectively. In addition, *google* (as a verb) was the "Word of the Decade 2000–2010."

B5.2 Historical and Diachronic Linguistics

Many studies of language change have been framed using perspectives from **historical linguistics**—the study of changes and shifts in language. Historical linguistics has also been called **diachronic linguistics**, which focuses on how linguistic features such as words, sounds, sentence structure, and semantic meanings have been used by speakers and writers of a language across time periods. Large-scale shifts in a language typically happen as a response to political, economic, and social pressures together with new inventions, innovations, and changes in popular culture. Historically, colonization, migration, and natural calamities have influenced large-scale shifts in linguistic usage. Some drastic shifts have even resulted in **language death,** often due to a societal decision to simply stop using a particular language altogether in favor of a new one. Evolving societal needs clearly dictate the creation and continuing use of new words and phrases. New industries, jobs, merchandise, equipment, or cultural experiences have produced terms and jargon that have infused mainstream language use.

Temporal change in language use, at least from the 1900s, has been related to trends in popular culture and entertainment. There have been many studies conducted of unique words in the English language contributed by books, radio, television shows, music, and movies. Modern day U.S. television shows such as *The Simpsons, Seinfeld, Saturday Night Live,* and *Friends* have originated words and phrases (e.g., *bagzooka, duh, man-hands, regift, shmoopie*) that have subsequently been adopted and used by speakers and writers in other settings, especially in everyday speech. However, the measurable influence of television on language may be limited to vocabulary use and some forms of pronunciation, and it is actually difficult to determine and document its impact upon a greater number of speakers of a language across time periods without specialized quantitative data. Younger age groups and social networks contribute to the consistent use of television-inspired vocabulary, but the definite *shelf life* of these linguistic features is not commonly documented.

A study by Naro (1981) suggests that there was a link between Brazilian dialogues in television soap operas and the shift to the standardization of Brazilian Portuguese spoken by many Brazilians. "Standardized" forms in this context are more formal, somewhat more academic, and often characterized as more grammatically correct than slang or everyday speech. These standardized forms also reflect dialogues spoken by characters representing higher socioeconomic status. Other similar studies did not find causal relationships between television language and mass-based language shifts (see, for example, Saladino, 1990 on Italian; or Stuart-Smith, 2006 on the television show *EastEnders* in London and its influence on the use of Southern English in England in the 1990s). However, the works of renowned British sociolinguist Peter Trudgill indicate that television shows may promote attitudes that could reflect a particular dialect positively. Trudgill (1986) posits that media and television combine with other factors of language contact in the "softening-up" process, leading to popular use of a dialect feature that was, perhaps, previously somewhat disdained by a larger group of speakers (see also, Stuart-Smith, 2007).

The U.S.-made television comedy *30 Rock*, created by Tina Fey, ended a critically acclaimed run of seven seasons in 2013, leaving behind what the U.S. media have referred to as a "linguistic legacy." This show has introduced words and phrases in its many episodes that its followers have continued to use or have redefined in episode glossaries or blog posts. For example, in the samples below, Harris, Heimbach, and Haglund (2013) document etymologies of *30 Rock* words, while Hood (2010) creates a glossary of favorite *30 Rock*–isms.

Text Sample B5.1 Sample Innovative Words from *30 Rock*

Blergh! The Linguistic Legacy of 30 Rock

Blergh

Variations (and spellings) of *blergh* or *blurgh* (particularly *blargh*) have been around for a while, but *30 Rock* put its own spin on it: *Blërg* isn't just a handy expression of frustration to use when the network won't let you curse, it's also the name of Liz's preferred line of Ikea furniture. (Is there a better example of frustration than putting together furniture that's missing half the pieces?) Google trends suggest that *30 Rock* pushed the word into the mainstream after it appeared in 2007.

Dealbreaker

The term *deal breaker* may seem old, but it's not, really: The earliest citation in the OED is from 1979, and Google Ngrams shows the phrase popping up even a few years before that—and not really taking off until the '90s. It initially meant something that might derail business or political negotiations, but once it became popular it quickly spread to other contexts. *30 Rock* wasn't the first to use *dealbreaker* in reference to relationships, but the show popularized its use as a spontaneous exclamation. As in, "*He never takes off his socks? Dealbreaker!*" These days, you're just as likely to hear the phrase describing a boyfriend's (or girlfriend's) quirks as an unacceptable provision in a contract.

Lizzing, Mind Grapes, Sabor de Soledad, and Beyond: A 30 Rock Glossary

Adultaraisin: Tracy's Ben and Jerry's ice-cream flavor

awes: helpful shorthand for those who don't have time to say the whole word *awesome*

the bubble: the world in which beautiful people live where they are protected from all criticism and all of life's unpleasantries and never get a true sense of their actual limitations

Cheesy Blasters: the number-one selling food in America outside of New York City. Its jingle describes its ingredients: "*You take a hot dog, stuff it with some jack cheese, fold it in a pizza, you got Cheesy Blasters.*" (see also: *Meatcat*)

Reflective Break

• Speakers and writers drive language change by using new words and phrases regularly, and these words and phrases will have to be included as an integral part of a group's linguistic repertoire before they can be considered as part of a societal dictionary. It takes years of sustained presence for words to spread into common usage. Clearly, coined words such as those from *30 Rock* may no longer be popular in 2020. What factors influence the continuing success and utilization of coined words from popular culture? How can we measure the impact of gender and age, social media and social networks on lexical innovations?

• What words and phrases from television programs have you used (knowing that they came specifically from these programs)? What influenced you to use them? What types/genres of programs are these?

B5.3 Diachronic Corpora of English

Diachronic (or **diachronous**) is a practical term for an event or observable behavior that happens across time periods. **Diachronic research** in the study of languages typically looks at trends in linguistic use over time, often in relation to historical and social influences. **Synchronic research,** on the other hand, focuses on the study of linguistic phenomena without reference to their historical settings or contexts. Most linguists in the early nineteenth century studied languages within the parameters of their own historical orientations. Grammars have also been analyzed in reference to their historical changes and applications over time. Linguist Ferdinand de Saussure's work in defining and distinguishing synchronic and diachronic linguistics has influenced the application of linguistic theories to areas such as language teaching and discourse analysis. Preeminence or primacy in language is examined using a synchronic approach, while a diachronic perspective is shown to be composed of successive synchronic stages. Most sociolinguists have characterized the synchronic approach in language change as "change as it happens" (i.e., real-time language change in progress). Thus, synchronic change shows observable variation in language without a definite time reference or consideration of particular social influence upon language development and usage.

Diachronic research has benefited tremendously from electronic corpora. The last 30 years has produced a number of texts that have been organized and coded to represent various time periods. For example, written texts of Old English have been scanned and saved electronically into machine-readable formats and earlier forms of correspondence, diaries, sermons, and poetry have been transcribed and collected to form a specialized corpus. It is now relatively easy to collect a diachronic corpus of written texts across languages from electronic library archives using readily available text converters. However, a diachronic corpus of spoken texts from the pre-1950s period (or before the advent of audio recorders) is harder to collect. Nevertheless, several studies have used specialized transcriptions of texts such as town meetings, court deliberations, radio broadcast, movie or television scripts, or plays to represent spoken dialogs of a certain time period (i.e., "speech-based discourse"). Biber and Burgess (2001), for example, looked at historical spoken language from 95 American and British dramas/plays divided into four historical periods: 1650–1699, 1700–1799, 1800–1899, and 1900–1990. These texts were taken from ARCHER (briefly described below). ARCHER's speech-based texts were coded to show the gender of authors and manually checked to indicate the gender of speakers in the conversational turns (or dialogues) in dramas. Results from this study of dramatic portrayal of female/ male discourse by female and male authors show connections between gender and loquacity or "verbosity" (measured by number of words per conversational turns) across time periods. Specifically, Biber and Burgess found that authors representing characters of their own gender are "speaking more" than those of the opposite gender.

The collection of diachronic corpora of English immediately caught the interest of numerous corpus-based researchers. It was obvious that many research questions related directly to language shift, lexicography and change, and historical linguistics were clearly answerable by data from corpora. Smaller corpora of Old English texts were slowly digitized and processed to produce word lists in the 1970s and 1980s, and register comparisons of literary pieces, sermons, and scientific articles have also been conducted. Before major improvements in electronic scanning technology, digitizing archival documents was tedious and extremely time-consuming, and was relegated to major institutions such as the Library of Congress and the Smithsonian Institutes in the United States. Earlier diachronic corpora were not freely distributed and were subjected to copyright restrictions. Times have certainly changed for the better; we now can readily collect historical texts or access freely available corpora online. Scanners and document-to-text converters are easily available to most researchers.

In the following sections, we introduce popular corpora which have been used for corpus-based diachronic research. One of the first comprehensive collections of historical texts was developed in Finland, the Helsinki Corpus of English Texts: Diachronic and Dialectal, which paved the way for other collections such as ARCHER (or A Representative Corpus of Historical English Registers) in the United States. Other important collections include the groups of letters that comprise the Corpora of Early English Correspondence in the United Kingdom. and more recent online corpora such as Google Books Ngram Viewer, Corpus of Historical American English, Diachronic Corpus of Present-Day Spoken English, the Time Corpus, and other collections that are briefly summarized below.

B5.3.1 The Helsinki Corpus of English Texts

The Helsinki Corpus of English Texts: Diachronic and Dialectal was developed in 1984 by Matti Rissanen and Ossi Ihalainen at the University of Helsinki, Helsinki, Finland. This corpus was one of the first corpora to prominently feature time-coded texts in order to extensively study linguistic changes in the English language with the advent of computer-based corpora. The Helsinki corpus was developed to incorporate texts representing a range of text types, geographic regions, social categories of speakers, and levels of style and modes of expression. There are two sections: Dialectal and Diachronic, with the diachronic section containing English texts from year 750 to 1700 (Table B5.1). A dialectal section features transcripts of interviews with British speakers representing rural dialects of the United Kingdom recorded in the 1970s. Rissanen and Ihalainen noted that their primary goal in the design of the Helsinki corpus was to show that language

TABLE B5.1 Composition of the Helsinki corpus

Periods	Number of Words
Old English −1150	413,250
Middle English 1150–1500	608,570
Early Modern English 1500–1710	551,000

Source: adapted from Kytö and Rissanen, 1993, p. 3

change must be approached through evidence coming from synchronic and diachronic variation inherent in the structure of English. They argue that analyzing quantitative data from corpora will provide more accurate information that can be generalized to represent changes in English across historical periods.

The diachronic texts from the Helsinki corpus as shown in Table B5.1 were collected from Old, Middle and Early Modern English periods from the United Kingdom. Most texts have 2,000 to 10,000 words with approximately 1.6 million words total. Texts were scanned from original paper documents obtained from libraries and computerized archives such as the Oxford Text Archive in the United Kingdom Old and Middle English texts include a variety of materials such as Chaucer's *Canterbury Tales*, *The Pricke of Conscience*, and *Cursor Mundi*. Some texts were obtained from another collection, the *Toronto Corpus of Old English Texts*, and have been "cleaned" for accuracy and spelling consistency.

Overall, the Helsinki corpus is well designed to match quantitative sociolinguistic approaches, with special care employed to make sure that texts represent historical periods appropriately. The developers of the corpus have focused equally on dialect differences, types of writing, settings (i.e., formal and informal settings), and author-based variables such as age, gender, and social status. The Helsinki corpus has also been used for synchronic dialect-based studies of dialect groups in the United Kingdom. The dialectal corpus has approximately 406,600 words representing four regions: East Anglia, the South-West, Yorkshire, and Clare (from Ireland). A related group of texts representing data from Scotland and the United States have been also added recently, and texts from the West Midlands of England will also be included in the corpus.

The texts from the dialectal corpus were taken from transcriptions of oral interviews of older men and women residing in rural areas of the United Kingdom. These interviews were longer than most sociolinguistic interviews from individual speakers to show a range of variation in rural grammatical forms. Note that the Helsinki corpus emphasizes the urban versus rural distinction in collecting speech samples from residents. As many studies in social dialectology in England have focused on urban settings (e.g., London, Birmingham), data from rural settings also contribute important distinctions that could be further explored across the urban-rural divide. Including urban and rural groups clearly allow social comparisons that can further inform studies in variationist sociolinguistics.

B5.3.2 A Representative Corpus of Historical English Registers (ARCHER)

A Representative Corpus of Historical English Registers or ARCHER (Biber & Finegan, 2001; Biber, Finegan, & Atkinson, 1994) was originally developed to analyze historical change in British and American English written and speech-based registers from 1650 to the present.

The overall corpus design of ARCHER is similar to the Helsinki corpus, and ARCHER also aims to cover a wide range of registers. In order to accomplish this, texts were sampled systematically across common written and spoken registers in the last three-and-a-half centuries. The general structure of ARCHER includes 10 major register categories, which were sampled in 50-year periods from 1650. The complete corpus comprises 1,037 texts and approximately 1.7 million words (certainly not a lot when compared to recent collections of diachronic texts available online such as the Corpus of Historical American English). Written registers collected for ARCHER include "personal styles of communication" (e.g., journals/diaries and personal letters), "prose fiction," (e.g., novels and short stories), "popular exposition" (e.g., newspaper texts), and "exploratory registers" (e.g., legal opinion, medical and scientific prose). Speech-based registers were collected from character dialogues in drama and fiction to represent casual, face-to-face conversation. In addition, (transcribed) church sermons were collected to represent planned monologues.

Unlike the Helsinki corpus, there have been relatively few studies based on ARCHER, so far. In addition, there is currently no attempt to add more historical texts to ARCHER, and there is also no online presence dedicated to the documentation of ARCHER-based studies.

Among these limited sets of studies, Biber, Finegan, and Atkinson (1994) reported initial investigations of features such as the use of zero and *that-* complementizers across historical periods and the evolution of medical and scientific research writing from 1650 to the 1990s. Biber and Finegan (2001) compared diachronic relations among speech-based and written registers, reporting that specialist expository written registers follow a different developmental course than popular written registers (e.g., letters, diaries, fiction, and news reports). They found that written registers, in general, have consistently shifted to become more *literate* across time and also increasingly more distinct compared to conversations.

As mentioned earlier, Biber and Burges (2001) used dramatic dialogues from ARCHER to study the historical shifts in the language of males and females in speech-based registers. Speech in this context was represented by dialogues from plays. The gender of speakers (characters) in these historical plays, as well as the gender of authors, were coded and used as independent study variables. Biber and Burges reported that the central determining factor influencing "involved" speech (e.g., use of personal pronouns, private verbs, and emphatics in speech) has become the distinction between cross-gender or same-gender dyads. That is, cross-gender dialogues (female to male) have shifted to become considerably more involved than same-sex dialogues (female to female or male to male) as represented in plays.

B5.3.3 The Google Books Ngram Viewer

The Google Books Ngram Viewer contains over 5.2 million books from Google Books, a division of Google that has conducted an extensive scanning of published books and historical manuscripts in order to create a database of global electronic texts. The number of currently scanned books comprises approximately

4 percent of all the books ever written in English (Bohannon, 2010). This mega-corpus contains over 500 billion words; the majority of them are in English (361 billion). Other available languages in the corpus include French, Spanish, German, Chinese, Russian, and Hebrew. The Ngram Viewer contains data that span 1550 to 2008. (Note that texts before the 1800s are extremely limited in this collection, and oftentimes there are only a few books per year.) From the 1800s, the corpus grows to 98 million words per year; by the 1900s, it reaches 1.8 billion and by the 2000s, 11 billion per year. Hence, texts collected for Google Books Ngram Viewer represent the largest corpus in existence, to date (Walker & Randall, 2012).

The Google Books Ngram Viewer is composed of raw data that is encoded by the number of n-grams. Before the Ngram Viewer was published, Peter Norvig, the head of research at Google Labs, had reservations about requests to develop an online interface due to many pending lawsuits about Google's book digitizing initiative. In order to avoid further problems with publishers and copyright owners of published materials, the Ngram Viewer makes use of texts converted into various n-grams. Thus, data from the whole corpus could not be downloaded as complete books and, in effect, "cannot be read by a human" (Michel et al., 2011, p. 176). The process of converting Google Books into n-grams has been tedious, and this explains why only 5.2 million books have been converted of the 15 million Google Books, so far.

It is important to note here that the Ngram Viewer was not created primarily for research applications in linguistics and/or corpus linguistics. The developers of the viewer emphasized that they have created a new approach to humanities research coined as "culturomics." Culturomics (http://www.culturomics.org/home) is a way to quantify culture by analyzing the growth, change, and decline of published words over centuries. This would make it possible to rigorously study the evolution of culture making use of distributional, quantitative data on a grand scale. In an effort to prove the adequacy and provide clear impetus for the Ngram Viewer, Google-affiliated researchers have been conducting a series of studies to validate the usefulness and various applications of their new program. One such study shows that over 50 percent of the words in the n-gram database do not appear in any published dictionary (Bohannon, 2010). In addition, it is argued that patterns and cultural influences of words could be clearly established and tracked across timeframes. The use of Google Books Ngram Viewer and culturomics, therefore, contributes academic and technical value to the study of culture, making it arguably a new tool for cultural research that has limitless possibilities.

B5.3.4 Corpus of Historical American English (COHA)

As with the Google Books Ngram Viewer, which has been available since late 2010, the Corpus of Historical American English was also first rolled out in 2010 with limited functionality. Information available from COHA has been continually updated since then with major upgrades in its data and search features, including interesting information on visualization and motion chart techniques as applied to COHA's diachronic distributional data. As previously mentioned, COHA was developed by Mark Davies, professor of linguistics at Brigham Young University (BYU). Davies also created many other interactive online databases for corpus analyses (e.g., Corpus do Português, Corpus del Español, and Corpus of Latter Day Saints General Conference Talks), which can be accessed from his personal Web site: http://davies-linguistics.byu.edu/personal/.

COHA's data, so far, cover the period from 1810 to 2012, and specific registers such as fiction, magazine, nonfiction, and newspaper texts can be searched. Following established functionalities from COCA, COHA also provides POS lists, collocates, list and chart options, and various sorting and comparison options (Figure B5.1). COHA has over 400 million words compared to the Ngram Viewer's 500 **billion** words. Davies argues, however, that this substantial difference in corpus size does not necessary affect the reliability of results when these two corpora are used and compared across a range of linguistic distributions (e.g., when searches were performed between COHA and Google Ngram Viewer, similar results were found when data were **normalized**) (Davies, 2011b, 2011d). Davies also believes that COHA can do exactly what the Google Books Ngram Viewer does, with the addition of specific features that directly apply to linguistics and corpus-based research including the ability to (1) employ concordancing tools, (2) display data in context, and (3) limit results by register characteristics not available on the Ngram Viewer. In addition, COHA allows more powerful searches; for example, synonyms and word comparisons across historical periods, which may produce much more insightful analyses about cultural and societal shifts (Davies, 2011d). The types of detailed COHA searches include the following:

- lexis, through mass comparison between historical periods
- morphology, via wildcards
- syntax, from POS-tagged data included in the program
- semantics, via collocates, synonyms, and customized lists.

In 2011, Davies launched an interface for Google Books Ngram Viewer that allows a more extensive search of the massive Google collection than the basic Ngram Viewer can provide. Davies's search platform is very similar to the standard COCA/COHA structure, providing options for wildcard, lemma, part of speech, synonyms, and collocate searches. This interface is certainly more advanced than Google's online viewer, with presentations of frequency data that go beyond simple line graphs or figures. In addition, Davies's interface allows users to copy the data to other applications for further analysis (Davies, 2011c), which is currently not possible in the Google interface. The Davies version is based on 155 billion words of American English from 1810 to 2009, with future plans for major upgrades. Davies also intends to integrate other Google Books collections into this new interface including texts from British and American English texts from the 1500s to the 1700s, as well as texts from Spanish, German, and French. Davies's interface also provides a guided tour of the site (http://googlebooks.

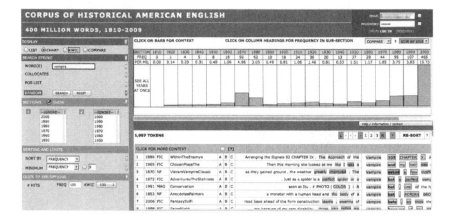

FIGURE B5.1 Search result for "vampire" in COHA

byu.edu/) showing its major features and an intuitive search form. A click for each search query automatically fills in the form and displays the results obtained from actual American English books collected by Google Books. Davies points out that his interface is not an official product of Google or Google Books (Davies, 2011c).

B5.3.4.1 Mark Davies on Corpus-Based Sociolinguistics

Mark Davies began his academic career in Spanish and linguistics, particularly focusing on syntax and historical linguistics. When asked about how he became interested in corpora and corpus linguistics, Davies recounted a very pragmatic rationale. In the late 1980s and early 1990s, he had been conducting research on Spanish and also Portuguese. As a nonnative speaker of these languages, he realized that he did not have the intuitions about these languages that his native-speaking counterparts had. Corpora offered ways to potentially have an edge in research and publishing in these areas. To Davies, corpora served as a "proxy access to intuitions" about Spanish and Portuguese—what linguistic features speakers of these languages actually use across registers.

According to Davies, many historical linguists, especially in languages other than English, are almost, by definition, corpus linguists because of the types of data they collect and analyze. With the advent of computers and digitized language, large amounts of data from various time periods could be stored, organized, and explored much more easily. Early in his career, Davies worked in more traditional models of functional language. In these models, there was often the distinction made between "acceptable and unacceptable" grammatical forms. With corpora, however, research has shown how historical language change is very gradual and that many linguistic features become more or less acceptable over longer periods of time than previously believed. His formal linguistics background taught Davies that lexis and syntax were separable. Working with corpora has instead shown him the crucial intersection of lexis and syntax in actual language in use.

From the early 2000s, since he has been at BYU, Davies's research career moved away from studying historical changes in Spanish and Portuguese. At least in the last 10 years, he has been busy creating corpora, especially in English, that can be accessed publicly online. Teachers, learners, and researchers around the world can conduct their own synchronic, diachronic, multilingual, multidialectal studies using the data he collects and the online database he manages. This has been a rewarding direction of scholarship for Davies who values how he has been able to make a difference in many researchers' lives. In fact, included on his BYU Web site is the option for researchers to list their studies (e.g., journal articles, chapters, books) that have incorporated datasets using his corpora. In the summer of 2013, more than 550 works have been included on this list.

Davies is well-known for his advocacy of using extremely large corpora to explore linguistic variation. He observes that for many researchers, including many corpus linguists, variation is a function of the narrow range of data that can be accessed through the small corpora they use. If a corpus is small, a researcher might be able to explore common grammatical structures, but the variation within those structures (e.g., the particular lexical items used) would be less visible. Larger corpora, on the other hand, allow researchers to explore less common structures but also the lexical and semantic variation in common structures in ways that smaller corpora cannot possibly show.

As for future directions in corpus-based sociolinguistics, Davies posits that social media will revolutionize the field. Our concept of what is a large corpus (e.g., BNC, the Brown-based corpora) will change. Davies describes how sociolinguists tend to be very interested in variation at the level of the individual. Traditionally, many corpus creators were not necessarily concerned with specific and detailed demographic variables, and thus were unlikely to include such information in their corpora. For example, although the BNC was tagged for demographic data, it was not constructed primarily with those questions in mind. However, social media sites such as Facebook and Twitter offer billions of words worth of linguistic output daily and also provide important demographics of the language users. "There is the possibility of having information about who the language users are, where they are from, what are their ages, what are some of the things they *like*, etc. We will then be able to explore those variables alongside enormous amounts of linguistic data," Davies concludes.

B5.3.4.2 Recent Linguistic Analysis of Data from COHA and Google Ngram Viewer

One obvious way to explore megacorpora such as Google Books Ngram Viewer and COHA is to conduct diachronic and trend studies comparing the distribution of various linguistic features across specific time periods. For example, Davies

(2011b) presents frequency changes in lexical items (e.g., *fellow, teenager, sublime, global warming, steamship*) used in published texts from 1810 to the present. Hilpert (2011) uses visualization techniques using Google Visualization (or Google Code) and the statistical/graphical software R in showing language change through COHA. Sociolinguistic time series studies of semantic shifts (semantic changes or change in meaning) across its designated registers could be conducted using COHA, although this could be further improved if particular demographic information on speakers/writers could be provided. While more generic trending information is provided by the Ngram Viewer from published books and manuscripts, such a dataset also allows for immediate macrolevel snapshots of quantitative language patterns across timelines from the 1800s to the present.

Specialized linguistic work from Google Books Ngram Viewer has, so far, focused on many cultural trends throughout history, as taken from or "recorded" in books. The culturomics team quantitatively looks at linguistic and cultural phenomena reflected in the English language. This reporting of linguistic trends is directly related to the fields of "lexicography, the evolution of grammar, collective memory, the adoption of technology, the pursuit of fame, censorship, and historical epidemiology" (Michel et al., 2011, p. 176). Some lexical and culturally specific data intended for popular reading obtained from the Google Ngram Viewer and culturomics include the following (Cohen, 2010):

Women in comparison with *Men* is rarely mentioned until the early 1970s, when feminism gained a foothold. The lines eventually cross paths about 1986.

Mickey Mouse and *Marilyn Monroe* do not get nearly as much attention in books as *Jimmy Carter*; there are many more references in English than in Chinese to *Tiananmen Square* after 1989; and *Grilling* has been used frequently from the late 1990s and outpaced *Roasting* and *Frying* in 2004.

Michel and colleagues (2011) also measured the endurance or transience of fame from the 1800s, reporting that written references to popular celebrities faded twice as quickly in the mid-twentieth century as they did in the early nineteenth. They also found technological advances and inventions (e.g., telephone, radio) took, on average, 66 years to be adopted by the larger culture in the early 1800s, and only 27 years between 1880 and 1920. They tracked the way irregular English verbs that did not add *-ed* at the end for past tense (i.e., *learnt*) evolved to conform to the common pattern (*learned*). And finally, as an application of quantitative, lexico/syntactic data, Michel and colleagues calculated that the English lexicon has grown by about 70 percent to more than a million words in the last 50 years with direct implications for lexicographic changes and updating dictionaries by pinpointing newly popular words and obsolete ones.

Spiegel (2013) reported how the Google Books database was used by a team of researchers from University of Bristol (Acerbi, Lampos, Garnett, & Bentley, 2013) to answer the question, **Were people happier in the 1950s than they are today? Or were they more frustrated, repressed, and sad?** These emotions were defined based on a collection of words (mostly nouns and adjectives) that directly identify (1) anger, (2) fear, (3) joy, (4) sadness, (5) disgust, and (6) surprise. For example, words such as *rage, fury, irritation*, and *wrath* were included in the "anger" group, while *pleasure, delight, bliss, elation*, and *ecstasy* were included in the "joy" group. A total of 146 different words that connote anger, 92 words for fear, 224 for joy, 115 for sadness, 30 for disgust, and 41 words for surprise were used for frequency searches using the Google Books database. Because the digitized Google Books database was temporally coded, it was easy for the researchers to program and track the use of these words over time from the 1900s. Frequency data thus allowed for the comparisons of these groups of emotion words at certain moments in history. Acerbi and colleagues (2013) were able to conduct positive and negative mood tracking through published books along a 20-year period. Values above zero—that is, positive values—suggested generally "happy" periods, while values on the negative side suggested generally "sad" periods. Below are summaries of the researchers' observations:

- The 1920s had the highest peak of joy-related words and very few groups fell on the negative side of the chart (i.e., *the roaring 20s*).
- The 1940s had the most number of negative mood words. In the United States, 1941 marked the beginning of America's entry into World War II, and overall, published academic papers and literature from 1940 to 1950 reflected a world struggling to cope with major economic and political and social unrest.
- Collectively, the usage of commonly understood emotion words was in decline throughout the twentieth century. Authors used words that express emotions, especially anger, disgust, and surprise, less in the year 2000 than authors 100 years earlier. However, fear-related words started to increase just prior to the 1980s.
- We tend to think that modern culture is more emotionally open than people in the past. As Spiegel (2013) noted, we currently live in a world of reality television, blogs, and Facebook/Twitter, and it seems like the explicit display of emotions is everywhere, shared to a degree like never before. However, according to this research, that is not the case, at least in how these sentiments are distributed or represented in published books.

Reflective Break

- It is promising and intriguing to be able to capture emotions throughout history from big databases like Google Books. Although such analyses are complicated and will have to be further interpreted, trend data offers a new window that might clearly provide details on cultural changes and shifts across time. What do you think are the limitations of these types of studies? What additional interpretive techniques could be used?

- Psycholinguist James Pennebaker, who also works with big-data and corpus tools, noted, "Our current emotional state completely biases our memories of the past and our expectations for the future" (Spiegel, 2013). He added that mining Google Books is a kind of emotional archaeology from traces and evidence left behind by writers' words. What other applications of Google Books can you think of? What sociolinguistic topic, in particular diachronic research questions, are you interested in pursuing using this database?

B5.3.5 TIME Magazine Corpus of American English

A complete archive of *TIME* magazine's articles has been shared online, and in 2007, Mark Davies also published the TIME Magazine Corpus of American English, following the structure and interface of COCA and COHA. The TIME corpus online can be searched to explore diachronic data of articles and special features from 1923 to 2006. The TIME corpus has over 100 million words and can be searched to produce comparative data per 10-year periods from the 1920s to the 2000s.

TIME magazine, established in 1923 by Briton Hadden and Henry Luce, was the first weekly news magazine in the United States. From the date of its founding to the present, *TIME* has covered American politics and culture and has also extensively featured global developments, celebrity news, style, and literary trends. *TIME*'s "**Person** of the Year" designation (previously "**Man** of the Year") has been prominently featured as an important annual event to recognize an individual or groups of people with the greatest impact on news headlines for a particular year. Charles Lindberg (1927), Adolf Hitler (1938), the Apollo 8 Astronauts (1968), New York mayor Rudolf Guliani (2001), "you" (2006) (represented by Internet content creators), and Facebook founder Mark Zuckerberg (2010) have all been among those designated as *TIME*'s Person/s of the Year.

Figure B5.2 shows a comparison of normalized frequencies of the word *communism* used in *TIME* articles from the 1920s to 2000s. In the 1950s, *communism* was used 115.91 times per one million words in the whole corpus, referring in most instances to Russian or Soviet Communism and also to news reports of efforts to contain communism in Asia.

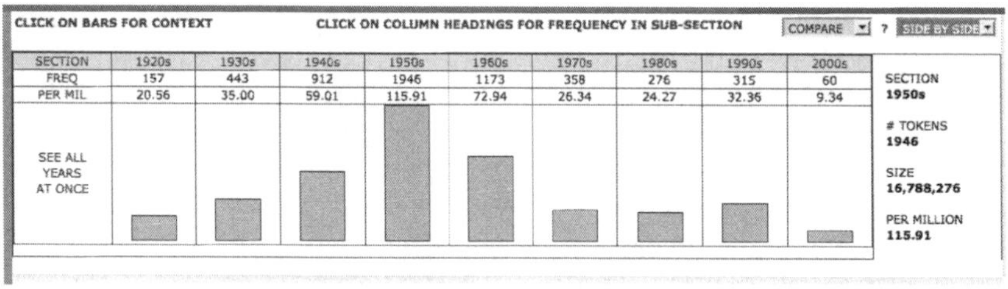

CLICK ON BARS FOR CONTEXT			CLICK ON COLUMN HEADINGS FOR FREQUENCY IN SUB-SECTION					COMPARE ▼ ? SIDE BY SIDE ▼	
SECTION	1920s	1930s	1940s	1950s	1960s	1970s	1980s	1990s	2000s
FREQ	157	443	912	1946	1173	358	276	315	60	SECTION
PER MIL	20.56	35.00	59.01	115.91	72.94	26.34	24.27	32.36	9.34	1950s

TOKENS
1946

SEE ALL
YEARS
AT ONCE

SIZE
16,788,276

PER MILLION
115.91

FIGURE B5.2 Normalized distributions of "communism" in the TIME corpus from the 1920s to the 2000s

Communism in the United States was largely considered as a "menace" and "un-American" in the 1950s, in part because of the Cold War between the United States and the Soviet Union and coverage of zealous U.S. congressional investigations initiated by senator Joseph McCarthy from Wisconsin of alleged Soviet spies and sympathizers in the federal government and within the community of artists, writers, and movie producers in Hollywood. *TIME* magazine reported extensively on McCarthy's congressional hearings, which later gave rise to the term *McCarthyism*, and also profiled personalities related to these various congressional investigations. By the 2000s, *communism* had lost its "un-American" connotations and only appeared in the TIME corpus 9.34 times per one million words. Below are excerpts from concordance lines of *communism* in the 1950s and 2000s from the TIME corpus:

Text Sample B5.2. Comparison of Sample Concordance Lines for *Communism* from the Time Corpus

1950s

free world in its struggle with	**Communism**,	and a warrior for peace
convinced himself that	**Communism**	is the inevitable foe of
Committee questions about	**Communism**.	
to resist the spread of	**Communism**.	

2000s

inspiration from the father of	**communism**	as well as from one of the
Chinese workers living under	**communism**	are allowed to have
over those differences, but	**communism**	is gone. Europe lives by

B5.3.6 Other Diachronic Corpora

Corpora of Early English Correspondence

The Corpora of Early English Correspondence was compiled specifically for diachronic sociolinguistics research and has four different versions: Corpus of Early English Correspondence (CEEC), Corpus of Early English Correspondence Sampler (CEECS), Corpus of Early English Correspondence Supplement (CEECSU), and Corpus of Early English Correspondence Extension (CEECE). These corpora have been explored utilizing approaches from socio- and historical linguistics and have produced interesting results that link language change to various social variables. Some of these findings are reported in Nevalainen and Raumolin-Brunberg (2003), Laitinen (2007), Nevala (2004), Nurmi (1999), and Palander-Collin (1999). An edited book entitled *The Language of Daily Life in England (1400–1800)* (Nurmi, Nevala, & Palander-Collin, 2009) collected various studies, which extensively document the linguistic characteristics of English correspondence across various personal and professional contexts.

Altogether, the CEEC has a total of 5.1 million words representing British English (Late Middle, Early Modern, Late Modern) from 188 collections of letters and 1,200 authors. For the most part, these corpora feature letters from literate, educated writers such as male members of the gentry, clergy, and professionals (lawyers and military officers). Female writers comprise only about 20 percent of the total texts. All letters are coded to also include writer's rank and occupation and other traceable background information. The CEEC research team intends to extend this database to also provide information on letter recipients.

Patha and Nurmi (2009) used the CEEC letters to study code-switching practices from a case study of letters sent by musician and music historian Charles Burney (1726–1814). Burney's letters featured code-switching from English to French, Italian, and Latin. The length of the code-switched segments varies between 1 and 33 words, and the average length of a segment is 2.6 words. In the excerpt below, Burney code-switched to more than one language in the course of a short segment (French and Italian):

Text Sample B5.3. Sample Text in the Study of Code-Switching in Historical Letters

> But, *en attendant*, let me tell you that our dear Pacchierotti has come back, (*entre nous, par une Trame de ma façon*). Though such is the distracted state of Opera Governm't, it is very doubtful whether any Theatrical use will be made during the whole winter of his Talents—but he is here—& I shall now & then hear him—I have made him very fond of a Cantata by Haydn, lately come from Vienna. "*Ah, come il core mi palpita*"—It is so much in his best style of singing that it seems *fatta apposta per lui*. (Charles Burney to Thomas Twining, 1783) (Patha and Nurmi, 2009).

The Diachronic Corpus of Present-Day Spoken English

The Diachronic Corpus of Present-Day Spoken English (DCPSE) is a parsed corpus of spoken British English only from the 1960s to the 1990s. The DCPSE has over 400,000 words taken from ICE-Great Britain representing spoken British English collected in the 1990s and approximately 400,000 words from the London-Lund Corpus (late 1960s to early 1980s spoken texts). DCPSE texts were selected to ensure a balanced sampling of spoken registers (e.g., telephone conversations, television talk show transcripts) from two already-available corpora of British English. The DCPSE features sociolinguistic information on texts, speakers, and authors and also detailed online help in understanding parsing and annotation conventions.

Transcriptions, parsing, and annotations followed the format from ICE-GB. The DCPSE is available on CD-ROM and can be purchased from the DCPSE Web site hosted by University College London (http://www.ucl.ac.uk/english-usage/index.htm or search "Diachronic Corpus of Present-Day Spoken English"). A sample DCPSE corpus is available for free online.

The York-Toronto-Helsinki Parsed Corpus of Old English Prose (YCOE) and The Penn-Helsinki Parsed Corpus of Middle English (PPCME2)

The York-Toronto-Helsinki Parsed Corpus of Old English Prose (YCOE) (1.5 million word syntactically annotated corpus of Old English prose) and The Penn-Helsinki Parsed Corpus of Middle English (PPCME2) compile texts of Old English prose such as the *Anglo-Saxon Chronicle, Canons of Edgar, Gospel of Nicodemus, Other Saints' Lives*, and *Honorius of Autun and Elucidarium*. Both corpora are both available for free for noncommercial users.

Variation Contacts and Change in English: VARIENG-Compiled Corpora

Finally, VARIENG, which stands for "Research Unit for the Study of Variation, Contacts and Change in English," is one of the best online resources for research on corpus-based English language variation and change. Links to diachronic corpora and bibliographies of comparative, historical studies are provided. The VARIENG team is primarily interested in how language is situated in social, cognitive, textual, and discourse contexts across time periods. Studies emphasizing discourse produced in speaker interaction and how language varies and changes in meaning and structure are highlighted. Access to the following diachronic corpora can be obtained by visiting the VARIENG site online (http://www.helsinki.fi/varieng/corpora/index.html):

- Corpus of Early English Medical Writing (CEEM)
  - Middle English Medical Texts (MEMT)
  - Early Modern English Medical Texts (EMEMT)
  - Late Modern English Medical Texts (LMEMT)
- Corpus of Scottish Correspondence (CSC)
- Helsinki Corpus of Older Scots (HCOS)
- Small Corpus of Political Speeches (SCPS)
- Helsinki Archive of Regional English Speech (HARES).

B6

WEB REGISTERS

B6.1 Corpus Linguistics and the Internet

Major advancements in Internet technology in the past 15 years have contributed significantly to the growth of corpus-based research. The collection of Web registers such as Weblogs, online newspaper articles and opinion columns, and various user-generated contents has become easily accessible and manageable, while more and more types of specialized texts (e.g., status updates, reader thread comments) have been generated and freely shared online. The Internet as a corpus (Crystal, 2006) or as a platform for corpus collection provides not only English texts but also other languages used online by multimillions of users worldwide. In addition, automated transcriptions and translations of Web-based audio and video clips have also been developed for various applications. Clearly, the captioning and automatic annotation of spoken discourse posted online can help in the collection of emerging spoken registers. In sum, the current availability of downloadable texts from the Web shows how far corpus linguistics has progressed from its precomputer period to the present.

Many encouraging studies dealing with the linguistic characteristics of online language have utilized computational and corpus-based approaches to produce a range of research data. An academic journal called *Language@Internet* specifically publishes research articles on language that is mediated by the Internet and also by mobile technology. This journal encourages the application of corpus tools and corpora in the study of language and digitally mediated communication. Web-based tools have now guided how we compile corpora for linguistic studies or big-data analytics. Big-data involves the collection, tracking, and analysis of millions (or billions) of texts from all Web sources in order to obtain quantifiable patterns or behavior. This mechanism enables negative or positive sentiment analysis, product or celebrity likability, and marketing and forecasting activities to be conducted using available data posted online.

There are still many challenges in achieving a well-principled and balanced collection of specialized online corpora for linguistic analysis, especially in multilingual contexts. In addition, the dynamic nature of Web-based language development also involves rapidly occurring major contextual and linguistic changes that are challenging to keep up with. For example, our traditional Web sites and Weblogs (later simplified as "blogs") have now evolved to include multimedia "microblogs" through popular social media sites such as Facebook and Twitter. These platforms, which provide links to multimodal sources of information, are also now very easily accessible from smart phones or tablet computers. Social news Web sites such as Reddit (http://www.reddit.com/) or dashboard blogging and photo blogging sites such as WordPress (www.wordpress.org), Tumblr (https://www.tumblr.com/), Pinterest (http://pinterest.com/), Foursquare (www.foursquare.com), and Instagram (http://instagram.com/) continue to add new varieties of written discourses that incorporate collaborative posting, photos, videos, gifs, and links to other sites. Tumblr had over 59.3 million blogs with 24.9 billion posts (most of them in English) as of April 2012, and in 2013, it was bought by Yahoo! for $1.1 billion (Simpson, 2013).

This section is a snapshot of studies focusing on Web registers, viewed through a sociolinguistic lens. As we noted in Section B1, the rapid growth of *geotagged* social media data has paved the way for Twitter-based analysis of regional variation and dialectology (Eisenstein, O'Connor, Smith, & Xing, 2010). Similarly, Facebook status updates have also been examined using narrative theory and how culture influences the self-construal and self-expression of Facebook users through their posts. Studies of blogging language have taken a predominantly corpus-based approach, together with content and rhetorical analysis to examine topics such as the social import of blogging and linguistic co-occurrence features of personal blogs (Grieve, Biber, Friginal, & Nekrasova, 2010).

Reflective Break

- Large-scale corpora such as the British National Corpus, the American National Corpus, the International Corpus of English, or the Corpus of Contemporary American English have yet to incorporate Web-based registers such as e-mails, blogs, and reader comments. How valuable are Web registers to these reference corpora? Do you think a diachronic study of Web registers (from 1994 to the present) will show marked patterns of linguistic variation? What linguistic features would be interesting to study in a diachronic research of Internet language?
- Copyright and privacy concerns prevent automatic corpus collection (by means of "crawling") of proprietary sites. Additionally, multilingual posts, reposts, and various metadata continue to pose challenges for corpus collection

and CL research. What other challenges to online corpus collection do you see? We provide ideas in the collection of a blog corpus in Section C1.

- **Suggested readings**: Researchers Susan Herring and John Paolillo have published interrelated articles on gender and Computer Mediated Communication (CMC) from 1996 to the present. Their work extensively documents sociolinguistic variables encoded in various subregisters of CMC texts. David Crystal's *Internet Linguistics: A Student Guide* (2011) discusses important research issues related to online language including blogs, tweets, and the multilingual Internet.

B6.2 Blogs

A blog is a Web site containing an archive of regularly updated online postings. The postings are typically made by one person (for personal blogs), presented in reverse chronological order, and made freely available to the public. These postings tend to consist primarily of raw text but may also contain hyperlinks and other media, including pictures, videos, and sound files. Often, blogs allow readers to submit comments following the posts, as well. In terms of content, blogs appear to fall into one of two major types: personal blogs in which an author discusses his or her own life and experiences—typically in the form of personal narrative entries—and thematic blogs in which an author discusses a topic which may include current events, politics, arts, entertainment, religion, or sports and technology. Herring and Paolillo (2006) additionally characterize thematic blogs into subgroups of *filter blogs*, which contain links to news articles and comments about their content, and *k-logs* (or knowledge logs), which contain information about a selected topic written by an expert.

B6.2.1 The Evolution of Blogging

In the mid-1990s, online diaries and commentary pages begin to appear, adding to the growing number of Internet postings outside of newsgroups. Two of the earliest online diaries were posted by Claudio Pinhanez (1994 to 1996, hosted by MIT lab) and Justin Hall (1994 to 2005).

These online diaries gave rise to the structure of personal blogs we are now familiar with. Online diaries had principal features associated with blogs: they are regularly updated and chronologically ordered online archives of postings written by a single person. These key features were also characteristic of portions of early Web sites that posted commentary on news, entertainment, and gaming (Grieve et al., 2010; Harmanci, 2005).

The late 1990s saw a rise in the popularity of blogging when free and easy-to-use blog publishing platforms became available—for example, Opendiary (1998), LiveJournal (1999), and Diaryland (1999). These sites provided opportunities for non-HTML programmers or Web designers to create their own blog sites. Also, blog hosting services such as **blogger.com** were introduced in the late 1990s. Blogger.com made it easy for all bloggers, especially beginners, to create their blog pages, post regular updates, and find potential readers. Blogger.com was eventually purchased by Google in 2003.

The term *Weblog* was coined by Jorn Barger in 1997 to describe the list of links and posts he collected in his Web site *Robot Wisdom* (Wortham, 2007). *Blog* was then used in 1999 first by Peter Merholz, separating *Weblog* into *we blog* in a play on words ("It's the Links, Stupid," 2006). An entry from *The Oxford English Dictionary* noted that the first time *blog* appeared online was in May of 1999 on Brad Graham's Weblog (www.bradlands.com) in a posting referencing Merholz:

> Cam points out lemonyellow.com and PeterMe decides the proper way to say 'Weblog' is 'wee'-blog' (Tee-hee!).

Merholz later used the word in context on his Weblog (www.peterme.com): "For those keeping score on blog commentary from outside the blog community." By 2002, *blog* was voted as the new word most likely to succeed by the American Dialect Society. Andy Carvin (2007), writing for National Public Radio, summarized a timeline tracking the development blogging in an article entitled "Timeline: The Life of the Blog":

- 1992: Tim Berners-Lee launched the first Web site.
- 1998: Open Diary became one of the first online tools to assist users in the publishing of online journals. It would later be followed by other journaling tools, including Pitas (1999), Blogger (1999), Xanga (2000), Movable Type (2001) and Wordpress (2003).
- 1999: The development of RSS, or Really Simple Syndication made it easier for people to subscribe to blog posts, as well as distribute them to other sites across the Internet.
- 2002: The launch of Technorati, one of the first blog search engines made it possible for users to track blog conversations on a continuous basis.
- 2004: Videographer Steve Garfield launched his video blog and declared 2004 "The Year of the Video Blog," more than a year before the birth of YouTube.
- February 2004: The launch of Flickr, a photo-sharing community that helped to popularize photo blogging.
- 2006: The launch of Twitter, one of the first micro-blogging communities that allows user to publish and receive short posts online or through text messaging and instant messaging.
- 2007: Technorati reported that it was tracking more than 112 million blogs worldwide.

The evolution (or decline?) of blogging: In 2013, Facebook, Twitter, and Tumblr dominate online social media activity. Although successful bloggers still maintain readership and online diaries continue to attract young writers, immediate abbreviated posts and updates are now mostly posted through microblogs. The snowballing change in traditional blogging is also greatly affected by the popularity of smart phones and tablet computers, which provide quick and easy access to Facebook and Twitter (or related apps) pages.

Reflective Break

- **Have you heard of this?** In the early 2000s, major political news stories in the United States started breaking in blogs before they were covered by network television or newspapers. An example of these blog-exclusive stories was the Trent Lott scandal in 2002 (Lott was a U.S. senator from Mississippi). From a recording of his speech at a birthday party for U.S. senator Strom Thurmond, Lott seemed to suggest that the United States would have been a better country if Thurmond had won the presidency in 1948. Thurmond ran on a platform of racial segregation and lost the election to Harry S. Truman. Mainstream media did not report this speech, but liberal political bloggers attacked Lott vigorously, bringing the issue to the attention of the public. Lott resigned as Senate Minority Leader following this controversy (Wortham, 2007).

  What do you think were the reasons why political blogging in the early 2000s gained major traction? Do you follow political bloggers from online sites such as The Huffington Post, Politico, or The Daily Beast in the United States?

- Tim O'Reilly (O'Reilly Media, www.rader.oreilly.com) proposed a "**Blogger's Code of Conduct**" for bloggers to observe civility on their blogs, in part by moderating comments and following generally acceptable behavior through self-regulation. The list includes eliminating anonymous reader comments, taking responsibility for blogsites' contents, and ignoring trolls. Is a blogger's code of conduct necessary? Why or why not?

B6.2.2 Sociolinguistic Analysis of Blogs

With blogging becoming an important and widely recognized variety of online language, numerous studies of blogs have investigated topics as social import, genre characteristics of blogging, and the rhetoric of blog posts. Herring and Paolillo (2006) analyzed a select group of linguistic features (e.g., the relative frequency of pronouns, determiners, and certain function words) to investigate gender differences in blogs, and Pushmann (2007) examined variation in expressions of futurity in blogs. Aside from gender, the social categories of bloggers in scholarly studies include age, occupation (e.g., journalists blogging for an online publication vs. private individual/writer not affiliated with any established Web site), and theme (e.g., politics, sports, entertainment).

One of the main distinctions made in earlier research was to establish the linguistic patterns of personal blogs and thematic blogs. Krishnamurthy (2002) suggested that the personal versus thematic dimension was the most important classifier of blog types followed by whether or not a blog was produced by an individual or a group of people. Herring, Scheidt, Bonus, and Wright (2004) noted that group blogs are relatively rare and are probably best analyzed as distinct individual blogs. Related to these topics, Pushmann (2007) established a *corporate blog* type in which corporations blog about their products for marketing purposes. Corporate blogs appeared to be best classified as thematic blogs, given their narrow focus and marketing or product/service promotion goals. Entertainment bloggers have popularized thematic blogs with their coverage of popular media, focusing especially on celebrities, music, film, and television. Newer models and categories have emerged since 2010 because of the dominance of microblogs for immediate postings and updates. The structure and format of traditional blogging sites have also dramatically changed with photo blogging and the use of animated gif images increasingly added as common features.

B6.2.2.1 Gender Differences in Blogging

In general, blog categories can be formal or informal depending on their contextual features. Online diaries (personal, private) are different from corporate blogs (public, often edited) with regard to such characteristics as their target audiences and the number and frequency of regular updates, as well as other characteristics. Herring and Paolillo (2006) analyzed the functional distribution of stylistic features that appear to be associated both with the type of blog and the writer's gender. They wanted to know whether gender and blog type categorized as (1) diary blog and (2) filter blog (featuring news articles and reader comments) were predictors of linguistic variation in blogging. The blog corpus for this study was collected from a list of single-authored blogs drawn from two sources: a sampling of 100 blogs collected using the "random" feature of the blog-tracking site **blo.gs** (http://blo.gs/ping.php), while the second was a larger sample of blogs collected by following links from four random source blogs. The final sample comprised 127 entries drawn from 44 different blogs, with 65 entries written by women and 62 written by men. They found that blogs that were primarily intended as diary entries contained more "female" stylistic features than filter blogs regardless of authors' gender. Herring and Paolillo noted that this primary finding problematized the characterization of the stylistic features of language and suggested a need for more fine-grained blog-type analysis. At the same time, however, they observed that conventional associations of gender with certain spoken and written genres were reproduced in blogs, along with their societal valuations.

As expected, diary entries showed much greater use of personalization overall than filter blog entries. First person, plural pronouns (including possessives—*we*, *our*) demonstrated clearer separation along both gender and blog type categories. Female authors and diaries preferred the use of *we* and its variants *us*, *our*, and so on. Second person (*you*, *your*) appeared to be disfavored by female authors, but these did not produce significant differences in blog type. Similar to results from

Argamon, Koppel. Fine, and Shimoni (2003), third person masculine (*he*) was favored by female authors and more often used in filters. Finally, both third person feminine (*she*) and third person plural (*they*) were favored in filters but showed no significant gender difference. In terms of blog type, diaries appeared to favor first person reference (especially first person singular), as one might expect of personal journals. In contrast, filter blogs had more third person reference, which was consistent with their focus on external and public events.

A study by Pedersen and Macafee (2007) analyzed blogging in the United Kingdom compared to blogging in the United States in order to explore gender differences in blogging themes and behavior. Pedersen and Macafee also measured the extent of gender inequalities in the United Kingdom compared to data from U.S. bloggers. They collected a randomized sample of 48 female and male British bloggers who provided answers to a questionnaire about their blogging practices and attitudes. Additional data were also collected from these writers' blogs. For both genders, blogging was reported to be primarily a leisure activity, and men and women found the same range of satisfaction in blogging. However, more women used blogging as an outlet for creative work, whether as a hobby or as a source of livelihood. To Pedersen and Macafee, this suggested that women bloggers in both countries have a lower public profile. Gender differences in blogging were found primarily in three areas: (1) women tended to describe themselves as more interested in the social aspects of blogging, while men tended to be more interested in information and opinion; (2) men demonstrated more technical sophistication; and (3) privacy of communication and personal entries was a major issue for women (and also for gay bloggers of both sexes) but not for men.

Related research in the United States suggested that men were "more avid consumers than women of online information," while women were more enthusiastic online communicators (Fallows, 2005). In the United Kingdom, Pedersen and Macafee (2007) reported that women used blogs primarily to engage in the various social aspects of blogging. For example, more women were interested to participate in group blogs and also tended to belong to larger numbers of "blog rings" (i.e., links of themed blogs with easy access to related contents and topics written by other women). Women bloggers emphasized a sense of community in blogging and also made more mention of social interaction as something they valued. Feedback from readers, personal comments, and responses suggesting related topics or links to other Web sites/blogs were greatly appreciated by blog authors. In sum, Pedersen and Macafee found interesting similarities and differences in how men and women bloggers from the United States and the United Kingdom viewed the functions of blogging and the various social applications of blog components.

B6.2.2.2 Gender and Age in Blogs

In addition to gender, the role of age as a social variable influencing the functional and linguistic characteristics of blogs has also been studied by linguists. Friginal (2009a) (see sample result from this study in Figure A2.1) analyzed gender- and age-based variation in blogs by looking at a range of co-occurring linguistic features in addition to those analyzed by Argamon and colleagues (2003). Friginal wanted to extend the same research questions pursued by Argamon and colleagues in order to contrast formal versus informal texts (blogs represented informal, unedited texts). The personal blog corpus in this study, with 367 texts and approximately 2.5 million words, was manually collected from blogs written by American men and women in four age groups: (1) men 31 and over, (2) men 30 and under, (3) women 31 and over, and (4) women 30 and under.

Overall, Friginal's results mirrored those from Argamon and colleagues' (2003) study relative to how men and women used personalized features of writing. Women personalized their blogs more than men by using features that referred explicitly to themselves in the texts and encoded relationships between themselves and their intended readers. Younger women used significantly more of these features than older men. In general, women also used more lexical and syntactic features that communicated personal feelings, emotions, and assessments in their blogging. The use of first and second person (singular and plural) pronouns meant that the writer referred succinctly to himself or herself when conveying information and communicating feelings, reactions, and ideas, while at the same time involving or drawing the reader into the discourse (e.g., "**You** *will agree with* **me** *that Britney had to go to Paris*"—female, 19 years old, student).

Closely related to stance markers are egocentric sequences (*I* + private verbs: e.g., *I think*, *I feel*), interpreted as showing egocentrism and tentativeness in expression of ideas and assertions. Based on previous research in conversations and some forms of writing (e.g., Coates 1996; Rubin & Green 1992), women were found to use more of these discourse features than men. Results from Friginal (2009a) showed that gender- and age-based variation existed in the distribution of egocentric sequences in blogs, as well. *I think* was the most frequently used sequence, and on average, women bloggers used more of these egocentric sequences than men (only *I believe* was used slightly more by men than women in the corpus). A larger variation in the frequencies could be seen in the contrasts between the normalized counts from younger women and older men in their use of egocentric sequences (younger women = 2.22 vs. older men = 1.16 per 1,000 words).

Argamon, Koppel, Pennebaker, and Schler (2007) also found gender- and age-influenced linguistic and textual differences in a similar study of blogs. Articles and prepositions and themes such as *religion, politics, business*, and the *Internet* were used more by men as well as older bloggers than by women. Personal pronouns, conjunctions, auxiliary verbs, and themes focusing on *conversations*. "*At home*," *fun, romance*, and *swearing* were used more by women and younger bloggers. This study by Argamon and colleagues found only three exceptions to this pattern: (1) *family*, which as a theme was used more by older bloggers and by females; (2) *music*, which was used more by younger bloggers and by males; and (3) *school*, for which there was no significant difference between male and female usage.

Argamon and colleagues (2007) stressed that correlated gender- and age-based factors clearly illustrated significant variations in blogs reflecting the systematic linguistic preferences of men and women bloggers across age groups. Perhaps more significantly, however, their findings served to combine earlier observations regarding age- and gender-based writing characteristics that had not been previously synthesized. Earlier studies investigating gender and language have shown gender-based differences along dimensions of involvedness or contextualization. Other studies have found age-based differences in the immediacy and informality of writing (see, e.g., Pennebaker, Mehl, & Niederhoffer, 2003). Their findings suggested that these two sets of results were closely related.

B6.3 Facebook/Twitter Posts

Social media microblogs from Facebook and Twitter (status updates and tweets) are blogs that are reduced in both actual and aggregate file size compared to traditional blogs. Facebook and Twitter accounts allow users to quickly exchange abbreviated content like short comments, individual images, or video links (Kaplan & Haenlein, 2011). In many cases, these exchanges take the form of threaded comments, similar to instant messages (IM), the structure of text messages, or how Internet users post responses on bulletin boards. Clearly, microblogging in 2013 has changed the conventions in blogging and has become a more accessible option to share immediate information.

Scholarly studies of microblogs have looked at users' behavior and posting activity, public sentiment about an event or a celebrity, and business or political prediction models. In addition, more than traditional blogs, social and marketing research has tapped into Facebook and Twitter for data on psychosocial behavior and consumer profiles. Facebook and Twitter services have also become a major platform for public relations research, as these posts can be used to forecast real-world outcomes. For example, Asur and Huberman (2010) calculated expected movie box-office revenues from a model based on the frequency of Twitter posts for upcoming movies in the United States. They found that sentiments and the range of chatter extracted from Twitter can effectively forecast a film's revenue and critical reception. In 2013, Google reported that a combination of indexes has allowed it to predict box-office results with 94 percent accuracy.

Among microblogs as well as traditional blogs, then, linguistic and sociolinguistic analysis could certainly be conducted. While the predictive nature of social media has been examined using computer modeling, describing the linguistic characteristics of this form of communication would deepen our current understanding of online language. Insofar as they are a record of natural language use, microblogs offer fertile ground for linguistic inquiry (Friginal & Waugh, 2013).

B6.3.1 Facebook

Facebook, created at Harvard University by Mark Zuckerberg, started as a private social networking site in 2004, eventually becoming a global social media conglomerate in less than five years. Facebook allows users to create personal profiles and group pages in order to interact with other users in real-time or asynchronously via "status updates." These status updates are published on a user's (or group's) profile and then as news feeds within a user's network. Facebook network contacts, called *friends*, typically draw on users' existing offline social networks, consisting of diverse audiences from close friends and family to coworkers and acquaintances. The status update prompt in 2013, *What's on your mind?*, replaced the previous prompt, *What are you doing now?*, in 2009. This prompt encourages posts about current personal events, feelings, and opinions, although it is clear that many users ignore this question for the most part. Facebook activity directly shows personal information and the constructed public image of individuals as shared with people within and outside their networks, if permitted by privacy settings. Privacy in Facebook has been an ongoing issue, and popular media has been warning users about unintended consequences of disclosing information on Facebook that can be accessed by anyone from potential employers to cyber criminals (Friginal & Waugh, 2013). In addition, Facebook itself can collect personal information and user tracking data for various marketing and advertising purposes, and third party Web analysts can extract multiple personal posts without users' permission for big-data analytics. The popularity of Facebook for personal and professional networking has certainly helped business, political, and entertainment entities to reach their target audiences online.

B6.3.2 Twitter

Twitter has also been growing exponentially since its launch in 2006 as a mass media tool used to disseminate real-time information to large audiences. This microblogging platform is also effective in gathering information about people's reactions to current events. Twitter users post short messages (called tweets) which are available to followers or to everyone online depending on the user's privacy settings. Tweets, which are currently limited to 140 characters, can also include hyperlinks and images; however, Álvarez, Muñoz, and Herington (2010) found that most tweets used only half of the available character space. Tweets are made more easily searchable by the optional inclusion of topic markers called "hashtags" (a "#" followed by the topic word) and references to other users ("@" followed by username). Users can subscribe to, or follow, other users' tweets based on shared interest—for example, entertainment topics and news and not necessarily on personal relationships. Most followers and users can reply to a tweet, but it is not necessarily expected in this platform, as in Facebook. Tweets can also be retweeted in their original or modified form, pushing the same tweet to subsequent followers' news feeds. Because of its focus on real-time, interactive sharing of information, Twitter has become very popular with celebrities and politicians.

Twitter has been utilized as the source for breaking news that is faster than any other form of media reporting. Major events such as the Boston Marathon bombing in 2013 and the violent Egyptian protests in 2011–2012 were reported first on Twitter by individuals from professional journalists to casual witnesses. Its accessibility and affordance for direct communication between emergency responders and affected individuals have proven useful during many recent disasters and natural calamities. It is clear that Twitter as a platform to spread immediate information and issue real-time announcements and warnings could be adopted for official emergency response (see, e.g., Mills, Chen, Lee, & Rao, 2009). As expected, Twitter activity spikes during significant events that move users to tweet their opinions, observations, and sentiments, such as major sporting events (e.g., the Olympics, World Cup, U.S. Super Bowl), deaths of celebrities, global pageants and award ceremonies, and national elections.

In general, however, a majority of Twitter's content is of a personal and phatic nature, and a recent Twitter trend study showed that there was only a small group of active users contributing to most of the site's content. Based on an analysis of more than 11 million registered users, only 10 percent of active users accounted for 86 percent of all activity in 2010 (Stratmann, 2010). In 2013, it was reported that popular celebrity users such as Lady Gaga, Justin Beiber, and Ashton Kutcher had millions of dummy or fake Twitter followers.

B6.3.3 Sociolinguistic Analysis of Microblogs

Research on Facebook and Twitter language has focused on a range of topics such as sociopsychological concerns, business and professional applications, public relations, and political campaigns and the relationship between online and offline political activities. Related research in the area of Natural Language Processing has explored the aforementioned sentiment analysis, first story detection for significant events, extraction of critical information during mass emergencies, redundancy detection to enable presentation of diverse and informative content, and extraction of verb duration in units of time. The applications of Facebook and Twitter in academic settings have also been investigated, especially the ways in which teachers can utilize these sites to encourage written interaction and practice, critical thinking, and engagement.

There are a growing number of studies that explore Facebook and Twitter posts from a sociolinguistic standpoint. Register analysis of microblogging using a corpus of posts and tweets can provide an important description of emerging linguistic patterns in social media. For example, Carr, Schrock, and Dauterman (2012) analyzed the frequency and function of various speech acts and humor in

Facebook status updates. They reported that self-expression and self-disclosure in Facebook influenced the popular use of expressive speech acts, followed by assertive speech acts. Humor was used in various contexts but attached to personal topics and references. As we discussed in Section B1, tweets have been effectively used in dialectology studies, with 58 percent of tweets, from a corpus of 500 tweets, 100 each from five U.S. cities, correctly assigned to their posters' city of origin in the United States. A related ongoing study is also looking at the identification of specific lexical features of tweets that may be part of an emerging regional "tweet dialect" (Juola, Ryan, & Mehok, 2011).

Several corpus-based qualitative studies have also investigated the linguistic features of Facebook status updates using a content analysis approach. For example, Page (2010) examined short, episodic narratives embedded in a corpus of Facebook status updates from a narrative theory perspective. Unlike traditional narratives (i.e., based on past events and making use of past tense verbs), Facebook narratives were often found to be framed in the present time. The focus on immediacy, recency, and future events, with stories unfolding over multiple posts in real-time, appeared to be prevalent way for users to post references to past events. With regard to content, Lee (2011) explored literacy practices in Facebook status updates, which combine features of blogging, texting, and instant messaging into a new hybrid subregister.

In an exploratory cross-linguistic comparison of tweets, Álvarez and colleagues (2010) noted differences in the frequencies of certain parts of speech and the use of emoticons and ellipses, which may substitute for these linguistic markers. Twitter's feature incorporating user-defined metadata into particular posts has created new communicative practices in this medium, which, arguably, influence how users frame and send messages to their known and unknown followers. Similarly, hashtags in tweets have expanded their meaning beyond simple metadata. Hashtags indicate a searchable topic and function as evaluation and emphasis, thus enabling them to convey a value stance. The fact that hashtags allow tweets to be found more easily by others with shared values suggests that they act as an invitation to form dynamic affiliations around common values. Such an invitation is an example of a new communicative practice that has evolved within this unique medium (Friginal & Waugh, 2013).

Reflective Break

- Think about gender- and age-based research questions that can guide your sociolinguistic study of Facebook and Twitter posts. What are ways to collect your corpus of microblogs?
- What are linguistic similarities and differences between traditional personal blogging and microblogging? Both subregisters are categorized as primarily informal but their contents, target readers, and production circumstances are

different. Do you think microblogs are more personal than traditional blogs (e.g., use of personal pronouns)?

B6.4 Newspaper Articles and Opinion Columns

Newspaper writing is not necessarily categorized as a Web-based register per se; however, newspaper articles have been frequently explored in CL because of the availability of news corpora (e.g., both the BNC and ANC offer newspaper texts) and ease in collecting specialized newspaper texts online. In addition, searchable Web sites such as COCA and COHA can immediately return keyword frequency counts and comparative charts from various newspapers. An archive of newspaper articles from the *New York Times* and many other established publications is also available.

A significant amount of news content is now produced and read online, and researchers have begun to address issues related to this shift from traditional paper-based publications to news content read on desktop computers, mobile phones, and tablets. Studies have analyzed the degree of reader preferences for online news platforms, business models that react to the shift to online news, and the quality of journalistic reporting in online news. There is also a wealth of comparative studies focusing on linguistic variations in newspaper writing that follow CL approaches.

Online opinion columns cover a range of topics: political and business commentaries, lifestyle, entertainment, travel, sports and leisure, and science and technology. Web-only publications such as Slate, The Huffington Post, Politico, and ESPN (ESPN has a separate magazine division) have designated pages for opinion writers and columnists. As noted by Haarmann and Lombardo (2009), research on opinion columns and editorials is common in CL and media studies as part of an umbrella of newspaper registers. Content analyses of opinion columns have focused on political debate, evaluation of competing policy views, and personal focus or thematic variation. Additional features from online opinion columns not available in print include links to related articles; embedded pictures, videos, and presentation slides; and reader comments or feedback.

Sociolinguistic studies of newspaper articles and opinion columns have focused on the gender of authors, topical or register variation (e.g., comparison of travel/leisure, sports, and news articles), and cross-linguistic comparisons. For example, Hardy and Friginal (2012) compared the distribution of informational discourse features, narrative markers, focus on addressees, and themes in online opinion columns written in English by Americans and Filipinos. They reported that language background influenced variations in how writers evaluated information and expressed critical ideas and opinions. Unlike American opinion columns, Filipino columns were more formal and scholarly, somewhat similar in linguistic composition to newspaper articles, and slightly less personal than those written by

Americans who favored individualized expressions (e.g., *I, my, this to me is . . . my take on this, you'll agree with me*) and personal narratives.

B6.5 Reader Comments/Feedback

Reader opinions, comments, or feedback have become very popular, as Web sites solicit reader response to articles or blog posts. The number of comments (and "clicks" to a Web site's page) has become a measure for a Web site's popularity with its target audience and a source of additional advertising revenue. Readers post reactions to online content, to which other readers may then respond. A variety of Web sites and platforms, including Yahoo!, ESPN, CNN news, USA Today, the Guardian (U.K.) online, regularly solicit and receive comments after an article (especially those that are controversial, funny, or viral). Various posts from celebrity bloggers and threaded discussions in Reddit have elicited reader replies, producing a wealth of texts which are typically unedited or loosely regulated. These reader comments can be automatically crawled from online sources and sampled across popular topics such as politics, movies, music, and sports. Studies of online comments posted on Web sites are often qualitative (see, e.g., Goss, 2007, which examines political disagreements in threaded postings). To date, it appears that little work has been done in describing the linguistic characteristics of language in reader comments.

B6.6 Other Web Registers

Mining the Internet for specialized registers for sociolinguistic studies promises to be a very productive research endeavor. There are many available established, exclusively online texts that might be collected to form a corpus, together with new or emerging subvarieties that have not yet been extensively explored. Clearly, the Internet offers many opportunities for researchers and students of sociolinguistics to collect unique data, design a specialized corpus, and analyze a broad range of linguistic features. For example, **personals** (e.g., from dating sites such as Match.com or eHarmony) could be analyzed to investigate the role of gender and age in how individuals write about themselves in the context of meeting someone. **Classified ads** including **job announcements** (e.g., jobsearch.com, monster.com, job.com) could be studied by comparing the structure of the advertisement across categories such as occupation or company, location/regional background, and salary. The way **eBay members** package their products for auction, provide additional information and pictures, and appeal to community members (e.g., comic book fans, antique collectors, collectors of sports memorabilia) could be extensively studied by focusing on linguistic markers used by these members (who do not belong to major corporations or established businesses) to sell and ship products individually. Text Sample B6.2 below shows how an eBay seller structured the description of the item to provide information to potential buyers (notice the affect and use of punctuation: *Fun!*, "*rata-tat-tat*").

Text Sample B6.2. Sample Product Information for eBay Auction

Fun Vintage Chicken Pecking Action Toy! Pre-Batteries! Hand Painted, Works Well!

Item condition: Used

"Good working condition, strings in good condition."

Here we have 5 very hungry chickens all pecking desperately for a very few grains of feed. This is a fun vintage "action toy" which activates by a circular rotation which makes the wood ball swing in a circle, alternately loosening and tightening the strings on each of the 5 chickens so that when a chicken's string is slack, she's pecking and when taut, head up! There is a fun, loud pecking "rata-tat-tat" as the beaks hit the board. Fun! The chickens are painted bright, sort of transparent colors, as shown, and it's an attractive piece just sitting around.

The toy is 10 1/3" long and the round board is 5 3/4" in diameter.

Thanks for looking! Have an enjoyable day.

Finally, **product reviews** found on several online retailers such as Amazon. com or also in app stores, iTunes (e.g., reviews of MP4 albums, movies, and television shows), and many other types of customer feedback (e.g., hotels, car rental companies, restaurants, and venues) could be collected to create various subcorpora of Web-based customer/user reviews. Online product reviews, for example, have been described as very personal in overall style, with consistent rhetorical strategies that match their target readers. Skalicky (2013) conducted a genre analysis of Amazon.com product reviews that have been rated as "most helpful" by users/readers. He found that product reviews that contain new information and those projected as coming from experts were preferred by the Amazon.com discourse community.

Reflective Break

- What did you notice from the eBay product information in Text Sample B6.2? How similar or different is this presentation from other advertising genres (e.g., print or corporate advertising)? It would be interesting to investigate the connection between writing clarity and quality in eBay advertising and what the community prefers, and also whether or not the product sold. How can we study this connection?
- What other Web registers do you think can provide you with an interesting corpus to study? What linguistic features will you compare?

- Are there qualitatively noticeable differences between celebrity and political tweets? What are your reasons for following people who are not your family or friends on Twitter? Have you paid attention to their use of language?

B6.7 Functional Linguistic Dimensions of Web Registers

Titak and Roberson (2013) conducted a corpus-based, multidimensional analysis to investigate the structural and functional linguistic variation in Web registers represented by **blogs, microblogs, workplace e-mails, discussion posts** and **reader feedback,** and **online newspaper** and **opinion columns.** An earlier, related study by Grieve and colleagues (2010) focused only on personal blog texts from blog sites hosted in the United States. In Section C2, we discuss Biber's multidimensional (MD) analysis approach in the study of linguistic variation. We also provide an overview of this analytical (statistical) technique and the principal steps in running the analysis. Thus, you might benefit from reading our introduction to MD analysis first to fully understand the study described below.

The primary goal of Titak and Roberson's study was to establish the linguistic dimensions of online, written American English from Web sites and platforms that originated within the United States. The corpus of Web registers was collected from various public domains from 2006 to the present. This corpus did not actually follow an a priori corpus design guiding the compilation of texts or defining the required size of each subcorpus. In addition, some of the texts (e.g., online opinion columns and newspaper articles) were obtained from already existing corpora such as the American National Corpus (ANC). However, their Web texts were sampled across topics and demographics of writers. For example, e-mails from the Enron Corpus, which were conveniently sampled from all the folders available at the Cognitive Assistant that Learns and Organizes Project (http://www.ai.sri.com/project/CALO), covered various business and workplace topics and were coded for gender and management positions in the company. The newspaper texts from the *New York Times* and the opinion columns from Slate online were randomly sampled from the ANC database. Texts were collected automatically and manually across registers and were cleaned to ensure that linguistic and POS-tags were consistent across the board. Blogs have the highest number of words (4.4 million), while workplace e-mails have the least (325,450). The corpus has approximately 16,501,785 words. Table B6.1 shows the composition of this Web registers corpus.

As a sociolinguistic study, the key focus of Titak and Roberson's (2013) analysis was register variation in online language. The application of Biber's MD analysis was based on the theoretical assumption that register differences in online language have underlying linguistic co-occurrence patterns. When applied to linguistic data, MD analysis can be used to identify the sets of features that tend to co-occur within e-mails, vis-à-vis status updates, as well as other online registers. Hence, the linguistic patterning from these registers illustrates the influence

TABLE B6.1. Composition of the Web registers corpus

Registers	Approximate Number of Words
1 Blogs	4,423,267
2 Facebook/Twitter Posts	3,504,762
3 Newspaper Articles	3,398,012
4 Workplace E-mails	325,450
5 Opinion Columns	1,298,671
6 Reader Comments	3,551,623
Total	16,501,785

Source: adapted from Titak and Roberson, 2013, p. 285

of production constraints (e.g., e-mails have variable lengths while Facebook posts follow a default limit of 420 characters per status post, as of late 2012, and 704 characters for Notes), setting, topic, and target readers. Titak and Roberson reported that the four functional dimensions of online language include (1) personal narrative focus versus descriptive, informational production; (2) involved, interactive discourse; (3) complex statement of opinion; and (4) past versus present orientation. The co-occurring linguistic composition of these four dimensions is shown in Table B6.2.

B6.7.1 Understanding Production Focus in Online Language

Dimension 1 (*Personal Narrative Focus vs. Descriptive, Informational Production*) from Titak and Roberson (2013) was composed of 28 linguistic features; 19 features were on the positive side of the scale, while the negative side had 9 (Table B6.2). The positive scale included features that suggest personal and subjective production of texts (e.g., private verbs, first person pronouns, and mental verbs), narrativity (e.g., demonstrative pronouns, emphatics, and the pronoun *it*), and syntactic features that serve to provide more elaborated information (e.g., coordinating conjunctions, subordinating conjunctions, all WH words, *that* clauses with factive verbs, and *that* clauses with *like*). This combination of features suggested that the style of writing was personal and at the same time detailed in its focus on events. The use of second person pronouns (i.e., "addressee focused" features) also suggested that the writer was addressing an audience assumed to consist of people known to him or her.

Many of the negative features in this dimension, including average word length, nouns, nominalizations (e.g., words ending in *tion* and *ment*), attributive adjectives, agentless passives, and passives indicated a nominal style that emphasized the transmission of information. Grieve and colleagues (2010) pointed out that

TABLE B6.2. Linguistic composition of the four dimensions of online language

Dimension	Loading	Features
1 Personal Narrative Focus vs. Descriptive, Informational Production	Positive	private verbs, verbs, second person pronouns, first person pronouns, demonstrative pronouns, emphatics, pronoun *it*, nominal pronouns, coordinating conjunctions, other adverbs, past tense verbs, subordinating conjunctionconditional, adverbial conjuncts, all conjunctions, all *WH* words, nonauxiliary verbs, *that* clauses with factive verbs, *that* clauses with *like*, factive adverb, mental verbs
	Negative	word length, nouns, prepositions, attributive adjectives, public verbs, nominalizations, agentless passives, passives, communication verbs
2 Involved, Interactive Discourse	Positive	private verbs, verbs, second person pronouns, first person pronouns, *be* as main verb, discourse particles, modals of possibility, infinitive verb, modal of prediction, subordinating conjunctionconditional, all *WH*-words, nonauxiliary verbs, *to* complement clauses controlled by verbs of desire intention and decision, all stance *to* complement clauses, stance *to* complement clauses controlled by verbs, activity verbs, mental verbs
	Negative	word length, nouns, prepositions, attributive adjectives
3 Complex Statement of Opinion	Positive	*that* deletion, public verbs, *that* complement clause controlled by verb, *that* complement clause controlled by factive noun, *that* clauses with factive verbs, that clauses using *like*, stance *that* complement clauses controlled by verbs, all stance *that* complement clauses, communication verbs
	Negative	(no negative features)
4 Past vs. Present Orientation	Positive	first person pronouns, past tense, third person pronouns, nonauxiliary verbs, activity verbs
	Negative	word length, attributive adjectives, nominalizations, process nouns

Source: adapted from Titak and Roberson, 2013, p. 286

passives typically illustrate nominal style, as passives tend to call attention to the noun phrase in the patient role. In addition, the negative side also contained verb categories such as communication verbs (e.g., *demonstrate, explain, show*) and public verbs (e.g., *speak, announce*), which illustrated that the texts on the negative side of this dimension were written to show descriptive evidence or data. Online writers may be addressing a range of intended readers from familiar to the unfamiliar, but the clear emphasis of writing here was on providing detailed information.

The text samples below show contrasts between a personal blog post, with more *positive* features of Dimension 1, and a newspaper article (more *negative* features). Texts with more positive features demonstrated a highly personal style of address, whereas the negative texts focused more on the delivery of information.

Text Sample B6.3. Dimension 1 Comparative Texts (from Titak and Roberson, 2013)

Blogs (Personal Blog)

I walk into the bathroom, *close* the door and just as *I took off* my shirt there's a hard, rapid knock on the door. My roommates are gone, my friends just *left*, and the door was unlocked . . . so *I* had no idea who it would be. *I pull* on a hoodie and *run* downstairs. Both the stair lights and the porch lights are out. There's a black figure there. *I open* the door and it *happens* to be a man *I met* in Perkins in the middle of the night two or three weeks ago. *I* had not *told* him my phone number or *where I lived*.

News (NYT)

Earlier in the day the printing *operation* at the *State House* was working furiously to churn out *copies* of the *many amendments* that were *surfacing* to the *arena bill*. The *arena measure*, which *McGreevey supports*, would also *create sports* and *entertainment districts* for *Harrison* to build a *soccer arena*, and *Pennsauken* to build a *minor league hockey rink*. The *districts* would be allowed to keep some of the sales *taxes collected* at the *venues* to pay off *construction costs*.

As shown in the two text excerpts, personal blog posts are typically narrative, and they discuss a topic more appropriate for an audience who is familiar with the blogger. These texts include a substantial number of verbs, WH words, first and second person pronouns, as well as the pronoun *it*. Texts with more negative features in this dimension (e.g., news articles and Facebook/Twitter posts) demonstrate informational style of address, with prepositions, *be* as the main verb, infinitive verbs, and nonauxiliary verbs. Nouns are very frequent in the texts.

To compare the six Web registers in Dimension 1, Titak and Roberson (2013) computed each register's average dimension scores, which are then plotted in the dimension scale below (Figure B6.1).

On average, blogs and e-mails involved a more personal and narrative style, whereas newspaper articles and Facebook/Twitter updates focused more on the delivery of nominal information. Surprisingly, this dimension showed the linguistic similarities between news articles and microblogs. Nouns (especially proper nouns) and prepositions were very common in these two groups of texts. This dimension also captured differences between personal blogs and microblogs. The

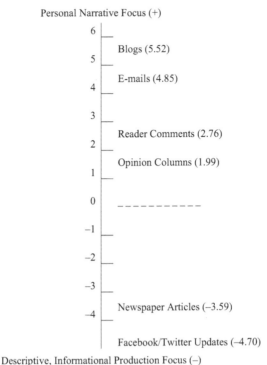

Personal Narrative Focus (+)

6

Blogs (5.52)

5

E-mails (4.85)

4

3

Reader Comments (2.76)

2

Opinion Columns (1.99)

1

0 – – – – – – – – – –

–1

–2

–3

Newspaper Articles (–3.59)

–4

Facebook/Twitter Updates (–4.70)

Descriptive, Informational Production Focus (–)

FIGURE B6.1 Comparison of average factor scores for Dimension 1: *Personal Narrative* vs. *Descriptive and Informational Production*; Kruskal-Wallis ANOVA, $p < .001$

Source: adapted from Titak and Roberson, 2013, p. 287

structure of Facebook/Twitter status updates, although very personal, was clearly limited in narrativity. Allowable average length of posts (measured in characters) has certainly influenced how posters composed their texts in this platform. Blogging, on the other hand, provided more opportunities for narration, "free writes," and use of addressee-focused features (e.g., *you, your*) directed to target readers.

Conducting Corpus-Based Sociolinguistic Studies

C1

DESIGNING YOUR OWN SOCIOLINGUISTIC CORPUS

C1.1 Corpus Collection

It is tempting to think that collecting a corpus, especially a do-it-yourself (DIY) corpus, is a study in itself. It is understandable for someone to say, "*I want to know how* [blank linguistic group] *talks, so I'll just make a corpus out of that.*" However, constructing your own corpus takes a lot more thought and planning than that. Before you begin constructing your corpus, it is essential that you first develop your research question. Although much can be understood through exploration of any dataset, the way that your corpus will be organized, compiled, and analyzed will depend upon the questions you want to answer.

Following a systematic procedure when collecting your corpus can be compared to medical experimental research. For example, in a pharmaceutical trial of a new medication, researchers take great care to control for many variables: the participants, the time of day the medication is taken, the amount of medication given for trials, and other medications the person is taking. For research based on your own corpus, there are also important considerations to maintain a sound design. The corpus' texts are your "participants"; in other words, these texts are your observations. To create a corpus well-designed for sociolinguistic research, it is critical that this be remembered. The same sampling issues associated with other social science research can be applied to creating a corpus by looking at your texts this way. The following sections describe what to do before collection and then how to collect and organize your corpus.

C1.1.1 Reading Previous Research and Finalizing Research Questions

Before you start compiling your corpus, it is important that you familiarize yourself with what has already been done. The most important reason for this is that there may be a preexisting, and perhaps even publicly available, corpus appropriate for the study you want to conduct. Another reason that you may want to read previous research is that maybe someone has already asked the same questions that you are asking. Studies that have investigated similar questions can help inform your own study. Perhaps the other study investigated the same target population you are interested in, but it was largely about linguistic variation across speakers based on their age, and maybe you are interested in differences based on gender or social status.

Because much of the current research in sociolinguistics follows qualitative and ethnographic approaches, studies that have looked at constructs that you find interesting may have some findings based on a very small number of participants. Corpus-based sociolinguistics offers a good way to find additional quantitative support that can be used to help make claims more generalizable. A corpus study that investigates the same constructs as a qualitative study also has the potential of disclosing the idiosyncrasies present when one has a very small sample size. Examine research questions if they are explicit in published studies and how the researchers have directly connected important parameters between their questions and their corpus. A principled collection of naturally occurring texts maintains a strict design. Consider an inclusion and exclusion criteria guided by your questions as you plan your corpus collection.

In a study that explored how the Israeli–Palestinian conflict has been covered and reported in American, Arab, and British Media, Kandil (2008) developed the following corpus-based research questions:

- Do the different news sources under investigation tend to use different linguistic forms (vocabulary and grammar) to represent the same events and the same participants in the Israeli–Palestinian conflict? If so,
  - Where do the differences lie?
  - Do these different forms have the potential of representing one side or the other in a more favorable way?
  - Is it likely that some of these forms can obscure the nature of the conflict?
- Is it true that the British media represented by the BBC is more evenhanded in its representation of the different parties and events involved in the conflict?
- In the case of the U.S. media, is there an internal difference between the two news outlets included, namely Fox News and CNN?

Based on these questions, Kandil needed to collect texts exclusively reporting on the Israeli–Palestinian conflict from American, Arab, and British media. With these questions, there are numerous ways to proceed and also several texts and contexts to include and to not include. Why the BBC, CNN, and Fox News, and Al-Jazeera? What are justifications for these choices? What subregisters to highlight (e.g., news reports vs. opinion columns)? Ultimately, a researcher needs to make a decision here, and narrowing focus and considerations is often necessary.

Below, Kandil (2008) provided the descriptions of his focus in corpus collection, with justifications as to how he arrived at his sources and use of additional materials:

This research will be conducted on four news reports corpora compiled from the websites of American, Arab, and British news channels. The news channels selected for this research are: Fox News and CNN from the United States, Al-Jazeera from Qatar, and the BBC from Great Britain. This choice is based on two public surveys of media credibility. The most recent one was conducted by the Global Public Opinion and Stakeholder Research (Globescan, 2006) on behalf of the BBC and Reuters. The Globescan survey was conducted in ten nations, including the United States, Britain, and Egypt. Among the findings that concern this study is what participants spontaneously pointed out as the most trusted source of news in each one of these countries. In the United States, CNN and Fox News received the highest ratings, each mentioned by 11% of the respondents. In Britain, BBC was mentioned by 32% and comes on top of the list. Results from Egypt were unique in that the majority of respondents (77%) mentioned that they trusted international news channels more than Egyptian ones. The survey analysts attributed this to the influence of Al-Jazeera, which was spontaneously mentioned by 55% of the Egyptian participants as the most trusted news source.

An earlier survey conducted by the PEW Research Center (2004) in the United States reveals more interesting information about Fox News and CNN. This survey also included information about a participant's political affiliation, mainly Democrat, Republican, or Independent. Even though Fox News appears on top of the Republicans' list of the most trusted news source, it does not appear in the top six for either Democrats or Independents. On the other hand, Democrats' most trusted news source is CNN, which also appears in the second position of both the Republicans and Independents.

The corpora will be compiled from the archives of these channels' websites starting from the year 2000 to the present. In the case of Al-Jazeera, the corpus will be compiled from their Arabic website, not the English website. One reason for this is that I want to capture the type of language directed at native Arabic speakers, which might differ from that directed to a broader international audience. Similarly, in the case of BBC and CNN, the corpora will be compiled from the national editions of their websites which target local rather than international audiences. To access the relevant news reports, I will search each website for articles that have the keywords Israel, Israeli(s), Palestine, or Palestinian(s) and their Arabic translations on the Al-Jazeera website. The complete reports will be copied and pasted into computer readable text files. The news reports for each month will be saved in a separate text file with the important file information such as the period covered included in a header at the beginning of the file. One advantage for saving the news reports for each month in a separate file is that it allows the researcher to know if a certain linguistic feature is pervasive in a corpus or if it is just due to the idiosyncrasies of a few texts. Information about the number of files in which a certain feature occurs is usually made available by corpus handling programs such as *Wordsmith Tools* (Scott, 1996). This type of information will not be apparent if texts are combined into one big file.

I expect the size of each corpus to be about 200,000 words. According to Baker (2006), this is a reasonable size for a discourse study. The corpora compiled for this study will fall under what has been called specialized corpora (Baker, 2006; Hunston, 2002; McEnery, Xiao, & Tono, 2006), or corpora that are designed to study aspects of a specific genre. For the purpose of a discourse study, this type of corpora needs to be big enough to allow patterns to show up using quantitative methods, but small enough to allow a more thorough human interaction with the corpus (Partington, 2003). Stubbs (1996) compared two very small corpora, consisting of 330 and 550 words each, and was still able to find patterns of difference. Shalom (1997) also used a relatively small corpus, less than 20,000 words, to study lexical and grammatical patterns in personal advertisements. In his study of White House press briefings, Partington (2003) used a corpus of 250,000 words. Similarly, Baker (2006) used three corpora, each consisting of no more than 200,000 words, in order to demonstrate how corpus-based techniques can be used to study discourse.

Finally, this study will also make use of large reference corpora in order to compare some linguistic features that will show up in the analysis of the specialized corpora mentioned above to the more conventional norms of the language. Some features in the Fox, CNN, and BBC English corpora will be compared against features in the Bank of English Corpus (BEC) and/or the Reuters Corpus Volume 1 (RCV1). My Arabic reference corpus will be the Corpus of Contemporary Arabic (CCA), designed by Latifa Al-Sualiti and Eric Atwell to represent the current state of the Arabic language (Al-Sulaiti & Atwell, 2006). (Kandil, 2008, pp. 20–23)

C1.1.2 Feasibility of Collection

Another area that needs to be considered is how your corpus will actually be collected. For example, what is the feasibility that you can actually collect, organize, annotate, analyze, and write about your data? Conducting a corpus-based study using a newly collected corpus for a course project, for example, is a very ambitious task. In that case, the construction of a corpus would need to begin relatively early in the term. One way that we suggest a DIY corpus be approached is to create a design plan similar to Kandil's (2008) plan, explanation, and justification above. Your design plan includes information about how texts will be collected, how they will be organized, the questions that you want to answer directly linked to the particular group of texts that will answer them, and how you can interpret anticipated results. Making sure that the constructs you are interested in are sufficiently represented and defined is thus important.

Having made clear what you want to investigate, you can then start to think about how you will answer those questions. If, for example, you are interested in the lexical bundles that are produced by teenage speakers of a particular dialect, you would need to consider what it would take to collect a corpus of one million words. The language of speech and writing has been shown to be quite different. Because of this, if your question involves the language as it is spoken, which is the case for most sociolinguistic studies, you also need to consider the difficulties associated with finding willing participants, recording speech, and transcribing tapes.

For these reasons, many corpus-based studies that have been conducted using DIY corpora have explored written language—and not just written language but actually digital or electronic written language. Texts that are found online, for example, are very easily copied and saved to .txt files (similar to how Kandil obtained texts from online archives from CNN, BBC, Fox, and Al-Jazeera). If your research question asks about student-written notes, on the other hand, you may be required to retype those notes from paper. Another option, if the writing on paper is typed or clearly handwritten, is to scan the paper samples then use an OCR or "optical character recognition" software to convert these hard copy texts into electronic files readable by the computer.

C1.1.3 Representativeness and Sampling

Because random sampling (consider reviewing Section A4.2.1) is difficult to achieve, you need to think about how you are going to create a balanced corpus that is representative of the population you are interested in. One useful way to do this is through **stratified random sampling** as determined by your corpus matrix. In this case, your secondary variables can help you select your participants or texts, and this creates a balanced quota for each group, which also helps you further define your inclusion/exclusion criteria. If you have enough time to collect your texts (especially online texts), then consider collecting more text samples across a wider range of categories. It will be very manageable for you to reach a million words by manually copying and pasting from online sources, but try to gain access to automated Web-crawling programs, which can fast-track your collection. Make sure that you only "crawl" public domain sites.

As we emphasized in Section A4.2, representativeness can be statistically measured following linguistic and sampling criteria. If you are studying a very rare linguistic form or structure—for example, the distribution of *wh-* cleft constructions in speech (e.g., "[*What I can say to you*] *is get out!*")—then you need a large corpus of spoken interactions to make sure that you extract enough occurrences of this structure. If you are looking only at distributions of nouns and verbs, then a normalized frequency of these POS-tagged features from a corpus of about 200,000 words may be enough, as these features occur very frequently in the texts. As also stated by Kandil (2008) above, Baker (2006) suggested that a corpus with 200,000 words may be enough for a discourse analysis study.

For specific statistical applications such as Factor or Cluster Analysis, you need to have a particular number of texts (i.e., observations) in order to satisfy basic assumptions of variables-to-observations ratio, normality, and homogeneity—also related to the statistical concept of representativeness. We revisit this topic in Section C2.

C1.1.4 Collection

Finally, we get to the description of actual corpus collection. Although it would be tempting to begin collecting your corpus as soon as possible, it is important to go through the processes described above first. For most of us, the corpora we collect are not meant to be used by other people. These corpora are also used primarily for academic purposes (and not for sale or resale).

Most corpus-based programs require the use of plain text files, which are saved as **.txt** (e.g., Notepad or Wordpad in many Windows-based personal computers). In these files, the text is minimally formatted. For example, it does not include bolding, underlining, or font differences. Most .txt files are saved using the encoding scheme ASCII (American Standard Code for Information Interchange). This is a useful system because of its simplicity and ability to be used in multiple formats and programs, including most corpus tools. With increasing amounts of research being completed in languages that do not use the Roman alphabet, however, there are limitations to ASCII. Where ASCII can represent 128 characters, Unicode, another encoding scheme, can represent more than 100,000 characters.

The .txt format is not commonly used in the sources from which corpus collectors find their texts. For example, most online sources are in **HTML** (hypertext markup language) format. This is a system for coding Web sites, creating the format that we see on Internet browsers. It is good to become familiar with the various ways to save texts and also in how to convert other files (e.g., Microsoft Word documents or PDFs). Look at options for batch converters online (e.g., convert PDF to text programs), which will make it easier for you when you need to process hundreds of .doc or .pdf files.

It is important to have an organization system in place for your texts. Organizing the data will help facilitate analysis later. In addition to ease of use, having a system in place will allow you to always know where to look in case you need text samples or information about a particular file. Creating header information and consistent use of titles, numbers, or codes can help you to better organize your folders. A spreadsheet with information about your files (e.g., annotations for length/number of words, speaker or writer, dates and locations) is also almost always necessary. We recommend treating corpus collection the same as one would treat any other data collection procedure: Write everything down. Keeping a research log can help organize your thoughts in the moment, but it can also help you when you need to revisit your data or if you begin to work on the data with a colleague.

Two useful ways to organize your data are (1) through a master spreadsheet and (2) purposeful file names. These complementary methods are described below:

- When we collect corpora, there are often dozens, hundreds, even thousands of texts involved. Such numbers can quickly become overwhelming if not well organized. In a corpus that explores disciplinary variation in writing, the Michigan Corpus of Upper-Level Student Papers or MICUSP, the text files were organized into folders based on different disciplines. These folders contain subfolders with texts organized according to other independent variables, such as level (e.g., graduate vs. undergraduate) or paper type.
- When all of these texts are saved in this way, one cannot necessarily see them all together. This is where a spreadsheet can help. When working with a corpus, we find it essential to create a master list of all of your texts. This type of list is imperative to include information about your texts in a searchable format. In a way, this acts like the demographic sheets you might keep about your participants in a more qualitative study. However, in this case, the sheet allows for quick searches.
- Your spreadsheet can easily be sorted based on your column categories. This is useful especially when dealing with a large number of texts, which may be organized into folders that do not reflect the variable you are interested at the time. Such a spreadsheet can also be directly imported into statistical software such as SPSS.
- Another useful organizational tool in corpus collection is to label your files in ways that show information that is important to your investigation. For example, MICUSP is labeled based on (1) discipline, (2) level of education, (3) participant number, and (4) the number of texts submitted by that participant. Your research question may not require the analysis of quite as many variables as the MICUSP project. In most cases, as a student, you may have one central variable that you are investigating such as age or gender. Instead of using disciplines for your file naming system, you could choose something that signifies your research question.

Sinclair (2005) provided a guide for corpus collection that can certainly help you compile your sociolinguistic corpus. Sinclair focused on the size and language samples, as well as representativeness and balance. He also emphasized the need to establish clear criteria for the inclusion or exclusion of texts and careful documentation of corpus design and composition:

1. Criteria for determining the structure of a corpus should be small in number, clearly separate from each other, and efficient as a group in delineating a corpus that is representative of the language or variety under examination.
2. Any information about a text other than the alphanumeric string of its words and punctuation should be stored separately from the plain text and merged when required in applications.
3. Samples of language for a corpus should wherever possible consist of entire documents or transcriptions of complete speech events, or should get as close to this target as possible. This means that samples will differ substantially in size.
4. The design and composition of a corpus should be documented fully with information about the contents and arguments in justification of the decisions taken.
5. The corpus builder should retain, as target notions, representativeness and balance. While these are not precisely definable and attainable goals, they must be used to guide the design of a corpus and the selection of its components.
6. Any control of subject matter in a corpus should be imposed by the use of external, and not internal, criteria.
7. A corpus should aim for homogeneity in its components while maintaining adequate coverage, and rogue texts should be avoided. (Sinclair, 2005, Chapter 1)

Reflective Break

- In studying the structure of written English often read by or distributed to Limited English Proficiency (LEP) immigrants and refugees in the United States, Roberts and Murphy (2012) designed a corpus that organized texts into the following categories: parenting, workplace, health, and civic participation. Each category in the corpus contained a variety of texts that immigrants are likely to encounter as they interact within these multiple roles in their daily lives. These texts were collected online, and not surprisingly, there were many publicly available options, especially from government Web sites and volunteer organizations. The table below (Table C1.1) lists the types, number of texts, and word counts of the **parenting** subcorpus collected by Roberts and Murphy.
- Roberts and Murphy (2012) had a specific, practical purpose in mind. They wanted to better serve language learners in their education. How can some of the same or similar variables provide insight into other sociolinguistic studies? For example, multiple registers were collected. How would that help understand the language use of a single population?

TABLE C1.1 Composition of the parenting subcorpus (Roberts & Murphy, 2012)

Text Type	No. of Texts	No. of Words
Student handbooks	19	241,660
Inception materials	26	29,123
School menus	9	5,023
Parental consent forms (permission slips)	10	3,654
Parent-teacher conference notices/sign-up sheets	15	7,272
School newsletters	21	74,427
Progress reports/grades/info about grading	14	15,137
Disciplinary material	11	68,719
Total	**125**	**445,015**

- What can you do to collect a spoken equivalent of this parenting subcorpus from Roberts and Murphy? Can you record interactions by LEP immigrants as they navigate their day-to-day life in the United States? What contexts or domains would be included in your audio recordings?

C1.2 Application: Collecting Your Own Corpus of Blogs

Manually collecting blogs for a sociolinguistic study is manageable but requires constant scanning and skimming of blog entries in order to maintain a principled and credible set of text files for inclusion in the corpus. Blogs are electronically available for downloading, so that data collection is relatively easy to do. Since there are many millions of such blogs, the blogosphere offers an unprecedented opportunity to study, in a natural context and over a vast scope, how different groups of people write. Again, using Web-crawlers that automatically copy and save new text entries from a designated blog can help you quickly and easily accumulate more blog texts. However, note that this process typically includes lots of unnecessary words, links, codes, and scripts in the text files that will have to be cleaned before conducting corpus analysis.

The manual collection of blogs online in studies by Friginal (2009a) and Grieve, Biber, Friginal, and Nekrasova (2010) was made possible by Globe of Blogs (www.globeofblogs.com), a Web site that indexes blogs according to the authors' location, gender, age, birthday, title, and topic. Globe of Blogs is a blog directory with 51,973 blogs registered in 2013. The stratified sampling of blogs included in this specialized corpus of over four million words involved careful selection of blog sites to ensure that the reported gender and age of authors were reliable. Reading or scanning blog postings was necessary to check whether the authors wrote the entries in their blogs themselves and did not simply copy and paste news articles and messages from other sources. In general, Friginal (2009a) and Grieve and colleagues (2010) did not control for topic or blog theme in their corpora, they also did not include blogs written for corporate and journalistic endeavors (such as news articles and company-sponsored blog sites) or those that were clearly written to advance a political or ideological agenda. The final version of these personal blog corpora thus comprised individual authors' observations and reflections about a wide range of topics and concerns, or accounts of day-to-day events and activities.

Argamon, Koppel, Pennebaker, and Schler's (2007) more extensive, large-scale study of blogs analyzed over 140 million words of English texts drawn from the blogosphere, exploring if and how age and gender affect writing blog style and topic. They gathered a collection of blogs from Blogger (www.blogger.com; also www.blogspot.com) in 2004. They automatically crawled and collected all blogs on the site that contained at least 500 total words, including at least 200 occurrences of common English words, and had an author-provided indication of both gender and age. They then randomly selected 10 percent of the documents as a holdout set, leaving an initial collection of 46,947 blogs. Over 60 percent of bloggers age 17 and below were females, while over 60 percent of bloggers older than 17 were males.

For purposes of analysis, non-English texts were automatically removed from each blog. To enable distinctively reliable age categorization, as a blog can span several years of writing, all blogs for what they called "boundary ages" (ages 18–22 and 28–32) were removed. Each blogger was categorized by age at time of collection: "10s" (ages 13–17), "20s" (ages 23–27), and "30+" (ages 33–47), and also by gender: "male" and "female." They made sure that the number of blogs per gender within each age category was similar. The final corpus included 19,320 different blogs, with a total of 681,288 individual posts. On average, there were approximately 35 posts and 7,300 words in each blog in the corpus.

Samford (2012) manually collected an exploratory sociolinguistic blog corpus consisting of 144 text files of blog entries written by American women and grouped into six age categories. The total number of words in the corpus was 583,688. Blog texts were collected from the Web site OpenDiary (http://www.opendiary.com/), which allows publicly available blogs to be searched following a number of options: age, gender, location, topic/theme, and related interests. Location and gender were easier to control in searching for blogs and blog pages usually included pictures of the author. Samford's blogs were strictly personal and individual, so a careful consideration of section criteria during manual collection was necessary. For example, to address topical concerns, if a blog had an overarching theme (e.g., book reviews, pregnancy and childcare, travel), it was not included in the collection. Metadata (such as date tags or signature lines) were not included in order to ensure that the texts represented only author-generated data and also to ensure that there were very limited reposts that could potentially skew corpus data. Only recent entries (those posted in 2012) were used.

C1.2.1 Ethical Considerations

Internet technology makes it easy to collect your blog corpus, whether manually or by means of automated software programs. As blogging research expands and more scholars and industry marketers focus on the analysis of blogs, ethical considerations are called for in how to properly represent blog authors and their ideas, as you proceed to use their blogs in your corpus-based research. Blogs in general are considered to be under public domain, which allows researchers to collect blog entries without the necessary author consent forms required by Institutional Review Boards (IRB) in most universities in the United States. However, the privacy and confidentiality of authors and their statements, ideas, pictures, or creative endeavors must be ensured. Author names and their addresses are not necessary in most sociolinguistic studies and can easily be replaced by a specific author ID number or basic location such as city and state.

Making a corpus public (e.g., MICUSP) may require obtaining copyrighted waivers for the texts collected. A corpus of copyrighted material, if only available to the collector is often a gray area. We would like to emphasize that if collecting for academic purposes such as course projects (without the expectation of conference presentations or publication), there is less to be concerned with. However, when publically presenting one's results, it is wise to err on the side of caution when collecting a corpus. Below are some suggestions from the Web site Daily Blog Tips regarding using copyrighted material (Scocco, 2007).

DOs

Do use material under public domain: you are free to use any work that is in public domain. This includes federal government documents, materials produced before 1923 and materials produced before 1977 without a copyright notice.

Do use other materials that are not subject to copyright: apart from facts and ideas there are many other classes of materials that cannot be protected under the Copyright Law. Those materials include names, familiar symbols, listings of ingredients or contents, short phrases, titles, slogans and procedures (notice that some of those materials might be protected by trademark, though).

DON'Ts

Don't assume that if you credit the author there is no copyright infringement: a lot of people wrongly think that if they credit the author of an article or image they are not violating the copyright law. You can only use copyrighted material if you have explicit permission from the author to do so (or if you make fair use of it).

Don't equate Creative Commons with "free for grab": while Creative Commons licenses are less restrictive than standard copyright they should not be interpreted a "free for grab." In order to understand what you can or cannot do with Creative Commons material you should check what kind of license it is using. Certain licenses will require you to credit the original author, while others will require that you release any modifications of the document under the same license.

(Scocco, 2007)

Scocco (2007) is quick to point out that he is not a lawyer. Likewise, we emphasize that this does not constitute legal advice. Instead, we recommend checking copyright laws in your location before proceeding to collect existing material. University ethics boards, legal consultants, and IRBs may also offer more information on the subject.

C1.3 Collecting Spoken Data

While relatively easy to collect written or previously transcribed data, most sociolinguistic studies ask questions about speech, including pronunciation and interactional behaviors. For many sociolinguists, the register of most interest is that of informal, unrehearsed, and self-reported speech. Labov (1984a) describes some of his working principles about speech and spoken data collection, including the following five principles, which have also influenced other research on sociolinguistic variation:

1   There are no single style speakers.
2   Styles can be ranged along a single dimension, measured by the amount of attention paid to speech.
3   The vernacular, in which the minimum attention is paid to speech, provides the most systematic data for linguistic analysis.
4   Any systematic observation of a speaker defines a formal context where more than the minimum attention is paid to speech.
5   Face-to-face interviews are the only means of obtaining the volume and quality of recorded speech that is needed for quantitative analysis. (Labov, 1984a, p. 29)

The first two principles recognize that speakers shift their styles of speech and such changes can vary depending on the amount of "attention" that they give to how they are speaking. The third principle shows the importance that variationists place on the vernacular among the various ways a person speaks. Labov (1984a) describes this as "the mode of speech that is acquired in pre-adolescent years" (p. 29), and it is the ideal target for sociolinguistic investigation. However, the last two principles recognize the paradox that observers pose for research: If individuals are being formally observed, they are less likely to reduce their attention to how they speak. It is thus important for interviewers or observers to conduct their research in ways that minimize the potential influence that their presence has on their participants.

The method used by many sociolinguists to accomplish this is the **sociolinguistic interview**. Although it is called an "interview," the sociolinguistic interview is not what one might think of as a traditional interview. Instead of an approach similar to an employer asking a potential employee questions, which tends to prompt specific answers, the sociolinguistic interview approach helps guide participants into speaking freely about themselves, giving personal narratives based on experience.

The sociolinguistic interview, according to Labov (1984a), has several essential characteristics. These include recording one to two hours of speech from each participant and collecting any necessary demographic information (e.g., age, job, language background, income) that would potentially be essential to the investigation. In today's modern research environment, high-quality digital recording devices can be used fairly easily. The quality is mentioned because research questions may include linguistic constructs such as minor differences in pronunciation that may not be detectable otherwise. Other requisites include setting up and directing conversations with participants in which the style moves toward the vernacular, isolating topics to those that are most interesting or relevant to the speakers.

Although getting people to freely talk openly to one another using their vernacular (while a researcher is present) may sound like a relatively easy task, sociolinguists have to work hard at creating such environments. Labov (1984a) describes how a series of principally determined questions, or an interview schedule, can be used to help guide sociolinguistic interviews. In her book *Analyzing Sociolinguistic Variation*, Sali A. Tagliamonte (2006, pp. 37–49) provides detailed, yet user-friendly, explanations and suggestions for conducting such interviews. One of her key pieces of advice is that conducting sociolinguistic interviews is not an immutable or static enterprise that is constant from one person to the next; each one will be different, depending on any number of variables, especially the personalities of those involved. However, one can continue to learn from experience, which will result in revisions to technique and interview schedules.

C1.4 Expert Perspective: A Brief Interview with Sali A. Tagliamonte

Sali A. Tagliamonte is a professor in the department of linguistics at the University of Toronto. She is a sociolinguist who often uses quantitative data collection and analysis in her research, together with contextual interpretive approaches. In the Labovian tradition of quantifiable measurements and relatively large sample sizes, Tagliamonte has become known for using corpora and corpus-based methods to explore variation in dialects of English. Speakers she studied early in her career were those of Samaná English, a dialect of English spoken by descendants of freedmen (former slaves) who had immigrated in 1824 from the United States to the Samaná Peninsula in the Dominican Republic. This was a particularly interesting speech community to study because as an isolated group, Samaná English evolved without much subsequent influence from other dialects of English, providing a glimpse into possibilities of how blacks in the United States may have spoken long ago. Poplack and Tagliamonte (1989), for example, compared Samaná English recordings from the 1980s to the recordings of the English spoken by former slaves who were born in the mid-1800s. In addition to such comparisons, Tagliamonte (1997) also studied how those more modern recordings of Samaná English compared to modern African American Vernacular English (AAVE). This allowed her to infer historical processes or how the dialects evolved even though she compared synchronic data (i.e., data from the same era).

In addition to research articles, Tagliamonte's monographs include such topics as historical developments of English, variation research methods, and past and present states of the field of variationist sociolinguistics. The latter of these, *Variationist Sociolinguistics: Change, Observation, Interpretation* (2012), does a particularly effective job of outlining the social variables that are often studied (e.g., social class, sex, dialect groups) as well as the types of linguistic variables that can be documented (e.g., phonological, morphological, syntactic, and discoursal). She has also extensively explored the language of Canadian and British adolescents, patterns of British English, and more recently Canadian dialects in Ontario.

Tagliamonte emphasizes her appreciation of how sociolinguistics can directly illustrate the interaction between language, culture, and history. When asked for any advice to those entering the field, she responded, "Everyone who wants to be a sociolinguist ought to get out there and do fieldwork." This advice is notable because although some may see big divides between ethnographic studies with small samples and large-scale corpus-based studies, that divide is not as fixed as it seems. Just because a study has a large sample and uses automated analysis, for example, it does not mean that researchers must be far removed from their data. Thus, Tagliamonte is very familiar with the context from which her data comes, and she knows exactly who the participants are. And, if she did not conduct the sociolinguistic interviews herself, then the anthropological observations of the collector in the field can help her understand the setting and participants. Such contextual information is not limited to the speakers, either. In her fieldwork, Tagliamonte prefers to immerse herself in the physical setting: taking pictures, talking with area residents, visiting graveyards, and so on. Tagliamonte describes how the understanding of context, which is gained by doing fieldwork and getting to know research participants—their lives and environment—helps her make meaningful connections between her findings from linguistic data and the culture and history of the speech community(ies) being investigated. This understanding of context is very useful for anyone interested in collecting and analyzing corpora who might be immediately tempted to just start with the analysis of decontextualized data.

One of the most rewarding parts of her academic life, Tagliamonte notes, is how sociolinguistics is grounded in the humanities. Her research and teaching involves understanding people. An example of this can be found in how she teaches: In an experiential learning course, she has students conduct fieldwork, talking to people, getting to know them. It not only can help them understand research methods, but it also helps them learn to be respectful and understand individuals who might come from different cultures than their own. As also described in her book

Analysing Sociolinguistic Variation (2006), Tagliamonte emphasizes that while collecting data in the field, one tries to elicit the most natural type of speech possible. As an approach to data collection, the sociolinguistic interview for Tagliamonte is not an interview at all. It is more like a person telling his or her life story in the way that is similar to how he or she would tell a story to family and friends. This is important because the goal of such interviews is to get participants to converse in ways that are most natural to them.

C2

MULTIDIMENSIONAL ANALYSIS OF LINGUISTIC VARIATION

C2.1 The Concept of Linguistic Co-Occurrence

In Section B6, we introduced a study that compared the linguistic characteristics of Web registers using multidimensional (MD) analysis. In this section, we provide an extensive discussion of this approach, with an overview of its research rationale, summary of MD studies, and a description of the procedures for conducting its statistical and functional analyses.

With computational tools such as grammatical POS-taggers and statistical tests that identify internal configurations of tagged data from corpora, it is possible to establish groups of co-occurring linguistic features and compare them across speaker demographics or registers. In the Web registers study (Titak & Roberson, 2013) in Section B6, for example, this framework was applied to compare the subregisters of blogs, Facebook (FB)/Twitter (TW) posts, e-mails, news/opinion columns, and reader comments across resulting groups of linguistic dimensions. This study also provided a functional interpretation of patterns of co-occurrence in Dimension 1. Blogs were very different from microblogs (FB/TW texts) in the personal narrative focus versus descriptive, informational production continuum. We learned that blogs frequently used past tense verbs, personal pronouns, and emphatic features, while FB/TW posts utilized more nouns, prepositions, attributive adjectives, and passives. Overall, these types of comparisons tell something about the detailed linguistic composition of spoken and written discourse. By identifying and clearly isolating these groups of statistically co-occurring linguistic features, we can further define both the internal and external qualities that form the building blocks of language, in general, and registers, in particular.

C2.2 Introduction to Multidimensional (MD) Analysis

Douglas Biber's (1988) *Variation across Speech and Writing* introduced corpus-based multidimensional (MD) analysis as a research methodology for exploring linguistic variation in spoken and written English texts. Much of the foundation of MD analysis came from Biber's dissertation research at University of Southern California in the early 1980s and work with Edward Finegan who helped conceptualize the methodological approach and provided opportunities to access computerized corpora for analysis. Biber and Finegan have published various collaborative books and edited collections of studies in linguistic variation. Edward Finegan is also the author of numerous books on language and linguistics, including *Language: Its Structure and Use* (2011) and *Attitudes toward English Usage: The History of a War of Words* (1980).

Biber's primary research goal was to conduct a unified linguistic analysis of spoken and written registers from 23 subregisters of the London-Oslo-Bergen Corpus (LOB) (for written texts) and London-Lund Corpus (for spoken texts). In the early 1980s, linguistic similarities and differences between spoken and written texts had already been the subject of numerous studies; however, most of these studies utilized an a priori set of individual or group comparisons of distributional data. By using a multivariate statistical procedure to identify intrinsic linguistic co-occurrence patterns across texts, Biber was able to substantially redefine a range of register characteristics of spoken/written discourse. Subsequently, he was able to establish a model of corpus-based research that could be applied to more specialized contexts.

MD output is derived from factor analysis (FA), which considers the sequential, partial, and observed correlations of a wide range of variables in order to produce groups of co-occurring factors. Biber used the first completed version of his tagger in 1983 through 1986, producing normalized tag counts that were applied in earlier studies on microscopic textual variations of spoken and written texts (e.g., Biber, 1986a, 1986b; Biber & Finegan, 1986). The first iterations of the Biber Tagger, thus, provided normalized part-of-speech (POS) counts, including counts for additional semantic categories (e.g., semantic categories of verbs, nouns, and adjectives) that were appropriate for FA. After POS-tagging all the texts from the LOB and London-Lund corpora and obtaining normalized frequencies of these tagged features per text, Biber ran an FA, which produced the following six groups (i.e., factors) of statistically co-occurring tagged features in the two corpora (Table C2.1).

The six original linguistic dimensions in Table C2.1 were then **functionally interpreted**. The question for Biber was, what do these patterns mean? Take a look at all the positive and negative features in Factor 1. So, if private verbs, first person pronouns, *that* deletions and contractions are used frequently together, what could a speaker or writer possibly be saying (or writing)? In addition to these positive co-occurrence features, there are negative features in this factor.

TABLE C2.1 Biber's co-occurring features of LOB and London-Lund

Factor	Co-Occurring Features—Positive	Co-Occurring Features—Negative
Factor 1	Private Verb (e.g., *believe, feel, think*)	Noun
	"*That*" Deletion	Word Length
	Contraction	Preposition
	Verb (uninflected present, imperative	Type/Token Ratio
	and third person)	Attributive Adjective
	Second Person Pronoun/Possessive	(Place Adverbial)
	Verb "*Do*"	(Agentless Passive)
	Demonstrative Pronoun	(Past Participial WHIZ Deletion)
	Adverb/Qualifier—Emphatic	(Present Participial WHIZ
	(e.g., *just, really, so*)	Deletion)
	First Person Pronoun/Possessive	
	Pronoun "*It*"	
	Verb "*Be*" (uninflected present tense,	
	verb and auxiliary)	
	Subordinating Conjunction—	
	Causative (e.g., *because*)	
	Discourse Particle (e.g., *now*)	*Features in parentheses are not
	Nominal Pronoun (e.g., *someone, everything*)	statistically strong features in
	Adverbial Hedge—(e.g., *almost, maybe*)	this factor
	Adverb/Qualifier—Amplifier (e.g.,	
	absolutely, entirely)	
	Wh- Question	
	Modals of Possibility (*can, may, might, could*)	
	Coordinating Conjunction—Clausal	
	Connector	
	Wh- Clause	
	Stranded Preposition	
Factor 2	Past Tense Verb	(Present Tense Verb)
	Third Person Pronoun (except "it")	(Attributive Adjective)
	Verb—Perfect Aspect	(Past Participial WHIZ Deletion)
	Public Verbs (e.g., *assert, complain, say*)	(Word Length)
	Present Participial Clauses	
Factor 3	Wh- Pronoun—Relative Clause—	Adverb—Time
	Object Position	Adverb—Place
	Wh- Pronoun—Relative Clause—	Other Adverbs
	Subject Position	
	Wh- Pronoun—Relative Clause—	
	"Pied Piping"	
	Coordinating Conjunction	
	Singular Noun—Nominalization	
Factor 4	Infinitive Verb	No negative features
	Modal of Prediction (*will, would, shall*)	
	Suasive Verb (e.g., *ask, command, insist*)	
	Subordinating Conjunction—Conditional	
	(e.g., *if, unless*)	
	Modal of Necessity (*ought, should, must*)	
	Adverb within Auxiliary (splitting aux-verb)	
	(Modals of Possibility)	

(Continued)

TABLE C2.1 (*Continued*)

Factor	Co-Occurring Features—Positive	Co-Occurring Features—Negative
Factor 5	Adverbial—Conjunct (e.g., *however, therefore, thus*) Agentless Passive Verb Passive Verb + *by* Passive Postnominal Modifier Subordinating Conjunction—Other (e.g., *as, except, until*)	(Type/Token Ratio)
Factor 6	That Clause as Verb Complement Demonstratives That Relative Clause—Object Position That Clause as Adjective Complement (Final Prepositions) (Existential *there*) Wh- Pronoun—Relative Clause—Object Position	(Phrasal Coordination)

Source: adapted from Biber, 1988, pp. 89–90

The presence of negative and positive features in this factor means that these two groups of features are in complementary distribution—which is a statistical term indicating that when one group is highly frequent or present in a text (or group of texts), the other group is significantly lacking or absent.

In Biber's qualitative interpretation of co-occurrence features, he came up with names to describe what that grouping of features means per factor. These names or labels then became **functional dimensions**, which describe the pragmatic and practical meanings, foci, and production constraints of these statistically co-occurring features from the target corpora (LOB and London-Lund in this case). Factor 1 became Dimension 1, functionally referred to as involved versus informational production. Biber interpreted the positive features of Factor 1 as "involved production" features of texts. The combination of private verbs (e.g., *think, feel*), demonstrative pronouns, first and second person pronouns, and adverbial qualifiers suggests that the speaker or writer is talking about his or her personal ideas, sharing opinions, and involving an audience (the use of *you* or *your*). The discourse is also informal and hedged (*that* deletions, contractions, *almost, maybe*). At the other end of the continuum, negative features combine to focus on the giving of information ("informational production") as a priority in the discourse. There are many nouns and nominalizations (e.g., *education, development, communication*), prepositions, and attributive adjectives (e.g., *smart, effective, pretty*) appearing together with very limited personal pronouns. This suggests that informational data and descriptions of topics are provided without particular focus on the speaker or writer. More unique and longer words are used (higher type/token ratio and average word length), and the texts appear to be formal in structure and focus. The two excerpts below describe the textual difference between the positive (involved) and negative (informational) sides of Dimension 1.

Text Sample C2.1. Involved versus Informational Texts from LOB and London-Lund (Biber, 1988)

Involved: Personal Letter

How **you doing? I'm** here at work waiting for **my** appointment to get here, **it's** Friday. Thank goodness, but **I** still have tomorrow, but this week has flown by, **I guess because I've** been staying busy, getting ready for Christmas and **stuff.** Have **you** done **your** Christmas shopping **yet? I'm** pretty proud of **myself. I'm almost** finished. **Me** an L went shopping at Sharpstown last Monday and **I** got a lot done, **I** just have a few little things to get. Thanks for the poster, **I** loved it, **I** hung it in **my** room last night, **sometimes I feel** like **that's** about right.

Informational: Official Document

The **restoration of** a further **volume of** the **collections of Hunterian drawings** has been completed **at the British Museum.** A **selection from** the **collection of Pharmacy Jars** was lent **to the Times Book Shopin connection with** their **Royal Society Tercentenary Exhibition.** Two **coloured engravings of** the **College in** the early **nineteenth century** were **presented to** the **Royal Australasian College of Surgeons by** the **President** when he visited **Melbourne.**

A comparison of the sub-registers of LOB and London-Lund shows that Dimension 1 primarily distinguishes between spoken and written texts. Spoken texts had predominantly positive features while written texts had more negative features. Biber noted that this important distinction provided a statistical description of **oral** versus **literate** discourse. Biber computed **dimension scores** per text to be able to plot subregister averages in a comparative figure. These dimension scores were also used to compute statistical significance tests. Figure C2.1 shows the subregisters of LOB and London-Lund plotted in Dimension 1 based on their average dimension scores.

Finally, the remaining six factors in Biber (1988) were functionally interpreted and labeled:

Dimension 2: Narrative vs. Nonnarrative Concerns
Dimension 3: Explicit vs. Situation-Dependent Reference
Dimension 4: Overt Expression of Persuasion
Dimension 5: Abstract vs. Nonabstract Information
Dimension 6: Online Informational Elaboration.

Note that a seventh factor was also obtained but was not functionally interpreted in *Variation across Speech and Writing.* These dimensions have clearly described the linguistic differences between spoken and written texts from LOB

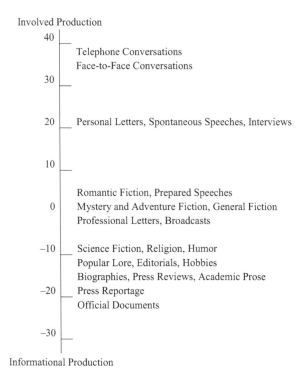

Involved Production

```
40 |
   |___  Telephone Conversations
   |     Face-to-Face Conversations
30 |___
   |
   |
20 |___  Personal Letters, Spontaneous Speeches, Interviews
   |
   |
10 |___
   |
   |     Romantic Fiction, Prepared Speeches
 0 |     Mystery and Adventure Fiction, General Fiction
   |     Professional Letters, Broadcasts
-10 |___  Science Fiction, Religion, Humor
   |     Popular Lore, Editorials, Hobbies
   |     Biographies, Press Reviews, Academic Prose
-20 |___  Press Reportage
   |     Official Documents
   |
-30 |___
   |
```

Informational Production

FIGURE C2.1 Comparison of average factor scores for Dimension 1: Involved Production (+) vs. Information Production (–)

Source: adapted from Biber, 1988, p. 128

and London-Lund and have been further interpreted broadly as the functional dimensions of the English language.

Reflective Break

- Take a look at the composition of features in Table C2.1 from Factors 1 to 6 and the dimension names given to these factors by Biber above. For example, Dimension 2: Narrative vs. Nonnarrative Concerns had the following co-occurring positive features: past tense verb, third person pronoun (except "*it*"), perfect aspect verbs, public verbs (e.g., *assert, complain, say*), and present participial clauses. Together, these features were interpreted as showing "narrativity." Do you see the logic of this interpretation? What do you think about this nature of functional analysis?
- Are Biber's dimension names useful in describing the meaning of these linguistic co-occurrence patterns? Are there potentially problematic areas you can think of in applying this interpretive technique?

C2.3 Summary of MD Studies

Biber's MD framework in the 1980s paved the way for follow-up books, manuscripts, and journal publications, including a quantitative exploration of cross-linguistic comparisons of differing languages (Biber, 1995), as well as an edited volume of papers applying Biber's 1988 dimensions to more specialized corpora (Conrad & Biber, 2001). After more than 25 years since the publication of *Variation across Speech and Writing*, new sets of dimensions have been established by conducting new FAs across many specialized discourse domains in English, as well as many other languages. For English, those studies include investigations of the following:

- televised cross-cultural interaction (Connor-Linton, 1989)
- elementary school spoken and written registers (Reppen, 1994, 2001)
- job interviews (White, 1994)
- 18th-century speech-based and written registers (Biber, 2001)
- stance and dialects of English (Precht, 2003)
- university spoken and written registers (Biber, 2006b)
- Google text types (Biber & Kurjian, 2007)
- metaphors (Berber Sardinha, 2007)
- moves in science research articles (Biber, Connor, Upton, & Jones, 2007; Kanoksilapatham, 2007)
- conversational text types (Biber, 2008)
- call center discourse (Friginal, 2009b)
- television sitcom dialogues vs. real-world conversation (Quaglio, 2009)
- world Englishes spoken and written registers (Xiao, 2009)
- blogs (Grieve, Biber, Friginal, & Nekrasova, 2010)
- written legal registers (Gozdz-Roszkowski, 2011)
- academic research articles across disciplines (Gray, 2011)
- 19th-century fictional novels (Egbert, 2012)
- movie and television scripts (Al-Surmi, 2012; Forchini, 2012)
- Filipino online and newspaper writing in English (Hardy & Friginal, 2012)
- ESL spoken and written exam responses (Biber & Gray, 2013)
- Michigan Corpus of Upper-Level Student Papers (MICUSP) (Hardy & Römer, 2013)
- web registers (Titak & Roberson, 2013)
- Chinese and English research article abstracts (Cao & Xiao, 2013).

Cross-linguistically, the approach has been applied to analyze register variation in an equally extensive set of languages, including the following:

- Nukulaelae Tuvaluan (Besnier, 1988)
- Somali (Biber, 1995; Biber & Hared, 1992)
- Korean (Kim & Biber, 1994)
- Taiwanese (Jang, 1998)

- Spanish (Asención-Delaney & Collentine, 2011; Biber, Davies, Jones, & Tracy-Ventura, 2006; Parodi, 2007)
- Czech (Kodytek, 2007)
- Dagbani (Purvis, 1998)
- Brazilian Portuguese (Berber Sardinha, Kauffmann, & Acuzo, forthcoming).

Together, the findings in these studies indicate that MD analysis can be effectively conducted using most corpora, including those from more controlled subregisters in a specialized corpus. MD analysis has also been remarkably useful in predicting the extent to which the occurrence of specific linguistic features varies across texts. For example, a low co-occurrence of past tense verbs and perfect aspect verbs, with a positive weight on Biber's (1988) original Dimension 2, could mean that the texts under investigation would have high frequencies of present tense verbs, attributive adjectives, and past participial which/that deletions (Forchini, 2012).

C2.4 MD Analysis in Present-Day CL Research: An Interview with Douglas Biber

Below is an excerpt of an interview with Douglas Biber conducted by Friginal (2013a) focusing on his reflections about his MD framework in present-day CL research. Biber is a regents' professor of applied linguistics at Northern Arizona University.

Biber has advanced U.S.-based corpus research, especially in grammar studies, corpora and linguistic variation, and language teaching applications of corpus data. The Biber Tagger is arguably the most effective and most valuable POS/grammatical tagger for corpus-based research used in seminal publications such as the *Longman Grammar of Spoken and Written English* (Biber, Johansson, Leech, Conrad, & Finegan, 1999). This tagger provides counts for functional linguistic features including word class, syntactic constructions, semantic class, and lexical-grammatical class. Biber's students and colleagues have applied his various analytical approaches and ideas about corpus design and representativeness to an extensive range of discourse domains and research contexts. He continues to influence many scholars in developing computational and statistical models for corpus research. Currently, he focuses on the analysis of historical written texts, Internet language, and spoken and written student outputs in language tests such as the Test of English as a Foreign Language (TOEFL). Biber, together with a small group of colleagues, founded the American Association for Corpus Linguistics Conference, which has now become the premier corpus linguistics conference in the United States.

In the following section, Biber responds to questions focusing on the applications of his MD framework to various corpus-based studies since the late 1980s. He also reflects on the surprising similarities and notable differences in the underlying dimensions of variation resulting from many recent MD studies. Finally,

Biber provides a synthesis of his responses to some criticisms of the MD approach and also poses questions that should be addressed or considered in similar corpus-based research methodologies.

What do you think about MD analysis's continuing popularity in CL research 25 years after the publication of *Variations across Speech and Writing***?**

Biber: It's hard to imagine what corpus-based linguistic research was like 30 years ago. Nearly all corpus investigations were carried out on main-frame computers. Corpora were stored on computer tapes, which had to be manually mounted on the computer by an operator before they could be processed; analyses of such corpora almost always ran as overnight jobs. Even the simplest corpus investigations—like generating a frequency-sorted list of words—were highly labor-intensive. As a result, most published corpus-based research during the early 1980s focused on word lists or describing the use of individual words, with research questions often constrained by considerations of computational feasibility rather than theoretical interest.

MD analysis was developed with a fundamentally different agenda. It started with a hotly debated theoretical question: What are the linguistic similarities and differences between speech and writing? The order of priorities was reversed from most contemporary research: The corpus analysis was motivated by the research question, rather than the research question being motivated by what could be reasonably extracted from a corpus. I think this is why MD analysis has remained so popular across the decades. It turned out to be a very powerful methodological approach, designed to address genuine research questions, uncovering important linguistic patterns of use that would not be noticed otherwise. The proof is in the pudding: Applications of MD analysis have consistently proven to be insightful across discourse domains and across languages.

What applications of MD analysis over the years have been surprising or most important to you?

Biber: The two major extensions of MD analysis since the 1980s have been its application to languages other than English (including many non-European languages) and its application to specialized discourse domains. These have been important for understanding the patterns of register variation within those languages/cultures/domains. Further, the cumulative results of these studies are theoretically important because they provide strong evidence for the existence of universal parameters of register variation, especially the existence of a fundamental "oral"/"literate" opposition (see Q3 below), and the persistent importance of a narrative dimension across discourse domains.

The applications of MD analysis that have surprised me the most have been the studies of restricted discourse domains. For example, several of my PhD students over the years have been eager to apply the MD framework to the analysis of register variation in restricted domains of use, such as White's (1994) analysis of job interviews, Friginal's (2009b) analysis of call center discourse, and Gray's

(2011) analysis of academic research articles. I was skeptical of these enterprises (especially in the earlier years) because I didn't believe there would be sufficient variation within those discourse domains for a stable statistical analysis. MD analysis relies on factor analysis, which is a correlational technique that requires variation. For example, imagine the correlation between pronouns and verbs in a corpus of face-to-face conversations. Both linguistic features will probably be consistently frequent in nearly all conversations. But the correlation between the two would probably be low in this case, just because there is not enough variation across the texts of the corpus. This problem can be even more acute with factor analysis, which involves the correlations among a large set of linguistic features. As a result, I was not optimistic about the prospects for MD analysis applied to restricted discourse domains. However, my skepticism was proven wrong: All applications of MD analysis to such domains have resulted in stable and interpretable dimensions of variation.

As you mentioned earlier, the co-occurring features of Dimension 1 [functionally, literate/oral; informational/involved] have been repeated in many MD studies across a range of corpora. What does this suggest about language in general and linguistic variation in particular?

Biber: MD studies of register variation have uncovered both surprising similarities and notable differences in the underlying dimensions of variation. From both theoretical and methodological perspectives, it is not surprising that each MD analysis would uncover specialized dimensions that are peculiar to a given language and/or discourse domain. After all, each of these studies differs with respect to the set of linguistic features included in the analysis and the set of registers represented in the corpus for analysis. Given those differences, it would be reasonable to expect that the parameters of variation that emerge from each analysis would be fundamentally different.

For that reason, it has been surprising to discover dimensions of variation that occur across languages and discourse domains. Two such dimensions have emerged in nearly all MD studies, making them candidates for universal parameters of register variation: a dimension associated with "oral" versus "literate" discourse and a dimension associated with narrative discourse. The robustness of narrative dimensions across studies indicates that this rhetorical mode is basic to human communication. Apparently, whether we're speaking or writing, for personal or informational purposes, in literate languages/cultures (e.g., English, Spanish) or "oral" languages/cultures (e.g., Tuvaluan, Bagdani), there is always need for discourse that describes past events contrasted with discourse focused more on the present.

The more surprising finding is the oral/literate opposition, which emerges as the very first dimension in nearly all MD studies. In MD studies based on reference corpora of spoken and written registers, this oral/literate dimension clearly distinguishes between speech and writing. However, MD studies of specialized discourse domains show that this is not a simple opposition between speech and writing. In fact, this dimension emerges in studies focused exclusively on spoken registers, as well as studies focused on written registers.

In terms of communicative purpose, the "oral" registers characterized by this dimension focus on personal concerns, interpersonal interactions, and the expression of stance. These registers are usually produced in real time, with little or no opportunity for planning, revising, or editing. In contrast, "literate" registers focus on the presentation of propositional information, with little overt acknowledgement of the audience or the personal feelings of the speaker/writer. These registers usually allow for extensive planning and even editing and revising of the discourse.

There have also been some criticisms of the MD approach. How have you addressed these criticisms?

Biber: In large part, criticism and observations about the MD approach are issues that should be addressed in all corpus-based research; for example, are linguistic features identified accurately in texts? What linguistic features and variants are included in the analysis? Is the corpus representative of the target language and/or discourse domain? What qualitative functional interpretations can be proposed to account for the quantitative patterns? What supporting evidence can be offered for those interpretations? When developing the MD approach, I have tried to develop procedures that give careful attention to these considerations—in contrast to many other corpus-based studies, which tend to disregard these issues altogether.

A related criticism concerns the accuracy and replicability of the computational tagging used in MD analyses, although this criticism disregards the actual goals of MD analysis: to achieve accurate linguistic analyses of register differences—not to demonstrate the power or accuracy of a particular tagger. In many cases, this goal has been achieved automatically with my tagging software; in other cases, the goal requires both automatic coding and interactive tag-editing. Any tagging software could be used, as long as it is followed by verification of the accuracy, and correction of mis-tags to ensure accurate counts of the linguistic features. Thus, the replication of the patterns of register variation should not be dependent on the particular software used for the analysis . . .

A major issue here concerns the representativeness of the corpus: For MD studies of a particular discourse domain, does the corpus represent the domain? And for general MD studies, how can we determine the extent to which a corpus represents the full range of register variation in a language? I have been interested in these methodological issues since the early 1990s [see Biber 1990, 1993]. Here again, this is an issue for all corpus-based research, not just for MD analysis. Any linguistic research that disregards register differences leads to incomplete descriptions and, in some cases, inaccurate conclusions. But corpus studies rarely include discussion of the extent to which the corpus represents the target population. Thus, there is a need in all corpus-based studies to develop better methods for evaluating the register-representativeness of the corpus itself.

C2.5 Overview of MD Analytical Procedures

Conducting your own FA, if you have limited background in statistics, will undoubtedly be difficult and seem very complicated. However, there are available resources that can help you run your dataset through statistical software packages such as SPSS or SAS, which are accessible in many university libraries or computer labs. These statistical software programs are also available for purchase. In the following sections, we provide an overview of the MD analytical framework. We are aware that the discussions here may not be enough to get you the final data (i.e., factors) you need. If you seriously intend to conduct your own MD analysis, we suggest that you start by reading the following:

- *Variations across Speech and Writing*, Biber (1988): for an extensive introduction and detailed rationale and steps Biber followed in working with LOB and London-Lund corpora in the early 1980s (using the statistical software package SAS).
- *Variation in English: Multi-Dimensional Studies*, Conrad and Biber (editors) (2001b): for applications of Biber's 1988 dimensions to more specialized domains (e.g., historical registers, student/adult speech and writing). An introduction to MD analysis and a chapter on FA methodology are provided, written by Biber and Conrad.
- "Conducting Biber's Multi-Dimensional Analysis Using SPSS," Friginal and Hardy (forthcoming): a chapter in Berber Sardinha and Veirano Pinto's (editors) *Multi-Dimensional Analysis 25 Years On* for detailed instructions in running MD analysis using SPSS. Sample data and various SPSS outputs are presented and discussed.
- "25 Years of Biber's Multi-Dimensional Analysis: Introduction to the Special Issue" Friginal (2013a): for additional overview on MD applications. This article introduces the special issue celebrating 25 years of MD studies from the journal *Corpora*. Four new MD studies are featured in this special issue.
- *Using Multivariate Statistics, 5th Edition*, Tabachnick and Fidell (2007) and *SPSS for Windows Workbook*, Osterlind and Tabachnick (2001): for in-depth coverage of factor analysis—statistical concepts, assumptions, and procedures.

Factor analysis employs the reduction of a large number of variables (i.e., POS-tagged linguistic features) into a small group of derived variables (i.e., factors) with *high shared variance* that can be interpreted to show various functional relationships. As a statistical test, FA considers the sequential, partial, and observed correlations within a wide range of data from which multiple correlations and groups of statistically co-occurring factors are then derived (Tabachnick and Fidell, 2007). In order to arrive at the final group of factors for MD analysis, Biber (1988) developed the four primary methodological requisites in conducting MD analysis (p. 63):

1   The use of computer-based text corpora, providing a standardized database and ready access to a wide range of variation in communicative situations and purposes.

2   The use of computer programs to count the frequency of certain linguistics features in a wide range of texts, enabling the analysis of the distribution of many linguistic features across many texts and registers.
3   The use of multivariate statistical techniques (FA) to determine co-occurring relations among the linguistic features.
4   The use of microscopic analyses to interpret the functional parameters underlying the quantitatively identified co-occurrence patterns.

You begin your work in MD analysis by organizing your registers/corpora, POS-tagging all your texts, and then conducting the statistical analysis. These steps are discussed below.

C2.5.1 Obtaining a Dataset for FA

Biber (1988) analyzed a corpus composed of 481 spoken and written texts (with 960,000 words) from the LOB and London-Lund corpora and these texts were POS-tagged using the Biber Tagger. Unfortunately, in terms of access, the Biber Tagger is not commercially available or accessible online. However, researchers may contact The Corpus Linguistics Research Program at Northern Arizona University for information about corpus tagging and analysis. Biber's tagged dataset included a wide range of linguistic features that clearly showed functional associations across a total of 16 major grammatical categories (e.g., tense and aspect markers, pronouns and pro-verbs, lexical classes, verb classes, coordination, etc.).

What tagging program can you use in addition to the Biber Tagger? Recent MD studies—for example, Xiao (2009) and Cao and Xiao (2013)—have grammatically and semantically tagged their corpora using **Wmatrix**, a corpus comparison and tagging tool (Rayson, 2003). Wmatrix combines data from the CLAWS POS-tagger and the University Centre for Computer Corpus Research on Language (UCREL) Semantic Annotation System (USAS) (Xiao, 2009). USAS is a program developed by UCREL at Lancaster University, with the latest version, CLAWS7, available for site and user licenses. This tool can be conveniently accessed and used online. UCREL also offer in-house tagging service with cost depending on the text(s) being tagged (http://ucrel.lancs.ac.uk/claws/).

Other accessible Web-based taggers and parsers include **Go Tagger** (http://web4u.setsunan.ac.jp/Website/GoTagger.htm) and **The Stanford Parser/Stanford Tagger** (http://nlp.stanford.edu/software/lex-parser.shtml). Although the current tagsets from these tools are limited to primary POS counts, they provide enough features to run an exploratory FA. Finally, the **Coh-Metrix** tagset is generally similar to the Biber Tagger with additional features focusing on lexical diversity and specificity markers. Data and related research from Coh-Metrix, including contact information for potential tagging requests, are located at http://cohmetrix.memphis.edu/cohmetrixpr/index.html.

*MICUSP_MDA.sav [DataSet1] - PASW Statistics Data Editor

File Edit View Data Transform Analyze Graphs Utilities Add-ons Window Help

1 : vrb_do   0   Visible: 119 of 119 Variables

	Text	wrdlen	vrb_priv	that_del	verb	vrb_do	@1stpers	it
1	bio.g0.01.1.txt	5.10	2.40	.0	62.40	.0	.90	11.80
2	bio.g0.02.1.txt	5.20	12.40	1.50	69.00	.50	1.80	6.60
3	bio.g0.02.2.txt	5.70	10.90	2.40	86.90	2.40	1.20	6.00
4	bio.g0.02.3.txt	5.80	4.90	.0	79.50	.0	4.90	4.90
5	bio.g0.02.4.txt	5.70	5.90	1.50	91.20	.0	.0	8.80
6	bio.g0.02.5.txt	5.20	9.90	.50	44.80	.0	2.30	2.60
7	bio.g0.02.6.txt	4.70	9.80	.40	52.50	.0	6.00	2.50
8	bio.g0.03.1.txt	5.10	2.40	.80	77.70	.0	16.50	5.10
9	bio.g0.03.2.txt	5.20	5.60	.40	50.70	.40	11.10	5.30
10	bio.g0.03.3.txt	5.20	3.90	1.60	42.90	.0	8.60	5.50
11	bio.g0.04.1.txt	5.70	5.60	.0	48.00	1.10	1.10	3.30
12	bio.g0.04.2.txt	4.60	15.60	.0	64.90	.0	19.00	2.70
13	bio.g0.04.3.txt	4.40	5.60	.0	58.10	.0	14.30	2.40
14	bio.g0.05.1.txt	5.20	1.30	.0	60.10	.0	.0	15.60
15	bio.g0.06.1.txt	5.20	3.70	.50	77.50	.30	.0	5.30
16	bio.g0.07.1.txt	5.10	13.20	.90	60.60	.90	.0	6.10
17	bio.g0.07.2.txt	5.30	6.80	.0	72.40	.0	1.70	4.50
18	bio.g0.07.3.txt	4.70	9.80	.30	61.80	.30	3.70	1.00
19	bio.g0.08.1.txt	4.60	10.00	.70	39.90	.30	3.10	4.10
20	bio.g0.09.1.txt	4.80	9.30	2.60	70.10	.0	2.50	6.80
21	bio.g0.10.1.txt	4.60	12.90	.60	56.60	.0	30.20	4.50
22	bio.g0.10.2.txt	4.60	13.60	1.10	71.70	.40	28.30	6.80

Data View   Variable View

Save this document   PASW Statistics Processor is ready

> SPSS Data Editor with normalized counts for average word length, private verbs, *that*-deletion, verbs, etc. for texts (i.e., observations) in the corpus.

FIGURE C2.2 Sample MD analysis dataset for FA in SPSS

After tagging, the next step is to count the frequencies of your POS-tagged features in the corpus. Automated "tag-count" programs are needed for this step, but most tagger outputs will return these specific counts in a spreadsheet. All these frequency counts must then be normalized per a certain number of words (Biber has often normalized distributions per 1,000 words in running FA). If you use a tagger that provides only primary counts, you may calculate the normalized counts separately.

In setting up your data, you might consider working in SPSS because it is cheaper and easier to use than many other software packages, including SAS. SPSS does not require the user to input codes to perform queries. Thus, someone who is familiar with the basics of statistics—and who can follow a guide like this (and others)—can begin to run tests fairly quickly. Another benefit to SPSS is that it uses a spreadsheet to organize data and variables. This spreadsheet is similar to MS Excel. In fact, much of the data can be saved in MS Excel, and you can also import Excel files into SPSS rather seamlessly. There are many online tutorials for SPSS that can help you in setting up your data. For example, Levesque (2012) has a good general tutorial: *Raynald's SPSS Tools* (http://www.spsstools.net/ index.html). The Academic Technology Service at the University of California Los Angeles also provides a tutorial for SPSS, *Resources to Help You Learn and Use SPSS* (http://www.ats.ucla.edu/stat/spss/). These sites offer basic information on entering and editing SPSS data. They also show how to run commands for tests such as FA and how to read output files. A sample SPSS dataset with normalized tag counts is shown in Figure C2.2.

C2.5.2 Data Preparation and Running Exploratory FA

Once your dataset is created, the next step is to finalize the composition of tag-counted linguistic features for FA runs. Identifying these features is critical and must be based on related literature or established grammatical categories and patterns. For *Variation across Speech and Writing*, Biber used a final group of 67 POS-tagged linguistic features informed by a survey of previous research on spoken/written differences across texts. A careful, principled selection of features is necessary and should be linguistically justifiable. These tagged features will often include several form-function pairings to address the shared functions of different grammatical categories. For example, in his study of business telephone interactions, Friginal (2009b) used features identified by White (1994) in conducting an MD analysis of job interviews. Linguistic features associated with spoken discourse (e.g., discourse markers, backchannels, imperative *let's*, and politeness/respect markers) were added to the final list of POS-tagged features to fully represent the range of linguistic variation expected in the corpus of telephone interactions.

Next, running several FAs to pilot various combinations of tag-counted features is necessary to screen out features that do not contribute to the correlations. These FA tests will help produce a cumulative variance that reflects the communalities and strengths of relationships among the remaining variables in the final dataset. Linguistic features that correlate below 0.30 in communality values (which can be seen in the FA output) are frequently excluded. In Friginal's study, a total of 70 features were used in the pilot FA runs, but these were narrowed down to a final set of 36 features after the removal of features that did not produce communality values above 0.30.

C2.5.3 Data Screening and Final FA

This is the primary step in your FA, which will produce your sets of factors. To continue, your data should include at least five times more participants (or texts) than variables. This is your suggested **sample size**. In corpus linguistics, this equates to more texts than linguistic features. MD analyses that use the Biber Tagger generally consider 40 to 80 linguistic features. Thus, the number of texts, or observations, in the corpus should be at least 200. However, fewer observations are required if there are several variables (linguistic features) that load highly, thereby differentiating the sample (Tabachnick & Fidell, 2007). The general rule of thumb in the case of sample size is to aim for having a high ratio of texts to linguistic features.

After finalizing your sample for analysis, "data screening" is necessary to test for multivariate outliers, multicollinearity, singularity, and normality in the distribution of variables. These tests are conducted to satisfy FA's multivariate assumptions. In other words, you conduct data screening to ensure that your dataset meets FA's statistical requirements. Most recent MD studies commonly report data for Kaiser-Meyer-Olkin Measure for Sampling Adequacy (KMO), which shows the strength of relationship across all variables; and Bartlett's Test for Sphericity (a chi-square measure), which reports partial and observed correlations in the dataset. Running FA in SPSS will provide options for actual tests such as "principal axis factoring" and options for "rotations" (e.g., Promax or Varimax). The choice of which test or rotation to use depends on specific research goals, the nature of the dataset, and whether or not shared variance or correlations between factors is preferred.

For those familiar with SPSS, the commands below outline the steps in producing the primary FA dialog box and the first set of outputs:

- Analyze
    - Dimension Reduction
    - Factor

Variables (move your feature counts over to the Variables box by highlighting them and clicking the bottom arrow)

- Extraction
    - Display
        - Unrotated Factor Solution
        - Scree Plot
    - Method
        - Principal Axis Factoring

    - Extract
        - Based on Eigenvalue
        - Eigenvalues greater than 1

- Continue
    - OK (clicking OK will produce the output)

The number of factors (often from three to six-factor solutions in MD analysis) can be determined based upon the resulting Eigen values shown in scree plots or the test's structure matrix. Specifying a preferred number of factors can also be accomplished through SPSS or SAS. A final factor matrix table showing each linguistic feature's communality value within the factor determines the composition of features that characterizes that factor. This step produced the 34 +/– features included in Biber's (1988) Dimension 1, with the following highest-loading factors: (+) private verbs (0.96), *that* deletion (0.91), and contractions (0.90); (–) nouns (–0.80) and word length (–0.58). Table C2.2 shows a sample FA output from SPSS, with the highlighted features identified as important components of the four factors (loading = /–0.30 or higher).

TABLE C2.2 Sample "Factor Matrix" (final output) for FA in SPSS

Rotated Factor Matrix	Factor			
	1	2	3	4
Type/Token	−.124	−.220	−.041	**−.308**
Word Length	**−.792**	−.100	−.155	−.188
Word Count	−.121	−.136	−.095	.013
Verb Private	**.364**	.163	**.450**	**.466**
That Deletion	**.328**	.167	**.446**	**.361**
Contraction	.184	.026	.059	−.035
Verbs	**.328**	**.608**	.159	.219
Second Person Pronoun	**.325**	−.030	.271	.029
Verb *Do*	.144	.240	.183	.177
Demonstrative Pronoun	**.313**	**.408**	.019	.035
Emphatics	**.414**	.217	.167	−.038
First Person Pronouns	**.445**	.102	**.440**	.160
Pronoun *It*	**.406**	**.428**	−.005	.165
Verb *Be*	.033	**.586**	.168	.082
Subordinating Conjunction	.196	.169	.122	.067
Discourse Particles	.229	.114	.081	.028
Nominal Pronoun	**.455**	.256	**.317**	.207
Adverbial Hedge	.258	.107	−.013	−.043
Adverbial Qualifier	**.338**	.230	.059	−.075
WH- Questions	.169	.040	.195	.180

C2.5.4 Computing Factor Scores and Interpreting Results

Each text in the corpus will have a factor score across the resulting groups of factors produced after running FA. These factor scores are computed from the original normalized counts of linguistic features that loaded on each of the factors. The normalized counts will have to be standardized to create a more comparable range of average factor scores. Note that these normalized counts can have a high range of 200-plus per 1,000 words for features such as nouns, or 0.001 per 1,000 words for less-frequent features (e.g., WH clauses, necessity modals). A z-score per variable can be used to standardize the dataset. Z-scores will transform the variables, producing means of 0.0 and standard deviations of 1. Calculating factor scores is necessary to compare the means of the groups/categories of texts in the target corpus across extracted factors. The groups of texts with high or low factor scores help in interpreting the meaning of the co-occurrence of linguistic features for microscopic, qualitative analysis. This functional interpretation of factors ultimately produces the linguistic dimensions that emphasize the discourse characteristics of the target corpus. Finally, significance tests (e.g., one-way or factorial ANOVA and independent t-tests) can be performed to determine whether or not differences in the means of factor scores per group of texts (across dimensions) are statistically significant. These mean scores are then plotted in dimensional scales for visual comparisons.

C2.6 Application: Interpreting Linguistic Co-Occurrence Patterns

Take a look at the composition of Friginal's (2009b) Factor 1 below (Table C2.3) from his call center study. We revisit this study in this section because it directly applied Biber's MD framework to sociolinguistic research that considers gender, role, and registers compared across three resulting dimensions. The Call Center Corpus has transcripts of turns (utterances) from 500 different Filipino call center agents serving 500 different American callers. Of the 500 agents, 252 are females and 248 are males. There are 255 female callers and 245 male callers in the transactions. The Filipino agents all have college degrees obtained from universities in the Philippines. The ages of agents range from 21 years old to 55 years old. The average age of Filipino agents in the corpus is 26. American callers were distributed throughout the United States. However, the geographic location of callers was not controlled or considered in the present analyses. Texts from the Call Center Corpus are also compared with two other corpora: switchboard telephone discussions and face-to-face conversations from the Longman Corpus. You might remember these corpora from Section B3.

TABLE C2.3 Sample positive/negative features for analysis

Factor 1	
Second Person Pronouns	.683
Word Length	.612
Please	.523
Nouns	.515
Possibility Modals	.445
Nominalizations	.394
Length of Turns	.376
Thanks	.325
Ma'am/Sir	.309
Pronoun *It*	−.687
First Person Pronouns	−.663
Past Tense Verbs	−.609
That Deletion	−.506
Private Verbs	−.439
WH Clauses	−.397
Perfect Aspect Verbs	−.345
I mean/You know	−.338
Verb Do	−.321

Source: adapted from Friginal, 2009b, p. 80

Friginal's Factor 1 had nine positive and nine negative features. Second person pronouns (0.683) and word length (0.612) loaded highly on the positive side; the pronoun *it* (–0.687) and first person pronouns (–0.663) on the negative. Remember that these features came from transcripts of task-based, business interactions on the telephone.

Questions

- What do these positive features mean, collectively? What do the negative features suggest? What functional name will you give this factor, which will ultimately be "Dimension 1"?
- Remember complementary distribution? When a text (i.e., transcript of a speaker's turns) has many co-occurring positive features in it, there are significantly fewer negative features in that same text. This phenomenon can help you analyze the functions of these two groups of features in Factor 1.

Another step that can help you analyze a particular factor is to obtain text samples from your corpus. Texts with high positive or high negative scores (after you have computed your factors scores) can help you further interpret Factor 1. Below are two sample texts:

Text Sample C2.2. Comparing Agent and Caller Turns

Agent 1: factor score equals 5.71
Agent: **Thank you** for calling [**phone company**] **payment services**, my name is [**Jane**], how
can I help **you?**
Agent: I **apologize** for the **inconvenience sir**, I'll, let me explain on that ok? **Please,** give
me your **cell phone number** so I can check on **your minutes**.
Agent: Ok, let me just verify the charges at the **moment, please** give me **your name** and
address on the **account please**
Agent: **Thank you** for that [Mr. Doe], let me just pull out **your account** to check **your balance**,
OK? [Mr. Doe], **you** have now zero **balance** on the **account** and uh, OK [Mr. Doe], **you** are notified of **your balance** when **you** reached below **$10,** below [interruption]
Caller 1: factor score equals –2.21
Caller: Yes, uh, when are you guys gonna go back telling us when how much time is left on these phone cards? I mean on these phones?
Caller: [333–333–3333], I think it has run out because I wanted to use it but it said it didn't have enough time.
Caller: [John A. Doe], 2635[something] Road, in [XX city], Ohio.
Caller: There never was a word said anytime. I never heard anything. How am I supposed to be notified?

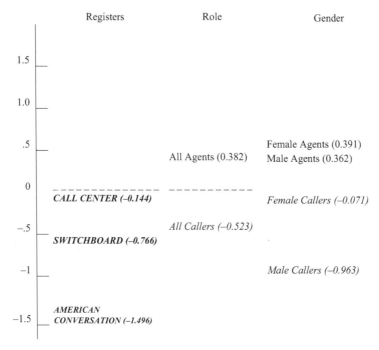

FIGURE C2.3 Group comparison of texts for Dimension 1

Source: adapted from Friginal, 2009b, p. 83

Question

• Based on these text samples, how do you characterize the production focus or primary intent of agents' and callers' turns? The caller had many first person pronouns and past tense verbs while the agent used repeated politeness markers. Do these samples help you in interpreting Factor 1?

And finally, Figure C2.3 shows Friginal's (2009b) Dimension 1 comparison, focusing on (1) registers, (2) role, and (3) gender of speakers. To briefly summarize, there are differences in the average group scores of texts on the positive and negative ends of the figure.

Questions

• Try to explain what this figure suggests, based on the linguistic composition of Factor 1. What features contributed greatly to the differences in the factor scores between agents and callers? Do you see a gender-based difference in this figure that could be further explored in research?
• The two telephone-based subregisters (call center and switchboard) differed from face-to-face conversation. Do you think the telephone as a medium contributed to this difference?

Interpretation

Friginal's Factor 1 was interpreted as addressee-focused, polite, and elaborated information (positive features) versus involved and simplified narrative (negative features).

Positive features include politeness and respect markers (e.g., *thanks, please, ma'am* and *sir*), markers of elaboration and information density (e.g., long words and turns, nominalizations, and more nouns), and second person pronouns (e.g., *you, your*), which indicate "other-directed" focus of talk. Possibility modals (*can, could, may, might*) also loaded positively on this factor. The features on the negative side of this factor, especially the pronoun *it*, first person pronouns, *that* deletion, private verbs, WH clauses, and the verb *do*, resemble the grouping in the dimension "involved production" identified by Biber (1988) and White (1994). These features are typical of spoken texts and generally contrast with written, informational, and planned discourse. Also on the negative side of the factor are past tense verbs, perfect aspect verbs, and the use of discourse markers *I mean* and *you know*. These elements point to an accounting of personal experience or narrative that tries to explain the occurrence of a particular situation. *I mean* and *you know* are considered by Schiffrin (1988) as markers of information and participation; *I mean* marks speaker orientation toward the meaning of one's own talk while *you know* marks interactive transitions.

This factor also distinguishes between caller or agent roles based on how they communicate a concern or provide a response. In other words, the merging of features in this dimension seems to represent the contrast between the dominant objectives of speakers' utterances. This means that participants who use more positive features are likely intending to give details, explanations, and solutions. In the process, these interactants use more nouns, nominalizations, and longer utterances or turns to deliver the information. In addition, the information density in these turns is high because of the higher average word lengths in the texts (Biber, 1988). The turns of participants are elaborated and also hint at giving detailed explanations, likelihood, or risks through the use of a significant frequency of possibility modals (e.g., "*A reboot can cause problems when you connect to the external modem*"). The high frequency of second person pronouns indicates that the transfer of information is highly addressee-focused.

The grouping of features on the negative side of the factor appears to illustrate personal narrative and experiences, and highly simplified information. The combination of past tense verbs, private verbs, the pronoun *it*, and discourse markers *I mean* and *you know* demonstrates the specific goal of the utterances to provide a personal account on how a situation happened. The involved production features (e.g., first person pronouns, WH clauses, the verb *do*, and *that* deletion) and *I mean* and *you know* serve a communicative purpose in the maintenance of the interaction, establish personal orientation (White, 1994), and purposely ask for response or assistance. Turns are not elaborated and respect markers are not frequently used. The majority of utterances on the negative side of the factor have smaller word counts and are significantly shorter in length.

C3

STUDYING TEMPORAL CHANGE

C3.1 Revisiting Diachronic Research

We mentioned in Section B5 that the analyses of diachronic corpora have been quite popular in corpus linguistics and for researchers in the subfields of historical linguistics, communication and media, and linguistic anthropology. Language change/shift, lexicography and change, and sociocultural variations in discourse appeal to many audiences, even outside the community of linguists. The merging of linguistic analysis and popular culture has captivated people, especially when topics have direct entertainment, functional, and cultural values. For example, Rey (2001) analyzed gender roles in *Star Trek* episodes from 1966 to 1993, collecting a specialized corpus that separated male and female dialogues into two files for extensive linguistic comparisons. *Star Trek*'s widespread global popularity has been the subject of many linguistic studies, and the show continues to attract more and more fans with an enduring movie franchise and various offshoots. *Star Trek into Darkness* was released to theaters in May 2013. The **Klingon language**, a language spoken by *Star Trek* characters also called Klingons, has an extensive dictionary and usage books patronized by many Trekkies. Rey found significant differences between the language of male and female characters in *Star Trek*—overall, female dialogues were personal and more involved compared to male dialogues. Diachronically, however, she found that significant changes have shifted, with male dialogs becoming more and more personal and involved (or also informal) over the years. Pronoun use, hedging, mental verb usage, and the distribution of emphatics and intensifiers have all increased in male dialogues from the 1960s to the late 1990s. She noted that a major contributing factor in this shift was likely due to more recent female characters (e.g., in *Star Trek: Deep Space 9*—running from 1993 to 1999) assuming positions of science/command officers instead of the more nurturing staff positions held by many female characters in the past.

The Helsinki corpus and ARCHER were collected primarily by linguists for linguistic studies, scanning archival documents and digitizing them for corpus collection and processing. Nowadays, these historical texts are readily available online or through various library sources. Scanners and document converters (e.g., PDF to text) have revolutionized the collection of historical documents and the push by Google, together with major libraries and private organizations, to extensively digitize important published documents has been instrumental in producing texts that can be used for corpus collection. E-books and e-readers and companies that host and sell them (e.g., Amazon through its Kindle e-book reader, iTunes library) have also made many source materials available for easy corpus collection. **Project Gutenberg** shares over 42,000 free e-books that can be downloadable as PDF files or read online or through Kindles/iPads. In the following sections, we introduce ideas and exercises that can help you plan a corpus-based diachronic research study using available materials online.

C3.2 Collecting Your Diachronic Corpus Online

The Internet is the gift that keeps on giving to corpus linguists. The exponential developments in online technology in the last decade have contributed tremendously to the growth of corpus-based research and, most especially, the ease of corpus collection. Collecting texts online from newspaper articles to actual books has become relatively convenient, while more and more Web sites have been posting various free text samples that can be downloaded to start a corpus collection. Students of sociolinguistics and corpus linguistics can immediately commence a corpus-based project just by dedicating some time to exploring online registers and Web sources. Copying and pasting text samples to a document (.doc) or text file (.rtf or .txt), although manual work, can be completed within a very manageable period of time.

We emphasize, of course, the need for all researchers to strictly follow copyright policies and privacy/confidentiality of information principles, especially with regard to those texts that come from personal blogs or sites such as Facebook and Twitter. Due diligence in making sure that sources are acknowledged properly and that proprietary materials are treated with appropriate care in their redistribution is compulsory. As we mentioned in Section B6, not every Internet source belongs to the public domain, although the language of the law is still quite ambiguous regarding this matter. The message here is to be careful in your collection of online texts whenever you begin a corpus-based project. Ask for permission from authors and Web site administrators whenever necessary, and contact your university's institutional review board (IRB) for guidance if you have questions about the materials you are collecting online for a corpus.

What diachronic texts can you collect online? In this section, we explore available public domain materials and the Web sites that share them, which can certainly help you collect enough texts/words for an exploratory corpus project (or for a semester-long class project). As mentioned above, in the past, many historical texts were available only in archives from major libraries; however, today they have been digitized and posted online. In the following sections, we provide sample Internet sources for public documents, government papers, and other varieties of written texts. The two application exercises below offer ideas for collecting and analyzing a corpus of U.S. presidential inaugural addresses and using COHA and the Google Books Ngram Viewer for a comparative study.

C3.2.1 Public Documents and Government Papers

Books and related written materials (including music, compositions, collections of poetry) in the **public domain** are those whose intellectual property rights have expired or have been legally forfeited or rendered irrelevant. In most current usage, public domain includes works that are publicly available (e.g., online), while according to the formal definition, this designation refers to works that are unavailable for private ownership or are available only for public use (Graber & Nenova, 2008). Interpretations of intellectual property rights are based on a country's existing laws, which may also prescribe a certain number of years for materials to become public. Shakespearean plays, compositions by Mozart, and historical religious publications are all examples of materials under public domain.

Historical publications, thus, could be your first options in collecting a diachronic corpus. Book publishers with extensive online components such as the Oxford University Press and Random House can lead you to copies of texts that might be suitable for a diachronic corpus. Bartleby (www.bartleby.com) offers a wide range of classic, full-text reference works that are searchable and directly available through Web links. This site has an extensive collection of references (e.g., books of quotations, speeches, *The King James Bible*, *Gray's Anatomy*), verses (e.g., anthologies, ballads, and poems), and fiction and nonfiction works. Books by Emily Dickinson, Walt Whitman, and Robert Frost are accessible online, together with *Harvard Classics*, *World Factbook*, and *Strunk's Elements of Style*. Imagine collecting your corpus of male and female authors' texts and comparing them across time periods. Who do you think will have a higher readability score or type/token ratio among T. S. Eliot, William Wordsworth, and Charlotte Smith? Which current authors would you pick for a suitable corpus comparison with Eliot, Wordsworth, and Smith?

C3.2.1.1 Sample Texts Available from Bartleby.com

Copies of the following prose quotations and orations are accessible from Bartleby.

Prose Quotations

- Prose Quotations from Socrates to Macaulay (1880). Lengthy selections (9,000 texts) highlighting English prose from Addison, Burke, Johnson, Locke, and Macaulay.

- *Forty Thousand Quotations: Prose and Poetical* (1917). Over 41,000 selections divided into 1,500 categories including and an entire volume's-worth of Shakespeare.
- John Bartlett's *Familiar Quotations*, 10th edition (1919). Includes over 11,000 quotations, the first new edition of John Bartlett's corpus to be published after his death in 1905, which has kept most of Bartlett's original work intact.
- Dwight Edwards's *Curiosities in Proverbs* (1916). Over 2,000 entries in a multicultural collection that features comparisons of similar proverbs in different languages.

World Famous Orations

Table C3.1 provides a sample of world famous classic orations also available online. These orations mirror persuasive addresses, cultural and historical changes, and personal expressions. There are not very many corpus-based studies of historical change as seen through orations and speeches. These texts (Greek and Roman) were collected and translated into English by various scholars (e.g., those edited by William Jennings Bryan and Francis W. Halsey).

TABLE C3.1 List of Greek and Roman orations from Bartleby

Greece (432 BC—324 BC)	Rome (218 BC—AD 84)
Homer	Publius Cornelius Scipio
Achilles' Reply to the Envoys	*To His Army Before Battle*
Pericles	Hannibal
I. In Favor of the Peloponnesian War	*Address to His Soldiers*
II. On Those Who Died in the War	Cato the Censor
III. In Defense of Himself	*In Support of the Oppian Law*
Cleon	Scipio Africanus Major
On the Punishment of the Mytileneans	*To His Mutinous Troops*
Nicias	The Gracchi
Against the Sicilian Expedition	*I. Fragments by Tiberius Gracchus*
Hermocrates	*II. Fragments by Caius Gracchus*
On the Union of Sicily Against Invaders	Caius Memmius
Lysias	*On a Corrupt Oligarchy*
Against Eratosthenes	Caius Marius
Socrates	*On Being Accused of a Low Origin*
I. In His Own Defense	Cicero
II. On Being Declared Guilty	Mark Antony
III. On Being Condemned to Death	*His Oration Over the Dead Body of Cæsar*
Isocrates	Catiline
On the Union of Greece to Resist Persia	*I. An Exhortation to Conspiracy*
Demosthenes	*II. To His Army Before His Defeat in Battle*
I. The Second Oration Against Philip	Julius Cæsar
II. On the State of the Chersonesus	*On the Punishment of the Catiline Conspirators*
III. On the Crown	

Reflective Break

- What linguistic variables can you compare when working with English-translated texts? The Greek and Roman texts above could be used for cross-linguistic, diachronic comparisons (Greece: 432 BC–324 BC; Rome: 218 BC–AD 84). What linguistic results would you expect to find in these two groups of speeches? Do you think these orators refer to themselves (e.g., use of *I, me, my*) frequently in these speeches?
- Speeches addressing armies before battles were very popular in these collections of ancient orations (e.g., Publius and Hannibal's above). How similar or different are these addresses to contemporary "battle speeches"? Think about movie battle speeches from *Patton, Full Metal Jacket*, or even *Braveheart*, or real-world settings such as speeches by U.S. president George W. Bush on the Iraq War.

C3.2.1.2 Documents in Law, History, and Diplomacy from the Avalon Project

The Avalon Project (http://avalon.law.yale.edu/) from Yale University is a digital repository of documents related to the fields of law, history, economics, politics, diplomacy and government. This extensive collection of legal and hitorical documents is divided into the following time periods: ancient, 4000 BC–AD 399; medieval, 400–1399; 15th century, 1400–1499; 16th century, 1500–1599; 17th century, 1600–1699; 18th century, 1700–1799; 19th century, 1800–1899, 20th century, 1900–1999; and 21st century, 2000–present. Diplomatic and political materials also come from various countries (and also include non-English documents). Controversial documents on human rights, sociocultural ideologies, and war are included in this collection. The Avalon Project is the best source for U.S. government official documents, including topics such as documentary record of American Revolution, African American slavery laws, Native American treaties, and American World War II documents. We provide a list of these U.S. legal documents below (Table C3.2) for your reference (highlighted documents have been previously studied or included in a specialized corpus of American English).

C3.2.1.3 The American Presidency Project

The American Presidency Project (http://www.presidency.ucsb.edu/) collects public papers of U.S. presidents, including most public messages, statements, speeches, and news conference remarks. Documents such as proclamations and executive orders were obtained from the Federal Register and the Code of Federal Regulations. Papers from presidents Herbert Hoover through Gerald Ford (1929–1977) are not included, nor are some documents from president Jimmy Carter's administration (from 1977). The documents in these sources are arranged

TABLE C3.2 Major U.S. document collections from the Avalon Project

African Americans—Biography, Autobiography and History	International Agreements and Diplomatic Documents
The American Constitution—A Documentary Record	**The Jefferson Papers**
American Diplomacy: Bilateral Treaties 1778–1999	**Laws of War: Hague and Geneva Conventions**
American Diplomacy: Multilateral Treaties 1864–1999	The Middle East 1916–2003: A Documentary Record
American History: A Chronology 1492–Present	**Native Americans: Treaties with the United States**
American Revolution—A Documentary Record	Nazi–Soviet Relations 1939–1941
Ancient, Medieval and Renaissance Documents	**Nuremberg War Crimes Trial**
Annual Messages of the Presidents	Presidential Papers
Chinese American Diplomacy	**Project DIANA—An Online Human Rights Archive**
The Cold War	September 11, 2001: Attack on America—A Collection of Documents
Cold War Diplomacy—Defense Treaties of the United States	**Slavery: Statutes and Treaties**
Colonial Charters, Grants and Related Documents	Terrorism—A Document Collection
Confederate States of America: Papers	**Treaties Between The United States and Native Americans**
Congressional Resolutions	**United Nations—Documents**
Cuban American Diplomacy	**United States Statutes**
Diplomatic Document Collections	United States Statutes Concerning Native Americans
The Federalist papers	United States Statutes Concerning Slavery
Inaugural Addresses of the Presidents	**World War II—Documents; 1940–1945**

in chronological order and can be directly searched and copied. Most presidential remarks were delivered from Washington, D.C., unless otherwise indicated in the file. Messages from the White House such as statements and letters are also collected and made available as public documents. The suggested application exercise below, which focuses on U.S. presidents' inaugural addresses, can also be adapted to cover other documents from U.S. presidents from George Washington to Barack Obama.

C3.2.1.4 Movie (and Television) Screenplays

And finally, how about a diachronic study of movie and television screenplays and scripts? There are many online sites offering downloadable copies of movie screenplays that could be organized to collect your own corpus. One popular site is called **Screenplays for You** (http://sfy.ru/) which has more than 1,000 English movie scripts listed alphabetically and coded with the title of the movie, year of production, and names of screen writer/s. (See sample page 1 of the screenplay for the movie *Raising Arizona* [1987] written by Ethan and Joel Coen.)

In Section B3.6, we examined sample results from a study by Quaglio (2009), which collected a corpus of the U.S. television sitcom *Friends* for comparison with face-to-face conversation from the Longman Grammar Corpus. Quaglio was able to obtain his *Friends* corpus online with permission from the show's producers (NBC-Universal). Al-Surmi (2012) collected TV scripts from U.S. daytime soap operas, and Forchini (2012) collected movie screenplays (e.g., *Erin Brockovich, Ocean's Eleven, Finding Forrester*, and *The Devil Wears Prada*) also from various online sources.

Text Sample C3.I. Page 1 of *Raising Arizona* (1987) Movie Script Written by Ethan Coen and Joel Coen (from a Draft Script)

OVER BLACK:
VOICE-OVER: My name is H.I. McDunnough . . .
A WALL
With horizontal hatch lines.
VOICE-OVER: . . . Call me Hi.
A disheveled young man in a gaily colored Hawaiian shirt is launched into frame by someone offscreen.
He holds a printed paddle that reads "NO. 1468–6 NOV. 29 79."
The hatch marks on the wall behind him are apparently height markers.

Reflective Break

- How would you linguistically characterize the register of screenplays? What unique structure and form of language could you immediately notice from reading scripts? Do you think screenplays can be read for entertainment (in the same way you would read a book/narrative)?
- Below are sample screenplays shared by **Screenplays for You**, organized chronologically by decade. What sociolinguistic research questions could you formulate from a corpus study analyzing these screenplays?

All the King's Men **(1949)** by Robert Rossen. Based on a novel by Robert Penn Warren.

Bad Day at Black Rock **(1955)** by Don McGuire and Millard Kaufman. Based on the story "Bad Day at Hondo" by Howard Breslin.

Birds, The **(1963)** by Evan Hunter. Based on the novel *Birds* by Daphne Du Maurier.

Cool Hand Luke **(1967)** by Donn Pearce and Frank Pierson. Based on the novel by Donn Pearce.

Barry Lyndon **(1975)** by Stanley Kubrick. Based on the novel by William Makepeace Thackeray.

When a Stranger Calls **(1979)** by Steve Feke and Fred Walton.

Starman **(1984)** by Bruce A. Evans and Raynold Gideon with Dean Riesner (uncredited).

Affliction **(1997)** by Paul Schrader. Based on a novel by Russell Banks.

Enemy of the State **(1998)** by David Marconi and Aaron Sorkin.

Sideways **(2004)** by Alexander Payne and Jim Taylor. Based on the novel by Rex Pickett.

C3.3 Application 1: Exploring a Corpus of U.S. Presidential Inaugural Addresses

U.S. presidential inaugural addresses comprise a distinct type of very formal discourse that stretches back almost to the founding of the country. The address is delivered orally as a speech in public, in a very formal ceremony, yet, this speech is written and extensively prepared, at least for most presidents. In 220 years of American history, there have been only 57 such speeches, starting with George Washington in 1789 through Barack Obama in 2013. They appear at regularly scheduled intervals. Up until 1933, when Franklin D. Roosevelt took office, presidents had been inaugurated every four years on March 4, about four months after the November elections. The date changed with the adoption of the 20th Amendment to the U.S. Constitution. Since Roosevelt's first term, inaugurals have been held every four years on January 20 (Reiter, 2011). These inaugural addresses serve a function that is ceremonial as well as deliberative, and the rhetoric in these speeches reflects that. The rhetoric also may be shaped by context and by other variables, including party affiliation, regional background, era of service, peacetime or wartime periods, and good or bad economic conditions (Reiter, 2011; Ryan, 1993). Clearly, diachronic changes can be investigated within a very specialized register of this type, focusing only on a small group of individuals (all males, so far) over the years.

There is much related research on the form, content, rhetorical style, and historical applications of presidential inaugurals. Recently, radio and television coverage of these speeches have become major events scrutinized immidiately by political commentators. Media and Internet broadcasts of Barack Obama's inaugural address in 2009, a historic address delivered by the first African American president of the United States, was met with great global enthusiasam. The ceremonial nature of this domain covers a lot of contexts that have also shifted over time. George Washington spoke in New York to a small group comprised mostly of supporters and elected senators and congressmen while George W. Bush in 2005, his second term, spoke in Washington, D.C., to an international audience who tuned in to listen to U.S. post-9/11 thoughts and sentiments and immediate future directions related to the ongoing turmoil in the Middle East at that time.

Reiter (2011) notes that some of the most-often quoted lines in American discourse have come from presidential inaugural speeches, including, "*We have nothing to fear but fear itself*," from Franklin D. Roosevelt's first inaugural (1933) and "*Ask not what your country can do for you, but what you can do for your country*," from John F. Kennedy's inaugural (1961). Barack Obama commented that for his historic first inaugural speech, his primary goal was to capture the moment in American history and culture and to present a future-oriented optimism to his national and international audiences. "*I think that the main task for me in an inauguration speech, and I think this is true for my presidency generally, is to try to capture as best I can the moment that we are in,*" Obama stated to ABC News. He also emphasized that he would note the "crossroads" at which the country finds itself as an African American man has been elected to the presidency. After that, he said, he wanted to "*project confidence that if we take the right measures, that we can once again be that country, that beacon for the world*" (Seelye, 2009). Many inaugural speeches follow this classic formula of laying out the challenges that lie before the nation and calling on basic American ideals and values to meet and overcome them.

C3.3.1 Qualitative Analysis of Inaugural Speeches

Trivia

- Longest presidential inaugural speech: 1841, William Henry Harrison (8,460 words)
- Shortest presidential inaugural speech: 1793, George Washington, second inaugural address (135 words).

Study the two excerpts below comparing George Washington's first inaugural address, in 1789, with Bill Clinton's second inaugular address, delivered on January 20, 1997—a difference of over 200 years. We highlighted the use of personal pronouns in these two excerpts and also italicized references to the country (e.g., note Clinton's explicit mention of America). An additional content analysis of Washington versus Clinton's speeches in these two excerpts can certainly provide you with ideas to pursue further in conducting a diachronic corpus-based analysis of all U.S. presidential inaugural addresses.

Text Sample C3.2. Comparing Presidential Speeches from Washington (1789) and Clinton (1997)

George Washington

New York, Thursday, April 30, 1789 (excerpt from 1,428 words total)

Fellow Citizens of the Senate and of the House of Representatives:

Among the vicissitudes incident to life no event could have **filled me** with greater anxieties than that of which the notification was transmitted by your order, and received on the 14th day of the present month. On the one hand, **I was summoned** by **my Country**, whose voice **I can never hear** but with veneration and love, from a retreat which **I had chosen** with the fondest predilection, and, in **my flattering hopes**, with an immutable decision, as the asylum of **my declining years**—a retreat which was rendered every day more necessary as well as more **dear to me** by the addition of habit to inclination, and of frequent interruptions in **my health** to the gradual waste committed on it by time. On the other hand, the magnitude and difficulty of the trust to which the **voice of my country called me**, being sufficient to awaken in the wisest and *most experienced of her citizens a distrustful scrutiny into his qualifications, could not but overwhelm with despondence one who (inheriting inferior endowments from nature and unpracticed in the duties of civil administration) ought to be peculiarly conscious of his own deficiencies*. In this conflict of emotions all **I dare** aver is that it has been **my faithful study** to collect **my duty** from a just appreciation of every circumstance by which it might be affected. All **I dare hope** is that if, in executing this task, **I have been** too much swayed by a grateful remembrance of former instances, or by an affectionate sensibility to this transcendent proof of the confidence of **my fellow-citizens**, and have thence too little consulted **my incapacity** as well as disinclination for the weighty and **untried cares before me**, **my error** will be palliated by the **motives which mislead me**, and its consequences be judged by **my country** with some share of the partiality in which they originated.

William J. Clinton

Washington, DC, January 20, 1997 (excerpt from 2,157 words total)

My Fellow Citizens:
   At this last presidential inauguration of the 20th century, **let us lift our eyes** toward the **challenges that await us** in the next century. **It is our great good fortune** that **time and chance have put us** not only at the edge of a new century, in a new millennium, but on the edge of a bright new prospect in human affairs, a moment that will **define our course**, and **our character**, for decades to come. **We must keep our old democracy forever young**. Guided by the ancient vision of a promised land, **let us set our sights** upon a land of new promise.
   The promise of America was born in the 18th century out of the bold conviction **that we are all created equal.** It was extended and preserved in the 19th century, when **our nation** spread across the continent, saved the union, and abolished the awful scourge of slavery. Then, in turmoil and triumph, that promise exploded onto the world stage to make this *the American Century*.
   And what a century it has been. *America became the world's mightiest industrial power*, saved the world from tyranny in two world wars and a long cold war; and time and again, reached out across the globe to millions who, **like us, longed for the blessings of liberty**.

Along the way, *Americans produced a great middle class and security in old age; built unrivaled centers of learning and opened public schools to all; split the atom and explored the heavens; invented the computer and the microchip; and deepened the wellspring of justice by making a revolution in civil rights for African Americans* and all minorities, and extending the circle of *citizenship, opportunity and dignity to women.*

Now, for the third time, **a new century is upon us**, and another time to choose. **We began** the 19th century with a choice, to spread **our nation** from coast to coast. **We began** the 20th century with a choice, to harness the Industrial Revolution to **our values** of free enterprise, conservation, and human decency. Those choices made all the difference.

Reflective Break

*   What do you think were the primary contributing factors accounting for the clear difference between Washington and Clinton's use of personal pronouns? Clinton used *we, our, us* and did not specifically refer to himself (*I, me, my*) in this excerpt. In contrast, the opposite is apparent with Washington. Could this particular difference in only one linguistic feature (personal pronoun) be influenced by temporal change? Have presidential inaugural speeches become much more inclusive? What are potential functional applications of these types of observations?
*   Explore differences in lexical and grammatical usage in these two samples. Identify words and grammatical structures from Washington's speech which you think are no longer common in formal, public speeches nowadays. Are you surprised (or not) by changes or potential pattens of language shifts from these two short excerpts in a span of over 200 years?
*   What topic or content areas can you further study from these two samples? How have related contextual variables—for example, audience, medium of delivery (radio/TV for Clinton)—influenced the nature of political public speeches over time?

C3.3.2 Corpus-Based Analysis of Inaugural Speeches

We are not aware of any strictly corpus-based published study of presidential inaugural addresses, so far. However, the *New York Times* dedicated an online page, first posted in 2009, that collected all presidential inaugural addresses; they can be searched and compared across word frequencies and links to concordances from the actual speeches. This page displays only the most common 60 or so lexical words, with no raw frequency counts provided. The page is available at

http://www.nytimes.com/interactive/2009/01/17/washington/20090117_ADDRESSES.html.

Clearly, this Web-based application produced by the *New York Times* is based on corpora and CL approaches to identify and produce frequencies, keywords, and KWIC outputs. By making it publicly available, researchers can immediately explore all presidential inaugural addresses and manually compare them using embedded **word cloud** visuals and graphs.

What are word clouds? A word cloud typically is a graphical representation of word frequency.

Another very popular online application with deep corpus linguistics roots are word clouds (or tag clouds) from word frequency generators such as Wordle (www.wordle.net) or Tagxedo (http://www.tagxedo.com/). These applications convert frequency data to graphical presentation of text contents. Keyword metadata or word tags from text files or Web sites can be used for these visualization techniques. Tags are identified from single words, and the importance of each tag is shown with increased font size and/or change in color (Halvey & Keane, 2007). This visualized format is convenient for quickly locating the most prominent word in the input text. Figure C3.1 shows a word cloud of a speech from Barack Obama (2013), and Figure C3.2 shows one from Abraham Lincoln (1865), with sample KWIC lines of their most frequent words (*must* for Obama and *war* for Lincoln).

Sample KWIC lines for *must*:

- Together, we resolved that a great nation **must** care for the vulnerable and protect its people from life's worst hazards and misfortune.
- Now, more than ever, we **must** do these things together, as one nation, and one people.
- We **must** harness new ideas and technology to remake our government, revamp our tax code, reform our schools, and empower our citizens with the skills they need to work harder, learn more, and reach higher.

FIGURE C3.1 Word cloud of Obama's second inaugural speech (2013); 2,095 total words delivered January 21, 2013

FIGURE C3.2 Word cloud of Lincoln's second inaugural speech (1865); 689 total words delivered March 4, 1865

- We **must** make the hard choices to reduce the cost of health care and the size of our deficit. But we reject the belief that America **must** choose between caring for the generation that built this country and investing in the generation that will build its future.

Sample paragraph with *war*:

- On the occasion corresponding to this, four years ago all thoughts were anxiously directed to an impending civil **war**. All dreaded it; all sought to avert it. While the inaugural address was being delivered from this place, devoted altogether to saving the Union without **war**, insurgent agents were in the city seeking to destroy it without **war**—seeking to dissolve the Union and divide effects by negotiation. Both parties deprecated **war**, but one of them would make **war** rather than let the nation survive and the other would accept **war** rather than let it perish, and the **war** came.

Reflective Break

- Campbell and Jamieson (1985) argued that presidential inaugural addresses are different from other forms of presidential speeches and documents. These addresses are examples of epideictic or ceremonial discourses which contain four generic elements. The presidential inaugural (1) unifies the audience by reconstituting its members as "the people" who can witness and ratify the ceremony, (2) rehearses communal values drawn from the past, (3) sets forth the political principles that will govern the new administration, and (4) demonstrates that the president appreciates the requirements and limitations of the executive function. Each of these must be achieved through means appropriate to epideictic address—that is, while urging contemplation not action (p. 396). Are these elements observable from the word clouds of Obama and Lincoln's speeches? What do these word clouds tell you about communal values present during the periods represented by these two presidents?

C3.3.3 Ideas in Conducting Your Corpus-Based Analysis of Inaugural Speeches

Collect your corpus of U.S. presidential inaugural addresses online. You will have many options or sources here, but we recommend that you start with Bartleby. com or Project Avalon. Organize your collection into one text (.txt) file per speech. You will have a total of 57 speeches.

Reiter (2011) suggested the following steps and considerations:

Social Variables

- **Political Party Affiliation**: beginning with creation of the Republican and Democratic parties in 1854.
- **Historical Economic Periods**: presidents elected during good and bad economic times; expansion and growth of the economy (good) or stagnation, inflation and high unemployment (bad) as evidenced by increases or decreases in real gross national product per capita.
- **Era**: early (18 addresses: Washington through Buchanan), middle (18: Lincoln through Hoover), and late (20: Franklin Roosevelt through Obama).
- **Regional Background**: South, Northeast, West/Midwest (regions based on where a president began his political career or based on data from U.S. Census Bureau).
- **Military Service**: presidents who were military veterans and nonveterans (based on history of military service).
- **Peacetime/Wartime Distinction**: presidents who were elected during peacetime and wartime (based on when the speech was given).

Linguistic Variables

- **Lexical Items**: singular and plural personal pronouns; *god* words (e.g., *god, almighty, divine, providence, heaven*); distributions of parochial, national, and global words (e.g., *states, America, world*); *I* use and *we* use—*I* or *we* collocations.
- **Wordiness**: type/token ratio comparisons; indicates the verbosity of the speaker or group of speakers.
- **Multidimensional Analysis**: using Biber's 1988 dimensions, especially involved versus informational production across time periods.
- **Cohesion and Coherence**: extracting distributions of cohesive devices in speech—for example, conjunctions and linking adverbials.
- **Readability Measures**: comparing readability measures of group of speeches across the social categories listed above.

- **Keyword Analysis**: comparing unique words that are statistically frequent in one group compared to other groups. For example, would political party affiliation influence the distribution of keywords? Do Democrats and Republicans have particular preference for words or terms?
- **Others?** What other linguistic variables can you suggest?

Research Questions

You can develop research questions similar to the following examples:

- Does the frequency of _____ vary in presidential inaugural addresses across variables such as party affiliation, geographical origin, and era of service?
- Do these variations point to historical changes in presidential rhetoric or in American political discourse? Do they reflect changes in American society and culture?
- What are particular keywords and functional characteristics of presidential inaugurals that influence or predict party affiliation, geographical origin, and era of service?

Obtaining Data

For the first research question above, you will have to use concordancing software such as *AntConc* (Anthony, 2012) to obtain word and phrase-level results (e.g., for distributions of words such as *god* or *almighty*). POS-tagged features will also provide you with additional information focusing on the frequency of nouns, adjectives, or adverbs. Normalized counts of these features will also be necessary in conducting modified MD analyses using Biber's 1988 dimensions for comparison.

Examine the sample result (Figure C3.3) below (Reiter, Feinberg, & Thompson, 2011). Every president has invoked the deity, but the words to do so have varied dramatically. More elaborate words (e.g., *almighty, divine providence, Holy Spirit, creator, divine*) gave way to *god*, and the use of that word has increased significantly over the past 80 years.

Analysis and Interpretation

If you pursue word or phrase-level comparisons (such as the sample results in Figure C3.3), your analysis will cover a description of the figures/data and your interpretation of what you think influenced the variation you found. How do you explain the significant increase in the use of *god* in Figure C3.3? Below is an interpretation provided by Reiter (2011):

It is clear that religious references are a staple of this form of rhetoric. Every inaugural except for Washington's second (the shortest on record at 135 words) contains at least one reference to the *Deity*. However, the words used by the various presidents to refer to the *Almighty Being* (Washington), *Parent of the Human Race* (Adams) and *Divine Author* (Madison) have changed markedly over time. The word *god* was used only three times by the early presidents, compared with 33 for the middle presidents and 63 for the later presidents (note that data in Figure C3.3 were normalized per 1,000 words in the corpus). The use of the lemma *providence* seems to have a negative correlation with *god*. Whereas the early presidents invoked the blessings of *providence* 17 times, the middle presidents used the term only seven times and the later presidents only once. The lemma *blessing*, too, has fallen out of favor among U.S. presidents. Early presidents used it 31 times, almost three times as often as the middle presidents (11 mentions) and four times as often as the later presidents (8 mentions).

A subsequent search of COHA shows an apparent correlation for the use of the lemma blessing.* For the period 1810–1859 (which roughly corresponds to the early presidents), blessing* appeared an average of 91 times per million words. From 1860–1929 (the middle presidents), that average dropped by nearly two-thirds, to 33 per million. From 1930 through 2009 (the later president), the frequency dropped 50% from the middle era, to 16 words per million. That result suggests there might be some broader trends to be mined from an analysis of the presidential inaugural corpus.

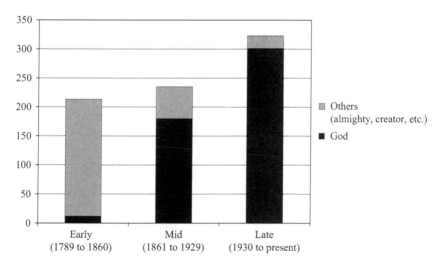

FIGURE C3.3 Comparison of *god* words in presidential inaugurals across historical periods (Reiter et al., 2011)

Another possible correlation, though seemingly weaker, emerges when results of searches for the word *women* in the three corpora are compared. In the presidential corpus, though *man* and *men* were used by the early presidents (20 and 34 mentions, respectively), it was not until the inaugural of Woodrow Wilson in 1913 that the word *women* was uttered in an inaugural addresses (*woman* had to wait even longer—until Harding's 1921 address, which came after the first presidential election in which all American women could vote). In all, there were zero mentions of *woman* or *women* by the early presidents; eight by the middle presidents; and 23 by the later presidents. The variation over time is not as extreme in COHA and the Google Books Ngram Viewer, but the direction seems to correlate. COHA shows an average of 135 times per million words for women between 1810 and 1860, rising to an average of 313 mentions per million from 1860–1930, and increasing again to an average of 359 from 1930 through 2009. For the Ngram Viewer, the comparable averages are 88 per million, 151 per million, and 254 per million.

These preliminary results suggest that for some words or clusters at least, there are marked differences in usage by U.S. presidents over time, and that these trends will correlate with usage in the larger corpora of American discourse. However, the principle of regression to the mean still holds.

C3.4 Application 2: Using COHA and the Google Books Ngram Viewer in Exploring Lexical Change

In Section B5, we presented Davies's Corpus of Historical American English (COHA), which is the largest structured corpus of historical English from multiple registers (fiction, magazine, newspaper, and nonfiction books). We also introduced the Google Books Ngram Viewer, which contains approximately 500 billion words from over 5.2 million books written in English, French, Spanish, German, Chinese, Russian, and Hebrew. A majority of books digitized by Google so far are in English (with 361 billion words). COHA allows you to quickly and easily search more than 400 million words of text of American English from 1810 to the present. You can see how words, phrases, and grammatical constructions have increased or decreased in frequency, how words have changed meaning over time, and how stylistic changes have taken place in American English. The Google Books Ngram Viewer, on the other hand, provides you with megacorpora of books with, to date, still-untapped linguistic applications in the study of global "culturomics." Both platforms offer visual representations of word frequencies across time periods.

Clearly, these two online resources can be used by students in sociolinguistics for a range of diachronic studies intended for semester-long class projects. For COHA, Davies (2011a) suggests a number of queries that can give you some ideas of what his interface can do. These are also ideas that can help you conduct an exploratory diachronic research. COHA's *Help* page provides a detailed description of search options (including searches for tagged features and collocations):

- Frequency over time of words and phrases related to changes in society and culture, or historical events, such as *emancipation, steamship, telegraph, flapper★, fascis★, teenage★, communis★*, and *global warming*. [The use of an asterisk allows the interface to include related words; for example, results for *communis★* will also include *communism, communist, communists*.]
- Changes in the language itself, such as the rise and fall of words and phrases:
  - **(decrease since the 1800s)**: bosom, grieved, bestow★, beauteous, fellow, sublime, lad, many a time, of no little, and for (used as a conjunction)
  - **(an increase and then decrease in frequency across time periods)**: *anyhow, mustn't, naughty, as though to, don't know as, far-out, swell* (as adjective), and *lousy*
  - **(an increase to the present time)**: a lot of, guys, unleash, sexual, calm down, screw up, freak out, mommy, and frustrating.
- Changes with syntactic constructions such as *end up* V-*ing, going to* V, V PRON *into* V-*ing* (e.g., *talked them into going*), phrasal verbs with *up* (e.g., *make up, show up*), post-verbal negation with *need* (*needn't mention*), the get passive (e.g., *get hired*), sentence-initial *hopefully*, semi-modals like *need to* and *have to*, and the rise (and possible recent decrease) of the progressive passive (e.g., *was being considered*).
- Stylistic constructions (half lexical, half syntactic) across different time periods: *so* ADJ *as to* V (*so good as to show me*), *be* V *but* (*they are but the last examples*), *have quite* V -*ed* (*until she had quite finished*), NOUN *be that of* (*her dress was that of a beggar*), or *a most* ADJ NOUN (*a most helpful child*). Davies (2012) found that these constructions are now used less frequently than before.
- Word list that is used more in one period than another, without specifying what words they might be; you can compare V in the 1970s–2000s (left) to the 1930s–1960s (right), ADJ in the 1970s–2000s (left) and the 1930s–1960s (right), or -*ly* Adverbs in the 1900s (left) to the 1800s (right).
- Change in meaning or usage over time through collocates. For example, the collocates of *sexual, gay, chip, engine*, or *web* have obviously changed over time.

For basic visual representations of many of the words suggested by Davies above, the Google Books Ngram Viewer can also be used for comparison. Remember that COHA provides other data sources while Google Books exclusively returns frequency data from published books alone.

In addition to culture-based lexico/syntactic diachronic studies, what else could be done with these online megacorpora? Are there pedagogical applications, especially in lexical studies of change?

Walker and Randall (2012) explored the applications of the Ngram Viewer and COHA in the analysis of academic word lists—in particular, Coxhead's (2000)

Academic Word List (AWL). The focus here was not necessarily to compare the strengths and/or weaknesses of these megacorpora when used together following similar search functions. Instead, this study looked at word lists as a conventional concept common in corpus-based studies with emphasis on pedagogical applications of corpus data, especially in the teaching of academic writing in English. The study of vocabulary use predates other areas of corpus investigation (Biber, Conrad, & Reppen, 1998), and vocabulary teaching materials developed from corpora have been very commonly used in many writing classrooms (and also incorporated into dictionaries and textbooks). Coxhead (2011) has called for further research on the AWL with larger corpora, noting that there is a continuing need to address learners' use of academic vocabulary for the AWL to be useful in various contexts over a decade after its publication. The Ngram Viewer and COHA seem to provide this opportunity for an update, in part, because these megacorpora have the volume of words and a variety of registers (at least for COHA) needed to check actual patterns of lexical distributions. The AWL has been widely used in English for Academic Purposes (EAP) and the teaching of second language writing in English.

Sample research question: How are words on the AWL reflected and distributed across time frames in the Google Books Ngram Viewer and COHA?

In pursuing this line of research, it may also be possible to answer whether or not there is evidence that an updated word list is necessary. You can choose any group of words from the AWL sublists (or other lists, in fact).

Results from both COHA and the Ngram Viewer from Walker and Randall (2012) validate an overall decline of frequencies for the AWL from 1998 to 2008 (from 1990 in the case of COHA). These results demonstrating an overall decreasing rate of use of common AWL words are not surprising. One clear fact known about language is that words have a life span (Crystal, 2006). Michel and colleagues (2011) noted that word usage is typically characterized by a spike at some point, followed immediately by a slow decline. Occasionally, words revive and have a short comeback at times, followed once again by a decline, measured by means of frequency distributions. However, such decline, when measured in a relatively short timeframe (e.g., 1990 to 2008) is very relevant if applied to standard word lists used for language teaching. As the AWL has been used as a reference for teachers of academic writing for a range of learners, including nonnative speakers of English, accurate distributions representing the present status of word usage in specific contexts is of greater importance. Another possible reason for the declining frequencies of these AWL words could be the consistent increase in the number of new words. A quick search for words such as *software, interface, develop,* and *document* in the Ngram Viewer showed increasing frequencies of these words in English books. Every year, there are approximately 8,500 new words added to the English language (Michel et al., 2011). The constant influx of new words gives a writer more options for presenting ideas and structuring academic arguments or explanations.

Reflective Break

Here are some more ideas to think about when using COHA and the Ngram Viewer. What else do you think could be added to this discussion?

- The Ngram Viewer and COHA are tools that will continue to stimulate the production of research studies on language variation and use. Statistically, when frequencies are normalized from these two databases and the investigated linguistic feature is not extremely rare, the large word count difference has very limited effect. COHA's present structure and range of features make it more ideal for corpus-based research than the Ngram Viewer. This database is monitored and regularly updated and Davies provides users with extensive *Help* features and also a bibliography of COCA/COHA-published studies over the years.
- COHA's search features (e.g., collocates, POS-tagged data, synonyms, etc.) and clearly defined registers are grounded in linguistic theory and are all well supported by previous research in corpus linguistics. In contrast, the Ngram Viewer's raw database has very limited search options and interactive features at present. However, while impossible to read as individual texts, Google allows users to download n-grams, which could then be processed further using specialized computer programs (note that COHA's database is not available for free download to users; see Davies's Google Books interface). A sampling of Google's texts of published books from 1500s to the present across major languages would represent a very important, globally available corpus for extensive linguistic analysis.
- The use of Google's corpora of books is going to be very valuable in a variety of natural language processing applications. Results of comparative and contrastive analysis of linguistic data from these texts across time periods will provide fascinating information about the human race.
- Keuleers, Brysbaert, and New (2011) suggest that Google Books Ngram Viewer can be effectively utilized for many types of studies in psycholinguistics. There are also potential applications of the Ngram Viewer for manipulation using other interfaces that aid dictionary research and linguistic tagging approaches (Sekine & Dalwani, 2010).

C4

APPLICATIONS: KEYWORD ANALYSIS, THE LINGUISTIC INQUIRY AND WORD COUNT (LIWC), AND USING POS-TAGGED DATA IN SOCIOLINGUISTIC RESEARCH

C4.1 Constructs and Tools

In Section A3.6, we summarized common linguistic constructs that can be investigated using corpus-based approaches. Several studies synthesized in this book revisited these constructs—frequency data, collocations, and co-occurrence patterns as they were applied to sociolinguistic analyses. Word (and POS-tags) frequency distributions across corpora have been our most basic output, providing easily interpretable sets of descriptive data. Our analyses then evolve to also include word relationships, multiword units (e.g., n-grams, lexical bundles, p-frames), and more specialized applications such as linguistic patterning and clustering. There remain many more constructs and tools to explore and apply in corpus-based sociolinguistics. Emerging computational models intended for big-data analytics can be adapted for variationist studies and advanced tagging techniques can still be developed (e.g., tagger for speech acts and pragmatic functions of language).

In this final applications section, we discuss research ideas and procedures for (1) conducting a keyword analysis, (2) using the physical and psychological processes captured by the Linguistic Inquiry and Word Count (LIWC) software, and (3) interpreting POS-tagged data.

C4.2 Keyness and Keyword Analysis

A keyword is "a word which occurs with unusual frequency in a given text" (Scott, 1997, p. 236). A determination of an unusually high frequency occurrence of words from one corpus is based upon a comparison with a target corpus and computed statistically from a measure of likelihood of occurrence. In Section B2.5.1 (Age and Corpora), we discussed Barbieri's (2008) keyword analysis of age-based variation from parallel corpora grouped according to speakers' ages ("younger corpus" vs. "older corpus"). Barbieri wanted to extract age-based keywords, captured statistically, from spontaneous conversation with younger and older speakers. She found that younger speakers used unusually frequent slang and swear words, stance makers, and "emotional involvement" markers (e.g., intensifiers, discourse markers, personal pronouns, and attitudinal adjectives) compared to older speakers.

In conducting a keyword analysis, you need two well-designed, parallel corpora, and you have to establish very clear goals for why you are comparing them. Keyword analysis data are obtained from computer programs such as *WordSmith Tools 6* (Scott, 2012) or *AntConc 3.2.4* (Anthony, 2012). For this section, we provide instructions for running a keyword analysis using the freeware *AntConc* to extract keywords and compute **keyness** values. Running the analysis in *AntConc* is relatively easy and does not require users to have an additional background in statistics. The results are intuitive and immediately interpretable, focusing primarily on a wordlist that is organized from the most frequent keyword down to the least frequent within the predetermined number of requested outputs (e.g., top 50 or top 100+).

C4.2.1 Steps in Keyword Analysis Using AntConc

AntConc (Anthony, 2012) was first shared online as a relatively simple concordance program, but it has progressed to become one of the best corpus and text analysis tools that is widely used in CL. Laurence Anthony of Waseda University continues to share *AntConc* for free and regularly updates the program for improved speed and quality of processing. In addition to generating simple concordance lines, n-gram outputs, and traditional word lists, *AntConc 3.2.4* can return keywords by comparing words that appear in the "target files" with the words from a "reference corpus" that are unusually frequent (or infrequent). Note that Anthony uses the term *reference corpus* to mean "comparison corpus" in this context. *AntConc* generates a keyword list by cross-tabulating frequencies of all lexical items in the two resulting word lists, from the most frequent to the least. Each word with a high frequency of occurrence is identified as a potential keyword in each of the two lists. These words are then ordered based on their "keyness" value. In keyword analysis, the calculation of keyness is typically done using Pearson's chi-square or Dunning's Log-Likelihood statistics. *AntConc's* default measure to compute keyness values is Log-Likelihood.

It is important to prepare your two corpora for keyword analysis using *AntConc*. Make sure that all files are transcribed using the same transcription convention; check for consistent spacing, spelling, and use of upper case and lowercase letters (although this could be addressed in *AntConc* by choosing an option that converts all upper case letters to lowercase). Also, scan for punctuation use, especially for contractions and possessives. Remove annotations or repetitive markups that do not belong to the actual speech or written texts you are comparing, as these will certainly skew your results. Once you have cleaned your two groups of texts, follow these steps in *AntConc* (Anthony, 2012):

1 Select a set of target files.
2 Go to the "Preferences" menu and chose the "Keyword Preferences" option.
3 Choose a statistical measure to assess the keyness of the target file words. The default setting of Log-Likelihood is recommended.
4 Choose a threshold for the number of keywords to be displayed (e.g., 50, 100, 200+).
5 Choose whether or not to view "Negative Keywords" (Negative Keywords are target file words with an unusually low frequency compared with the frequency in the reference corpus).
6 Choose a reference corpus of text (.txt) files, in the same manner that the target files are chosen.
7 The reference corpus directory will be shown, and the list of reference corpus files will appear at the bottom of the Keyword Preferences option menu.
8 Click "OK" in the Keyword Preferences menu, and return to the main Keywords window.
9 Choose suitable options for displaying the list of generated Keywords.
10 Press the "Start" button. At any time, the generation of the keyword list can be halted using the "Stop" button.
11 Clicking on the keyword will generate a set of KWIC lines using the text as the search term.

Figure C4.1 shows a screenshot of *AntConc* keyword analysis output with keyword ranks, raw frequency, and keyness. This comparison looked at personal blogs written by female bloggers compared against personal blogs by male bloggers.

Now, look at the following top 50 keywords comparing personal blogs written by male and female bloggers. Using the female blogs as target files and the male blogs as the comparison/reference files, we obtained these results (Table C4.1).

Reflective Break

*   What jumped out at you after analyzing the top 50 keywords from personal blogs by female bloggers compared to male bloggers? What happens when you group these keywords into categories that might further explain gender-based variation in blogging? Note that in her study of age-based keywords, Barbieri (2008) analyzed over 400 keywords and qualitatively grouped them together to form part of her linguistic conclusions. She summarized that younger speakers used more slang, expletives, and emotion words more than older speakers. What do you think are the contextual factors influencing more references to day/time/month (Friday, Saturday, A.M./P.M., October) in Table C4.1 by female bloggers compared to male bloggers?
*   The two groups of blog texts used in this sample analysis were not coded or cleaned for topics. Do you think topic is an important consideration in

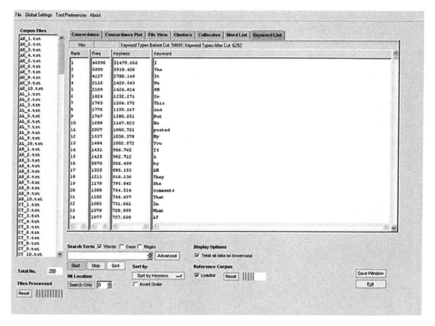

FIGURE C4.1 Sample keyword analysis output from *AntConc 3.2.4* (Anthony, 2012)

conducting a keyword analysis? What other variables should you consider in making sure that you have a logical and accurate comparison?

• What sociolinguistic corpora would you like to compare using keyword analysis? Draft your research questions and reflect on the potential functional applications of your study.

C4.3 Linguistic Inquiry and Word Count

The Linguistic Inquiry and Word Count or LIWC (pronounced as *Luke*) is a text analysis program developed by Pennebaker, Chung, Ireland, Gonzales, and Booth (2007). The primary goal of this application is to examine the emotional, cognitive, and structural components occurring in individuals' verbal and written speech samples. Evidence from a synthesis of these psychometric properties can support the generalization that people's physical and psychological well-being are manifested in the words they use in various communicative contexts. For example, in writing, studies by Campbell and Pennebaker (2003) and Pennebaker, Mayne, and Francis (1997) suggested that individuals who tend to use relatively high rates of positive emotion words—matched with a moderate number of negative emotion words and an increasing number of cognitive words—and who also switch their use of pronouns benefit the most from writing activities, leading to improvements in mental and physical health. Newman, Pennebaker, Berry, and Richards

TABLE C4.1 Female bloggers' keywords compared to those of male bloggers

Rank	Frequency	Keyness	Keyword
1	46,596	31,479.666	I
2	5,800	3,918.406	the
3	4,127	2,788.149	it
4	2,116	1,429.543	we
5	2,109	1,424.814	PM
6	1,824	1,232.271	so
7	1,783	1,204.572	this
8	1,775	1,199.167	and
9	1,747	1,180.251	but
10	1,699	1,147.823	he
11	2,007	1,040.721	our
12	1,537	1,038.378	my
13	1,484	1,002.572	you
14	1,431	966.765	if
15	1,425	962.712	a
16	5,870	926.499	by
17	1,325	895.153	AM
18	1,211	818.136	they
19	1,178	795.842	she
20	1,102	744.497	that
21	1,083	731.661	in
22	1,079	728.959	what
23	1,077	727.608	at
24	1,058	714.771	maybe
25	1,029	695.179	posted
26	55,369	678.374	their
27	988	667.48	there
28	857	578.978	when
29	756	510.744	well
30	750	506.69	as
31	715	483.045	no
32	27,391	476.784	of
33	699	472.236	god
34	683	461.426	now
35	670	452.643	new
36	594	401.299	for
37	554	374.275	not
38	518	349.954	one
39	512	345.901	Friday
40	501	338.469	then
41	497	335.767	to
42	495	334.416	after
43	466	314.824	all
44	464	313.473	how

(Continued)

TABLE C4.1 (*Continued*)

Rank	Frequency	Keyness	Keyword
45	462	312.121	oh
46	461	311.446	just
47	458	309.419	September
48	428	289.151	October
49	425	287.125	Saturday
50	416	281.044	why

(2003) found that **deceptive communication** could be characterized by the use of fewer first person singular pronouns (e.g., *I*, *me*, *my*), fewer third person pronouns (e.g., *he, she, they*), more negative emotion words (e.g., *hate, anger, enemy*), fewer exclusive words (e.g., *but, except, without*), and more motion verbs (e.g., *walk, move, go*).

A well-designed sociolinguistic corpus with a primary focus on mental processes (e.g., reflections from personal blogs, diaries, and narrative interview data) would be very appropriate for LIWC, although other registers such as gender and age-based academic writing or cross-cultural varieties of English texts may also be explored through LIWC. For example, LIWC psychometric results from a study based on age-categorized blogs reported that the general topic of *money* was far more often associated with bloggers older than 39 years old; the word *house* was also more frequently used by older bloggers (Nguyen, Phung, Adams, & Venkatesh, 2011). Pinkasovic (2013) suggested that women, as they age, may become more focused on their homes than when they were younger and that this focus may be revealed in their language usage. LIWC's analytical structure is unique compared to other popular linguistic taggers because of its additional focus on personal and psychological measures. The concept here is similar to many sentiment analysis tools utilized by big-data forecasters online.

LIWC returns a different form of tags from typical POS-taggers. It is well developed to analyze individual or multiple language text files relatively quickly, with a higher level of accuracy. The program counts and normalizes proportions of four groups of processes: **linguistic** (e.g., pronouns, word count, conjunctions), **psychological** (e.g., social, affective, cognitive, social), **personal concern** (e.g., work, leisure, home, money, religion), and **spoken category** (e.g., assent, fillers, nonfluencies). All these processes are manifested through the groups of words that most effectively and characteristically capture them. The counting and normalizing system is basically provided by a dictionary and information from test data that applied LIWC to various spoken and written corpora. Below is the composition of each of LIWC's processes—psychological, personal concern, and spoken category (we did not include *linguistic processes*—they consist of linguistic features such as pronouns, verbs, adverbs, prepositions, etc.)

TABLE C4.2 Composition of LIWC's psychological, personal concern, and spoken category

Word Categories	Sample Words from the LWIC Dictionary
Psychological Processes	
Social processes	mate, talk, they, child
Family	daughter, husband, aunt
Friends	buddy, friend, neighbor
Humans	adult, baby, boy
Affective processes	happy, cried, abandon
Positive emotion	love, nice, sweet
Negative emotion	hurt, ugly, nasty
Anxiety	worried, fearful, nervous
Anger	hate, kill, annoyed
Sadness	crying, grief, sad
Cognitive processes	cause, know, ought
Insight	think, know, consider
Causation	because, effect, hence
Discrepancy	should, would, could
Tentative	maybe, perhaps, guess
Certainty	always, never
Inhibition	block, constrain, stop
Inclusive	and, with, include
Exclusive	but, without, exclude
Perceptual processes	observing, heard, feeling
See	view, saw, seen
Hear	listen, hearing
Feel	feels, touch
Biological processes	eat, blood, pain
Body	cheek, hands, spit
Health	clinic, flu, pill
Sexual	horny, love, incest
Ingestion	dish, eat, pizza
Relativity	area, bend, exit, stop
Motion	arrive, car, go
Space	down, in, thin
Time	end, until, season
Personal Concerns	
Work	job, majors, xerox
Achievement	earn, hero, win
Leisure	cook, chat, movie
Home	apartment, kitchen, family
Money	audit, cash, owe
Religion	altar, church, mosque
Death	bury, coffin, kill
Spoken categories	
Assent	agree, OK, yes
Nonfluencies	er, hm, umm
Fillers	blah, I mean, you know

Source: adapted from Pennebaker et al., 2007, pp. 5–6

C4.3.1 Using LIWC in Sociolinguistic Research

Information on purchasing LIWC can be found in the LIWC Web site (http://www.liwc.net/). Running the program is easy and interpreting results is intuitive once you have read the LIWC manual for details on what the resulting percentages mean in the output file (the output is on .txt format which can easily be converted to a spreadsheet). A feature added in the LIWC Web site in 2013 applies this analytical process to Twitter personality analysis.

An exploratory study by Pinkasovic (2013) compared the speeches of African American civil rights leaders Martin Luther King, Jr. and Malcolm X. Pinkasovic noted that both X and King were gifted orators who used the podium as their primary platform for which they communicated and disseminated their views related to African American rights, religion, and social change. They had two different approaches and communication foci, however, and their respective followers maintained projections of their messages and mandates differently. King was the religious pacifist, whereas X was the more aggressive, antiestablishment figure. Cone (2001, p. ix) noted that "more than twenty years after their assassinations, their names arouse passionate acceptance or rejection, and few people, black or white, have unbiased opinions about them."

Various examinations of King's and X's speeches (including sermons by King) have been conducted, focusing, for the most part, on qualitative discourse analysis. For example, Vail (2006) looked at the metaphoric and temporal contexts of King's speeches in conjunction with isolated and contextualized features of politics during the civil rights period in the United States. King's "I Have a Dream" speech, his most memorable and most popular speech, has also been analyzed for orality and related oral dimensions. Studies of X's political discourse have also examined similar rhetorical features and strategies. What was clear to Pinkasovic (2013) was the surprising lack of corpus-based analyses comparing the linguistic and rhetorical characteristics of speeches by X and King. Furthermore, a CL approach has not been applied to compare and contrast X's and King's ideologies as manifest in their recorded rhetoric across a variety of contexts (e.g., political and public speeches, lectures, religious sermons, speeches delivered to a private audience, and audio and video recorded public speeches and interviews).

Pinkasovic (2013) collected a subset of speeches and sermons from King and X exclusively online, accessing materials from public libraries and Web sites dedicated to these leaders, their followers, and the civil rights movement in the United States. A specialized corpus of King's and X's speeches could be further categorized into speech events, intended audiences, topics, and also length. Indeed, such corpus can be aggregated and compared or contrasted using LIWC. A clear goal for Pinkasovic was to examine, on the extreme, what King may have said to merit some of X's followers labeling him a "twentieth century religious Uncle

Tom pacifist" and to discover what X may have uttered to incite some of King's disciples to label X a "messiah of hate" (Cone, 2001, p. 173). On a more general level of comparison, this type of corpus data could provide a detailed description of African American discourse during the civil rights movement relative to political and temporal changes in the United States.

Below are three groups of results from Pinkasovic (2013), showing (1) the frequency of language utilizing affective processes, and positive and negative emotion; (2) each speaker's use of words of anxiety, anger, and sadness, relative to their general word usage in their speeches; and (3) use of words pertaining to family, friends, and religion. Note that the results in the figures below were sorted by category to indicate the percentage that words within a specific LIWC process were used (in comparison to the total words used in the corpus).

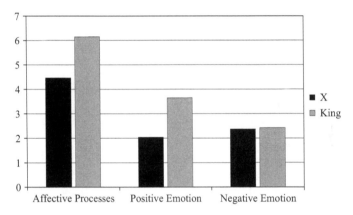

FIGURE C4.2 Emotive words used as a percentage of total word use in King's and X's speeches (Pinkasovic, 2013)

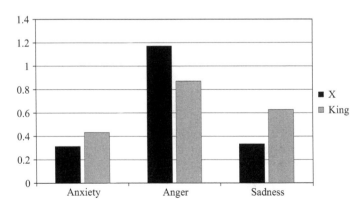

FIGURE C4.3 King's and X's use of words of anxiety, anger, and sadness (Pinkasovic, 2013)

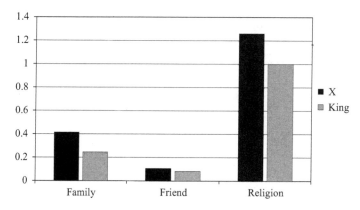

FIGURE C4.4 King's and X's use of words referring to family, friends, and religion (Pinkasovic, 2013)

Reflective Break

- In Figure C4.2, while King was shown to use more positive emotion in his speech, both X and King used essentially the same amount of negative emotion. It is evident, however, that King used significantly more positive than negative emotion in this speeches. Pinkasovic (2013) commented that the fact that King utilized positive emotion considerably more than negative emotion may have led to contemporary conceptualizations of King as "a promoter of love and nonviolence." Although X had considerably less positive emotion than King, the nearly equivalent usage of negative emotion by both X and King did not necessarily support the impression of X as "a preacher of hate and violence" (Cone, 2001, p. 181). Do you agree with this interpretation from Pinkasovic? What other conclusions could you make from the three figures above?
- What are the implications of these results? How will you apply LIWC to similar studies of political or creative discourse? Which speakers or authors will you compare?
- In using LIWC, make sure you that you know how to correctly interpret the tagged output. LIWC outputs do not return frequency counts. LIWC works by counting the number of tokens in a given text, tagging them using its category/dictionary system, and then counting the frequency that a given category's words are used. This frequency is compared to the overall number of words or tokens in the text. A single token may fall under several categories, and the percentages for that category will be adequately reflective. For example, "The word *cried* is part of five word categories: sadness, negative emotion, overall affect, verb, and past tense verb . . . if it is found in the target text, each of these five sub-dictionary scale scores will be incremented" (Pennebaker et al., 2007, p. 4).

C4.4 Using POS-Tagged Data

The term *World Englishes* refers to localized varieties of English used around the world (Bolton, 2005). The concentric circles of Englishes from native, core-Englishes to expanding regional varieties were developed and modeled by Braj Kachru (1996, 1992) to illustrate the global spread of English from its norm-providing varieties (L1 or L2 norm) to norm-dependent varieties (e.g., English in China or Egypt). The study of World Englishes has typically been approached from linguistic and sociocultural perspectives. The classification of new or emerging Englishes and colonization models in countries like India (colonized by the British) and the Philippines (colonized by the Americans) are common topics of comparative studies in this subfield. English as a Lingua Franca (ELF) and English as an International Language (EIL) are related areas of study, but both have been operationalized differently to address a particular audience and diverse linguistic constructs. For example, ELF emphasizes the use of English in task-based, inter-cultural communication between nonnative English speakers and may focus more on the performance of communicative tasks or speaker identities.

World Englishes have been widely studied using corpora. In particular, the International Corpus of English (ICE) has been used in many research articles published by the journal *World Englishes*. One of this journal's most frequently downloaded articles from 2010 to 2012 was a study by Xiao (2009), which was a multidimensional analysis of ICE components, following Biber's (1988) framework. Xiao's dimensions, extracted from ICE, included (1) interactive casual discourse versus informative elaborate discourse, (2) elaborative online evaluation, (3) presentational concern, (4) human versus object description, (5) future projection, (6) subjective impression and judgment, (7) lack of temporal/locative focus, (8) concern with degree and quantity, and (9) concern with reported speech.

Xiao found interesting variations in ICE texts across his nine dimensions. For example, in Dimension 5 (future projection—e.g., future time expressions from modals *will, would, shall*; conditionals; and expressions of definiteness), British English had the highest dimension score in most written registers and private conversations, while Indian English had the lowest. In the same dimension, patterns of English usage for future projection in Hong Kong and Singapore appeared to be closer to British English, while Philippine English patterns resembled those of Indian English. Xiao attempted to interpret this particular result, while referencing the need for additional research, as well as the need to examine such data from a socio-cultural perspective. He cited Shastri (1988) who suggested that the Indian mind and its communicative expressions in English may not be inclined to thinking much in terms of the future. This postulation could definitely be investigated further.

C4.4.1 POS-Tagged Data from ICE

In this subsection, we present POS-tagged data from ICE India, Philippines, and Singapore—three parallel corpora of "Asian Englishes." As referenced in Section B1, the ICE project represents various regional varieties of English collected by research teams in countries including East Africa (Kenya and Tanzania), South Africa, Jamaica, Hong Kong, and Malaysia. Native or national varieties such as English in Great Britain, Ireland, Canada, and New Zealand also have completed spoken and written texts for ICE, while the U.S. version is still under construction as of late 2013. Copies of ICE can be obtained free for noncommercial and academic research applications from the ICE Web site (http://ice-corpora.net/ice/). Tagged versions (using CLAWS7) of ICE India, Singapore, Hong Kong, New Zealand, Canada, and Jamaica are also available.

The ICE was designed primarily for synchronic, comparative studies of global Englishes based on parallel corpora of spoken and written texts. Each component corpus follows a common design, with five hundred 2,000-word texts sampled from a wide range of spoken (60%) and written (40%) registers (Nelson, 1996). Most components were collected in the 1990s. The ICE is limited by its total word count of only one million words per corpus. Also, many subregisters (e.g., broadcast interviews, demonstrations, student essays) have a total of only 10 texts, and there are no plans, it appears, to update the composition of each corpus to include Web registers or computer-mediated speech. With the current ICE design, it may be more appropriate to study ICE from a macrocomparison model by combining all spoken and all written texts together.

In the sample results below, we provided the normalized tagged counts of these registers from ICE India, Philippines, and Singapore. The 42 POS-tags came from the Biber Tagger (Biber, 2006b).

List of Tag Categories Coded in Table C4.3

1 Type/Token (ratio formula used here indicates that a high type/token ratio results from the use of many new lexical items)
2 Word Length (average word length per letter)
3 Word Count (total word count per register)
4 Private Verbs (e.g., *believe, feel, think*)
5 "*That*" Deletion
6 Contraction
7 Verb (uninflected present, imperative, and third person)
8 Second Person Pronoun/Possessive
9 Verb "*Do*"
10 Demonstrative Pronoun
11 Adverb/Qualifier—Emphatic (e.g., *just, really, so*)
12 First Person Pronoun/Possessive
13 Pronoun "*It*"
14 Verb "*Be*" (uninflected present tense, verb, and auxiliary)
15 Subordinating Conjunction—Causative (e.g., *because*)
16 Discourse Particle (e.g., *now*)
17 Nominal Pronoun (e.g., *someone, everything*)
18 Adverbial—Hedge (e.g., *almost, maybe*)

TABLE C4.3 ICE components tagged results using the Biber Tagger (data normalized per 1,000 words)

	1	2	3	4	5	6	7
ICE Component	type/token	word length	word count	private verbs	that deletion	contractions	verbs
India Spoken	46.82	4.30	2284.93	15.71	5.01	0.24	98.08
India Written	55.10	4.80	2224.38	6.80	1.16	0.11	59.50
Philippines Spoken	47.94	4.22	2258.32	18.36	6.32	1.05	90.13
Philippines Written	56.19	4.82	2250.31	8.02	1.76	0.04	60.75
Singapore Spoken	48.32	4.17	2215.82	22.88	8.34	0.88	104.51
Singapore Written	55.77	4.74	2186.85	9.28	1.78	0.15	65.61

	8	9	10	11	12	13	14
ICE Component	second persons	verb do	demonstrative pronouns	emphatics	first Person	it	verb be
India Spoken	17.98	1.44	5.48	3.88	33.39	14.04	2.40
India Written	5.44	0.47	2.22	1.86	11.77	8.72	1.80
Philippines Spoken	22.31	1.66	4.24	7.41	43.33	14.97	2.73
Philippines Written	4.95	0.48	2.75	2.84	14.69	8.97	1.88
Singapore Spoken	34.40	1.89	5.83	6.53	38.74	16.76	2.84
Singapore Written	9.37	0.59	2.96	2.87	16.06	9.85	2.43

(Continued)

TABLE C4.3 (Continued)

	15	16	17	18	19	20	21
ICE Component	subordinating conjunction	discourse particles	nominative pronouns	hedges	amplifiers	wh questions	modals of possibility
India Spoken	2.49	1.62	3.95	0.53	4.92	0.26	6.22
India Written	0.99	0.37	1.64	0.32	1.90	0.52	5.06
Philippines Spoken	3.37	3.84	4.49	1.28	3.48	0.00	6.13
Philippines Written	1.39	0.41	2.12	0.43	1.83	0.57	5.54
Singapore Spoken	3.27	4.49	4.21	1.50	5.78	0.01	7.98
Singapore Written	1.03	0.44	2.22	0.39	1.91	0.62	6.61

	22	23	24	25	26	27	28
ICE Component	coordinating conjunctions	wh clauses	stranded prepositions	nouns	prepositions	attributive adjectives	past tense verbs
India Spoken	1.86	0.87	0.05	235.15	87.21	31.66	24.79
India Written	5.35	0.29	0.92	318.67	122.78	56.48	25.39
Philippines Spoken	1.45	1.26	0.00	230.87	82.50	27.84	27.69
Philippines Written	7.59	0.54	1.21	316.40	116.00	49.91	26.08
Singapore Spoken	1.73	1.50	0.00	218.68	80.55	27.24	23.60
Singapore Written	5.77	0.63	1.17	293.96	112.58	51.30	28.09

ICE Component	29 third person	30 perfect aspect verbs	31 public verbs	32 wh object pronouns	33 wh subject pronouns	34 wh pied-pipings	35 coordinating conjunctions
India Spoken	22.37	9.42	5.50	0.90	2.79	0.54	1.82
India Written	17.97	7.93	3.14	0.76	2.99	0.71	2.59
Philippines Spoken	20.35	5.92	5.66	0.87	2.14	0.28	1.81
Philippines Written	20.82	6.45	5.23	0.89	3.01	0.54	2.67
Singapore Spoken	23.56	7.40	6.07	0.86	1.98	0.23	1.64
Singapore Written	23.11	7.16	4.14	0.85	3.45	0.47	2.99

ICE Component	36 nominalizations	37 time adverbs	38 place adverbs	39 other adverbs	40 infinitive adverbs	41 modals of prediction	42 suasive verbs
India Spoken	35.69	10.89	8.10	32.13	9.56	6.53	1.32
India Written	55.30	3.71	4.96	30.54	10.67	4.76	1.14
Philippines Spoken	35.19	9.32	7.19	35.20	10.59	8.07	1.13
Philippines Written	55.46	4.41	4.45	29.71	12.38	5.58	1.29
Singapore Spoken	29.80	10.87	7.73	40.18	12.93	7.90	0.99
Singapore Written	52.20	4.50	4.77	34.52	13.73	6.32	1.20

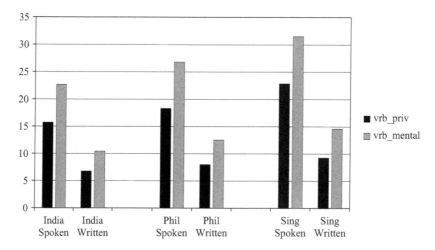

FIGURE C4.5 Distribution of private and mental verbs across spoken and written ICE corpora

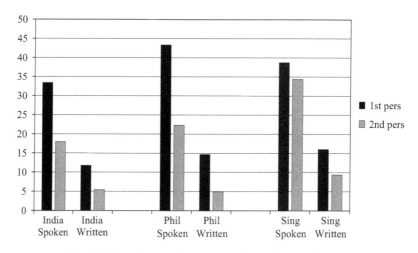

FIGURE C4.6 Distribution of personal pronouns (first and second) across spoken and written ICE corpora

19 Adverb/Qualifier—Amplifier (e.g., *absolutely*, *entirely*)
20 *Wh-* Question
21 Modals of Possibility (*can, may, might, could*)
22 Coordinating Conjunction—Clausal Connector
23 *Wh-* Clause
24 Stranded Preposition
25 Noun

26 Preposition
27 Attributive Adjective
28 Past Tense Verb
29 Third Person Pronoun (except "*it*")
30 Verb—Perfect Aspect
31 Public Verbs (e.g., *assert, complain, say*)
32 *Wh-* Pronoun—Relative Clause—Object Position
33 *Wh-* Pronoun—Relative Clause—Subject Position
34 *Wh-* Pronoun—Relative Clause—with Prepositional Fronting ("*pied piping*")
35 Coordinating Conjunction—Phrasal Connector
36 Singular Noun—Nominalization
37 Adverb—Time
38 Adverb—Place
39 Adverb—Other Adverbs
40 Infinitive Verb
41 Modal of Prediction (*will, would, shall*)
42 Suasive Verb (e.g., *ask, command, insist*)

Reflective Break

- Study the normalized frequencies of POS-tagged features from ICE India, Philippines, and Singapore in Table C4.3. What comparative studies can you conduct from these results? What are your immediate observations about these numbers?
- Can you compare these data from ICE India, Philippines, and Singapore with results from native Englishes in ICE such as ICE Great Britain and ICE Canada? (Note that ICE America is still under construction, but its written texts are now available from the ICE Web site.) What features do you think will show greater variability?
- India and Singapore follow British English as their norm-providing variety; the Philippines was under U.S. rule from the early 1900 to the late 1940s (after World War II) and follows American English as its exonormative model in pronunciation and grammar. With this in mind, how will you compare our sample tagged data in Table C4.3 to study the influence of native English models to nonnative varieties?
- Interpret Figures C4.5 and C4.6. What did you notice? A credible interpretation of these results calls for more understanding of Englishes in India, the Philippines, and Singapore within the context of their sociocultural backgrounds. As a researcher, what will be the ideal ways for you to be able to learn more about these countries without visiting them? Who can you talk to and how will you synthesize information?

BIBLIOGRAPHY

Acerbi, A., Lampos, V., Garnett, P., & Bentley, R.A. (2013). The expression of emotions in 20th Century books. *PLoS ONE, 8*(3), 1–6. doi: 10.1371/journal.pone.0059030

Adolphs, S., Brown, B., Carter, R., Crawford, P., & Sahota, O. (2004). Applying corpus linguistics in a health care context. *Journal of Applied Linguistics, 1*(1), 9–28.

Al-Sulaiti, L., & Atwell, E. (2006). The design of a corpus of contemporary Arabic. *International Journal of Corpus Linguistics, 11*(2), 135–171.

Al-Surmi, M. (2012). Authenticity and TV shows: A multidimensional analysis perspective. *TESOL Quarterly, 46*(4), 671–694. doi: 10.1002/tesq.33

Albanyan, A., & Preston, D.R. (1998). What is standard American English. *Studia Anglica Posnaniensia, 33*, 29–46.

Alderson, J.C. (2007). Judging the frequency of English words. *Applied Linguistics, 28*(3), 383–409. doi: 10.1093/applin/amm024

Álvarez, I.A., Muñoz, A.M., & Herington, R. (2010). *Twitter a new global genre: A contrastive study of the use of language in English and Spanish.* Paper presented at the Annual Meeting of the British Association for Applied Linguistics, Aberdeen, UK.

Anthony, L. (2012). AntConc (Version 3.3.5). [Software]. Available from http://www.antlab.sci.waseda.ac.jp/

Anton, J., & Setting, T. (2004). The American consumer reacts to the call center experience and the offshoring of service calls. Available from http://www.kellyconnect.com/eprise/main/web/us/kcnt/en/kc_offshoring.pdf

Argamon, S., Koppel, M., Fine, J., & Shimoni, A.R. (2003). Gender, genre, and writing style in formal written texts. *Text, 23*(3), 321–346. doi: 0165–4888/03/0023–0321

Argamon, S., Koppel, M., Pennebaker, J., & Schler, J. (2007). Mining the blogosphere: Age, gender, and the varieties of self-expression. *First Monday, 12*(9). doi: http://dx.doi.org/10.5210%2Ffm.v12i9.2003

Asención-Delaney, Y., & Collentine, J. (2011). A multidimensional analysis of a written L2 Spanish corpus. *Applied Linguistics, 32*(3), 299–322. doi: 10.1093/applin/amq053

Asur, S., & Huberman, B.A. (2010). *Predicting the future with social media.* Paper presented at the Web Intelligence and Intelligent Agent Technology (WI-IAT), Toronto, ON.

Austin, J.L. (1975). *How to do things with words* (Vol. 88). Cambridge, MA: Harvard University Press.

Bailey, G. (2002). Real and apparent time. In J.K. Chambers, P. Trudgill, & N. Schilling-Estes (Eds.), *The handbook of language variation and change* (pp. 312–332). Oxford: Blackwell.

Baker, P. (2006). *Using corpora in discourse analysis*. New York: Continuum.

Baker, P., Gabrielatos, C., Khosravinik, M., Krzy anowski, M., McEnery, T., & Wodak, R. (2008). A useful methodological synergy? Combining critical discourse analysis and corpus linguistics to examine discourses of refugees and asylum seekers in the UK press. *Discourse & Society, 19*(3), 273–306. doi: 10.1177/0957926508088962

Barbieri, F. (2008). Patterns of age-based linguistic variation in American English. *Journal of Sociolinguistics, 21*(1), 58–88.

Bargiela-Chiappini, F., & Harris, S. (1997). *Managing language: The discourse of corporate meetings*. Amsterdam: John Benjamins.

Barlow, M. (1998). Corpus of Spoken, Professional American-English. Available from http://www.athel.com/cpsa.html

Barlow, M. (2012). MonoConc Pro 2.2 (MP2.2) [Software]. Available from http://www.monoconc.com/

Bauer, L. (1994). Introducing the Wellington Corpus of Written New Zealand English. *Te Reo, 37*, 21–28.

Beeching, K. (2002). *Gender, politeness and pragmatic particles in French*. Amsterdam: John Benjamins.

Bekkerman, R., McCallum, A., & Huang, G. (2004). Automatic categorization of email into folders: Benchmark experiments on Enron and SRI corpora. *UMass CIIR Technical Report IR-418*. Available from http://www.cs.umass.edu/~ronb/papers/email.pdf

Benson, E.J. (2009). Everyone wants in: Want + prepositional adverb in the Midland and beyond. *Journal of English Linguistics, 37*(1), 28–60. doi: 10.1177/0075424208329373

Berber Sardinha, T. (2007). Metaphor in corpora: A corpus-driven analysis of applied linguistics dissertations. In L. Cameron, M. Zanotto, & M. Cavalcanti (Eds.), *Confronting metaphor in use: An applied linguistic perspective* (pp. 127–147). Amsterdam: John Benjamins.

Berber Sardinha, T., Kauffmann, C., & Acuzo, C.M. (forthcoming). Dimensions of register variation in Brazilian Portuguese. In T. Berber-Sardinha, & M. Veirano-Pinto (Eds.), *Multi-dimensional analyses: Twenty-five years on*. Amsterdam: John Benjamins.

Berryman-Fink, C.L., & Wilcox, J.R. (1983). A multivariate investigation of perceptual attributions concerning gender appropriateness in language. *Sex Roles, 9*, 663–681.

Besnier, N. (1988). The linguistic relationships of spoken and written Nukulaelae registers. *Language, 64*, 707–736.

Biber, D. (1986a). On the investigation of spoken and written differences. *Studia Linguistica, 40*, 1–21.

Biber, D. (1986b). Spoken and written textual dimensions in English: Resolving the contradictory findings. *Language, 62*(2), 384–414.

Biber, D. (1988). *Variation across speech and writing*. Cambridge: Cambridge University Press.

Biber, D. (1990). Methodological issues regarding corpus-based analyses of linguistic variation. *Literary and Linguistic Computing, 5*(4), 257–269. doi: 10.1093/llc/5.4.257

Biber, D. (1993). Representativeness in corpus design. *Literary and Linguistic Computing, 8*(4), 243–257.

Biber, D. (1995). *Dimensions of register variation: A cross-linguistic comparison*. Cambridge: Cambridge University Press.

Biber, D. (2001). Dimensions of variation among eighteenth-century speech-based and written registers. In S. Conrad, & D. Biber (Eds.), *Variation in English: Multi-dimensional studies* (pp. 200–214). New York: Longman.

Biber, D. (2006a). Stance in spoken and written university registers. *Journal of English for Academic Purposes, 5*(2), 97–116. doi: 10.1016/j.jeap.2006.05.001

Biber, D. (2006b). *University language: A corpus-based study of spoken and written registers.* Amsterdam: John Benjamins.

Biber, D. (2008). Corpus-based analyses of discourse: Dimensions of variation in conversation. In V.K. Bhatia, J. Flowerdew, & R. Jones (Eds.), *Advances in discourse studies* (pp. 100–114). London: Routledge.

Biber, D. (2009). A corpus-driven approach to formulaic language in English: Multi-word patterns in speech and writing. *International Journal of Corpus Linguistics, 14*(3), 275–311. doi: 10.1075/ijcl.14.3.08bib

Biber, D., & Burges, J. (2000). Historical change in the language use of women and men. *Journal of English Linguistics, 28*(1), 21–37. doi: 10.1177/00754240022004857

Biber, D., & Burges, J. (2001). Historical shifts in the language of women and men: Gender differences in dramatic dialogue. In D. Biber, & S. Conrad (Eds.), *Variation in English: Multi-dimensional studies* (pp. 157–170). London: Longman.

Biber, D., Connor, S., Upton, T.A., & Jones, J.K. (2007). Vocabulary-based discourse units in biology research articles. In D. Biber, U. Connor, & T.A. Upton (Eds.), *Discourse on the move: Using corpus analysis to describe discourse structure* (pp. 175–211). Philadelphia: John Benjamins.

Biber, D., & Conrad, S. (2009). *Register, genre, and style.* New York: Cambridge University Press.

Biber, D., Conrad, S., & Cortes, V. (2004). *If you look at . . .*: Lexical bundles in university teaching and textbooks. *Applied Linguistics, 25*(3), 371–405.

Biber, D., Conrad, S., & Reppen, R. (1998). *Corpus linguistics: Investigating language structure and use.* Cambridge: Cambridge University Press.

Biber, D., Davies, M., Jones, J.K., & Tracy-Ventura, N. (2006). Spoken and written variation in Spanish: A multi-dimensional analysis. *Corpora, 1*, 7–38.

Biber, D., & Finegan, E. (1986). An initial typology of English text types. In J. Aarts, & W. Meijs (Eds.), *Corpus linguistics II* (pp. 19–46). Amsterdam: Rodopi.

Biber, D., & Finegan, E. (1989). Styles of stance in English: Lexical and grammatical marking of evidentiality and affect. *Text, 9*, 93–124.

Biber, D., & Finegan, E. (2001). Diachronic relations among speech-based and written registers in English. In S. Conrad, & D. Biber (Eds.), *Variation in English: Multi-dimensional studies* (pp. 66–83). New York: Longman.

Biber, D., Finegan, E., & Atkinson, D. (1994). ARCHER and its challenges: Compiling and exploring "A Representative Corpus of Historical English Registers". In U. Fries, G. Tottie, & P. Schneider (Eds.), *Creating and using English language corpora* (pp. 1–14). Amsterdam: Rodopi.

Biber, D., & Gray, B. (2013). *A corpus-based analysis of writing and speaking task types on the TOEFL iBT.* Paper presented at the American Association for Corpus Linguistics 2013, San Diego, CA.

Biber, D., & Hared, M. (1992). Literacy in Somali: Linguistic consequences. *Language Variation and Change, 4*, 41–75.

Biber, D., Johansson, S., Leech, G., Conrad, S., & Finegan, E. (1999). *Longman grammar of spoken and written English.* Harlow, UK: Pearson.

Biber, D., & Kurjian, J. (2007). Towards a taxonomy of web registers and text types: A multi-dimensional analysis. In M. Hundt, M. Nesselhauf, & C. Biewer (Eds.), *Corpus linguistics and the web* (pp. 109–132). Amsterdam: Rodopi.

Biber, D., Reppen, R., & Friginal, E. (2010). Research in corpus linguistics. In R.B. Kaplan (Ed.), *The Oxford handbook of applied linguistics* (2nd ed., pp. 548–570). Oxford: Oxford University Press.

Blum-Kulka, S., House, J., & Kasper, G. (1989). *Cross-cultural pragmatics: Requests and apologies*. Norwoord, NJ: Ablex.

Bohannon, J. (2010). Google opens books to new cultural studies. *Science, 330*(6011), 1600. doi: 10.1126/science.330.6011.1600

Bolton, K. (2005). Where WE stands: Approaches, issues, and debate in world Englishes. *World Englishes, 24*, 69–83.

Brazil, D. (1985). *The communicative value of intonation in English.* Birmingham, UK: University of Birmingham, English Language Research.

Brazil, D. (1997). *The communicative role of intonation in English* (2nd ed.). Cambridge: Cambridge University Press.

Breiteneder, A. (2009). English as a lingua franca in Europe: An empirical perspective. *World Englishes, 28*(2), 256–269. doi: 10.1111/j.1467–971X.2009.01579.x

The British National Corpus version 2 (BNC World). (2001). Distributed by Oxford University Computing Services on behalf of the BNC Consortium. Available from http://www.natcorp.ox.ac.uk/

The British National Corpus version 3 (BNC XML Edition). (2007). Distributed by Oxford University Computing Services on behalf of the BNC Consortium. Available from http://www.natcorp.ox.ac.uk/

Brockman, J. (2010). Who's taking your call? *CFI Group's 2010 Contact Center Satisfaction Index*. Available from http://www.cfigroup.com/resources/whitepapers_register. asp?wp=46

Brown, C. (2006). *Rating tobacco industry documents for corporate deception and public fraud: A corpus linguistic assessment of intent*. Unpublished doctoral dissertation, University of Georgia, Athens, GA.

Brown, C., & Rubin, D.L. (2005). Causal adverbs in tobacco industry documents: The pragmatics of responsibility. *Journal of Pragmatics, 37*, 799–811. doi: 10.1016/j.pragma. 2004.10.015

Brown, P., & Levinson, S. (1987). *Politeness: Some universals in language*. Cambridge: Cambridge University Press.

Burnard, L. (2000). *Reference guide for the British National Corpus (World Edition)*. Oxford: Oxford University Computing Services.

Cameron, D. (2001). *Working with spoken discourse*. London: Sage.

Campbell, K., & Jamieson, K. (1985). Inaugurating the presidency. *Presidential Studies Quarterly, 15*(2), 394–411.

Campbell, R.S. & Pennebaker, J.W. (2003). The secret life of pronouns: Flexibility in writing style and physical health. *Psychological Science, 14*, 60–65.

Cao, Y., & Xiao, R. (2013). A multi-dimensional contrastive study of English abstracts by native and nonnative writers. *Corpora*.

Carr, C.T., Schrock, D.B., & Dauterman, P. (2012). Speech acts within Facebook status messages. *Journal of Language and Social Psychology, 31*(2), 176–196. doi: 10.1177/0261927x12438535

Carvin, A. (2007, December 24). Timeline: The life of the blog. *The Evolution of the Blog* (National Public Radio). Available from http://www.npr.org/blogs/health/2013/04/01/175584297/mining-books-to-map-emotions-through-a-century

Caskey, D.M. (2011). *Speak like a wo(man): A corpus linguistic and discourse analysis of gendered speech.* Master of Arts in TESOL, Western Carolina University.

Cassidy, F.G. (1985). *Dictionary of American regional English.* Cambridge, MA: Harvard University Press.

Cauldwell, R.T. (1997). Tones, attitudinal meanings, and context. *Speak Out! Newletter of the IATEFL Pronunciation Special Interest Group, 21,* 30–35.

Center for Disease Control. (2002). Annual smoking-attributable mortality, years of potential life lost, and economic costs—United States, 1995—1999. *Morbidity and mortality weekly report, 51 (14).* Available from http://www.cdc.gov/mmwr/preview/mmwrhtml/mm5114a2.htm

Chafe, W.L. (1986). Evidentiality in English conversation and academic writing. In W.L. Chafe, & J. Nichols (Eds.), *Evidentiality: The linguistic coding of epistemology* (pp. 261–272). Norwood, NJ: Ablex.

Chambers, S.A. (2003). Telepistemology of the closet; or, the queer politics of Six Feet Under. *The Journal of American Culture, 26*(1), 24–41.

Charles, M. (2006). The construction of stance in reporting clauses: A cross-disciplinary study of theses. *Applied Linguistics, 27*(3), 492–518. doi: 10.1093/applin/aml021

Charles, M. (2007). Argument or evidence? Disciplinary variation in the use of the Noun *that* pattern in stance construction. *English for Specific Purposes, 26*(2), 203–218. doi: http://dx.doi.org/10.1016/j.esp.2006.08.004

Cheng, W. (2007). Concgramming: A corpus-driven approach to learning the phraseology of discipline-specific texts. *CORELL: Computer Resources for Language Learning, 1,* 22–35.

Cheng, W., Greaves, C., & Warren, M. (2005). The creation of a prosodically transcribed intercultural corpus: The Hong Kong Corpus of Spoken English (prosodic). *ICAME Journal, 29,* 47–68.

Cheng, W., Greaves, C., & Warren, M. (2008). *A corpus-driven study of discourse intonation.* Amsterdam: John Benjamins.

Cheng, W., & Warren, M. (2005). //CAN i help you //: The use of rise and rise-fall tones in the Hong Kong Corpus of Spoken English. *International Journal of Corpus Linguistics, 10*(1), 85–107.

Christie, C. (2002). Politeness and the linguistic construction of gender in parliament: An analysis of transgressions and apology behaviour. *Working Papers on the Web, 3.* Available from http://extra.shu.ac.uk/wpw/politeness/christie.htm

Clopper, C.G., & Pisoni, D.B. (2006). The Nationwide Speech Project: A new corpus of American English dialects. *Speech Communication, 48*(6), 633–644. doi: http://dx.doi.org/10.1016/j.specom.2005.09.010

Coates, J. (1996). *Women talk: Conversation between women friends.* Cambridge, MA: Blackwell.

Coates, J. (2004). *Women, men and language: A sociolinguistic account of gender differences in language* (3rd ed.). New York: Pearson Longman.

Cohen, P. (2010, December 17). In 500 billion words, new window on culture. *New York Times,* A3. Available from http://www.nytimes.com/2010/12/17/books/17words.html?pagewanted=all

Cohen, W. (2009). Enron email dataset. Available from https://www.cs.cmu.edu/~enron/

Collins, P.C., & Peters, P. (1988). *The Australian Corpus Project*. Paper presented at the Corpus linguistics: Hard and soft: Proceedings of the Eighth International Conference on English Language Research on Computerized Corpora, Helsinki.

Cone, J.H. (2001). Martin and Malcolm on nonviolence and violence. *Phylon, 49*, 173–183.

Connor-Linton, J. (1989). *Crosstalk: A multi-feature analysis of Soviet-American spacebridges*. Doctoral dissertation, University of Southern California, Los Angeles.

Conrad, S., & Biber, D. (2000). Adverbial marking of stance in speech and writing. In S. Hunston, & G. Thompson (Eds.), *Evaluation in text: Authorial stance and the construction of discourse* (pp. 56–73). Oxford: Oxford University Press.

Conrad, S., & Biber, D. (2001a). Multi-dimensional methodology and the dimensions of register variation in English. In S. Conrad, & D. Biber (Eds.), *Variation in English: Multi-dimensional studies* (pp. 13–42). New York: Longman.

Conrad, S., & Biber, D. (Eds.). (2001b). *Variation in English: multi-dimensional studies*. New York: Longman.

Coulthard, M., & Brazil, D. (1981). The place of intonation in the description of interaction. In D. Tannen (Ed.), *Analyzing discourse: Text and talk* (pp. 94–112). Washington, DC: Georgetown University Press.

Coulthard, M., & Montgomery, M. (Eds.). (1981). *Studies in discourse analysis*. London: Longman.

Coxhead, A. (2000). A new academic word list. *TESOL Quarterly, 34*, 213–238.

Coxhead, A. (2011). The Academic Word List 10 years on: Research and teaching implications. *TESOL Quarterly, 45*(2), 355–361.

Crawford, M. (1995). *Talking difference: On gender and language*. London: Sage.

Cresti, E., & Moneglia, M. (2005). *C-ORAL-ROM: Integrated reference corpora for spoken Romance languages*. Amsterdam: John Benjamins.

Crystal, D. (2006). *Language and the internet*. Cambridge: Cambridge University Press.

Crystal, D. (2011). *Internet linguistics: A student guide*. New York: Routledge.

Daly, N., Holmes, J., Newton, J., & Stubbe, M. (2004). Expletives as solidarity signals in FTAs on the factory floor. *Journal of Pragmatics, 36*(5), 945–964. doi: http://dx.doi.org/10.1016/j.pragma.2003.12.004

Daniels, A.J. (n.d.). 1920's to 1940's phrases & slang. Available from http://www.angelfire.com/comics/howardfineandhoward/20sTo40sPhrases.html

Davies, M. (2008). *The Corpus of Contemporary American English: 450 million words, 1990-present*. Available from http://corpus.byu.edu/coca

Davies, M. (2009). The 385+ million word Corpus of Contemporary American English (1990–2008+): Design, architecture, and linguistic insights. *International Journal of Corpus Linguistics, 14*(2), 159–190. doi: 10.1075/ijcl.14.2.02dav

Davies, M. (2011a). *A comparison of Google Books and the Corpus of Historical American English (COHA): Researching lexical, morphological, syntactic, and semantic changes in American English*. Paper presented at the American Association for Corpus Linguistics 2011, Atlanta, GA.

Davies, M. (2011b). The Corpus of Historical American English and Google Books/culturomics. Available from http://corpus.byu.edu/coha/compare-googleBooks.asp

Davies, M. (2011c). *Google Books corpus*. Available from http://googlebooks.byu.edu/

Davies, M. (2011d). N-grams and word frequency data from the Corpus of Historical American English (COHA). Available from http://www.ngrams.info

Davies, M. (2012). Distributions of words from five registers of COCA from 1990 to 2012. Available from http://corpus.byu.edu/coca/

Davies, M. (2013). *GloWbE: Corpus of Global Web-Based English*. Available from http://corpus2.byu.edu/glowbe/.

De Haan, P. (1989). *Postmodifying clauses in the English noun phrase: A corpus-based study*. Amsterdam: Rodopi.

Di Ferrante, L. (2012). *Small talk in the workplace: A discourse analysis of AAC and non-AAC users using corpus linguistics*. Unpublished pilot study, Texas A&M University-Commerce, Commerce, TX.

Drager, K. (2013). Experimental methods in sociolinguistics: Matched guise and identification tasks. In J. Holmes, & K. Hazen (Eds.), *Research methods in sociolinguistics: A practical guide* (pp. 58–73). Hoboken, NJ: Wiley-Blackwell.

Eckert, P. (2004). Adolescent language. In E. Finegan, & J. Rickford (Eds.), *Language in the USA: Themes for twenty-first century* (pp. 361–374). Cambridge, UK: Cambridge University Press.

Eckert, P., & McConnell-Ginet, S. (1992). Think practically and look locally: Language and gender as community-based practice. *Annual Review of Anthropology, 21*, 461–490.

Economidou-Kogetsidis, M. (2005). "Yes, tell me please, what time is the midday flight from Athens arriving?": Telephone service encounters and politeness. *Intercultural Pragmatics, 2–3*, 253–273.

Egbert, J. (2012). Style in nineteenth century fiction: A multi-dimensional analysis. *Scientific Study of Literature, 2*(2), 167–198. doi: 10.1075/ssol.2.2.01egb

Eisenstein, J., O'Connor, B., Smith, N.A., & Xing, E.P. (2010). *A latent variable model for geographic lexical variation*. Paper presented at the Proceedings of the 2010 Conference on Empirical Methods in Natural Language Processing, Cambridge, MA.

Fairclough, N. (1993). Critical discourse analysis and the marketization of public discourse: The universities. *Discourse & Society, 4*(2), 133–168. doi:-10.1177/0957926593004002002

Fallows, D. (2005). *How women and men use the Internet*. Washington, DC: Pew Internet and American Life Project.

Feinberg, M., Willer, R., Stellar, J., & Keltner, D. (2012). The virtues of gossip: Reputational information sharing as prosocial behavior. *Journal of Personality and Social Psychology, 102*(5), 1015–1030. doi: 10.1037/a0026650

Fellows, K.L., & Rubin, D. (2005). Identities for sale: how tobacco industry marketers construed Asians, Asian Americans, and Pacific Islanders. *Journal of Intercultural Communication Research, 35*, 265–292.

Finegan, E. (1980). *Attitudes toward English usage: The history of a war of words*. New York: Teachers College Press.

Finegan, E. (2011). *Language: Its structure and use* (6th ed.). Boston: Wadsworth Cengage Learning.

Firth, J. (1957). *Papers in linguistics*. Oxford: Oxford University Press.

Fleishman, S. (1998). Gender, the personal, and the voice of scholarship: A viewpoint. *Signs, 23*(4), 975–1016.

Flowerdew, L. (2005). An integration of corpus-based and genre-based approaches to text analysis in EAP/ESP: countering criticisms against corpus-based methodologies. *English for Specific Purposes, 24*(3), 321–332. doi: 10.1016/j.esp.2004.09.002

Forchini, P. (2012). *Movie language revisited: Evidence from multi-dimensional analysis and corpora*. Bern: Peter Lang.

Fries, C. C. (1940). *American English grammar: The grammatical structure of present-day American English with especial reference to social differences or class dialects*. New York: Appleton-Century-Crofts.

Friginal, E. (2009a). A corpus-based study of gender and age in blogs. *Language Forum, 35*(2), 19–37.

Friginal, E. (2009b). *The language of outsourced call centers: A corpus-based study of cross-cultural interaction.* Amsterdam: John Benjamins.

Friginal, E. (2011). Interactional and cross-cultural features of outsourced call center discourse. *International Journal of Communication, 21*(1), 53–76.

Friginal, E. (2013a). 25 years of Biber's multi-dimensional analysis: Introduction to the special issue. *Corpora, 8*(2), 137–152.

Friginal, E. (2013b). Evaluation of oral performance in outsourced call centres: An exploratory case study. *English for Specific Purposes, 32*(1), 25–35. doi: http://dx.doi.org/10.1016/j.esp.2012.06.002

Friginal, E., & Hardy, J.A. (forthcoming). Conducting Biber's corpus-based multidimensional analysis using SPSS. In T. Berber Sardinha, & M. Veirano Pinto (Eds.), *Multi-dimensional analyses: Twenty-five years on.* Amsterdam: John Benjamins.

Friginal, E., Pearson, P., Di Ferrante, L., Pickering, L., & Bruce, C. (2013). Linguistic characteristics of AAC discourse in the workplace. *Discourse Studies, 15*(3), 279–298. doi: 10.1177/1461445613480586

Friginal, E., & Waugh, O.S. (2013). *Linguistic variation in social media.* Unpublished manuscript, Department of Applied Linguistics and ESL, Georgia State University, Atlanta.

Fuertes-Olivera, P.A. (2007). A corpus-based view of lexical gender in written Business English. *English for Specific Purposes, 26*(2), 219–234. doi: http://dx.doi.org/10.1016/j.esp.2006.07.001

Gabrielatos, C., Torgersen, E.N., Hoffman, S., & Fox, S. (2010). A corpus-based sociolinguistic study of indefinite article forms in London English. *Journal of English Linguistics, 38*(4), 297–334. doi: 10.1177/0075424209352729

Gee, J.P. (2011). *An introduction to discourse analysis: Theory and method* (3rd ed.). New York: Routledge.

Globescan. (2006). BBC/Reuters/Media Center Poll. Trust in the Media 'Media More Trusted Than Governments'—Poll. Available from http://globescan.com/news_archives/bbcreut.html

Goss, B.M. (2007). ONLINE "LOONEY TUNES": An analysis of reader-composed comment threads in The Nation. *Journalism Studies, 8*(3), 365–381. doi: 10.1080/14616700701276117

Gozdz-Roszkowski, S. (2011). *Patterns of linguistic variation in American legal English.* Bern: Peter Lang.

Graber, C.B., & Nenova, M.B. (Eds.). (2008). *Intellectual property and traditional cultural expressions in a digital environment.* Northampton, MA: Edward Elgar Publishing.

Granger, S. (1983). *The be + past participle construction in spoken English with special emphasis on the passive.* New York: Elsevier Science Publishers.

Gray, B. (2011). *Exploring academic writing through corpus linguistics: When discipline tells only part of the story.* Unpublished doctoral dissertation, Northern Arizona University, Flagstaff.

Gray, B., & Biber, D. (2013). Lexical frames in academic prose and conversation. *International Journal of Corpus Linguistics, 18*(1), 109–136.

Greenbaum, S. (Ed.). (1996). *Comparing English worldwide: The International Corpus of English.* Oxford: Clarendon Press.

Grieve, J. (2009). *A corpus-based study of dialect variation in the United States.* Unpublished doctoral dissertation, Northern Arizona University, Flagstaff.

Grieve, J. (2011). A regional analysis of contraction rate in written Standard American English. *International Journal of Corpus Linguistics, 16*(4), 514–546. doi: 10.1075/ijcl.16.4.04gri

Grieve, J. (2012). A statistical analysis of regional variation in adverb position in a corpus of written Standard American English. *Corpus Linguistics and Linguistic Theory, 8*(1), 39–72. doi: 10.1515/CLLT.2012.003

Grieve, J., Biber, D., Friginal, E., & Nekrasova, T. (2010). Variation among blogs: A multi-dimensional analysis. In A. Mehler, S. Sharoff, & M. Santini (Eds.), *Genres on the web: Corpus studies and computational models* (pp. 45–71). New York: Springer-Verlag.

Gu, Y. (2002). Towards an understanding of workplace discourse: A pilot study for compiling a spoken Chinese corpus of situated discourse. In C.N. Candlin (Ed.), *Research and practice in professional discourse* (pp. 137–186). Hong Kong: City University of Hong Kong Press.

Gu, Y. (2007). Segmenting and annotating a multimodal corpus (with special reference to SCCSD). Keynote speech at the 3rd International Corpus Linguistics Conference, University of Birmingham, UK.

Haarmann, L., & Lombardo, L. (2009). Introduction: Evaluation and stance in war news. In L. Haarmann, & L. Lombardo (Eds.), *Evaluation and stance in war news: A linguistic analysis of American, British and Italian television news reporting of the 2003 Iraqi War* (pp. 1–26). London: Continuum.

Halvey, M., & Keane, M.T. (2007). *An assessment of tag presentation techniques.* Poster presentation at WWW 2007, Banff, AB.

Handford, M. (2010). *The language of business meetings.* Cambridge: Cambridge University Press.

Hannerz, U. (1967). Gossip, networks and culture in a black American ghetto. *Ethnos, 32*(1–4), 35–60.

Hardy, J.A., & Friginal, E. (2012). Filipino and American online communication and linguistic variation. *World Englishes, 31*, 143–161. doi: 10.1111/j.1467–971X.2011.01728.x

Hardy, J.A., & Römer, U. (2013). Revealing disciplinary variation in student writing: A multi-dimensional analysis of 16 disciplines from MICUSP. *Corpora, 8*(2), 183–207.

Harmanci, R. (2005, February 20). Time to get a life—pioneer blogger Justin Hall bows out at 31. *San Francisco Chronicle.* Available from http://www.sfgate.com/news/article/Time-to-get-a-lihttp://www.sfgate.com/news/article/Time-to-get-a-life-pioneer-blogger-Justin-Hall-2697359.phpfe-pioneer-blogger-Justin-Hall-2697359.php

Harris, A., Heimbach, A., & Haglund, D. (2013). Blergh! The linguistic legacy of 30 Rock. *Slate.* Available from http://www.slate.com/blogs/browbeat/2013/01/30/_30_rock_catchphrases_that_will_survive_blergh_dealbreaker_egot_and_more.html

Harris, S. (2003). Politeness and power: Making and responding to 'requests' in institutional settings. *Text, 23*(1), 27–52.

Henry, A., & Roseberry, R.L. (2001). Using a small corpus to obtain data for teaching genre. In M. Ghadessy, A. Henry, & R.L. Rosenberry (Eds.), *Small corpus studies and ELT: Theory and practice* (pp. 93–134). Amsterdam: John Benjamins.

Heritage, J., & Clayman, S. (2010). *Talk in action: Interactions, identities, and institutions.* Malden, MA: Wiley-Blackwell.

Hernández, N. (2006). *User's guide to FRED (Freiburg Corpus of English Dialects).* Freiburg im Breisgau, Germany: Universität Freiburg.

Herring, S., Scheidt, L., Bonus, S., & Wright, E. (2004). Bridging the gap: A genre analysis of weblogs. *Proceedings of the Thirty-Seventh Hawai'i International Conference on System Sciences* (pp. 234–256). Los Alamitos, CA: IEEE Computer Society Press.

Herring, S.C., & Paolillo, J.C. (2006). Gender and genre variation in weblogs. *Sociolinguistics, 10*(4), 439–459. doi: 10.1111/j.1467–9841.2006.00287.x

Hewings, M. (Ed.). (1990). *Papers in discourse intonation.* Birmingham, UK: English Language Research.

Hilpert, M. (2011). Dynamic visualizations of language change: Motion charts on the basis of bivariate and multivariate data from diachronic corpora. *International Journal of Corpus Linguistics, 16*(4), 435–461. doi: 10.1075/ijcl.16.4.01hil

Hoffmann, S., Evert, S., Smith, N., Lee, D., & Berglund-Prytz, Y. (2008). *Corpus linguistics with BNCweb-a practical guide* (Vol. 6). Available from http://usir.salford.ac.uk/id/eprint/16802

Holmes, J. (1995). *Women, men and politeness.* London: Longman.

Holmes, J. (2000). Victoria University of Wellington's Language in the Workplace project: An overview. *Language in the Workplace Occasional Papers, 1,* 1–17. Available from http://www.vuw.ac.nz/lals/lwp/resources/

Holmes, J. (2003). Small talk at work: Potential problems for workers with an intellectual disability. *Research on Language and Social Interaction, 36*(1), 65–84.

Holmes, J. (2005). Leadership talk: How do leaders 'do mentoring', and is gender relevant? *Journal of Pragmatics, 37*(11), 1779–1800. doi: http://dx.doi.org/10.1016/j.pragma.2005.02.013

Holmes, J. (2009). Disagreeing in style: Socio-cultural norms and workplace English. In C. Ward (Ed.), *Language teaching in a multilingual world: Challenges and opportunities* (pp. 85–102). Singapore: SEAMEO Regional Language Centre Anthology Series 50.

Holmes, J., & Fillary, R. (2000). Handling small talk at work: Challenges for workers with intellectual disabilities. *International Journal of Disability, Development & Education, 47*(3), 273–291.

Hood, B. (2010). Lizzing, mind grapes, sabor de soledad, and beyond: A 30 Rock glossary. *Vulture.* Available from http://www.vulture.com/2010/09/30_rock_glossary.html

Hülmbauer, C. (2009). "We don't take the right way. We just take the way that we think you will understand"–The shifting relationship between correctness and effectiveness in ELF. In A. Mauranen, & E. Ranta (Eds.), *English as a lingua franca: Studies and findings* (pp. 323–347). Newcastle upon Tyne: Cambridge Scholars Publishing.

Hunston, S. (2002). *Corpora in applied linguistics.* New York: Cambridge University Press.

Hutchby, I., & Wooffitt, R. (2008). *Conversation analysis.* Oxford: Polity.

Hyland, K. (1994). Hedging in academic writing and EAF textbooks. *English for Specific Purposes, 13*(3), 239–256. doi: http://dx.doi.org/10.1016/0889–4906(94)90004–3

Hyland, K. (1998). *Hedging in scientific research articles* (Vol. 54). Amsterdam: John Benjamins.

Hyland, K., & Tse, P. (2005). Evaluative *that* constructions: Signaling stance in research abstracts. *Functions of Language, 12*(1), 39–63.

Ihalainen, O. (1985). He took the bottle and put 'n in his pocket: The object pronoun it in present-day Somerset. In W. Viereck (Ed.), *Focus on: England and Wales* (pp. 153–161). Amsterdam: John Benjamins.

Ihalainen, O. (1990). A source of data for the study of English dialectal syntax: the Helsinki Corpus. In J. Aarts, & W. Meijs (Eds.), *Theory and practice in corpus linguistics* (pp. 83–104). Amsterdam: Rodopi.

Ihalainen, O. (1991). A point of verb syntax in south western British English: An analysis of a dialect continuum. In K. Aijmer, & B. Altenberg (Eds.), *English corpus linguistics: Studies in honour of Jan Svartvik* (pp. 290–302). London: Longman.

Ishikawa, Y. (2011). A corpus-based research on THANKS in British dialogue. *Proceedings of the International Conference on Languages, Literature and Linguistics IPEDR, 26* (pp 384–389).

It's the links, stupid. (2006, April 20). Special report. *The Economist*. Available from http://www.economist.com/node/6794172

James, D., & Drakich, J. (1993). Understanding gender differences in amount of talk: A critical review of research. In D. Tannen (Ed.), *Gender and conversational interaction* (pp. 281–312). New York: Oxford University Press.

Jang, S.-C. (1998). *Dimensions of spoken and written Taiwanese: A corpus-based register study.* Unpublished doctoral dissertation, University of Hawai'i at Manoa, Honolulu, HI.

Jespersen, O. (1952). *A modern English grammar on historical principles.* Copenhagen: E. Munksgaard.

Johansson, S., & Hofland, K. (1989). *Frequency analysis of English vocabulary and grammar.* Oxford: Oxford University Press.

Juola, P., Ryan, M., & Mehok, M. (2011). *Geographic localizing Tweets using stylometric analysis.* Paper presented at the American Association of Corpus Linguistics 2011, Georgia State University, Atlanta.

Kachru, B.B. (Ed.). (1992). *The other tongue: English across cultures* (2nd ed.). Urbana: University of Illinois Press.

Kachru, B.B. (1996). World Englishes: Agony and ecstasy. *Journal of Aesthetic Education, 30*(2), 135–155.

Kachru, Y. (2008). Language variation and corpus linguistics. *World Englishes, 27*(1), 1–8. doi: 10.1111/j.1467–971X.2008.00532.x

Kandil, M. (2008). *The Israeli-Palestinian conflict in American, Arab, and British media: Corpus-based critical discourse analysis.* Unpublished doctoral dissertation proposal, Department of Applied Linguistics and ESL, Georgia State University, Atlanta.

Kanoksilapatham, B. (2007). Rhetorical moves in biochemistry research articles. In D. Biber, U. Connor, & T.A. Upton (Eds.), *Discourse on the move: Using corpus analysis to describe discourse structure* (Vol. 28, pp. 73–119). Philadelphia: John Benjamins.

Kaplan, A.M., & Haenlein, M. (2011). The early bird catches the news: Nine things you should know about micro-blogging. *Business Horizons, 54*, 105–113. doi: 10.1016/j.bushor.2010.09.004

Keck, C.M., & Biber, D. (2004). Modal use in spoken and written university registers: A corpus-based study. In R. Facchinetti, & F. Palmer (Eds.), *English modality in perspective: Genre analysis and contrastive studies* (pp. 23–40). New York: Peter Lang.

Kellogg, C. (June 10, 2011). The Sarah Palin email extravaganza. Weekend reading anyone? *Los Angeles Times*. Available from http://latimesblogs.latimes.com/jacketcopy/2011/06/sarah-palin-emails-weekend-reading.html

Kendall, T. (August 16, 2011). 50 years of language study began on Martha's Vineyard. *The Martha's Vineyard Times*. Available from http://www.mvtimes.com/2011/08/16/50-years-language-study-began-marthas-vineyard-6918/

Kerswill, P., Cheshire, J., Fox, S., & Torgersen, E.N. (2008). Linguistic innovators: The English of adolescents in London. Final report submitted to the ESRC.

Keuleers, E., Brysbaert, M., & New, B. (2011). An evaluation of the Google Books Ngrams for psycholinguistic research. In J. Heister, E. Pohl, & K.-M. Würzner (Eds.),

Lexical resources in psycholinguistic research (Vol. 3, pp. 23–26). Potsdam, Germany: Universitätsverlag Potsdam.

Kim, Y.-J., & Biber, D. (1994). A corpus-based analysis of register variation in Korean. In D. Biber, & E. Finegan (Eds.), *Sociolinguistic perspectives on register* (pp. 157–182). New York: Oxford University Press.

Klimt, B., & Yang, Y. (2004). *Introducing the Enron Corpus.* Paper presented at the First Conference on Email and Anti-Spam (CEAS), Mountain View, CA.

Knowles, G., Wichmann, A., & Alderson, P. (Eds.). (1996). *Working with speech: Perspectives on research into the Lancaster/IBM Spoken English Corpus.* London: Longman.

Kodytek, V. (2007). *On the replicability of the Biber model: The case of Czech.* Unpublished manuscript, Northern Arizona University.

Kortmann, B., Herrmann, T., Pietsch, L., & Wagner, S. (Eds.). (2005). *A comparative grammar of British English dialects: Agreement, gender, relative clauses.* Berlin: Mouton De Gruyter.

Kortmann, B., & Wagner, S. (2005). The Freiburg English Dialect Project and Corpus. In B. Kortmann (Ed.), *A comparative grammar of British English dialects* (pp. 1–20). Berlin: Mouton de Gruyter.

Kretzschmar, W.A., Darwin, C., Brown, C., Rubin, D.L., & Biber, D. (2004). Looking for the smoking gun: Principled sampling in creating the Tobacco Industry Documents Corpus. *Journal of English Linguistics, 32*, 31–47. doi: 10.1177/0075424204263024

Kretzschmar, W.A., McDavin, V., Lerud, T., & Johnson, E. (1993). *Handbook of the linguistic atlas of the middle and south atlantic states.* Chicago: University of Illinois Press.

Krishnamurthy, S. (2002). *The multidimensionality of blog conversations: The virtual enactment of September 11.* Paper presented at the Internet Research 3.0: NET / WORK / THEORY, Association of Internet Researchers (AoIR), Maasricht, The Netherlands.

Kučera, H., & Francis, W.N.F. (1967). *Computational analysis of present-day American English.* Providence, RI: Brown University Press.

Kurath, H. (1949). *Word geography of the Eastern United States.* Ann Arbor: University of Michigan Press.

Kytö, M., & Rissanen, M. (1993). General information. In M. Rissanen, M. Kytö, & M. Palander-Collin (Eds.), *Early English in the computer age: Explorations through the Helsinki Corpus* (pp. 1–17). Berlin: Mouton de Gruyter.

Labov, W. (1962). *The social history of a sound change on the island of Martha's Vineyard.* Master's essay, Columbia University, New York.

Labov, W. (1966). *The social stratification of English in New York City.* Washington, DC: Center for Applied Linguistics.

Labov, W. (1972a). *Language in the inner city.* Philadelphia: University of Pennsylvania Press.

Labov, W. (1972b). *Sociolinguistic patterns.* Philadelphia: University of Pennsylvania Press.

Labov, W. (1984a). Field methods of the project on linguistic change and variation. In J. Baugh, & J. Sherzer (Eds.), *Language in use: Readings in sociolinguistics* (pp. 28–54). Englewood Cliffs, NJ: Prentice-Hall.

Labov, W. (1984b). Intensity. In D. Schiffrin (Ed.), *Meaning, form, and use in context: Linguistic applications* (pp. 43–70). Washington, DC: Georgetown University Press.

Labov, W. (1990). The intersection of sex and social class in the course of linguistics change. *Language Variation and Change, 2*, 205–254.

Labov, W. (2001). *Principles of linguistic change: Social factors.* Cambridge, MA: Blackwell.

Labov, W., Ash, S., & Boberg, C. (2006). *The atlas of North American English: Phonetics, phonology and sound change.* Berlin: De Gruyter Mouton.

Ladegaard, H.J. (2012). The discourse of powerlessness and repression: Identity construction in domestic helper narratives1. *Journal of Sociolinguistics, 16*(4), 450–482. doi: 10.1111/j.1467–9841.2012.00541.x

Laitinen, M. (2007). Explaining present-day variation: Agreement patterns of HE and THEY with singular antecedents. *Neupphilologische Mitteilungen, 108*(4), 537–562.

Lakoff, R. (1975). *Language and woman's place.* New York: Oxford University Press.

Lakoff, R. (1990). *Talking power: The politics of language in our lives.* New York: Basic Books.

Lave, J., & Wenger, E. (1991). *Situated learning: Legitimate peripheral participation.* Cambridge: Cambridge University Press.

Leap, W. (1995). *Beyond the lavender lexicon: Authenticity, imagination, and appropriation in lesbian and gay languages.* Amsterdam: Gordon and Breach Publishers.

Leap, W. (1996). *Word's out: Gay men's English.* Minneapolis: University of Minnesota Press.

Lee, C.K.M. (2011). Micro-blogging and status updates on Facebook: Texts and practices. In C. Thurlow, & K. Mroczek (Eds.), *Digital discourse: Language in the new media* (pp. 110–130). Oxford: Oxford University Press.

Levesque, R. (2012). *Raynald's SPSS tools.* Available from http://www.spsstools.net/index.html

Levinson, S.C. (2006). On the human "interactional engine". In N.J. Enfield, & S.C. Levinson (Eds.), *Roots of human sociality: Culture, cognition and interaction* (pp. 39–69). Oxford: Berg.

Lindemann, S. (2002). Listening with an attitude: A model of native-speaker comprehension of non-native speakers in the United States. *Language in Society, 31*(3), 419–441. doi: 10.1017.S0047404502020286

Locher, M.A. (2004). *Power and politeness in action: Disagreements in oral communication* (Vol. 12). Berlin: De Gruyter Mouton.

Macaulay, R.K.S. (2009). *Quantitative methods in sociolinguistics.* New York: Palgrave Macmillan.

Mauranen, A. (2007). Hybrid voices: English as the lingua franca of academics. In K. Flottum, T. Dahl, & T. Kinn (Eds.), *Language and discipline perspectives on academic discourse* (pp. 244–259). Cambridge: Cambridge Scholars Press.

McCafferty, K. (2001). *Ethnicity and language change: English in (London) Derry, Northern Ireland* (Vol. 7). Amsterdam: John Benjamins.

McCarthy, M., & Handford, M. (2004). Invisible to us: A preliminary corpus-based study of spoken business English. In U. Connor, & T.A. Upton (Eds.), *Discourse in the professions: Perspectives from corpus linguistics* (pp. 167–201). Amsterdam: John Benjamins.

McEnery, A., & Xiao, Z. (2004). Swearing in modern British English: The case of *fuck* in the BNC. *Language and Literature, 13*(3), 235–268. doi: 10.1177/0963947004044873

McEnery, T., & Wilson, A. (2001). *Corpus linguistics* (2nd ed.). Edinburgh, UK: Edinburgh University Press.

McEnery, T., Xiao, R., & Tono, Y. (2006). *Corpus-based language studies: An advanced resource book.* New York: Routledge.

McGrath, C. (August 10, 2003). Sexed texts. *The New York Times.* Available from http://www.nytimes.com/2003/08/10/magazine/10WWLN.html

Meyerhoff, M. (2005). *Introducing sociolinguistics.* New York: Routledge.

Michel, J.-B., Shen, Y.K., Aiden, A.P., Veres, A., Gray, M.K., Team, T.G.B., . . . Aiden, E.L. (2011). Quantitative analysis of culture using millions of digitized books. *Science, 331*(6014), 176–182. doi: 10.1126/science.1199644

Mills, A., Chen, R., Lee, J., & Rao, H.R. (2009). Web 2.0 emergency applications: How useful can twitter be for emergency response. *Journal of Information Privacy & Security, 5*(3), 3–26.

Mills, S. (2003). *Gender and politeness* (Vol. 17). Cambridge: Cambridge University Press.

Mitra, T., & Gilbert, E. (2012). *Have you heard? How gossip flows through workplace email.* Paper presented at the Sixth International Association for the Advancement of Artificial Intelligence (AAAI) Conference on Weblogs and Social Media, Dublin, Ireland.

Mulligan, T.S., & Bustillo, M. (July 6, 2006). Death puts Lay conviction in doubt. *Los Angeles Times.* Available from http://articles.latimes.com/2006/jul/06/business/fi-lay6

Naro, A.J. (1981). The social and structural dimensions of syntactic change. *Language, 57*(1), 63–98.

Nelson, G. (1996). The design of the corpus. In S. Greenbaum (Ed.), *Comparing English worldwide: The International Corpus of English* (pp. 27–35). Oxford: Clarendon Press.

Nesi, H. (2008). BAWE: An introduction to a new resource. In A. Frankenberg-Garcia, T. Rkibi, M. Braga da Cruz, R. Carvalho, C. Direito, & D. Santos-Rosa (Eds.), *Proceedings of the Eighth Teaching and Language Corpora Conference* (pp. 239–246). Lisbon, Portugal: ISLA.

Nesi, H. (2011). BAWE: An introduction to a new resource. In A. Frankenberg-Garcia, L. Flowerdew, & G. Aston (Eds.), *New trends in corpora and language learning* (pp. 213–228). London: Continuum.

Nevala, M. (2004). Accessing politeness axes: On forms of address and terms of reference in early English correspondence. *Journal of Pragmatics, 36*(12), 2125–2160. doi: 10.1016/j. pragma.2004.02.001,

Nevalainen, T., & Raumolin-Brunberg, H. (2003). *Historical sociolinguistics: Language change in Tudor and Stuart England.* London: Longman.

Newman, M.L., Pennebaker, J.W., Berry, D.S., & Richards, J.M. (2003). Lying words: Predicting deception from linguistic styles. *Personality and Social Psychology Bulletin, 29*, 665–675.

Newton-Small, J. (2011). Sarah Palin's email etiquette. *Time: Swampland.* Available from http://swampland.time.com/2011/06/12/sarah-palins-e-mail-etiquette/—ixzz 2T0XRwGkS

Nguyen, T., Phung, D., Adams, B., & Venkatesh, S. (2011). Prediction of age, sentiment, and connectivity from social media text. In A. Bouguettaya, M. Hauswirth & L. Liu (Eds.), *Web Information System Engineering—WISE 2011: 12th International Conference* (pp. 227–240). Berlin: Springer-Verlag.

Nurmi, A. (1999). Auxiliary do in fifteenth-century English: Dialectal variation and formu-laic use. In I. Taavitsainen, G. Melchers, & P. Pahta (Eds.), *Writing in nonstandard English* (pp. 225–242). Amsterdam: John Benjamins.

Nurmi, A., Nevala, M., & Palander-Collin, M. (2009). *The language of daily life in England (1400–1800).* Amsterdam: John Benjamins.

Orton, H., Sanderson, S., & Widdowson, J. (1978). *The linguistic atlas of England.* London: Croom Helm.

Osterlind, S., & Tabachnick, B.G. (2001). *SPSS for Windows workbook* (4th ed.). Boston: Allyn and Bacon.

Overstreet, M., & Yule, G. (1997). On being inexplicit and stuff in contemporary American English. *Journal of English Linguistics, 25*(3), 250–258. doi: 10.1177/007542429702500307

Page, R. (2010). Re-examining narrativity: Small stories in status updates. *Text and Talk— An Interdisciplinary Journal of Language, Discourse & Communication, 30*(4), 423–444.

Palander-Collin, M. (1999). Male and female styles in 17th century correspondence: I THINK. *Language Variation and Change, 11*(02), 123–141.

Parodi, G. (2007).Variation across registers in Spanish: Exploring the El Grial PUCV Corpus. In G. Parodi (Ed.), *Working with Spanish corpora* (pp. 11–53). New York: Continuum.

Partington, A. (2003). *The linguistics of political argument: The spin-doctor and the wolf-pack at the White House.* London: Routledge.

Patha, P., & Nurmi, A. (2009). Negotiating interpersonal identities in writing: Code-switching practices in Charles Burney's correspondence. In A. Nurmi, M. Nevala, & M. Palander-Collin (Eds.), *The language of daily life in England (1400–1800)* (pp. 27–52). Amsterdam: John Benjamins.

Pearson, P., Pickering, L., Di Ferrante, L., Bouchard, J., Lomotey, C.F., & Menjo, S. (2011). *Small talk at work: Comparison of AAC and non-AAC user corpora.* Paper presented at the American Association for Corpus Linguistics 2011, Atlanta, GA.

Pedersen, S., & Macafee, C. (2007). Gender Differences in British Blogging. *Journal of Computer-Mediated Communication, 12*(4), 1472–1492. doi: 10.1111/j.1083–6101.2007.00382.x

Pennebaker, J.W., Chung, C.K., Ireland, M., Gonzalez, A., & Booth, R.J. (2007). *The development and psychometric properties of LIWC2007.* LWIC Inc: Austin, TX. Available from http://www.LIWC.net.

Pennebaker, J. W., Mayne, T., & Francis, M. E. (1997). Linguistic predictors of adaptive bereavement. *Journal of Personality and Social Psychology, 72,* 863–871.

Pennebaker, J.W., Mehl, M.R., & Niederhoffer, K.G. (2003). Psychological aspects of natural language use: Our words, our selves. *Annual Review of Psychology, 54*(1), 547–577. doi: 10.1146/annurev.psych.54.101601.145041

Pennebaker, J.W., & Stone, L.D. (2003). Words of wisdom: Language use over the life span. *Journal of Personality and Social Psychology, 85,* 291–301. doi: 10.1037/0022–3514.85.2.291

PEW Research Center. (2004). News audiences increasingly politicized: Online news audience larger, more diverse. Available from http://www.people-press.org/files/legacy-pdf/215.pdf

Philipsen, G. (1975). Speaking "like a man" in Teamsterville culture patterns of role enactment in an urban neighborhood. *Quarterly Journal of Speech, 61,* 13–22.

Pickering, L. (2001). The role of tone choice in improving ITA communication in the classroom. *TESOL Quarterly, 35*(2), 233–255.

Pickering, L. (2004). The structure and function of intonational paragraphs in native and nonnative speaker instructional discourse. *English for Specific Purposes, 23*(1), 19–43. doi: http://dx.doi.org/10.1016/S0889–4906(03)00020–6

Pickering, L. (2006). Current research on intelligibility in English as a lingua franca. *Annual Review of Applied Linguistics, 26,* 219–233.

Pickering, L., & Bruce, C. (2009). *AAC and Non-AAC Workplace Corpus (ANAWC).* Atlanta, GA: Georgia State University.

Pickering, L., Friginal, E., Vine, B., Bouchard, J., & Clegg, G. (2013). *The function of stance markers in the workplace: Comparison of two workplace corpora in New Zealand and the United States.* Paper presented at the American Association for Applied Linguistics Conference, Dallas, TX.

Pickering, L., & Wiltshire, C. (2000). Pitch accent in Indian English TAs' teaching discourse. *World Englishes, 19*(2), 173–183.

Pinkasovic, B. (2013). *The speeches of Malcom and Martin: An exploratory corpus study.* Unpublished manuscript, Department of Applied Linguistics and ESL, Georgia State University, Atlanta.

Pitzl, M.-L. (2010). *English as a lingua franca in international business: Resolving miscommunication and reaching shared understanding.* Saarbrücken:VDM.

Poplack, S., & Tagliamonte, S.A. (1989).There's no tense like the present:Verbal-s inflection in early Black English. *Language Variation and Change, 1,* 47–84.

Precht, K. (2003). Great versus lovely: Stance differences in American and British English. In C.F. Meyer, & P. Leistyna (Eds.), *Corpus analysis: Language structure and use* (pp. 133–152).Amsterdam: Rodopi.

Precht, K. (2008). Sex similarities and differences in stance in informal American conversation. *Journal of Sociolinguistics, 12*(1), 89–111. doi: 10.1111/j.1467–9841.2008.00354.x

Preston, D.R. (Ed.). (1993). *American dialect research: Celebrating the 100th anniversary of the American Dialect Society, 1889–1989.* Amsterdam: John Benjamins.

Purvis, T.M. (1998). *A linguistic and discursive analysis of register variation in Dagbani.* Unpublished doctoral dissertation, Northern Arizona University, Flagstaff.

Pushmann, C. (2007). *Blogs or flogs? Genre conventions and linguistic practices in corporate web logs.* Paper presented at the Telematica Instituut, Enschede, The Netherlands. Slides available from http://www.slideshare.net/coffee001/blogs-or-flogs-genre-conventions-and-linguistic-practices-in-corporate-web-logs

Quaglio, P. (2009). *Television dialogue: The sitcom "Friends" versus natural conversation.* Amsterdam: John Benjamins.

Quirk, R., Greenbaum, S., Leech, G.N., & Svartvik, J. (1972). *A grammar of contemporary English.* London: Longman.

Rayson, P. (2003). *WMatrix: A statistical method and software tool for linguistic analysis through corpus comparison.* Unpublished doctoral dissertation, Lancaster University, Lancaster, UK.

Rayson, P. (2008). From key words to key semantic domains. *International Journal of Corpus Linguistics, 13*(4), 519–549. doi: 10.1075/ijcl.13.4.06ray

Rayson, P., Leech, G., & Hodges, M. (1997). Social differentiation in the use of English vocabulary: Some analyses of the conversational component of the British National Corpus. *International Journal of Corpus Linguistics, 2,* 133–150.

Reinhardt, J. (2010). Directives in office hour consultations:A corpus-informed investigation of learner and expert usage. *English for Specific Purposes, 29*(2), 94–107. doi: http://dx.doi.org/10.1016/j.esp.2009.09.003

Reiter, J. (2011). *Lexical variation in inaugural addresses: A research proposal and preliminary results.* Unpublished manuscript, Department of Applied Linguistics and ESL, Georgia State University, Atlanta.

Reiter, J., Feinberg, I., & Thompson, N. (2011). *Lexical variation in presidential inaugural addresses.* Unpublished manuscript, Department of Applied Linguistics and ESL, Georgia State University, Atlanta.

Reppen, R. (1994). *Variation in elementary student writing.* Doctoral dissertation, Northern Arizona University, Flagstaff.

Reppen, R. (2001). Register variation in student and adult speech and writing. In S. Conrad, & D. Biber (Eds.), *Variation in English: Multi-dimensional studies* (pp. 187–199). New York: Longman.

Rey, J.M. (2001). Changing gender roles in popular culture: Dialogue in *Star Trek* episodes from 1966 to 1993. In D. Biber, & S. Conrad (Eds.), *Variation in English: Multi-dimensional studies* (pp. 138–156). London: Longman.

Roberts, J., & Murphy, C. (2012). *Multidimensional Needs-Based Literacy Corpus (MNBLC) for LEP adult learners: A specialized corpus proposal.* Unpublished manuscript, Department of Applied Linguistics and ESL, Georgia State University, Atlanta.

Römer, U. (2005). "This seems somewhat counterintuitive, though . . . "—Negative evaluation in linguistic book reviews by male and female authors. In E. Bonelli-Tognini, & G. Del Lungo Camiciotti (Eds.), *Strategies in academic discourse* (pp. 97–115). Amsterdam: John Benjamins.

Römer, U. (2010). Establishing the phraseological profile of a text type: The construction of meaning in academic book reviews. *English Text Construction, 3*(1), 95–119. doi: 10.1075/etc.3.1.06rom

Rubin, D.L., & Greene, K. (1992). Gender-typical style in written language. *Research in the Teaching of English, 26*(1), 7–40.

Rühlemann, C. (2007). *Conversation in context: A corpus-driven approach.* London: Continuum.

Ryan, H. (1993). *The inaugural addresses of twentieth-century presidents.* Westport, CT: Praeger.

Saladino, R. (1990). Language shift in standard Italian and dialect: A case study. *Language Variation and Change, 2*(01), 57–70.

Samford, W. (2012). *Cognitive and emotional elements of female online journals in relation to age: An exploratory corpus study.* Unpublished manuscript, Department of Applied Linguistics and ESL, Georgia State University, Atlanta.

Saville-Troike, M. (1982). *The ethnography of communication: An introduction.* Oxford: Basil Blackwell.

Schegloff, E.A. (2005). On integrity in inquiry . . . of the investigated, not the investigator. *Discourse Studies, 7*(4–5), 455–480. doi: 10.1177/1461445605054402

Schiffrin, D. (1988). *Discourse markers.* Cambridge, UK: Cambridge University Press.

Scocco, D. (2007). Copyright Law: 12 Dos and Don'ts. *DailyBlogTips.* Available from http://www.dailyblogtips.com/copyright-law-12-dos-and-donts/

Scott, M. (1996). *Wordsmith: Software tools for Windows* Available from http://www.lexically.net/downloads/version6/wordsmith6.pdf

Scott, M. (1997). PC analysis of key words—and key key words. *System, 25*(2), 233–245.

Scott, M. (2012). WordSmith Tools (Version 6). [Software]. Available from http://lexically.net/wordsmith/

Searle, J.R. (1969). *Speech acts: An essay in the philosophy of language* (Vol. 626). Cambridge, MA: Cambridge University Press.

Seelye, K.Q. (2009, January 17). The past as a guide for Obama's address. *New York Times,* p. A26. Available from http://www.nytimes.com/2009/01/18/us/politics/18speech.html?pagewanted=1&_r=0

Seidlhofer, B. (2007). Common property: English as a lingua franca in Europe. In J. Cummins, & C. Davison (Eds.), *International handbook of English language teaching* (pp. 137–153). New York: Springer.

Seidlhofer, B. (2012). Anglophone-centric attitudes and the globalization of English. *Journal of English as a Lingua Franca, 1*(2), 393–407. doi: 10.1515/jelf-2012-0026

Sekine, S., & Dalwani, K. (2010). *Ngram search engine with patterns combining token, POS, chunk and NE information.* Paper presented at the Proceedings of the Seventh International Conference on Language Resources and Evaluation (LREC'10), Valletta, Malta.

Shalom, C. (1997). That great supermarket of desire: Attributes of the desired other in personal advertisements. In K. Harvey, & C. Shalom (Eds.), *Language and desire: Encoding sex, romance and intimacy* (pp. 186–203). London: Routledge.

Shastri, S.V. (1988). The Kolhapur Corpus of Indian English and work done on its basis so far. *ICAME Journal, 12,* 15–26.

Shastri, S.V., Patilkulkarni, C.T., & Shastri, G.S. (1986). *Manual of information to accompany the Kolhapur Corpus of Indian English, for use with digital computers* Available from http://khnt.hit.uib.no/icame/manuals/kolhapur/

Shetty, J., & Adibi, J. (2004). The Enron dataset database schema and brief statistical report. *Information Sciences Institute Technical Report, University of Southern California, 4.*

Sidnell, J. (2009). *Conversation analysis: An introduction* (Vol. 37). Malden, MA: Wiley-Blackwell.

Simkins-Bullock, J.A., & Wildman, B.G. (1991). An investigation into the relationships between gender and language. *Sex Roles, 24*(3/4), 149-160.

Simpson, C. (May 19, 2013). Yahoo! just bought Tumblr for $1.1 billion. *The Atlantic Wire.* Available from http://www.theatlanticwire.com/technology/2013/05/yahoos-messy-tumblr-acquisition-going-fall-apart/65371/

Simpson, R., Briggs, S.L., Ovens, J., & Swales, J.M. (2002). *The Michigan Corpus of Academic Spoken English.* Ann Arbor: Regents of the University of Michigan.

Simpson-Vlach, R., & Leicher, S. (2006). *The MICASE handbook.* Ann Arbor: University of Michigan Press.

Sinclair, J., & Brazil, D. (1982). *Teacher talk.* Oxford: Oxford University Press.

Sinclair, J.M. (2000). Lexical grammar. *Naujoji Metodologija, 24,* 194–224.

Sinclair, J.M. (Ed.). (1987). *Collins COBUILD English language dictionary.* New York: Collins.

Sinclair, J.M. (2005). Corpus and text—basic principles. In M. Wynne (Ed.), *Developing linguistic corpora: A guide to good practice* (pp. 1–16). Oxford: Oxbow Books. Available from http://www.ahds.ac.uk/guides/linguistic-corpora/chapter1.htm.

Skalicky, S. (2013). Was this analysis helpful? A genre analysis of the Amazon.com discourse community and its "most helpful" product reviews. *Discourse, Context & Media, 2*(2), 84–93. doi: 10.1016/j.dcm.2013.04.001

Spice, B. (2011). CMU research finds regional dialects are alive and well on Twitter: Slang terms like y'all, yinz, koo, coo and suttin predict location of tweet authors. Available from http://www.cmu.edu/news/archive/2011/January/jan7_twitterdialects.shtml

Spiegel, A. (2013, April 1). Mining books to map emotions through a century. *All Things Considered* (National Public Radio). Available from http://www.npr.org/blogs/health/2013/04/01/175584297/mining-books-to-map-emotions-through-a-century

Stephen, L. (2002). Sexualities and genders in Zapotec Oaxaca. *Latin American Perspectives, 29*(2), 41–59.

Stratmann, J. 2010. Social media monitoring tools–2010 review (intro). Available online at: http://www.freshnetworks.com/blog/2010/03/social-media-monitoring-tools-2010-review-intro/

Stuart-Smith, J. (2006). "We fink, so we are from Glasgow": TV and accent change in Glaswegian. Presented December 12, 2006, Radboud University. Nijmegen, The Netherlands.

Stuart-Smith, J. (2007). The influence of the media. In C. Llamas, L. Mullany, & P. Stockwell (Eds.), *The Routledge companion to sociolinguistics* (pp. 140–148). London: Routledge.

Stubbe, M. (2001). From office to production line: Collecting data for the Wellington Language in the Workplace Project. *Language in the Workplace Occasional Papers, 2.* Available from http://www.vuw.ac.nz/lals/lwp/resources/

Stubbs, M. (1996). *Text and corpus analysis.* Oxford: Blackwell.

Stubbs, M. (2001). Texts, corpora, and problems of interpretation: A response to Widdowson. *Applied Linguistics, 22*(2), 149–172.

Svartnik, J. (1990). *The London-Lund Corpus of Spoken English: Description and research.* Lund Studies in English 82. Lund, Sweden: Lund University Press.

Switchboard: A users' manual. (2004). University of Pennsylvania. Available at http://catalog.ldc.upenn.edu/docs/LDC94S15/manual.txt

Szmrecsanyi, B. (2010). Geography is overrated. In S. Hansen, C. Shchwarz, P. Stoeckle, & T. Streck (Eds.), *Dialectological and folk dialectological concepts of space* (pp. 215–231). Berlin: Walter de Gruyter.

Tabachnick, B.G., & Fidell, L.S. (2007). *Using multivariate statistics* (5th ed.). Boston: Pearson.

Tagliamonte, S.A. (1997). Obsolescence in the English perfect? Evidence from Samana English. *American Speech, 72*(1), 33.

Tagliamonte, S.A. (2006). *Analysing sociolinguistic variation.* Cambridge: Cambridge University Press.

Tagliamonte, S.A. (2008). So different and pretty cool! Recycling intensifiers in Toronto, Canada. *English Language and Linguistics, 12*(2), 361–394. doi: 10.1017/S1360674308002669

Tagliamonte, S.A. (2012). *Variationist sociolinguistics: Change, observation, interpretation.* Malden, MA: Wiley-Blackwell.

Tagliamonte, S.A., & Roeder, R.V. (2009). Variation in the English definite article: Socio-historical linguistics in t'speech community. *Journal of Sociolinguistics, 13*(4), 435–471. doi: 10.1111/j.1467–9841.2009.00418.x

Tannen, D. (1986). *That's not what I meant!* New York: HarperCollins.

Tannen, D. (1996). *Gender and discourse.* Oxford: Oxford University Press.

Taylor, C. (2011). Negative politeness forms and impoliteness functions in institutional discourse: a corpus-assisted approach. In B.L. Davies, M. Haugh, & A.J. Merrison (Eds.), *Situated Politeness* (pp. 209–231). New York: Continuum.

Temples, A.L., & Nelson, G. (2013). Intercultural computer-mediated communication: Insights from corpus-based analysis. In D. Belcher, & G. Nelson (Eds.), *Critical and corpus-based approaches to intercultural rhetoric* (pp. 154–179). Ann Arbor: Michigan University Press.

Teubert, W. (2005). My version of corpus linguistics. *International Journal of Corpus Linguistics, 10*(1), 1–13.

Thorne, S., Reinhardt, J., & Golombek, P. (2008). Mediation as objectification in the development of professional discourse: A corpus-informed curricular innovation. In J. Lantolf, & M. Poehner (Eds.), *Sociocultural theory and the teaching of second languages* (pp. 256–284). London: Equinox.

Titak, A., & Roberson, A. (2013). Dimensions of web registers: An exploratory multidimensional comparison. *Corpora, 8*(2), 237–266.

Tognini-Bonelli, E. (2001). *Corpus linguistics at work.* Philadelphia: John Benjamins.

Trudgill, P. (1986). *Dialects in contact.* Oxford: Blackwell.

Vail, M. (2006). The "integrative" rhetoric of Martin Luther King Jr.'s "I Have A Dream" speech. *Rhetoric & Public Affairs, 9*(1), 51–78.

Vaux, B. (2005). Dialect Survey. Available from http://www4.uwm.edu/FLL/linguistics/dialect/index.html

Vine, B. (2009). Directives at work: Exploring the contextual complexity of workplace directives. *Journal of Pragmatics, 41*(7), 1395–1405. doi: http://dx.doi.org/10.1016/j.pragma.2009.03.001

Walker, M., & Randall, J.B. (2012). *Exploring mega-corpora: Google Ngram Viewers and the Corpus of Historical American English.* Unpublished manuscript, Department of Applied Linguistics and ESL, Georgia State University, Atlanta.

Warner, M. (1991). Introduction: Fear of a queer planet. *Social Text*(29), 3–17. doi: 10.2307/466295

Warren, M. (2004). //So what have YOU been WORking on REcently//: Compiling a specialized corpus of spoken business English. In U. Connor, & T.A. Upton (Eds.), *Discourse in the professions: Perspectives from corpus linguistics* (pp. 115–140). Philadelphia: John Benjamins.

Waugh, O.S. (2011). *"I'm not going to speculate": Lexical bundles in White House press briefings.* Unpublished manuscript, Department of Applied Linguistics and ESL, Georgia State University, Atlanta.

Weinberger, S.H. (2013). *Speech Accent Archive.* Fairfax, VA: George Mason University. Available from http://accent.gmu.edu

Wenger, E. (1998). *Communities of practice: Learning, meaning, and identity.* Cambridge: Cambridge University Press.

White, M. (1994). *Language in job interviews: Differences relating to success and socioeconomic variables.* Unpublished doctoral dissertation, Northern Arizona University, Flagstaff.

Widdowson, H.G. (2000). On the limitations of linguistics applied. *Applied Linguistics, 21*(1), 3–25. doi: 10.1093/applin/21.1.3

Wisenburn, B., & Higginbotham, D.J. (2008). An AAC application using speaking partner speech recognition to automatically produce contextually relevant utterances: Objective results. *Augmentative and Alternative Communication, 24*(2), 100–109.

Wortham, J. (December 17, 2007). After 10 years of blogs, the future's brighter than ever. *Wired Magazine.* Available from http://www.wired.com/entertainment/theweb/news/2007/ 12/blog_anniversary

Xiao, R. (2009). Multidimensional analysis and the study of world Englishes. *World Englishes, 28*(4), 421–450. doi: 10.1111/j.1467–971X.2009.01606.x

Xiao, Z., & McEnery, A. (2005). Two Approaches to Genre Analysis. *Journal of English Linguistics, 33*(1), 62–82. doi: 10.1177/0075424204273957

INDEX